MARSHALL'S
BEST GAMES OF CHESS

(Formerly Titled: My Fifty Years of Chess)

By

FRANK J. MARSHALL
United States Chess Champion 1909-1936

Frank J. Marshall and Thomas Emery

The world needs no introduction to Frank James Marshall, our great American Chess Master, who has played all over the world and achieved successes unparalleled in history.

What the world may not know, however, is that our Frank would probably have done even better in chess tournaments if he had not always been so eager to play for a win. An artist of the chess board, he always played to win so long as there was the remotest possibility of succeeding. As a result, he lost many a game which he could have drawn if he had not set out with that idea in mind.

It has been my privilege to have known Frank over a period of twenty years and to have worked with him during that time. No finer sportsman than Frank Marshall ever sat down to a chess board, nor could anybody hope to have a better friend.

Of this one can be certain: Marshall's name will live to eternity. To paraphrase Shakespeare, " Age cannot wither him, nor custom stale his infinite variety."

THOMAS EMERY.

New York, 1942.

Dedicated to

GUSTAVUS A. PFEIFFER

A True and Valued Friend

Who helped to establish us in our home at
the Marshall Chess Club and whose generous
and continuous assistance has smoothed the
path of life for me and my family.

———

FOREWORD

A recent story in LIFE magazine described me as a "preoccupied old gentleman who looks like a Shakespearean actor, smokes strong cigars incessantly and takes a chess board to bed with him so he can record any plays he may think up."

A fair enough pen-portrait, I suppose, but I resent being called an "old gentleman" just the same. After all, I am only 64 and my friends tell me that I have never really grown up. And the chess board I take to bed with me is just one of those little pocket sets. You can never tell when you will get a good idea for a move.

Am I preoccupied? I suppose so. And what am I preoccupied about? Chess, of course. My entire life has been devoted to the game. I have been playing it for over fifty years. I started when I was ten years old and I am still going strong. In all that time I don't believe a day has gone by that I have not played at least one game of chess—and I still enjoy it as much as ever. Such is the fascination of the royal game, with its endless variety and limitless possibilities.

My chess career has been rich in experiences, some amusing, others tragic, all of them interesting. Chess has taken me to the far corners of the earth, has brought me some fame, though little fortune. In my travels I have met thousands of people and made many lasting friendships.

Chess has fully repaid me in the real things of life, the sharing of colorful experiences with my wife and son, the devotion and loyalty of old friends, the good fellowship of a host of chess players throughout the world, the constant mental stimulus of the greatest of games.

In the first part of this book I tell the story of my life in chess from the time I started as a boy up to the present day. Of necessity, these reminiscences are brief as the major portion of this volume must be devoted to the recording of my best games. These will be found in Part 2. They have been carefully selected from the thousands I have played during the past 50 years. One or two have been included for their historical value, a few "swindles" for entertainment, but the vast majority represent my outstanding efforts, the games which best illustrate my style of play in the different periods of my career. Some have never appeared in print before; others have been published, at various times, in magazines or books, but usually with inadequate notes. For the first time, a complete collection of my best games, thoroughly annotated, is presented in this volume.

My good friend THOMAS EMERY, a strong chess amateur and patron of the game, first suggested the idea of publishing this book. When we discussed the idea, we had in mind a collection of "study" games we had played together, analysis of openings, interesting positions which had developed from our analysis. From this modest beginning, the present volume, with its complete record of my life and games, has evolved. Some of the original material is contained in Part 3. To Tom Emery, I extend my grateful thanks for his assistance.

I acknowledge with gratitude the invaluable aid rendered by I. A. HOROWITZ and KENNETH HARKNESS, Editors of CHESS REVIEW, who, with their associates, supervised the assembly, arrangement and production of this book.

I also take this opportunity to salute the names of some of my old friends who have helped me in my chess career. I allude to GEORGE EMLEN ROOSEVELT, President of the Marshall Chess Club; WILLIAM J. A. BECK, life member of the club; EDWARD CORNELL, EDWARD B. EDWARDS, HENRY LEEDS and LOUIS J. WOLFF, Governors of the club; FRITZ BRIEGER, President of the Queens Chess Club. I thank them all for their generous support and encouragement throughout my fifty golden years of chess.

FRANK JAMES MARSHALL

New York, 1942

MARSHALL'S
BEST GAMES OF CHESS
(Formerly Titled: My Fifty Years of Chess)

PART ONE

My Chess Career

EARLY YEARS

As a child I had an unusual aptitude for chess. I took to it naturally, like a duck to water. Although I learned the game when I was very young, let me hasten to add that I was a perfectly normal, healthy and active youngster. Most people think of a chess "prodigy" as a small, unpleasant child with a bulging forehead who spends all his days with his head bowed over a chess board.

I wasn't in the least like that. I went to public school like any other boy, fought with my brothers the way brothers always fight, played baseball, lacrosse and hockey with the other kids. Chess was just one of my activities but, from the very first, it held a strange fascination for me.

The possession of a feeling for chess is not in any way abnormal or unusual. It is just like "card sense" or an ear for music. Some people may never play chess well, just as others can never carry a tune, but most of us have sufficient powers of visualization, logic and analysis to enable us to play and enjoy chess. Only a few have a real genius for the game, or are able to devote enough time and study to develop the necessary knowledge and experience which will enable them to become chess masters, but that is not important. Most people play chess as a hobby and recreation. The "coffee-house" players probably get more fun out of chess than most professionals.

Personally, I am not sorry that I took up chess as a profession. I enjoy playing in the Club with an old friend just for the fun of it, or matching my wits against the world's leading masters in an international tournament. I got the thrill of my life when I walked through the Cambridge Springs tournament without losing a game but I still get a kick out of seeing a combination work out in a friendly game.

It was my father who first taught me to play chess. He was of English birth and my mother of Scotch-Irish descent. I was born on August 10th, 1877, at Eighth Avenue and Fiftieth Street, New York City. When I was eight years old, my family moved to Montreal. We lived there for eleven years.

In our home in Montreal, my father played chess in the evenings with his friends. One night, he asked me if I would like to play him a game. I suppose he had noticed that I had been watching him and decided to try me out.

3

It would be romantic to say that I won the first game of chess I ever played, but it just wouldn't be true. As a matter of fact, my father was a fairly good player and it was quite a long time before I was able to win a game from him. My early games were just like any other games between a beginner and an experienced player. "Chess sense" in itself was not sufficient when pitted against experience. I still had to learn a great deal about the tactics of the game.

In the first few games I played with my father, I was hopelessly beaten, but this did not discourage me. He pointed out my mistakes and helped me to overcome them. We played together two or three times a week and my game gradually improved. In six months, we were on about equal terms. Within a year, I was able to give my father a Rook and beat him.

As I look back to those early days, I realize that the hours I spent alone with my father over the chess board developed strong bonds of companionship and affection between us, a relationship which lasted until the day of his death. I am sure he had no idea that I would make chess my life's work, but I am glad he lived to see the boy who played chess with him in Montreal become recognized as an international master.

From the very first, I was an attacking player, forever on the offensive. This often got me into trouble. However, I am glad that my father did not curb this instinct too much. As a chess player I suppose I am a little like Jack Dempsey as a fighter. Dempsey used to start slugging at the opening gong and never gave his opponent a chance to get started. As he was a good slugger, he won a lot of fights. Sometimes he would meet a fighter who was a good boxer and who went on the defensive. He couldn't hurt Jack much but he made him look bad.

I have been much the same way in chess. I have always liked a wide open game and tried to knock out my opponent with a checkmate as quickly as possible. I subscribe to the old belief that offense is the best form of defense. However, I always had great difficulty with defensive players. Sometimes they made me "look bad" too—but I still prefer my own style of chess!

When I was about 11 years old, my father decided that I must have stronger competition than he was able to give me. He introduced me to the players at the Hope Coffee House, in Montreal. Stiffer opposition again developed my game and before very long I was able to beat the coffee-house players easily.

I then joined the Montreal Chess Club and developed into a strong club player. Incidentally, there is no quicker way of improving your chess game than joining a chess club. It gives you the opportunity of playing with members who are stronger than yourself. You quickly learn all the different styles of play, the various openings, traps, etc. When you fall for a trap against a strong player, or blunder in an opening, you can look it up in your books or in the club library and find out where you went wrong. You will never forget it.

I spent most of my spare time at the Montreal Chess Club. If I wasn't playing with another member, I was playing over master games. My favorite "author" was Paul Morphy. His brilliant games inspired me. I used to play them over and over again.

One of my greatest thrills was to play against world-famous chess masters who visited the club from time to time and gave simultaneous exhibitions. I particularly remember the time when William Steinitz, then champion of the world, visited the club. It was in 1893 and I was sixteen years old.

I can see Steinitz now as he appeared to me then—a short, heavy-set bearded man with a large head. As he walked round the tables I noticed that he limped. Near-sighted, he leaned over each board and peered at the pieces. Each time he came to my board, he gave me an encouraging smile. One of the greatest waiting players of all time, he had such a fierce desire to win, that even in simultaneous exhibitions he hated to draw games.

I tried hard to win my game against Steinitz (Game No. 1), but I was too inexperienced. However, my efforts apparently impressed him. After the exhibition was over, he complimented me on my game and predicted a great future for me. Needless to say, I was tremendously flattered.

Two days later I got my name in the papers for the first time— and what a thrill that was! Underneath a portrait of a very solemn and self-conscious young man, seated beside a chess board, the following item appeared in *Le Monde Illustré* of Montreal, Nov. 15th, 1893:—

"This portrait is of a young chess player whose reputation is growing daily among our amateurs.

This future champion, Frank J. Marshall, is the son of Alfred Marshall of this city and is 16 years old. Despite his youth, he has proved, in various circumstances, that he is the equal of our best local players.

"He belongs to the Montreal Chess Club and the members of this Club consider him a very strong adversary. His game combines rapidity and originality. By inclination, he always prefers the attack to the defense.

"On Monday evening, November 13th, in a series of simultaneous games against sixteen opponents by Mr. Steinitz, the champion of the world, young Marshall played one of the boards. His original and strong defense caused the Master to say that he had never met an amateur of his age who had given him so much trouble. Mr. Steinitz predicted a brilliant future for him if he continues to play chess."

If I continued to play chess? Nothing could have stopped me. There was nothing else I wanted to do. Chess began to absorb my whole life. My head was full of it, from morning to night — and in my dreams as well. Gradually, it crowded out every other interest. I knew that I was going to devote my life to chess.

When I left school, I got various jobs in Montreal but visions of Queens and Rooks and Knights and Bishops kept floating into my head and interfered with my work. In one clerical job I held, I thought I was getting on all right until the boss found out that it was a pocket chess set in my desk drawer which was responsible for my studious attitude.

Shortly after the Steinitz exhibition, H. N. Pillsbury came to Montreal and gave a simultaneous blindfold exhibition. I was surprised to find that he was quite a young man—just 21 years old at that time. He was extremely likeable and very friendly with everyone. I succeeded in winning my game from him (No. 2). At the time, of course, it was a major triumph in my life. As I look back at the game, however, I realize that he probably gave me chances.

Pillsbury was a marvelous genius, one of America's greatest chess masters. He never played for the score, refused to accept many proffered draws and occasionally lost the games. Unfortunately, he took little care of his health and constant blindfold play left its mark on him. He died at the early age of 34.

In 1894 I won the championship of the Montreal Chess Club (Game No. 3) and began to look for more worlds to conquer. Fortunately for me, my family returned to New York a couple of years later and I joined the Manhattan and Brooklyn Chess Clubs. There I got my first taste of master chess, competing with players like Hermann Helms, C. S. Howell, W. E. Napier and others.

Shortly after I returned to New York I won a short match with V. Sournin, now of Washington, D. C. (Game No. 4). In 1897 I won the junior championship of the New York Chess Association; this was considered quite a feat for a lad of twenty. The following year I won a match with Sydney P. Johnston, of Chicago, and came in second in the Brooklyn Chess Club championship tournament, won by Napier.

In 1899, I gained some recognition by my game with Wainwright in the International Cable Matches. Finally, in the same year, I won the championship of the Brooklyn Chess Club. The period of my chess youth was over. I was ready for bigger things.

*   *   *   *   *

Frank J. Marshall in 1900

WINNING MY SPURS
(1899-1903)

"The characteristic that most impresses one in Frank Marshall, the young Brooklyn Chess Champion, is his fearlessness and utter disregard of persons when face to face with them at the chess board. His vis-a-vis might be Lasker, yet Marshall would meet him with alacrity."—Brooklyn Daily Eagle, 1899.

Just one year later after the above item appeared in the Brooklyn Daily Eagle, I met Lasker himself across the board and defeated him — but first I had to prove my worthiness; I had to win my spurs.

In 1899 the Manhattan and Brooklyn Chess Clubs honored me by their decision to send me abroad to compete in the International Tournament at London. I gladly accepted; I was only too eager to meet and play against the international Masters.

It was at this time that I met Leo Nardus and won his lasting friendship. He was then visiting New York and we met at the Manhattan Chess Club. He insisted upon my entering the International Tournament and gave generously toward the fund raised for my expenses. In the years that followed, I never made a trip to Europe that did not culminate in a reunion with him. I visited him last at his beautiful home in Tunis. I wonder what changes the war has wrought in his life.

When I arrived in London, I found that the championship of the Brooklyn Chess Club was not considered sufficient to justify the acceptance of my entry into the Masters Tournament. Like a prize-fighter who wants to challenge the champion, I was told to go out and make a reputation for myself.

To say that I was disappointed is putting it mildly. There I was in London, sent over as the representative of the leading New York chess clubs, and they wouldn't even let me play. However, in connection with the major event, a minor tournament with 12 competitors was being held. The tournament officials had entered my name in this section.

Swallowing my pride, I decided to play in the minor tournament. To my surprise, I then found that Mieses and Marco were also playing in this section. Too many applications for the major tourney had been received and the officials had placed these two recognized masters in the minor event. I knew then that this was my opportunity to show what I could do. Everybody expected Mieses or Marco to win with ease.

I went "all out" in this contest, played as hard as I knew how. I won first prize, losing only one game. Some of the games sparkled with fireworks. (See Games 5 and 6). The general aggressiveness and enterprise of my style, together with a winning score of 8½—2½, gave me what I was seeking—an international reputation. In memory of this important event in my life, I still treasure the little golden knight which was presented to me at this tournament.

In 1900, I again went to Europe, to compete for the first time against the world's leading masters in the International Tournament at Paris. A total of 17 entries was accepted, including Dr. Emanuel Lasker (who won the world's championship from Steinitz in 1894), Pillsbury, Tchigorin, Maroczy, Janowski, Burn, Schlechter, Showalter, Mieses and other famous masters.

It was an experience I will never forget. I was full of confidence in my own ability but I had never met competition like this before. I realized that my entire future in chess might depend on the showing I made in this tournament.

It began on May 18th and I started well by winning my game in the very first round. In the second round, however, I lost to Janowski. In the third, I won from Mason and then met Brody in the fourth. I drew with him but, according to the rules of the tourney, we had to play a second game; the first draw didn't count! I won the second game and was thus credited with a full point.

When I sat down to play Dr. Lasker in the fifth round (Game No. 7), I was both nervous and thrilled. At last I was facing a world's champion. How would I fare? Would he dispose of me in short order, or would he, perhaps, underrate this young newcomer from America? Even if I could hold him to a draw it would mean something to me. In this period Lasker was at the very peak of his form.

When the game started, I forgot all about my opponent and concentrated on the board. With my fifth move I played for an open game, the kind in which I feel most at home. At his eleventh turn Dr. Lasker made what seemed to be a very risky pawn capture with his Knight. Was he being careless? I studied the situation for quite a while and decided I had a good chance to win that Knight. Careful play was needed but finally on the 22nd move, I won the piece. I was a piece up against Lasker!

But the game wasn't over by any means. Probably surprised to find himself in this predicament, Lasker fought on for 36 more moves, almost succeeded in drawing the game. His efforts failed, however, and he resigned after I had made my 58th move. This was the only game in the tournament which Lasker lost.

I won in the sixth and seventh rounds and drew with Tchigorin and Schlechter in the eighth and ninth. Each draw required two games. In the tenth, I had Black against Pillsbury, the American Champion (Game No. 8). Before we started, he reminded me of our game seven years before, in Montreal.

"You're all grown up now, aren't you?" he said, with his friendly smile. "And you've come a long way too."

"I'll never forget that game," I told him. "It was the first I ever won from a master — even if you were blindfolded!"

"But you're not blindfolded now," I added, "so here's your chance for revenge!"

Against Pillsbury, I adopted the Petroff Defense. I was taking no chances and played for equality. On his 13th move, however, he gave me an opportunity for attack, overlooking a combination which led through to a win. He resigned in 26 moves. In my first appearance in an International Masters Tournament I had defeated both Lasker and Pillsbury!

In the following round I had a terrific battle on my hands with Showalter. The game went to 111 moves and I finally lost. In the 12th, I won from Rosen and then defeated Amos Burn in the 13th. This game (No. 9) was an amusing affair. I attribute the win largely to the fact that my opponent never had time to get his pipe lit! Marco was under the impression that I had swindled Burn and tried the same defense when we met in the next round (Game No. 10), but he met the same fate as the Britisher.

In the semi-final round I won from Mieses and entered the last round with a score of 12—3. My last opponent was Maroczy who had 11—4. If I had won this game, I would have placed second to Lasker. Unfortunately, I lost to Maroczy and dropped to a tie with him for 3rd and 4th. My final score was 12—4. Lasker won the event with a score of 14½—1½. Pillsbury was second with 12½—3½. Thus concluded my initiation into the ranks of the leading international masters.

* * * * * *

The four years which followed my sensational debut of 1900 proved to be a period of adjustment to my new status of international chess master. I had the saddening experience, common to most young masters after a period of initial success, of falling into a period of doldrums characterized by indifferent play and cheerless results. In short, I soon found that I was not invincible.

In the Monte Carlo Tournaments of 1901, 1902 and 1903, for example, my showing was only fair. My play at Hanover (1902) was of about the same character, with the result that I was only succeeding in disappointing myself and those who had faith in me. The chess world, which had been electrified by my defeats of Lasker and Pillsbury at Paris, began to think that I was just a "flash in the pan" and not to be taken too seriously.

And yet I knew I was capable of good chess, in fact was producing it in individual games, with victories over top-notchers such as Pillsbury, Tarrasch, Maroczy, Schlechter, Janowski. In the Monte Carlo tourney of 1903 I scored a very satisfying victory over Pillsbury (Game No. 13). And my win against Col. Moreau (Game No. 14) was the most spectacular of the tournament! It was played on March 13, 1903, and a most unlucky thirteenth it proved to be for the colonel! As you will note by referring to the game, I was able to turn in this score with an announced mate in eleven moves as the finale. If you would like to test your skill, cover up the moves below the diagram of the final position and see if you can figure out the mate. Remember, this mate was announced — so don't cheat by shifting the pieces!

To return to my chess career: the obligatory King's Gambit Tournament held in the summer of 1903 by the Vienna Chess Club promised to break the monotony of disappointment; no sooner had I received the invitation to play at Vienna than I felt that at long last my luck was due to change. The nature of the openings which had to be adopted was my guarantee of lively play — that was all the chance I asked in order to redeem myself in the eyes of the chess world. My anticipations proved correct, I did well from the very start, came a good second to Tchigorin and ahead of such outstanding players as Pillsbury, Schlechter, Teichmann, Maroczy and Mieses. No less than five games have been included from this tournament, all played in my happiest mood (Nos. 17-21). And coming second to Tchigorin was no disgrace, for the old Russian had made a lifelong study of the King's Gambit and had a deeper knowledge of this intricate opening than has ever been possessed by any other man.

At this time, I was living in England. For three years I had been appearing in so many European tournaments that I decided it was easier to live there. Between tourneys, I was engaged by various British clubs to give lectures and exhibitions. I still remember, with a great deal of pleasure, the month I spent with the Glasgow Chess Club (see Game No. 15!). A fine club they have there; and still carrying on, I hear, despite the bombs.

Before I close this chapter, I must refer the reader to my game with Atkins (No. 16), which contains one of my most notable combinations.

* * * * *

CAROLINE D. MARSHALL

in 1904

" . . . the girl who became my
wife, the mother of my son, my
devoted companion for the past
37 years."

THE YEAR OF YEARS
(1904-1905)

To condense into relatively few lines the notable events of 1904-1905, the most important years of my life, is no easy matter. Heartened by my excellent showing in the Vienna Tournament, I continued my good work at the Monte Carlo tourney of 1904. With first prize within my grasp, I refused Maroczy's offer of a draw in the last round, and with what seems incredibly youthful confidence, went on to try for a win; the result being a dismal loss and a drop to third place. But I learned something valuable from this heart-breaking experience, as may be seen from the following sentence taken from a letter I wrote to a friend after the tournament: "When will I learn that a draw counts more than a loss?"

Nevertheless, my play at Monte Carlo — study that monumental battle with Marco in Game No. 22! — had enhanced my reputation considerably. The good impression was further fortified by my dividing first prize with Swiderski a little later in the Rice Gambit Tournament at Monte Carlo. Swiderski, *en passant*. was a peculiar fellow. He made very few friends, had a gentle but melancholy disposition, was a fine

11

violinist, ate raw meat, committed suicide a few years later. The tournament was somewhat out of the ordinary as well. Because of Professor Rice's interest in his brain child, he showered generous payments on the analysts, who turned up the most marvelous attacks which were then followed by the most ingenious defenses, which in turn led to even more marvelous attacks, and then . . . but you get the idea! This was all great fun, but playing the gambit in a tournament was quite a job: you had to remember so much that a game with this opening was like an examination on French verbs!

Later in this same year came my greatest triumph: the International Tournament at Cambridge Springs. It was at this Pennsylvania resort that most of the leading chess masters of the world gathered to compete in one of the outstanding international events ever held in this country. The foreign contingent consisted of Dr. E. Lasker, R. Teichmann and J. Mieses (Germany), C. Schlechter and G. Marco (Austria), D. Janowski (France), M. Tchigorin (Russia) and T. F. Lawrence (England). The American entries were Pillsbury, Showalter, Hodges, Barry, Napier, Fox and Delmar.

A formidable field, indeed, and yet I began the tournament with quiet confidence. It was one of those times when a player feels that he is "in the pink." I played with just the right blend of enterprise and prudence, not too riskily, not too cautiously; an admirable system, as it turned out. I finished in first place, a full two points ahead of Lasker and Janowski, who tied for second and third prizes. My final score of 13—2 was made up of eleven wins and four draws (with Lasker, Marco, Tchigorin and Napier).

One thing that helped me in this tournament was my familiarity with the styles of play of the American masters. Some of the Europeans underestimated the American players, with sad results visible in the score table! Poor Pillsbury, already suffering from the illness which was to prove fatal two years later, did badly; but Showalter, on the other hand, covered himself with glory by coming a good fifth. The crucial point of the tournament arrived in the eleventh round, when I fought it out with Janowski for a gruelling 76 moves. My victory in that game clinched the tournament for me.

It was shortly after the Cambridge Springs tourney that fate dealt me a cruel blow in the death of my father, but then comforted me by allowing me to meet Carrie, the girl who became my wife, the mother of my son, my devoted companion for the past 37 years.

Carrie has travelled with me wherever chess has taken me. She has been a constant help and inspiration. As my business manager, she has fought all my battles for me. Carrie has devoted her whole life to my interests and the welfare of chess. Today she is the secretary of the Marshall Chess Club and a very exacting job it is.

I remember well the occasion on which I first met Carrie. It was on August 27th, 1904, at the wedding of her brother Charles. That very night I went to Carrie's mother and said:

Frank Marshall in 1905. Photo was taken in Paris on the occasion of his match with Janowski. He is wearing the medal awarded to him at St. Louis. 1904.

"I have fallen in love with your daughter and I'm going to steal her." Her mother laughed, but that's just about what happened. A few weeks later I had to leave New York to play at St. Louis (about which, more later), and to give more exhibitions. I returned just before Christmas and began a "blitz" courtship which lasted for about two weeks. I was leaving on January 7th for Paris to play Janowski, so I rushed things a bit.

We were married at 11:30 a. m. on January 6th, 1905. At 9 o'clock the next morning we sailed together for Paris. As Carrie put it:

"I thought I had better marry him, as he told me it was my last chance."

A word about the St. Louis tourney. The American champion Pillsbury was ill and unable to play. The tournament committee then announced that the winner would become champion of the United States. In fact, after I had won the tournament they presented me with a medal inscribed "Frank J. Marshall, champion." However, I did not agree with the action of the committee and publicly acknowledged that I regarded Pillsbury as still the champion. I hoped that it would be possible on my return from Europe, to play a match with him. Unfortunately, Pillsbury died in 1906, before a match could be arranged. The tragic end of this great master, still in his early thirties, with his wonderful gift for the game, his friendly personality and pleasant manners, was a great blow to chess the world over, but especially for us in this country.

The chess world, from then on, accepted me as the American Champion; but the situation was rather ambiguous and uncomfortable for me until 1909, when I won the match with Showalter, who had been champion before Pillsbury; I then felt that I had a clear right to the title.

Coming back to our trip to Paris: on the way over, there was a group in the smoking room playing chess all the time. The day before we arrived, I went in and watched them. When I saw one of the players make a "lemon," I couldn't restrain myself from telling him he had a won game if he hadn't made that move. Whereupon his opponent said to me:

"If you play chess, why haven't you shown up before? I've beaten everybody else on board the ship."

'I didn't feel like playing," I told him.

"Well, why don't you play now?" he asked. "Sit down, I'll give you a rook."

"No you won't," I answered, "I'll give *you* a rook."

This was too much for my new-found friend. "Nobody can give me a rook," he spluttered. "I'll bet you fifty dollars you can't."

"Well, I could take the bet, but it wouldn't be fair. My name is Marshall!"

When he learned he was talking to the winner of the Cambridge Springs Tournament, my friend calmed down a bit. I let him off his bet, but he insisted on buying us a dinner in Paris.

The match with my friendly enemy Janowski proved to be a battle royal, but I finally won by 8—5, with four draws. As I probably played more games with Janowski than with any other player (about 75, I believe!), a word or two about him is in order. At his best, he turned out games that were bywords for power and elegance. But he had little foibles about the kind of game he liked — his weakness for the two Bishops was notorious — and he could be tremendously stubborn. Janowski could follow the wrong path with more determination than any man I ever met! He was also something of a dandy and quite vain about his appearance.

Later in that same year (1905), I won first prize at the beautiful Dutch resort Scheveningen. Duras and Spielmann, at that time just at the beginning of their careers, were my closest competitors. I then went on to a very strong tournament at Ostend, the first of four interesting contests at this famous Belgian watering-place. I found myself in a slump again, finishing a bit above the middle of the score table, although I produced some excellent chess in individual games and took one of the brilliancy prizes (Game No. 29). A little later, however, at Barmen, I redeemed myself in a tournament of about the same strength. This was a great battle all the way, Janowski and Maroczy tying for first and second with 11½, myself third with 11, and Schlechter and the new star Bernstein, fourth and fifth with 10.

Frank and Caroline Marshall, with their son, Frank, Jr., in 1907. Photo was taken at Ostend, Belgium.

COMMUTING TO EUROPE
(1906-1909)

Carrie and I then returned to our home in Brooklyn, and my son, Frank Junior, was born shortly after our homecoming. The following year I went to Europe alone, as Carrie had to take care of young Frankie. Incidentally, I have lost count of the number of times I have crossed the Atlantic to participate in European chess tournaments! Certainly in the five years following my marriage, I seemed to spend a great deal of time on shipboard.

In the Ostend 1906 Tournament I took seventh prize with a score of 16½—13½. Perhaps my poor showing was due to the fact that Carrie was not with me. I hardly ever seemed to do well when she wasn't around. Still, my showing was not so bad after all, for the arrangements for this tournament can only be described as "whacky." First, we started off with 36 (!) players. Then we were broken up into four groups, and everyone in Group A played against everybody in Group B; likewise for everybody in Group C against everybody in Group D. The three players with the lowest scores in each section dropped out, and then Group A played Group C, while Group B played Group D, after which the two lowest players in each group dropped out. *Then* Group A

15

played Group D, and Group B played Group C and the two lowest scores were again discarded. After that, we had eight players left, and they played a tournament among themselves!! There ought to be a law against ideas like that.

Later in the year I redeemed my reputation by winning a very strong tournament at Nuremberg without loss of a game. Most of the big guns took part in the tourney, so it was almost as great a triumph as at Cambridge Springs. One thing that made this tournament hard was another experiment: an attempt to abolish the time limit! I notice that *The Year Book of Chess* has this to say on the subject: "The rules were: No time limit for the first six hours of a game, afterwards 15 moves an hour and a penalty of one shilling for each minute in excess of this. To avoid these absurd restrictions Leonhardt and Przepiorka at a certain juncture of their game agreed to make a number of meaningless moves so as to escape the fine and gain time. Other players copied this procedure. The most amusing incident was in the game Salwe-Tarrasch. Not only did Dr. Tarrasch suffer defeat in this game, but having consumed a great deal of time in endeavoring to stave off this disaster, had to pay four pounds and fifteen shillings for the privilege! After this the rule was altered as follows: No time limit shall be enforced the first day, but only on adjourned games." As for myself, I didn't let these weird rules bother me much, but just went about the business of playing good chess (Games No. 38 to 41).

In connection with peculiar tournament rules, I should have mentioned that in the Monte Carlo Tournaments of 1901 and 1902 they had the amazing regulation that a draw yielded only a quarter of a point to each player, and another game had to be played between the same opponents. The winner of the supplementary game got a half-point more, while if the game was again drawn, each player got another quarter-point! I suppose that all such ideas have to be tried once, just to see how foolish they are. In the 1901 tournament Janowski beat out Schlechter by three-quarters of a point, while the following year Maroczy snatched first prize from Pillsbury by *one-quarter* of a point!

In 1907 I was again invited to play at Ostend, and this time the tournament had still another special feature (it certainly was a great decade for experiments, wasn't it!?). There were two tournaments, one for "ordinary" masters, with an elephantine entry of 30 players, and a "Championship Tournament" for six world title aspirants. Carrie and I decided that we would go abroad together and take Frankie along, although he was only 16 months old. This new life was all very strange to Carrie, but she proved to be a real trouper. We had memorable experiences together in our travels abroad during this period.

The Championship Tournament proved to be a real humdinger, as indicated by the final scores: Tarrasch 12½—7½, Schlechter 12—8, Janowski and Marshall 11½—8½. Burn and Tchigorin were too old and badly outclassed. Each player had to play four games with each of the other players, and while this was a bit too much like match play for

In 1909, Marshall established clear title to the United States Chess Championship by defeating Jackson W. Showalter in a match. He held the title for 27 years, until he voluntarily retired in 1936.

my taste, I held my own and turned out some fine games (Games No. 42-45). Speaking of matches, I had several unfortunate results about this time. Everyone knows that I have always done better in tournaments than in match play, and no wonder: I've always had a passion for new faces, new places, novelties in opening play, slashing attack and counter-attack. The grim business of wearing down your opponent has never appealed to me very much.

Later that year (1907) we went on to Carlsbad, where the local club provided a chess master's dream of an ideal tournament — gorgeous natural surroundings, fine accommodations, friendly atmosphere and excellent prizes. It was during our stay here, by the way, that Frankie made the acquaintance of the Emperor Franz Josef! My play was only fair — seventh prize in a very strong field.

I made the same kind of showing the following year in the tournaments at Vienna and Prague, both held to celebrate the sixtieth (!) anniversary of the old emperor's accession to the throne. Both of these cities had an attractive quality which charmed me; and both had quite a number of intelligent and cultured amateurs who had distinguished themselves in their chosen professions and also managed to attain a fair degree of skill in chess. At Vienna I divided ninth and tenth prizes with Mieses and Leonhardt and at Prague I shared the seventh, eighth and ninth prizes with Leonhardt and Salwe. A curious feature of these

17

tournaments was that Schlechter, then in top form, tied for first prize in both contests! My play at Carlsbad, Vienna and Prague furnished at least the consolation of resulting in some very nice games (Nos. 46-53).

Later on in that same year, however, I carried off a first prize with no losses (11 wins, 7 draws) at Dusseldorf. A little later, at Lodz, I came second to Rubinstein (Salwe was last) in a triangular tournament in which each man played eight games with each of the other players. Lodz was a hospitable town, fanatically interested in chess. We were treated royally, and produced a great deal of interesting chess.

Still more activities of the same year: I lost a return match with Janowski and won a very lively match from Mieses. This period was a very trying one for me, as financial troubles made it difficult to apply the necessary amount of concentration.

After my European ramblings in 1908, my activities were confined to America the following year. In that year the chess world received a new great master when Capablanca scored his victory over me in an exhibition match. I must admit that I expected him to be a pushover: I made no preparation for the match, took the whole thing very lightly. My experience gave me a wholesome respect for his ability. Later in the same year I defeated Showalter decisively, thus finally settling the vexing problem of the United States Championship.

* * * * *

CHAMPIONSHIP YEARS
(1910-1914)

In 1910, I resumed my European activities by playing in a strong tournament in Hamburg, where I divided fifth and sixth prizes with Teichmann. This was a very exciting race, as may be seen from the fact that only 3 points separated first from tenth place. It was in this tournament that I had the pleasure of winning one of my most sensational games (No. 61, against Tarrasch). I introduced a new move in the Max Lange Attack, which was being exhaustively analyzed around that time, with many efforts made to refute it. My new move reestablished the strength of the attack and it has stood up for over twenty years. Ever since that game, few masters have permitted the Max Lange to be played against them. I believe, however, that I have finally found the refutation of the move myself! It is given at the end of this book in the chapter devoted to some recent analysis of openings, made with my friend Tom Emery.

•1911 was a busy year. It began auspiciously with my victory over a strong American field, including Capablanca, in the New York Tournament. Then came the great San Sebastian tourney, with a hand-picked field of distinguished masters. It was here that Capablanca, whose sudden death we all mourn, made his brilliant international debut. It is an occasion that stands out vividly in my memory, even though a hundred other tournaments clamor for remembrance. Capa was 23 years old, handsome, cultured, full of youthful eagerness to demonstrate his ability. As usual, the veterans at San Sebastian underrated the youthful newcomer, with practically no tournament experience. I did not share their viewpoint; I was still licking the wounds of the defeat I had received two years before.

When Capa first arrived at San Sebastian, he seemed a little awe-stricken to find himself in such distinguished company. His natural self-confidence, however, soon asserted itself and in the very first round he administered a crushing defeat to Dr. Bernstein. The rest is history: Capa came first, followed by Rubinstein, Vidmar and myself. I started off very well, and had a chance for first prize right up to the last two rounds, when I weakened. Some of the other competitors complained that Capa had been lucky, but after all it was their business not to give him undue chances.

After winning a brief match with Leonhardt, I went on to the great tournament at Carlsbad. This had a very strong field, with an entry list of no less than 26 players, and lasted over a month. I tied for fifth and sixth prizes with Nimzovich. From a sporting point of view, this distinguished tournament had a very satisfactory conclusion in the well earned triumph of Teichmann, who was a very fine player but handicapped by being blind in one eye. It has often been said that this tournament produced more fine games than any other ever held.

1912 was an even busier year for me. It began with another tournament at San Sebastian, a double-round affair with a formidable entry, in which I came sixth. There followed another strong tournament at Postyen, in which I obtained third prize; and then I took sixth prize at Breslau, where I played the most famous move of my life (Game No. 75); finally, I took first prize in the Budapest tournament, which had a small but very choice entry and was held to test the Tarrasch Defense to the Queen' Gambit.

This was the famous "Rubinstein year," in which that great master won the first prize at San Sebastian, Postyen, Breslau and Wilna! Finally, to round off my activities for the year, I played still another match with Janowski. This took place in the pleasant atmosphere of Biarritz, and I had the satisfaction of trouncing my ancient rival in decisive fashion.

My two 1913 tournaments took a curious course. At New York, Capa beat me out by half a point, but a month later I reversed the procedure at Havana. By that time, of course, Capa was the national hero

The five original Grandmasters of Chess—Lasker, Alekhine, Capablanca, Marshall and Tarrasch—appear in this reproduction of a historical postcard sent by Marshall to his wife and son from the Grand International Masters Tournament at St. Petersburg, 1914. These "five woodshifters" eliminated six other masters, including Rubinstein, Nimzovich and Janowski, then played a double round for the final prizes.

of Cuba. The first prize hinged on our individual game (No. 81). The setting and the game itself were quite extraordinary. There was a tremendous crowd, which filled the street outside. Capa had a win, which would have given him first prize, but the tension and excitement were too much for him. He played some weak moves and I eventually won the game and the first prize. When the result was announced, the crowd let out a terrific roar. At first I thought they were after my blood for defeating their idol and asked for an escort to my hotel. It turned out, however, that the good Cubans were just showing their sportsmanship and were cheering *me!*

In the Spring of the fateful year 1914 I took part in one of the most notable chess events which has ever taken place — the St. Petersburg Grand International Masters Tournament.

The participants included the reigning world champion, Dr. E. Lasker and two future world champions, Capablanca and Alekhine. The latter, a young man of 21 in the uniform of the Military School of St. Petersburg, and the youthful Aaron Nimzovich, had both qualified for the tournament by tying for first place in the Russian National which had just concluded.

Russia was also represented by Akiba Rubinstein and Dr. O. S. Bernstein; Germany by Dr. S. Tarrasch; France by D. Janowski; Great Britain by J. H. Blackburne and I. Gunsberg; the U.S.A. by myself.

The St. Petersburg Chess Society was responsible for the organization and conduct of the Tournament, the Tsar himself subscribing 1000 roubles towards the prize fund. As it turned out, the prizes were more than covered by the record gate of 6000 roubles.

The schedule called for a round-robin tournament between the eleven competitors, followed by a double-round play-off between the five leaders. In the first stage I did pretty well, tying with Alekhine for 4th and 5th with a score of 6—4. Capablanca finished at the top (8—2), followed by Dr. Lasker and Dr. Tarrasch, each with 6½—3½. In the second stage, however, I broke down completely, scoring only 2 points. The tournament was won by Dr. Lasker, who nosed out Capa by half a point. Alekhine placed third, Dr. Tarrasch fourth, and I received fifth prize. It was at this tournament (see Games 83 and 84) that the Tsar of Russia conferred on each of the five finalists the title "Grandmaster of Chess."

After visiting several places in Russia and Germany, giving exhibitions, I went to Mannheim. The tournament there was little more than half over when it ended abruptly by the outbreak of World War I. It was surprising how quickly the place became infested with soldiers. They seemed to spring up from nowhere. The one French representative, D. Janowski, and the three Russians, Alekhine, Flamberg and Bogoljubow, were promptly placed under arrest. The German players, including Krueger, Carls and John, at once joined the colors. Dr. Tarrasch saw two of his sons depart for the front. The remaining players were invited to make themselves scarce.

I made for the Dutch border and arrived in Amsterdam after many adventures. Usually a seven-hour trip, it took me 39 hours. Somewhere on the border I lost my baggage, containing all my belongings and the presents I had received in St. Petersburg and elsewhere. After a few days in Paris and London, I finally obtained "special accommodations" on the S. S. Rochambeau and returned home.

Five years later, much to my astonishment, my trunks arrived in New York, with their contents intact!

*　*　*　*　*

Hudson Maxim (right) was a frequent visitor at the Marshall Chess Divan in Keene's Chop House. His "War Game" was one of the attractions.

CHAMPIONSHIP YEARS
(1915-1936)

These years have been so eventful that it would take pages and pages to chronicle them properly. The period 1915-1922 suffered from the blighting effect of the war, and I have only a handful of games to show for it. We had some fine tournaments with an almost exclusively American entry, and Capablanca's presence livened things up for us. But these events lacked the color and excitement of international competition.

One event, however, took on added importance as the years went on. This was the founding of Marshall's Chess Divan at Keene's Chop House, 70 West 36th Street, New York, in 1915. The object was to establish in New York a central meeting place for lovers of chess, much on the same lines as such famous resorts as Simpson's Divan in London and the Cafe de la Regence in Paris.

It was my idea to make the Divan a place of instruction where young players would be encouraged and where all chess players could feel free to gather. Hudson Maxim was a frequent visitor at the Divan and his "War Game" was one of the attractions. The game was played on an enlarged board, made necessary by the increased army of pieces and the addition of the "flying machines."

The friends who visited us at the Divan formed the nucleus of the present Marshall Chess Club, with its notable membership and palatial quarters. We occupied various premises from 1915 to 1922, when we

22

Famous masters who took part in the International Tournament at New York, 1927. Seated, are Spielmann and Marshall. Standing, left to right, are Maroczy, Nimzovich, Dr. Vidmar, Dr. Alekhine, Capablanca and Director Lederer.

decided to incorporate the club. Alrick H. Man was the first President and our first club house, purchased by a group of members, was at 135 West 12th Street. In 1931, this building was sold and the more commodious house at 23 West 10th Street, the club's present quarters and also my home, was purchased. Here we are glad to greet old friends and help to develop the young players of today. Many of the leading players of the country are members and new talent is constantly being encouraged.

In 1923 came my match with Edward Lasker, the logical culmination to Lasker's excellent showing in American tournaments for almost a decade. Lasker put up a fine fight, as may be seen from the final score: 5—4 in my favor.

But the greatest event of all during this post-war period was the New York tournament of 1924. True, I had just retained my title and had won a tournament with a fine entry at Lake Hopatcong; but after ten years' absence from the international arena, how would I fare against the European masters, especially the young Hypermoderns whose theories were all the rage? As the tournament turned out, all these fears were groundless. I more than held my own, won the fourth prize and let Reti, Tartakover, Bogoljubow, Maroczy and others trail behind me. That was a most satisfying experience!

The following year, I went to Europe for the first time in a decade. Everything seemed different and sadder. Some old friends had been killed or wounded in the war. Others had been bereaved or lost their fortunes. But the interest in chess was greater than ever. I was quite pleased with my play at Baden-Baden, Marienbad and Moscow, in each

The victorious United States Chess Team at Stockholm in 1937. Left to right are Fritz Brieger (who accompanied the team), Samuel J. Reshevsky, Isaac Kashdan, I. A. Horowitz, Reuben Fine, Team Captain Frank J. Marshall.

of which I won high prizes. The interest in Moscow had even at that time reached an extraordinary pitch, and on some days traffic was paralyzed by the crowd that gathered outside of the building where we played. The Russians were very enthusiastic about us, and I still wear a comfortable smoking jacket that was presented to me during the tourney.

In 1926 I had another gratifying victory in my first prize in the first National Championship of the American Chess Federation in Chicago, coming ahead of Torre, Maroczy, Kupchik, Kashdan and Lasker among others.

In recent years team competitions have been featured much more than they were in earlier years. Thus the Metropolitan Chess League matches in New York have come to be regarded as one of the classic chess events in this country; many are the exciting battles I've had in these team matches, especially against the Manhattan Chess Club.

Of much greater importance, of course, are the International Team Tournaments. I have taken part in five of these contests, playing at Hamburg, and captaining the teams at Prague, Hastings, Warsaw and Stockholm. The United States team was victorious in four of these events. There are few sensations so satisfying as the feeling of cooperation toward a common goal against able opponents. These matches are gruelling, but the results make them well worth while.

In 1936, I came to a grave decision. I had held my title for almost three decades. Many youthful contenders for the crown had arisen, and I felt they all deserved a fair chance. It was time to step aside and make way for new blood; it was no longer as in the old days, when I was practically the only player to represent America in international competition. Now our country was being worthily represented by Reshevsky, Fine, Kashdan, Horowitz, Dake and others. The outcome of these reflections was that I decided to retire with the understanding that the new champion would be determined by open competition. Sammy Reshevsky won the first tournament and he has won the other three (the last ended in a tie with Kashdan), proving that the title rests in worthy hands,

*   *   *   *

RETIREMENT YEARS
(1937-1942)

These years have been quiet years; no longer for me the trans-Atlantic voyages, the interminable train trips, the killing tempo of one tournament hard upon another. But these years have not been empty years; I have had time to see more of my good friends of the Marshall Chess Club, to reflect upon the many events of my chess career, to appraise them and put them in order, to take a leisurely look at what the

CAROLINE D.
MARSHALL In 1942

"Carrie has devoted her whole life to my interests and the welfare of chess. Today she is the secretary of the Marshall Chess Club."

Frank J. Marshall, in 1942, plays for his club in the final round of the Metropolitan League matches.

youngsters are doing, to compare them with Lasker and Pillsbury and Schlechter and all the other great men I knew.

But, like the old warhorse who smells the smoke of battle, I still take part in competitive chess when I have the opportunity. I no longer have the physical stamina required for the difficult schedules of most tournaments, but I still play for my club in the Metropolitan League Matches and I have competed regularly in the Championship Tournaments of the Marshall Chess Club. These are *real* contests, putting many an international tournament in the shade. It must be remembered that it was in the Marshall Chess Club that such players as Reuben Fine, Erling Tholfsen, A. E. Santasiere, Milton Hanauer, Sidney Bernstein, Fred Reinfeld, Arthur Dake, Albert Simonson, Herbert Seidman and many others were developed. And we're still continuing to turn out gifted young players!

And so, taking a long look backward at my fifty years of chess playing, I turn these games over to you. They are the product of much toil and some suffering and of one ideal that was always with me: to play the most interesting and beautiful chess of which I was capable. I hope you will like these games.

PART TWO
My Best Games

LIST OF GAMES

I. EARLY YEARS (1893-1896)

II. WINNING MY SPURS (1899-1903)

III. THE YEAR OF YEARS (1904-1905)

IV. COMMUTING TO EUROPE (1906-1909)

V. CHAMPIONSHIP YEARS (1910-1914)

VI. CHAMPIONSHIP YEARS (1915-1936)

VII. RETIREMENT YEARS (1937-1941)

I
EARLY YEARS
(1893-1896)

1. Montreal, Que., 1893
FRENCH DEFENSE

This is my first recorded game. The occasion was a simultaneous exhibition by Steinitz, then champion of the world. I was 16 years old at the time.

W. Steinitz	F. J. Marshall
White	Black
1 P—K4	P—K3
2 P—Q4	P—Q4

The standard opening moves of the French Defense. I was usually more aggressive than this. However, I broke loose later, as you will see.

| 3 Kt—Q2 | Kt—K2 |

Steinitz usually played 3 P—K5 and today 3 Kt—QB3 is probably the most popular third move for White. My own reply was poor. Black should play . . . P—QB4.

| 4 B—Q3 | QKt—B3 |

Another poor move. Again Black should have played P—QB4. The text-move blocks the QB pawn and limits the scope of the Queen. Moves like this are responsible for losing games.

| 5 P—QB3 | Kt—Kt3 |

By no means the best. 5 . . . P—K4 is much better. Then, if 6 P x KP, Kt x P threatening the Bishop; or if 6 P x QP, Kt x P obtains more freedom. If 6 Kt—B3, P x QP; 7 BP x P (7 P x KP, Kt x P). P x P and at least Black does not lose a pawn.

| 6 Kt—Kt3 | P—K4 |
| 7 Q—K2 | B—B3 |

| 8 Kt—B3 | B—Q3? |

With this move I tried to lay a trap for Steinitz and started an entirely unsound combination. 8 . . . B—K2 is better but I didn't realize that my attack was unsound and made the text-move with the deliberate intention of sacrificing a piece!

| 9 P x QP | B x P |
| 10 P x P | O—O?? |

By castling at this point, Black must lose a piece. I could have avoided this by playing 10 . . . B x KKt. Then, if 11 KtP x B, B—K2. I had no such intentions. When I castled I hoped that Steinitz would play 11 P x B, whereupon I would launch an attack with 11 . . . R—K1; 12 B—K3, Kt—B5. This attack might have justified the sacrifice of a piece.

| 11 B x Kt! | . . . . |

Steinitz smiled a little at my inexperience as he upset all my plans with this move, winning a piece outright and skilfully avoiding my attack.

| 11 . . . . | R—K1 |

I continued hopefully with my attack, but White's 11th move had already demolished it.

12 B—B2	Kt x P
13 Kt x Kt	R x Kt
14 B—K3	Q—R5!

Apparently I was trying to put over one of those "swindles" for which I later became famous! If White makes the mistake of castling on the King's side he will be mated. Thus if 15 O—O, R x B; 16 P x R, Q x Pch; 17 K—B2, B—Kt6 mate.

Position after Black's 14th move

Marshall

Steinitz

15 O—O—O   . . . .

I am afraid Steinitz saw that one! He castled on the Queen's side and avoided the swindle.

15 . . . .   Q—QR5

Undaunted, I transferred my attack to the other side of the board.

16 K—Kt1   QR-Q1
17 P—KB4   . . . .

This simple but strong move forced me to declare my intentions before I was ready.

17 . . . .   B—B5
18 Q—B3   R—QR4

Offering the exchange. I didn't think he would take my Rook with his Knight, but he did!

19 Kt x R   Q x Pch
20 K—B1   Q—R8ch
21 B—Kt1   Q x Kt

Black has nothing better. His various attacks have all been skilfully parried and his last attempt has failed, leaving him a Rook down. Now it is just a matter of time. A few more moves and White must win.

22 Q—K4   B—R7
23 Q x Pch   K—B1
24 R—Q4   P—QB3
25 KR—Q1   Q—B2
26 Q—R8ch   Resigns

My inexperience made me too impetuous in this game. I am afraid I must have "underestimated my opponent"!

---

2.   Montreal, Que., 1893

QUEEN'S GAMBIT DECLINED

Another early game which I won from H. N. Pillsbury, the American champion. However, Pillsbury was playing in a simultaneous exhibition and was blindfolded! This is the kind of game which is very difficult to play blindfold.

H.N. PILLSBURY   F.J. MARSHALL

White   Black

1 P—Q4   P—Q4
2 P—QB4   Kt—KB3

An inferior move which permits White to gain control of the center. P—K3 or P—QB3 are better second moves for Black.

3 P x P   Q x P
4 Kt—QB3   Q—Q1

Black loses a tempo as the result of his second move.

5 P—K4   . . . .

5 Kt—B3 would prevent Black's next counter-attacking move.

5 . . . .   P—K4

Offering the sacrifice of a pawn which, if captured, cannot be held.

6 P—Q5   . . . .

There is nothing better. If 6 P x P, Q x Qch; 7 K x Q, Kt—Kt5, recovering the pawn. However, White's text move leaves holes for the Black bishop to enter.

6	B—Q3
7 P—KB4	P x P

White loses a pawn without any compensation. Pillsbury was taking chances as he was playing against an inexperienced youth. Or he may have been giving me an opportunity. Masters sometimes do that in simultaneous exhibitions.

8 Kt—B3	B—KKt5

Pins the Knight and prevents the advance of White's pawn to K5.

9 B—Q3	Kt—R4

Black begins a strong attack. His last move clears the way for the Queen, places the Knight in a strong position and guards the pawn a second time.

10 O—O	B—B4ch

Forcing the King into a corner where he can be checked by the Knight in the later stages of the combination.

11 K—R1	Q—B3
12 Kt—K2	. . . .

Forced. Black threatens . . . Kt—Kt6ch, followed by . . . Q—R3.

12	P—KKt4
13 Q—B2	B—Kt3
14 B—Q2	R—Kt1

Brings the rook into the attack and also forestalls 15 B—B3 which would win the Rook if it remained on the same diagonal as the Queen.

15 P—K5	Q—R3
16 P—QR4	Kt—Kt6ch
17 Kt x Kt	P x Kt
18 B—B3	. . . .

Clears the rank to enable the Queen to defend the threatened mate.

18	B x Kt
19 P x B	P—Kt5
20 P—B4	B—B7

21 R x B	. . . .

Forced. Otherwise, 21 . . . Q x P mate.

21	P x R
22 Q x P	P—Kt6
23 Q—Q2	Kt—Q2
24 P—K6	. . . .

Aggressive to the last, Pillsbury tries to get a counter-attack going.

24	P x P
25 P x P	Kt—B4
26 B—B4	R—Q1
27 Q—Kt2	Kt—K5

Of course, the Knight cannot be taken.

28 R—KB1	. . . .

Position after White's 28th move.

Marshall

Pillsbury

28	R—Q8!

The finishing blow. If 29 R x R, Kt—B7ch; 30 K—Kt1, P x Pch; 31 K x Kt R x Qch; 32 K x R, Q—Kt3 ch and White cannot avoid loss of material.

29 B—K1	R x B
30 R x R	Kt—B7ch
31 K—Kt1	P x Pch
32 K x Kt	R x Qch

33 K x R	Q x BP
34 B—K2	Q—Q7
Resigns	

For if 35 K x P, Q x R; or if 35 K—B2, Q x Rch; 36 K x Q, P—R8 (Q)ch.

---

3.   Montreal, Que., 1894

EVANS' GAMBIT DECLINED

This game is from the Montreal Chess Club Championship Tournament. I made an unsound sacrifice but my opponent was apparently afraid of me and didn't accept it. The finish is devastating.

F.J. Marshall	R. Short
White	Black
1 P—K4	P—K4
2 Kt—KB3	Kt—QB3
3 B—B4	B—B4
4 P—QKt4	B—Kt3

Declining the gambit. This is supposed to be better for Black than the acceptance. However, White gets dangerous attacks in both branches.

| 5 P—B3 | . . . . |

To support P—Q4, but too slow. 5 O—O is stronger. Another good suggestion, by Ulvestad, is 5 P—QR4, followed by B—R3.

5	P—Q3
6 O—O	B—Kt5
7 P—Q4	P x P
8 B x Pch?	K—B1?

Black should have played 8 . . . K x B. The sacrifice is unsound.

| 9 B—Q5 | KKt—K2 |

9 . . . Kt—B3 is better as, after 10 P—KR3, Black could play 10 . . . B x Kt without the dangerous recapture by the White Queen with a check. The text move enables White to finish with a killing attack.

| 10 P—KR3 | B—R4 |
| 11 P—KKt4 | B—Kt3 |

Position after Black's 11th move

Short

Marshall

12 Kt—Kt5!	Q—Q2
13 Kt—K6ch	K—K1
14 Kt x KtPch	K—B1
15 B—K6	Q—Q1
16 B—R6	B x P
17 Kt—R5ch	K—K1
18 Kt—B6 mate.	

4.   New York, 1896

DUTCH DEFENSE

Played while I was still in my teens. At the time, theoretical opinion about this opening was still in an experimental state. Although it may seem as if Black had an easy time of it, the fact is that such games require considerable patience and confidence.

V. Sournin	F. J. Marshall
White	Black
1 P—Q4	P—KB4
2 B—Kt5	. . . .

With the rather optimistic expectation that Black will fall for 2 . . .

P—KR3; 3 B—R4, P—KKt4? 4 B—Kt3, P—B5; 5 P—K3 saving the Bishop because of the threatened Q—R5 mate!

As far as I am concerned, the move that spoils this defense is 2 P—K4 (see Games 54 and 64).

| 2 . . . . | P—KR3 |
| 3 B—R4 | P—B4! |

Putting his finger on the weak point of White's play.

| 4 P—K4 | . . . . |

P—KB3 was better.

| 4 . . . . | Q—Kt3 |

Creating a flight square for the King and thus parrying the threat of Q—R5 mate. At the same time, White is unprepared for the counter-attack on his Queen-side.

5 QP x P	Q x KtP
6 Kt—Q2	P—KKt4
7 Q—R5ch	K—Q1
8 R—Kt1	Q—B3

It would have been even more exact to play . . . Q—Kt2, gaining time for Kt—KB3. White's sacrifice of the piece, obviously intended on move four, has solely nuisance value. However, Black's position is uncomfortable, with his slow development and a King anchored in the center.

9 KKt—B3	P x B
10 P—K5	Q—Kt2
11 Kt—B4	Kt—QB3
11 Q x P(R4)	Q—Kt5

Forcing the exchange of Queens and consequently easing his game considerably.

| 13 B—Q3 | P—KR4! |

It would not be so good for Black to exchange, for after 14 Kt x Q the Knight would be threatening to go to Kt6 with good effect. The text has the great virtue of putting Black's KR3 at the disposal of his pieces.

14 O—O	Kt—R3
15 KR—Q1	KR—Kt1
16 Q x Q	RP x Q
17 KKt—Q2	P—K3

Black is gradually consolidatng his game, rounding out his Pawn position and bringing new pieces into play.

| 18 Kt—Kt3 | Kt—B2 |
| 19 R—K1 | B—Kt2 |

And now the KP goes. Black has at last seized the initiative, and his considerable material advantage begins to tell.

| 20 P—QB3 | QKt x P |
| 21 QR—Q1 | R—Kt1 |

In order to create more open lines (. . . P—Kt3 etc.).

22 Kt—Q4	Kt x Kt
23 B x Kt	B x Kt
24 R x B	K—B2

Guarding against BxP. The foregoing exchanges were, of course, much in Black's favor.

25 B—Kt5	P—Kt3
26 P x Pch	R x P
27 P—QR4	P—R3
28 B—B1	R—R1

As will be seen, the occupation of the KR file brings quick results.

| 29 P—QB4 | P—K4 |
| 30 R—Q3 | QR—R3 |

To this there is no good reply; if 31 P—R3, P—K5; 32 R—QKt3, P x P; 33 P x P, Kt—Kt4 threatening . . . Kt x Pch or . . . Kt—B6ch with decisive effect.

31 P—Kt3	R x P
32 B—Kt2	Kt—Kt4!
33 R x P	. . . .

There is a nice finish now.

Position after White's 33rd move

Marshall

Sournin

33	Kt—B6ch
34 R x Kt	. . . .

Or 34 B x Kt, P x B; 35 R x P, R—R8ch; 36 K—Kt2, R(1)—R7 mate. White's King is blocked by his own Rook.

34	B—Kt2!

White resigns. If 35 R(5) x P, P x R; 36 B x P, R—R8ch!

II
WINNING MY SPURS
(1899-1903)

5. London 1899 (Minor Tourney)

TWO KNIGHTS' DEFENSE

One of my earliest brilliancies!

F.J. Marshall	Dr. J.F. Esser
White	Black
1 P—K4	P—K4
2 Kt—KB3	Kt—QB3
3 B—B4	Kt—B3
4 P—Q4	P x P
5 O—O	Kt x P

I would have enjoyed playing the Max Lange Attack after 5 . . . B—B4; 6 P—K5, P—Q4; 7 P x Kt, P x B; 8 R—K1ch, B—K3; 9 Kt—Kt5 etc.

6 R—K1	P—Q4
7 B x P	Q x B
8 Kt—B3	Q—Q1

An illogical retreat. As long as the Queen has been developed, why not play it to KR4 or QR4?

9 R x Ktch	B—K2
10 Kt x P	Kt x Kt

This allows White to command the Q file with great effect, and it is therefore inferior to 10 . . . P—B4; 11 R—B4, O—O; 12 Kt x Kt, Q x Qch; 13 Kt x Q, P x Kt — in which case the two Bishops compensate somewhat for the weak Queen-side Pawns.

11 R x Kt	B—Q2
12 B—B4	Q—B1
13 Kt—Q5	B—Q1
14 Q—R5!	O—O

White has worked up a mighty attacking position (one of the threats was 15 R—K1ch, B—K3; 16 B x P! B x B; 17 R x Bch!) and castling seems urgently called for. But now the real fireworks begin!

Position after Black's 14th move

Dr. Esser

Marshall

| 15 B x P! | B—K3 |

The Bishop is poison, for if 15 ... B x B? 16 Kt—K7ch, K—R1; 17 Q x Pch! and mate next move.

| 16 B x B | B x Kt |

16 ... Q x B avoids the combination, but then 17 QR—Q1 leaves Black in a hopeless state.

| 17 B—B6! | . . . . |

Perfectly sound and much more enterprising than the obvious 17 Q x B, R x B; 18 Q x Rch, Q x Q; 19 R x Qch, R x R; 20 K—B1, R—Q7; 21 R—B1 followed by K—K1 etc.

| 17 . . . . | Q—B3 |

Relatively best was 17 ... P x B; 18 Q x B etc.

18 B x P	K x B
19 Q x B	Q x P
20 Q—K5ch	. . . .

An even quicker win was 20 R—Kt4ch, K—R1; 21 Q—K5ch, P—B3; 22 Q—K7.

| 20 . . . . | P—B3 |

| 21 Q—K7ch | K—Kt3 |

Very sad, but on 21 ... R—B2 or ... K—R1; 22 R—Kt4 decides at once.

| 22 R—KR4 | K—Kt4 |
| 23 Q—Kt7ch! | K x R |

Shortens the agony.

24 Q—R6ch	K—Kt5
25 P—R3ch	K—B4
26 Q x RPch	Resigns

---

6. London, 1899

(Minor Tournament)

BISHOP'S OPENING

I still have a soft spot in my heart for the final mating position!

E. M. JACKSON	F. J. MARSHALL
White	Black
1 P—K4	P—K4
2 B—B4	Kt—KB3
3 P—Q3	P—Q4

The theorists frown on this move because it is likely to lose a Pawn. However, it has been my experience that White loses time and weakens his position in gaining the Pawn, so that the sacrifice becomes a worthwhile investment.

| 4 P x P | Kt x P |
| 5 Q—K2 | . . . . |

Aha! He goes after the Pawn.

| 5 . . . . | Kt—QB3 |
| 6 P—B4? | B—QB4 |

White's last move was very risky. If now 7 P x P, O—O (threatens ... Kt x P); 8 Kt—KB3, B—KKt5 with the strong threats of ... Kt x P or ... Kt—Q5.

7 Kt—KB3	B—Kt5
8 P—KR3	B x Kt
9 Q x B	Kt—Kt3

Nowadays I would simply play 9 ... Kt x P; 10 B x Kt, P x B; 11 Q x P, O—O with a clear advantage. The text leads to more complicated play.

10 B—Kt5	O—O
11 B x Kt	P x B
12 P—B5	....

Having played for the win of a Pawn, he gets cold feet now and tries to close the center. However, if 12 P x P, R—K1; or if 12 B—K3, B x B; 13 Q x B, Kt—Q4; or 12 Q x P, Q—Q5 (or 12 ... Q—R5ch) —always with advantage to Black.

| 12 .... | P—K5! |

I must have my open file!

| 13 P x P | R—K1 |

With his King stranded in the center, White's game is most uncomfortable.

| 14 Kt—B3 | .... |

Kt—Q2 has been suggested, but then 14 ... Kt—Q4 (threatening ... Kt—K6 or ... Kt—B3) is troublesome.

| 14 .... | Kt—Q4! |

Now if 15 B—Q2, Kt x Kt; 16 B x Kt, Q—R5ch; 17 P—Kt3ch, R x Pch with a winning position.

| 15 P—KKt3 | Kt—Kt5 |
| 16 Q—K2 | .... |

Or 16 Q—Q1, Q—B3 and the attack must triumph.

| 16 .... | Q—Q5 |

Here too, 16 ... Q—B3 (intending ... B—Q5 followed by ... Kt—Q4) was probably the strongest.

17 K—B1	Kt—Q4
18 K—Kt2	Kt x Kt
19 P x Kt	Q x Pch
20 Q x Q	R x Q

| 21 K—B3 | QR—K1 |

Black has regained his Pawn and has a tremendous lead in development, but the broken Pawn position necessitates his continuing to play for attack.

22 B—Q2	R—K7
23 QR—Q1	R—B7ch
24 K—Kt4	P—R4ch!

This involves careful calculation, as will be seen.

25 K x P	P—Kt3ch
26 P x P	R—K4ch
27 K—Kt4	P—B4ch
28 K—R4	....

He can hold out longer with 28 K—R5, P—B5ch; 29 K—Kt4, P x P; 30 K x P, R—K3! 31 P—KR4, R x P ch; 32 B—Kt5, R x P etc. but Black should win. The same applies to the next move.

28	K—Kt2!
29 B—B4?	K x P!
30 B—Kt5	R—B5ch!!

White resigns. A beautiful mating position.

Final Position

Marshall

Jackson

7. Paris, 1900

QUEEN'S GAMBIT DECLINED

Throughout my career, I did not succeed in winning very many games from the great Dr. Emanuel Lasker. Strangely enough, I won this game from him the first time we ever met across the board. Forty years later, I won my last game with Dr. Lasker—and it proved to be the last important game of his life.

This game shows the great resourcefulness of the then World Champion. After I had won a piece he all but drew.

F. J. MARSHALL	DR. E. LASKER
White	Black
1 P—Q4	P—Q4
2 P—QB4	P—K3
3 Kt—QB3	Kt—KB3
4 B—Kt5	P—B3
5 P—K4	. . . .

For a number of years I was fond of this move in similar positions. Eventually I discarded it, as it cannot lead to a permanent initiative.

5	P x KP
6 Kt x P	B—Kt5ch
7 Kt—B3	P—B4

It begins to appear as if White will have trouble with his Queen-side Pawns.

8 P—QR3	B x Ktch
9 P x B	Q—R4
10 B—Q2	Kt—K5
11 Kt—B3	Kt x QBP?!

Although careful analysis proves this move to be playable, the results it achieves are hardly worth the risk involved.

| 12 P x P! | . . . . |

If 12 Q—Kt3, P x P; 14 Kt x P, Q—K4ch freeing himself from the terrible pin. But the text-move threatens Q—Kt3; hence Black's reply is forced.

12	Kt x Q
13 B x Q	Kt—Kt7
14 P—QR4	. . . .

The following critical and ingenious play hinges on White's attempt to trap the Knight, and on Black's efforts to save the piece.

| 14 . . . . | B—Q2 |

The only reply to the threatened R—R2. Black appears to be in great difficulty, since after 15 Kt—K5 he cannot go in for 15 . . . Kt x RP? 16 Kt x B nor 15 . . . B x P? 16 B—B3. However, there is a way out in reply to 15 Kt—K5, namely 15 . . . Kt—B3! But White has a surprise reply!

Position after Black's 14th move

Dr. Lasker

Marshall

| 15 P—B6! | B x P |

If 15 . . . QKt x P? 16 B—B3 wins the Knight.

| 16 Kt—K5 | B—K5? |

One of the few instances in which Lasker fails to rise to the occasion. Necessary was 15 . . . Kt—Q2! 16 Kt x B, P x Kt; 17 B—B3, QR—Kt1; 18 B x P (not 18 R—

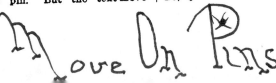

R2? Kt x BP!), R—Kt1; 19 B—Q4, P—K4; 20 B—B3, Kt—B4; 21 P—R5, P—B3. The position of the advanced Knight would then be safe but awkward.

| 17 | P—B3 | P—B3 |
| 18 | B—B3? | . . . . |

Not the best. More exact was P x B, P x Kt; 19 B—B3, Kt x RP; 20 R x Kt with an easy win.

18	. . . .	B—B7!
19	K—Q2	Kt x RP
20	K x B	Kt x B
21	Kt—Q3!	Kt—Q4
22	P x Kt	P x P

Black has managed to secure three Pawns for the piece, and White still has his work cut out for him.

| 23 | Kt—B5 | . . . . |

Kt—B4, winning the QP, was simpler; but the text, played with the idea of immobilizing the Queenside Pawns, also has its points.

23	. . . .	P—QKt3
24	B—Kt5ch	K—B2
25	Kt—R4	Kt—B3!

The only reply to the threatened Kt x P. If now 26 B x Kt, KR—QB1 etc.

| 26 | Kt—B3 | KR—QB1 |
| 27 | KR—Q1 | Kt—K2 |

After . . . P—Q5; 28 Kt—K4 Black has no useful discovered check.

| 28 | K—Kt2 | R—B2 |
| 29 | B—Q3 | . . . . |

Not 29 Kt x P? R—B4. Black's Queen-side Pawns are now harmless and White can concentrate on the job of combining useful simplification with threats against the Pawns.

| 29 | . . . . | P—QR4 |
| 30 | Kt—R4 | R—B3 |

31	QR—B1!	R—QKt1
32	R x R	Kt x R
33	R—QB1	Kt—K4
34	R—B7ch	K—K3

The passive 34 . . . K—Kt1 would lose much more rapidly.

| 35 | B—Kt5 | P—Kt4 |

White now disregards the KRP because he still intends to work on the Queen-side Pawns first. The QP cannot last long.

36	R—R7	P—Q5
37	R—R6	K—Q4
38	K—B2	R—Kt2

For if 39 Kt x Pch? K—B4. But White takes his time.

39	R—R8	Kt—B3
40	K—Q2	Kt—Kt5
41	R—Q8ch	K—K4
42	Kt—Kt2	R—QB2
43	Kt—B4ch	K—B4
44	R x P	. . . .

After the win of this Pawn, the rest is easy: 44 . . . R—B4; 45 B—K8, R—Q4; 46 Kt—K3ch, K—K4; 47 Kt x R, K x R; 48 Kt x Kt, P x Kt; 49 B—B7, P—R4; 50 B—Kt8, P—R4; 51 B—B7, P—R5; 52 P—R3, P—Kt4; 53 B—K8, K—B5; 54 B—Q7, P—Kt6; 55 B x BP, K—Kt5; 56 B—Q3, P—Kt7; 57 K—B2, K—R6; 58 K—Kt1 and Black resigned.

---

8. Paris, 1900
PETROFF DEFENSE

In this, my first encounter with the immortal Pillsbury on even terms, I began by playing for equality; but then I saw an opportunity to go in for a combination which apparently took him by surprise.

H. N. Pillsbury	F. J. Marshall
White	Black
1 P—K4	P—K4

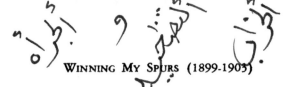

2 Kt—KB3   Kt—KB3
3 P—Q4   . . . .

I have never seen any reason to fear this move, although it was much favored by Steinitz, Pillsbury and Tchigorin. Any attempt to secure an advantage must begin with a 3 Kt x P.

3 . . . .   P—Q4
4 KP x P   P x P
5 B—QB4   . . . .

Either 5 B—Kt5ch or 5 Q x P would give more chance of obtaining some initiative. Black gets a good game with the following checks.

5 . . . .   B—Kt5ch!
6 P—B3   Q—K2ch!

If now 7 Q—K2, Q x Qch and Black stands well for the ending because White's Pawn position is somewhat weak.

7 B—K2   P x P
8 P x P   B—QB4
9 O—O   O—O
10 P—B4   R—K1
11 B—Q3   B—KKt5
12 B—Kt2?   . . . .

After this White's game becomes uncomfortable. (Note that 12 R—K1?? would lose a piece after 12 . . . B x Kt.) Best was 12 QKt—Q2, QKt—Q2 with a good game for Black.

12 . . . .   Kt—K5
13 QKt—Q2?   . . . .

He should have tried 13 B x Kt, Q x B; 14 QKt—Q2 although this would leave Black with an excellent position. The text gives Black an opportunity for a winning combination.

(see diagram next column)

13 . . . .   Kt x P!
14 R x Kt   B x Rch
15 K x B   Q—K6ch

Position after White's 13th move

Marshall

Pillsbury

16 K—Kt3   Q x B
17 K x B   R—K7!

The key to the whole combination. White is helpless.

18 K—R3   Kt—Q2·

Simpler than 18 . . . P—KR4 (threatening . . . Q—B4ch and mate next move); 19 Q x R!? Q x Q; 20 R—K1, Q—Q6; 21 R—K8ch and despite Black's considerable material superiority, the win is not easy with his Queen-side pieces bottled up.

19 R—B1   P—KR4
20 Q—B2   Kt—B4
21 P—Kt3   . . . .

If 21 Q x Q, Kt x Q; 22 R—B2, P—KKt4! 23 K—Kt3, P—Kt5; 24 Kt—R4, Kt—K8; 25 R—B1, R x Kt; 26 B—B3, R—QB7! and wins. If, here, 23 Kt x P, Kt—K8; 24 R—B1, R x Kt; 25 B—B3, R—Q6ch; or if 23 P—Kt4? Kt—B5ch; 24 K—Kt3, R—Kt7 mate.

21 . . . .   P—KKt4!
22 P—Kt4   . . . .

Despair. There is no defense.

22 . . . .   R x Kt

23 Q x Q	R x Q
24 R—B3	P—B4!
25 K—Kt2	BP x P
26 Kt x P	R—Q7ch

Resigns

9. Paris, 1900
QUEEN'S GAMBIT DECLINED

Britisher Amos Burn was a very conservative player and liked to settle down for a long session of close, defensive chess. He loved to smoke his pipe while he studied the board.

As I made my second move, Burn began hunting through his pockets for his pipe and tobacco.

| F. J. MARSHALL | AMOS BURN |
| White | Black |

1 P—Q4	P—Q4
2 P—QB4	P—K3
3 Kt—QB3	Kt—KB3
4 B—Kt5	B—K2

Not much thought needed on these moves, but Burn had his pipe out and was looking for a pipe cleaner.

5 P—K3	O—O
6 Kt—B3	P—QKt3
7 B—Q3	B—Kt2
8 P x P	P x P

He began filling up his pipe. I speeded up my moves.

| 9 B x Kt | B x B |
| 10 P—KR4 | . . . . |

Made him think on that one—and he still didn't have the pipe going. The threat is B x Pch, K x B; Kt—Kt5ch, known as the Pillsbury attack.

| 10 . . . . | P—Kt3 |

| 11 P—R5 | R—K1 |
| 12 P x P | RP x P |

Now he was looking for matches.

| 13 Q—B2 | B—Kt2 |

Position after Black's 13th move

Amos Burn

Marshall

| 14 B x P! | P x B |

He struck a match, appeared nervous. The match burned his fingers and went out.

| 15 Q x P | Kt—Q2 |

Another match was on its way.

| 16 Kt—KKt5 | Q—B3 |

He was puffing away and lighting up at last. No time left.

| 17 R—R8ch | Resigns |

For if 17 . , .K x R; 18 Q—R7 mate.

Poor Burn. I think I swindled him out of that one. If he could only have got that pipe going, it might have been a different story. He took it good-naturedly and we shook hands. Then his pipe went out.

10. Paris, 1900

QUEEN'S GAMBIT DECLINED

Only two days after the previous game, Marco, who was noted for his analytical ability, adopted the same line of play against me. Naturally I accepted the challenge with pleasure; but Marco did not find the best moves, and eventually succumbed very rapidly!

F. J. MARSHALL	G. MARCO
White	Black
1 P—Q4	P—Q4
2 P—QB4	P—K3
3 Kt—QB3	Kt—KB3
4 B—Kt5	B—K2
5 P—K3	P—QKt3
6 Kt—B3	B—Kt2
7 B—Q3	O—O

The customary 7 . . . QKt—Q2 is simpler and safer; but Marco was, of course, deliberately steering for the play that follows.

| 8 P x P | P x P |

If 8 . . . Kt x P; 9 B x B, Q x B; 10 Kt x Kt, B x Kt; 11 R—B1 with a clear positional advantage.

9 B x Kt	B x B
10 P—KR4	P—Kt3
11 P—R5	P—B4

The Tournament Book suggests . . . Kt—Q2 followed by . . . R—K1 and . . . Kt—B1 as offering a more solid defense.

| 12 RP x P | RP x P |

And here again, 12 . . . KBP x P might be preferable — to defend along the second rank.

| 13 Kt—K5! | B x Kt |
| 14 P x B | Q—Kt4 |

Not only to win a Pawn, but to prevent White's Q—Kt4 followed by O—O—O with strong attacking prospects.

| 15 Q—B3 | Q x KP |
| 16 O—O—O | K—Kt2? |

A fatal lapse. As Marco later pointed out, 16 . . . Kt—Q2 is better, but White would still have retained good attacking chances. After the text it is all over.

| 17 Q—R3! | Kt—B3 |

If 17 . . . P—Q5; 18 Q—R6ch wins.

Position after Black's 17th move

Marco

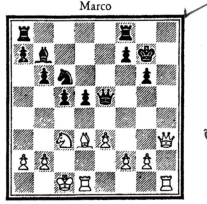

Marshall

18 P—B4!	Q—K3
19 Q—R6ch	K—B3
20 Q—Kt5ch	K—Kt2
21 P—B5!	Q—K4

Or 21 . . . Q—B3; 22 Q—R6ch, etc.

| 22 P—B6ch! | Q x P |
| 23 Q—R6ch | Resigns |

---

11. Monte Carlo, 1902

ENGLISH OPENING

White invites trouble by neglecting his development and weakening his position in order to grab a Pawn. The trouble arrives soon enough!

J. MASON	F. J. MARSHALL
White	Black
1 P—QB4	P—K4
2 Kt—QB3	P—KB4
3 P—K4	. . . .

More positional would be 3 P—KKt3 or 3 P—K3. The text can only help Black to open up the KB file.

| 3 . . . . | Kt—KB3 |
| 4 P—Q3 | Kt—B3 |

Offering the Pawn to gain time for development.

5 P x P	B—Kt5
6 B—Q2	O—O
7 P—Kt4	. . . .

Consistent enough, if he is to hold the Pawn; but White's game is already beginning to wobble.

| 7 . . . . | P—Q4 |
| 8 P x P? | . . . . |

White is headed for a catastrophe. 8 P—KR3 should have been tried.

8	B x Kt
9 B x B	Q x P
10 Q—B3	Q—B4
11 Kt—K2	Kt—Kt5

Regaining the Pawn, in the event of 12 B x Kt, and leaving White nothing to show for his ruined position.

| 12 R—B1 | . . . . |

(see diagram next column)

| 12 . . . . | Kt x KtP! |

With this move, which has been "in the air" for some time, White's position is smashed up irretrievably.

13 Q x Kt	Kt x Pch
14 K—Q2	B x P
15 B—Kt4	. . . .

Position after White's 12th move

Marshall

Mason

As good or bad as anything else.

15	Q x Bch
16 Q x Q	Kt x Q
17 Kt—B3	QR—Q1ch
18 K—K3	Kt—B7ch
19 K—B3	. . . .

19 R x Kt would tame the attack, but then Black's material advantage would win easily.

| 19 . . . . | R—Q5 |
| 20 KR—Kt1 | . . . . |

K—Kt3 would hold out a bit longer. White has nothing left now but forced moves.

20	B—K5ch
21 K—Kt3	R—B6ch
22 K—Kt4	B—Q4ch
23 K—Kt5	P—R3ch
24 K—R5	B—B2ch
25 R—Kt6	R—B4 mate

---

12. Hanover, 1902
ALBIN COUNTER GAMBIT

At this tournament I met my old friend W. E. Napier. He was born in England, but has spent most of his life in the United States. As a young man he competed often with C. S. Howell, A. W. Fox and myself. He was sent abroad by his parents to study music, but he preferred chess and so played in quite a few European tournaments; at one time he was champion of Great Britain. He is still active today, plays a fine game of chess and writes unusually well on the subject.

F. J. MARSHALL   W. E. NAPIER

White	Black
1 P—Q4	P—Q4
2 P—QB4	P—K4
3 QP x P	P—Q5
4 Kt—KB3	Kt—QB3
5 QKt—Q2	B—K3
6 P—KKt3	P—KKt3

Too slow. The basic idea of the gambit is rapid development with a view to counter-attack; hence the favored continuations are . . . Q—Q2 followed by . . . O—O—O; or . . . KKt—K2—Kt3; or . . . P—B3. When Black sheds aggressiveness in order to regain the Pawn, he usually comes off second-best.

7 B—Kt2	B—Kt2
8 Kt—Kt3	. . . .

A good idea. He surrenders the QBP, which is of no great value, in return for the hostile QP, whose presence often has a cramping effect on White's development.

8	B x BP
9 QKt x P	Kt x Kt
10 Kt x Kt	B—Q4

Not 10 . . . KB x P? 11 Q—R4ch. It appears that Black cannot avoid parting with his QB in a disadvantageous manner.

11 Q—R4ch	P—B3
12 P—K4	B—K3
13 Kt x B	P x Kt
14 O—O	B x P

See the first note. Black has re-gained the Pawn, but he is behind in development, and he is burdened with a bad weakness in the isolated KP.

15 Q—Kt3!	Q—K2
16 B—R3	K—B2
17 B—K3	Kt—B3
18 P—B4	B—B2
19 P—B5	. . . .

This smashing advance wins a Pawn, establishes a powerful advanced KP which will eventually carry the day and opens up the KB file for lasting pressure. Black is able to prolong his resistance quite a bit, however, by placing his Bishop at K4 in a very useful defensive position.

19	K—Kt2
20 P x KP	B—K4
21 R—B2	KR—Q1
22 QR—KB1	K—R1

If instead 22 . . . P—KR3; 23 Q—B2 is very strong (possibilities: B—B5 or Q—B1).

23 B—Kt5	Q—B4

Or 23 . . . R—KB1; 24 B—R6 followed by P—Kt4—5. White's immediate objective is, of course, to remove the obstructive Knight, gaining access to KB7 and thereby making possible the winning advance of the KP.

24 B x Ktch	B.x B
25 K—Kt2	B—Kt2
26 Q x P	Q—B5
27 Q—Kt3	Q x Pch
28 Q—B3	. . . .

(see diagram next page)

The Bishops of opposite colors cannot save Black; the position is too much against him. Thus if now 28 . . . Q x Qch; 29 R x Q, B x P; 30 P—K7, R—K1; 31 R—B8ch, K—Kt2; 32 R(1)—B7ch, K—R3; 33 R x R, R x R; 34 B—Q7 and wins. No better is the more conservative line 29 . . . **B—B1; 30 R—B7, R—K1**

Position after White's 28th move

Napier

Marshall

(if 30 . . . B—B4; 31 P—K7, R—K1; 32 R—K1, K—Kt1; 33 B—K6, K—R1; 34 B—Q7); 31 P—K7! B x P; 32 B—Q7 etc.

28	Q—QKt5
29 Q x P	QR—Kt1
30 P—Kt3	Q—K2
31 P—QKt4	. . . .

R—B7 was simpler. However, the Pawn cannot very well be taken: 31 . . . Q x P; 32 R—B7 with a winning position; or 31 . . . R x P; 32 R—B7 forcing the advance of the KP with a quick win in sight.

| 31 . . . . | R—Kt3 |
| 32 Q—K4 | R(3)—Q3 |

32 . . . R x KtP; 33 R—B7! is also hopeless for Black.

33 R—B7	R—Q7ch
34 K—R1	Q—Q3
35 P—K7	R—K1
36 Q—K6!	Q—Q6

After the exchange of Queens he would be helpless against R—B8ch.

| 37 R—B8ch | B x R |
| 38 Q—K5ch! | Resigns |

For mate is unavoidable.

---

13. Monte Carlo, 1903

QUEEN'S GAMBIT DECLINED

Again Pillsbury overlooks a tactical finesse!

H. N. PILLSBURY   F. J. MARSHALL

White	Black
1 P—Q4	P—Q4
2 P—QB4	P—QB3
3 Kt—KB3	Kt—B3
4 Kt—B3	Kt—K5

During this period I adopted the Stonewall formation a number of times in order to experiment with its attacking possibilities (see also Game No. 51).

| 5 P—K3 | . . . . |

It is surprising to see Pillsbury, who was so famous for his expert knowledge of this opening, voluntarily imprisoning his QB. As the game goes, he gets no value whatever from this piece; hence 5 B—B4 was preferable.

5	P—K3
6 B—Q3	P—KB4
7 Kt—K5	Q—R5
8 Q—B2	. . . .

And this, too, has little point. The recommended continuation nowadays is 8 O—O, Kt—Q2; 9 P—KB4, B—Q3; 10 P x P, KP x P; 11 B x Kt, BP x B; 12 B—Q2 (Gruenfeld). Then if . . . P—KKt4?? 13 B—K1, Q—R3; 14 Kt—B7!! and wins. But in those days there was still a lot of No Man's Land to be traversed in the field of opening theory!

8	Kt—Q2
9 O—O	B—Q3
10 P—B4	P—KKt4!?

A Pawn sacrifice characteristic of my style. Black gains a lasting initiative with the open KKt file, and even if the attack peters out, he has little reason to fear the ending, as White's QB is so ineffectual.

11	Kt—B3	Q—R4
12	B x Kt	BP x B
13	Kt x KtP	Kt—B3
14	Q—K2	Q—Kt3
15	P—QB5	B—B2
16	K—R1	P—KR3
17	Kt—R3	KR—Kt1
18	B—Q2?	....

Evidently not realizing the strength of Black's reply. KR—Kt1 was more accurate.

18	....	P—Kt3!
19	P—QKt4	P x P
20	KtP x P	....

After 20 QP x P, P—K4 (if 20 ... B—R3; 21 P—Kt5, P x P; 22 Kt x KtP, B x Kt? White's Queen retakes with check) Black's attacking possibilities are enhanced. Nevertheless this continuation was preferable to the following forced loss of the exchange.

20	....	B—R3
21	Q—B2	B x R
22	R x B	R—Kt1
23	B—B1	B—R4
24	Kt—Q1	K—Q2
25	R—Kt1	Q—R4
26	Q—B2	R—KKt2

The QKt file will eventually be the highway to Black's victory; but first he wants to see what can be accomplished on the other wing.

| 27 | Kt(1)—B2 | QR—Kt1 |
| 28 | Q—Q1 | .... |

The exchange of Queens only facilitates Black's task; but White is strictly limited to the defensive, as he must always be on guard against a possible ... RxP.

28	....	Q x Q
29	Kt x Q	.R—Kt1
30	P—Kt3	Kt—Kt5!
31	R—Kt2	R—Kt8
32	R—QB2	R—KKt1
33	K—Kt2	B—Q7!

Thus the White Bishop comes to an inglorious end. The simplifying text prepares a decisive return of the exchange, after which Black's command of the seventh, plus a passed KP, wins easily.

Position after Black's 33rd move

Marshall

Pillsbury

| 34 | B x B | R x Kt |
| 35 | R—Kt2 | R—Kt1! |

If now 36 R—B2, R(1)—Kt8 and Zugzwang sets in!

36	R x R	R x Bch
37	K—Kt1	R—Q8ch
38	K—Kt2	Kt x Pch
39	K—B2	Kt—Kt5ch
40	K—Kt2	....

Or 40 K—K2, R—KR8 wins easily.

| 40 | .... | R—Q7ch |
| 41 | K—Kt1 | P—K6! |

If 41 ... RxKRP? 42 R—Kt8!

| 42 | R—Kt1 | P—K7 |

Black falters, although the win is still mechanical. More exact, however, was 42 ...R x KRP winning the Kt and retaining the KP.

| 43 | Kt—B2 | P—K8(Q)ch |

44 R x Q   Kt x Kt

The remaining moves were: 45 R—K5, Kt—Kt5; 46 R—R5, R x QRP; 47 P—R3, Kt—K6; 48 P—Kt4, R—Kt7ch; 49 K—R1, R—KB7; 50 R x P, R x P; 51 R—R7ch, K—Q1; 52 P—Kt5, P—R4; 53 P—Kt6, Kt—B4; 54 P—Kt7, Kt x KtP; 55 R x Kt, R x P; 56 R—QR7, P—R5; 57 K—Kt2, R—QB5; 58 R—R5, K—K2; 59 K—Kt3, K—B3; 60 P—R4, K—B4; 61 R—R6, R x BP; 62 R x RP, R—B6ch; 63 K—R2, R—B5 and White resigned.

This game was widely praised by the critics; but I still regret my 42nd move!

---

14.   Monte Carlo, 1903

MUZIO GAMBIT

"What's this?" I can hear the reader exclaim, "A Muzio Gambit in a tournament game?" Well, the tourney was nearing its close, and I was determined to have some fun. The game was played on March 13, which proved to be an "unlucky thirteenth" indeed for Col. Moreau!

F. J. MARSHALL   C. MOREAU

White   Black

1 P—K4   P—K4
2 P—KB4   P x P
3 Kt—KB3   P—KKt4
4 B—B4   P—Kt5
5 O—O   . . . .

5 Kt—B3, as in Game no. 17, is a powerful alternative.

5 . . . .   P x Kt
6 Q x P   Q—B3
7 P—K5   Q x P
8 B x Pch!?   . . . .

Here I hark back to the days of my idol Morphy. The man who named this "the wild Muzio" certainly knew what he was talking about!

8 . . . .   K—Q1

The normal continuation 8 . . . K x B; 9 P—Q4, Q x Pch; 10 B—K3 leaves White with a powerful and lasting attack. However, Black's last is no improvement, as White has a strong attack at relatively less cost.

9 P—Q4   Q x Pch
10 K—R1   B—R3
11 B—Q2   Q—Kt2
12 B—Kt3   Kt—QB3
13 B—B3   Kt—K4

If 13 . . . Kt—B3; 14 Kt—Q2 followed by Kt—K4 is very strong.

14 Q—Q5   P—Q3
15 R—Q1   B—Q2?

Threatens . . . B—B3, but too slow. The right way was 15 . . . P—B6 and if 16 P x P, B—B5.

16 B—R4   B—B3?

This loses. The maneuver . . . P—B6 followed by . . . B—B5 was absolutely essential.

17 B x B   P x B
18 Q x Kt   Q—Kt5

Or 18 . . . Q x Q; 19 B x Q picking up the KR as well.

19 Kt—R3   K—Q2
20 Kt—B4   P—B6

Now too late; but there was no defense, for if 20 . . . Kt—K2; 21 Kt x P wins easily.

(see diagram next page)

Black threatens mate on the move, but White comes first with an announced mate in eleven moves:

21 R x Pch   P x R

If 21 . . . K—B1; 22 Q—K8ch, K—Kt2; 23 Kt—R5ch, K—Kt3; 24 Q x P mate.

22 Q x Pch   K—B1

If 22 . . . K—K1; 23 R—K1ch,

White announces mate in eleven!

Moreau

Marshall

K—B2; 24 Kt—K5ch, K—Kt2; 25
Kt x Qch, K—B2; 26 Kt x Bch, Kt x
Kt; 27 Q—B6ch, K—Kt1; 28 Q—
Kt7 mate.

23 Q x Pch	K—Q1
24 R—Q1ch	K—K2
25 Q—Q6ch	K—K1
26 R—K1ch	K—B2
27 Kt—K5ch	K—K1
28 Kt—Kt6ch	B—K6

Or 28 . . . K—B2; 29 Kt x R mate.

| 29 R x Bch | Q—K3 |
| 30 Q x Qch | K—Q1 |

31 B—R5 mate

---

15.   Glasgow, 1903
RUY LOPEZ

Black's slow and cramped development allows the formation of a
murderous attack.

F. J. MARSHALL	ALLIES
(Blindfold)	
White	Black
1 P—K4	P—K4
2 Kt—KB3	Kt—QB3

3 B—Kt5	Kt—B3
4 O—O	Kt x P
5 P—Q4	B—K2
6 P x P	. . . .

Varying from the then fashionable 6 Q—K2.

6	O—O
7 Q—Q5	Kt—B4
8 B—K3	Kt—K3
9 Kt—B3	Q—K1

Here or on the next move it is
absolutely essential for Black to
seek freedom with the liberating
. . . P—B3! Instead, the cumber-
some development actually selected by Black soon results in storm
clouds on the King-side.

10 QR—K1	P—QKt3
11 Q—K4!	B—Kt2
12 Kt—Q5	R—Kt1
13 B—Q3	P—Kt3

Creating a weakness on the
black squares which soon proves
fatal; and yet there was no alternative. See the previous note.

14 Kt—B6ch   . . . .

Because of the mating threat this
move creates (after the following
forced capture), I preferred it to
the win of the exchange by 14
B—KR6, Kt—Kt2; 15 Kt—B6ch,
B x Kt; 16 P x B etc.

14	B x Kt
15 P x B	Kt(B3)—Q5
16 Q—R4!	Kt x Ktch

Or 16 . . . B x Kt; 17 B x Kt etc.

17 P x Kt   Q—Q1

If 17 . . . B x P; 18 B—QB5 with
a winning game.

18 B—KKt5   K—R1

White threatened 19 Q—R6 and
20 R x Kt. If 18 . . . Kt x B; 19 Q x
Kt, R—K1; 20 R—K7, R x R; 21
P x R, Q—K1; 22 Q—B6 and Black
must eventually succumb.

| 19 P—KB4 | R—Kt1 |
| 20 R—K3 | Kt—B1 |

Guarding against the menace of 21 Q x Pch, K x Q; 22 R—R3 mate. If instead 20 . . . P—KR4; 21 R—R3 (threatening Q x Pch), R—K1; 22 P—B5 and wins.

21 KR—K1	P—B4
22 R—R3	P—B5
23 R (1)—K3!	P x B

There is nothing to be done.

The final position

Allies

Marshall

White announced mate in three: 24 Q x Pch, Kt x Q; 25 R x Ktch, K x R; 26 R—R3 mate.

---

16. Cable Match, 1903

QUEEN'S GAMBIT DECLINED

I think the reader will agree that the manner in which I extricate myself from a difficult position. makes this game well worthy of inclusion.

F. J. Marshall	H. E. Atkins
(U. S. A.)	(Great Britain)
White	Black
1 P—Q4	P—Q4

2 P—QB4	P—QB3
3 Kt—QB3	Kt—B3
4 P x P	. . . .

Throughout my whole career, I have been very partial to this early exchange and have achieved excellent results with it. Despite its apparent simplicity, the move leaves plenty of scope for interesting play and often Black finds himself in unexpected difficulties!

4	P x P
5 B—B4	Kt—B3
6 P—K3	P—K3
7 B—Q3	B—K2
8 Kt—B3	O—O
9 Kt—K5	. . . .

It might have been preferable to postpone this in favor of more development by O—O or QR—B1 or Q—Kt3.

9	Kt x Kt
10 P x Kt	Kt—Q2
11 Q—B2	. . . .

Beginning a faulty attacking policy. Simply O—O was better.

11	P—KKt3
12 P—KR4	Kt—B4!
13 P—R5	Kt x Bch
14 Q x Kt	P—KKt4!

Avoiding the opening of the KR file. From now on, it is Black who lays down the law.

15 B—Kt3	P—B4
16 P x P e. p.	B x P
17 R—Q1	Q—Kt3
18 R—Q2	B—Q2
19 O—O	QR—B1

Threatening to win the exchange with 20 . . . B x Kt and 21 . . . B—Kt4. What with Black's criss-cross Bishops and pressure on the QB file, White's game now becomes more precarious.

| 20 R—B1 | B—Kt4 |
| 21 Q—B2 | R—B5 |

22 Q—Kt3	Q—B3
23 R(2)—B2	R—B1
24 Q—R3!	B—R3

Position after Black's 24th move

Atkins

Marshall

Appreciatively and apprehensively, I had watched Atkins strengthen his game move by move with his well-known positional skill. Fortunately, I had already had inklings of a marvelous saving combination! Just in time, too; for . . . P—Kt4 promises to be deadly against ordinary play.

25 P—Kt3!!

An amazing move, isn't it?! If now 25 . . . R x Kt; 26 R x R, B x R; 27 R x B, Q x R; 28 Q—K7! and although Black is a Rook ahead he must concede a draw with 28 . . . R—B1 (if 28 . . . R—B3? 29 P—R6! and wins!); 29 Q x KPch, R—B2 forced; 30 Q—K8ch, R—B1 forced; 31 Q—K6ch etc.

White could also try for a win with 27 Q—K7, Q—K1; 28 Q x Qch, R x Q; 29 R x B with a somewhat better game, although a draw should be the legitimate outcome.

25 . . . .   R—B4?

Had Black foreseen what was coming, he would have taken the draw. After the text, he is lost.

26 Kt x P!!   R x R

All his moves are forced now.

| 27 R x R | Q x R |
| 28 Kt x Bch | K—B2 |

If 28 . . . K—Kt2; 29 Q—K7ch, K—R3; 30 Q—KB7, Q—Q8ch; 31 K—R2, R—KR1; 32 P—B3 wins. Or 28 . . . K—R1; 29 Q—K7 with the fatal threats 30 P—K4 or B—K5.
But the text seems to repulse the attack, for Black threatens 29 . . . Q—B8ch in addition to . . . K x Kt.

29 Q—Q6!!   K x Kt

If 29 . . . R—B2; 30 Kt—Kt4 wins quickly. Or 29 . . . Q—B2; 30 Kt—K4! and there is no satisfactory defense.

30 B—K5ch   K—B4

If 30 . . . K—B2; 31 Q—Q7ch, K—B1; 32 B—Q6ch, K—Kt1; 33 Q x KPch, K—Kt2; 34 P—R6ch and mate next move.

31 P—B3!   Resigns

After 31 . . . P—Kt5 there follows 32 P—K4ch, K—Kt4; 33 Q—K7ch, K—R3; 34 Q—Kt7ch, K x P; 35 Q x KtPch, K—R3; 36 B—Kt7 mate. The interpolation of 31 . . . Q—B8ch would not affect the outcome.

---

17. Vienna, 1903

MUZIO GAMBIT

Probably no other opening demonstrates so convincingly the value of rapid development.

F. J. MARSHALL	G. MAROCZY
White	Black
1 P—K4	P—K4
2 P—KB4	P x P
3 Kt—KB3	P—KKt4
4 B—B4	P—Kt5

A good but dull defense is 4 . . .
B—Kt2 followed by . . . P—KR3.
The text is more aggressive . . .
and more risky.

    5 Kt—B3   ....

I believe that this move, first
played by the great MacDonnell,
is stronger than castling.

    5 . . . .   P x Kt
    6 Q x P   P—Q4

Black is a piece ahead but very
much behind in development.
Therefore, he gives up a Pawn in
the hope of facilitating his development. Note that 6 . . . Q—R5ch?
is pointless, for after 7 P—Kt3 the
reply 7 . . . P x P?? would lead to
mate in two.

    7 Kt x P   ....

A good alternative is 7 B x P, P—
QB3; 8 B—Kt3, B—K3; 9 B x B;
P x B; 10 Q—R5ch or 10 Q x P with
promising attacking chances.

    7 . . . .   P—QB3

This does not contribute to his
development and in fact, as the
game goes, it does not even prevent White from occupying Q5!
Better seems 7 . . . Kt—QB3 or
else 7 . . . B—K3.

    8 Kt x P   Q—B3
    9 P—B3   ....

In order to be able to castle
without having to fear . . . Q—
Q5ch.

    9 . . . .   B—R3

This appears to leave Black with
a losing game. If 9 . . . B—K3
White has a promising game with
10 Kt x B, P x Kt; 11 Q x Q, Kt x Q;
12 B x P with three Pawns for the
piece (12 . . . Kt x P? 13 B—B8).
Better, however, is Tarrasch's
suggestion 9 . . . Q—R5ch; 10 P—
Kt3, B—Kt5; 11 Q—B2, Q—K2 etc.

    10 P—Q4   Kt—K2
    11 O—O   O—O

Evidently overlooking White's
ingenious reply. Against the preferable 11 . . . Kt—Q2 Denker offers the interesting continuation 12
Kt—R5! Q x Q; 13 R x Q, B x B; 14
Kt—Kt7ch, K—Q1 forced; 15 B x
P! (threatening Kt—K6 mate!),
Kt—B1; 16 R x B and White's three
Pawns and overwhelmingly superior development will outweigh the
piece.

Position after Black's 11th move

Maroczy

Marshall

    12 Kt—Q5!   Kt x Kt

Forced (if 12 . . . Q x Q; 13 Kt x
Ktch regaining the piece at once,
and if 12 . . . Q—Q3; 13 Kt—B6ch
wins).

    13 Q x Q   Kt x Q
    14 B x B   QKt—Q2

14 . . . Kt x P loses after 15 B x R,
Kt—Q7; 16 B x Pch, K x B; 17 B—
K6ch, Kt x R; 18 R x Ktch, K—K2;
19 B x B etc.

    15 B x R   K x B
    16 P—K5   Resigns

For if 16 . . . Kt—Q4; 17 B x Kt,
P x B; 18 P—K6, Kt—Kt3; 19 R x P
ch, K—Kt1 (or 19 . . . K—K1; 20
R x RP and the KP cannot be cap-
tured); 20 R—B6, K—Kt2; 21
QR—KB1 winning easily.

18. Vienna, 1903

KING'S GAMBIT

Just as in Game no. 11, White's P—KKt4 leads straight to disaster!

J. MIESES	F. J. MARSHALL
White	Black
1 P—K4	P—K4
2 P—KB4	P x P
3 Kt—KB3	P—KB4

This unusual move was played quite a bit in the Gambit Tournament. For one thing, it rules out the headaches of the Muzio and Allgaier Gambits.

| 4 P x P | .... |

Very tame for Mieses. 4 P—K5 holds out the best prospects for securing the initiative.

4	P—Q4
5 P—Q4	B—Q3
6 P—B4!?	P—B3

White's last move is played with a view to opening up new attacking lines, for instance 6 . . . P x P? 7 B x QBP, B x P? 8 Q—Kt3 etc.

7 Kt—B3	Kt—B3
8 B—Q3	Q—K2ch
9 K—B1	....

9 K—B2 is answered by . . . Kt—Kt5ch. However, 9 Q—K2 is preferable to the text, which keeps the KR out of play permanently.

| 9 .... | O—O |

A Pawn sacrifice to remove Black's King from the center.

| 10 P x P | P x P |
| 11 Q—Kt3 | Kt—B3 |

Better than 11 . . . Q—KB2; 12 Kt x P! Kt x Kt; 13 B—B4 etc.

12 Kt x P	Kt x Kt
13 Q x Ktch	K—R1
14 B—Q2	Q—B3

| 15 P—KKt4? | .... |

In making this formidable-looking advance, Mieses was evidently under the impression that Black's reply was impossible. 15 K—B2 is better, although 15 . . . Kt—K2 leaves Black with a superior game.

| 15 .... | P x P e. p.! |
| 16 B—KKt5 | Kt—Kt5! |

Position after Black's 16th move

Marshall

Mieses

Black has the advantage in all variations; for example 17 Q—Kt3, B—K3!! and then (a) 18 Q—Q1, Q—B2; (b) 18 B x Q, B x Q; 19 P x B, Kt x B; 20 B—R4, R x P etc.; (c) 18 Q x Kt, B x Q; 19 B x Q, B—Q4! etc.

Another amusing possibility is 17 Q—B4, B x P!; 18 B x Q, B x Bch etc.

17 Q—K4	Q x BP
18 Q x Q	B x Q
19 B x B	R x B

The exchanges have established an easily won game for Black.

20 K—Kt2	QR—KB1
21 QR—KB1	P x P
22 B—Q2	Kt—Q6

Preventing 23 Kt x P because of the reply . . . R—B7ch.

23 B—K3	Kt—K8ch!

Taking advantage of the fact that White cannot go in for 24 Kt x Kt, R x R etc.

24 R x Kt	R x Kt

Threatening . . . R—Kt6ch.

25 R x P	B x R
26 K x B	R—K1

Resigns

---

19. Vienna, 1903

BISHOP'S GAMBIT

In gambit openings the cardinal rule for each player is to "git thar fustest with the mostest men." Maroczy disregards this policy and comes to grief as a result.

G. MAROCZY	F.J. MARSHALL
White	Black
1 P—K4	P—K4
2 P—KB4	P x P
3 B—B4	P—Q4
4 B x P	Q—R5ch

This old-fashioned move still had a strong vogue at the turn of the century. Nowadays 4 . . . Kt—KB3 is preferred.

5 K—B1	P—KKt4
6 P—Q4	B—Kt2
7 Kt—QB3	Kt—K2
8 Kt—B3	Q—R4
9 P—KR4	P—KR3
10 Q—Q3	QKt—B3
11 Kt—K2	. . . .

11 Kt—Kt5 has been played in this position. Black can simply reply 11 . . . K—Q1; or he can sacrifice a Pawn with 11 . . . O—O, relying on his attacking chances and superior development to outweigh the Pawn minus.

11	B—Q2
12 Q—Kt3	. . . .

I had foreseen this move, but did not think it worth while to guard against it; in a position of this character, it is tempting fate to take the Queen away from the defense and to neglect one's development. White should have continued with B—Q2, K—B2 etc.

12	Kt x B!
13 P x Kt	Kt—K2
14 Q x P?	O—O
15 P—B3	QR—Kt1

Position after Black's 15th move

Marshall

Maroczy

16 Q x RP	. . . .

16 Q x BP leads to much the same kind of play: 16 . . . **B—Kt4!** 17 **P—B4** (if 17 Q x Kt? KR—K1 etc.), Kt x P! 18 **Q—B5** (if 18 P x Kt, KR—K1), KR—B1! 19 **Q x Kt,** B x P followed by . . . KR—K1 etc.

16	B—Kt4
17 Q—B5	B x Ktch
18 K x B	P—Kt5

Now if 19 Kt—Kt1, Kt x P with winning attack.

19 P—Q6	. . . .

In view of the exposed state of his King, White would be happy to exchange Queens, even at the cost of a piece. With several

Pawns for the Knight, he would have good chances in an ending . . . but it never comes to that.

19 . . . .   P x Ktch
20 P x P   Kt—B4!
21 P x P   Kt—Kt6ch

This appears risky, but proves to be quite feasible. White's reply is forced.

22 K—Q2   Q x BP

Threatens mate.

23 KR—K1   QR—K1
24 R x R   R x R

Still threatening mate. It is comical to see how White's advanced QBP remains poised to queen for 15 moves without ever getting around to it.

25 K—B2   Q—K5ch
26 K—Kt3   Q—Kt2ch
27 K—B2   Q—K5ch
28 K—Kt3   Q—Kt2ch
29 K—B2   B—B1!!

An important gain of time. Its value will be apparent on move 34.

30 Q—B4   R—K7ch
31 B—Q2   R x Bch
32 K x R   Q x Pch
33 K—Q1   . . . .

Or 33 K—Q3, Q—K7 mate! If 33 K—K1, Q x Rch; 34 K—B2, Kt—K5ch; 35 K—K2, Q—Kt7ch; 36 K—Q3, Kt—B7 mate, or 35 K—B3, Kt—Q7ch etc.

33 . . . .   Q x Rch
34 K—B2   Kt—B4!

As a result of Black's 29th move, White cannot queen with a check. If he plays 35 P—B8(Q), there follows 35 . . . Kt—K6ch; 36 K—Q3 (if 36 K—Kt3, Q—Q8ch followed by mate). Q—B8ch winning easily.

35 Q—R4   Kt—K6ch

White resigns, for if 36 K—Q2,

Q—Kt7ch; 37 K—Q3, Q—Kt8ch! 38 K—Q2, Q—Kt2 winning the advanced QBP, which cannot be protected by 39 Q—Q7 or 39 Q—R5 because of 39 . . . Q—QKt7ch forcing mate in a few moves.

———————   5 . 4 . 20

20. Vienna, 1903

KING'S GAMBIT

This was the most exciting of my games with Pillsbury. It was cut and thrust all the way!

F.J. MARSHALL   H.N. PILLSBURY

White	Black
1 P—K4	P—K4
2 P—KB4	P x P
3 Kt—KB3	P—KKt4
4 B—B4	B—Kt2

Avoiding the risky intricacies of the Muzio Gambit (4 . . . P—Kt5 etc.).

5 P—KR4	P—KR3
6 P—Q4	P—Q3
7 Q—Q3	P—Kt5

This involves a certain amount of danger, as the advanced Pawns will be exposed to attack. On the other hand, the development of Black's KKt now becomes possible.

8 Kt—Kt1	Q—B3
9 P—B3	P—KR4
10 Kt—QR3	Kt—K2
11 Kt—K2	Kt—Kt3
12 P—KKt3!	. . . .

Taking advantage of the fact that Black cannot very well reply 12 . . . P—B6 because of 13 B—Kt5, P—B7ch (only move!); 14 K—B1, Q—B6; 15 Q x Q, P x Q; 16 Kt—B4 after which Black will lose the Pawns at KB7 and KB6.

| 12 . . . . | P x P |
| 13 R—B1!? | . . . . |

13 Q x P was safe and simple, but

then White's R—B1 would be forestalled by 13 . . . B—K3. I therefore resolved to plunge into the ensuing complications, although they should have eventually turned out to my discomfiture!

13	Q x RP
14 B x Pch	K—Q1
15 B x Kt	P—Kt7ch
16 R—B2	R—B1

Adding a new piece to the attack, and hence even stronger than . . . Q—R8ch.

17 B—K3	B—R3!
18 B x B	. . . .

Paradoxically, this is best. Consider the following variations given by Marco:-

I 18 Kt—KKt1, R—B6! and wins.

II 18 B—B5, QB x B; 19 P x B, R—K1! (or 19 . . . P—Kt8(Q)ch.; 20 Kt x Q, B x B and wins.)

III 18 O—O—O, B x Bch; 19 Q x B, R x R with advantage to Black.

Despite the obvious power of the hostile attack, White does not despair, because Black's Queen-side pieces are still undeveloped.

18	P—Kt8(Q)ch
19 Kt x Q	Q x Rch
20 K—Q1	Q x Ktch
21 K—B2	R—B7ch
22 B—Q2	Q x R

The fantastic massacre has left Black with a Rook and the exchange ahead, and with two passed Pawns as well. But this material advantage is somewhat academic, as White's counter-attack now sets in. Due to Black's lack of development, his King must pretty well fend for himself.

23 Q—K3	R x Bch
24 Q x R	B—Q2

The annotators have suggested that . . . P—B3 gives an easier defense.

25 Q—Kt5ch	K—B1

26 B—B5!	P—Kt3!

26 . . . BxB would lead to a draw after 27 Q—Kt8ch, K—Q2; 28 Q—B7ch, K—B3; 29 Q—Q5ch, K—Q2; 30 Q x Bch etc. But with a Rook ahead, Pillsbury wants to win, despite his gruesome time pressure.

27 Q—Kt8ch	K—Kt2
28 B x B	Kt x B
29 Q—Q5ch	P—B3

Simpler was 29 . . . K—Kt1; 30 Q—Kt8ch, Kt—B1! 31 Q x Ktch, K—Kt2 and wins.

30 Q x QP	R—Q1

This was later criticized, but it should have won.

31 P—Q5	. . . .

Position after White's 31st move

Pillsbury

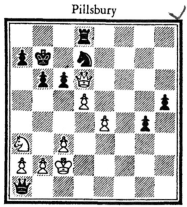

Marshall

31	R—KB1?

Black is now lost. This mistake is all the more curious, as he was no longer pressed for time. The Viennese amateur Dr. Kaufman subsequently demonstrated a highly ingenious win for Black as follows: 31 . . . Kt—B4!! 32 Q x R (32 Q x Pch, K—Kt1; 33 Kt—Kt5 is insufficient because of 33 . . . R—QB1), Q—B8!! 33 P x Pch! K x P.

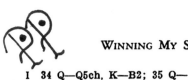

Muzio.
Muzio

I 34 Q—Q5ch, K—B2; 35 Q—K5ch, K—Kt2. There is no perpetual check, and the King-side Pawns can advance.

II 34 Kt—Kt1, P—Kt6; 35 Q—Q5ch, K—B2; 36 Q—K5ch, K—Kt2; 37 Q x KtP? Q—K7ch; 38 Kt—Q2, Q x Ktch! etc.

III 34 Kt—Kt1, P—Kt6; 35 Kt—Q2, P—Kt7! 36 Q—B8ch, K—Kt4 and wins.

32 P x Pch	K—R1
33 P x Kt	R—B7ch
34 K—Kt3	Q x KtPch
35 K—R4	Resigns

For if 35 . . . P—Kt4ch; 36 K—R5, Q x Pch; 37 K—R6 etc. A very delightful encounter, equally creditable, I believe, to both masters.

---

21. Vienna, 1903

BISHOP'S GAMBIT

In a previous encounter with Tchigorin (Monte Carlo), he had blundered badly, losing a piece on the seventh move. This was to be quite a different kind of game!

This great Russian master was a bundle of nervous energy, and he constantly swung his crossed foot back and forth. Speaking only his native Russian, he was handicapped in getting along with the other masters.

M. TCHIGORIN	F.J. MARSHALL
White	Black
1 P—K4	P—K4
2 P—KB4	P x P
3 B—B4	P—Q4
4 B x P	Q—R5ch
5 K—B1	P—KKt4
6 P—KKt3	. . . .

This move, a great favorite with Tchigorin, has to be met with care. Thus if 6 . . . P x P; 7 Q—B3! gives White the better game.

6	Q—R3

7 Kt—QB3	Kt—KB3
8 P—Q4	Kt—B3
9 K—Kt2	B—Q2

Another good line of play is 9 . . . B—KKt5; 10 Q—Q3, O—O—O (from a game Tchigorin-Pillsbury in the same tournament).

10 P—KR4	. . . .

Although it is obvious that White's King will be exposed, Tchigorin shirks no danger in his desire to demonstrate that Black's King-side Pawns are weak.

10	KR—Kt1!
11 Kt—B3	KtP x P
12 Kt—K2	P—R6ch
13 K—B1	. . . .

Position after White's 13th move

Marshall

Tchigorin

13	P x P!!?

A pretty combination which, however, leads only to the prosaic result of a somewhat better ending for Black. Later analysis showed that the quieter 13 . . . Kt—KR4 would have been more advantageous for me: 14 P x P, R—Kt7! 15 P—B5, Q—Kt2; 16 R x P, Q—Kt5 etc.

14 B x Q	. . . .

Perhaps White's best course would have been the refusal of the Queen sacrifice with 14 Kt x P, Q—Kt3; 15 KR—Kt1.

14 . . . .   P—Kt7ch
15 K—Kt1   B x B!

With the exquisite point that if 16 R—R2?? B—K6 mate! Meanwhile the threat is 16 . . . B—K6ch; 17 K—R2, Kt—Kt5ch; 18 K x P, Kt—K4ch; 19 K—R4, Kt x Ktch; 20 K—R5, B—Kt5 mate!

16 Q—Q3   Kt—KKt5
17 R x P   B—K6ch
18 K x P   . . . .

Better seems 18 Q x B, Kt x Q; 19 R x P etc.

18 . . . .   Kt—B7ch
19 R—Kt3   . . . .

Forced; if 19 K—R2? B x R! wins!

19 . . . .   R x Rch
20 K x R   Kt x Q
21 P x Kt   . . . .

And here the simplifying B x Kt was better.

21 . . . .   Kt—Kt5!

This cannot very well be answered by 22 B x P because of 22 . . . R—Kt1; 23 B—Q5, Kt x B; 24 P x Kt, R x P with a winning game.

22 R—KB1   . . . .

22 R—KR1 appears to be stronger, but against it I had worked out the following winning line: 22 . . . Kt x B; 23 R x P, K—K2; 24 P x Kt, R—Kt1ch; 25 K—R2, B—Kt5; 26 Kt(3)—Kt1, B—B4; 27 R—R5, K—B3 and White is helpless against the all-powerful Bishops.

22 . . . .   Kt x B

But not 22 . . . Kt x QP; 23 B x Pch!

23 P x Kt   K—K2

24 Kt—K5   R—Kt1ch
25 K—B3   B—R6!

Black has the better game. The fall of the tripled Pawns is already in prospect, and White must look for compensation elsewhere.

26 R—Q1   B—Kt4
27 R—KR1   B—B4
28 Kt—Kt3   B—Kt3
29 Kt—K4   . . . .

White must remove one of the terrible Bishops.

29 . . . .   P—KR3
30 Kt—B5   P—Kt3
31 Kt—K4   P—KB3
32 Kt x Bch   . . . .

Inferior would be 32 Kt—B6ch, K—Q2; 33 Kt x RP, R—QR1.

32 . . . .   R x Kt
33 K—Kt4   B—K6ch
34 K—B5   R—Kt8
35 R x R   . . . .

35 R—R3; R—B8ch; 36 K—Kt6, B—Kt4 is also in Black's favor.

35 . . . .   B x R
36 P—Q6ch!   . . . .

Avoiding the hopeless continuation 36 Kt x P, B x P; 37 Kt—Kt8 ch, K—Q3; 38 K—K4, B—Kt2! 39 P—Q4, P—KR4 and White can resign. After the text, the ending is still interesting and difficult.

36 . . . .   P x P
37 Kt x BP   B x P
38 Kt—Kt8ch   K—Q2
39 Kt x P   . . . .

A pretty variation would be 39 P—Kt3, P—KR4; 40 K—Kt5, K—K3! 41 K x P, B—K6; 42 K—Kt6 (else . . . K—B2 wins), K—Q4; 43 Kt—K7ch, K—Q5; 44 Kt—B6ch, K x P; 45 Kt x P, P—Q4 and wins.

39 . . . .   B x P
40 K—K4   K—B3

41 P—Q4	P—Kt4
42 Kt—B5	P—Kt5
43 Kt—K7ch	K—Q2
44 Kt—Q5	P—R4
45 K—Q3	K—B3
46 K—B4	B—B8
47 Kt—K7ch	K—Q2

The King must get to K5 to menace the QP.

48 Kt—Q5	K—K3
49 Kt—Kt6	B—Q7
50 K—Q3	B—B6
51 K—B4	B—K8
52 Kt—Q5	K—B4
53 Kt—Kt6	. . . .

After 53 K—Q3, K—Kt5 followed by . . . K—B6 etc. and Black would win in a more laborious manner.

53	K—K5

If 54 Kt—Q5, B—R5! and Black wins; for example 55 Kt—B7, B—B7; 56 Kt—K6, B—K6; 57 P—Q5 (57 K—Kt5, B—Q7!), B—Q7.

54 Kt—B8	P—Q4ch
55 K—B5	P—R5
56 Kt—Q6ch	K—Q6
57 Kt—Kt5	. . . .

Or 57 K x P, P—Kt6; 58 P x P, P—R6 etc.

57	P—R6!

White resigns, as he is helpless against . . . P—Kt6. Says Marco: "One of Marshall's best games. A classic from A to Z."

III
THE YEAR OF YEARS
(1904-1905)

22. Monte Carlo, 1904
SCOTCH GAMBIT

This is one of the most memorable games of all my years of play. Seventy-six moves and never a dull moment!

F.J. MARSHALL   G. MARCO

White   Black

1 P—K4	P—K4
2 Kt—KB3	Kt—QB3
3 P—Q4	P x P
4 B—B4	B—B4
5 P—B3	P—Q6

This conservative move makes it hard for White to get any attack.

6 O—O	P—Q3

7 Q x P	Kt—B3
8 P—QKt4	B—Kt3
9 P—QR4	. . . .

The weakening of the Queen-side Pawns causes trouble later on.

9	P—QR3
10 R—K1?!	. . . .

With this move, which intends an attack with P—K5 if Black's King remains in the center, White initiates a line of play which soon calls for the speculative sacrifice of a piece.

10	Kt—Kt5
11 R—R2!?	. . . .

After the humiliating retreat 11 R—B1 there would follow 11 . . . KKt—K4; 12 Kt x Kt, Kt x Kt; 13

Q—K2, Kt x B; 14 Q x Kt, B—K3
with an excellent and safe position
for Black. Therefore White prepares to sacrifice.

11	KKt—K4
12 Kt x Kt	Kt x Kt
13 Q—Kt3	. . . .

The colorless 13 Q—K2, Kt x B;
14 Q x Kt, B—K3 would lose the
exchange without compensation.

13	Kt x B
14 Q x KtP	R—B1
15 P—K5!	. . . .

Obviously 15 B—R6, Q—K2 is
not good enough for White.

| 15 . . . . | Kt x P? |

After this the game gets very
wild. Best was 15 . . . P x P; 16
R(2)—K2, B—K3; 17 B—R6, Q—
K2; 18 Q x RP, O—O—O; 19 B x R,
R x B with advantage.
If 15 . . . P—Q4; 16 B—Kt5,
Q—Q2; 17 R(2)—K2! Q—K3; 18
B—R6, Q—K2; 19 B—Kt5, Q—K3;
20 B—R6 and White has a draw.

| 16 K—R1 | B—K3 |
| 17 R(2)—K2 | Q—K2 |

He has to give back the piece
(17 . . . K—Q2; 18 R x Kt, P x R; 19
R—Q1ch).

| 18 P—KB4 | Kt—Q6 |

Appears very powerful, but
White's answer takes away most
of the sting.

| 19 P—B5! | Kt—K4! |

Best! If 19 . . . Kt x R; 20 B—
Kt5, Q—Q2; 21 R x Kt and wins,
or 19 . . . Kt x B; 20 R x Kt, O—
O—O; 21 R x B etc.

20 P x B	P x P
21 B—R6	Q x Q
22 B x Q	R—B4

Despite the removal of the Queens,
the play continues to be highly
critical.

23 B x Kt	R x B
24 R x R	P x R
25 P—Kt3	R—Q1
26 K—Kt2	R—Q6
27 R x P	K—B2

The ending is not easy for White
because of his weak Queen-side
Pawns.

| 28 R—K2 | B—K6! |

Preventing R—Q2, which would
force the exchange of Rooks, and
thereby preventing the development of the Knight at even this
late date.

29 R—B2	B—R3
30 R—B2ch	K—K2
31 R—B3	R—Q8
32 R—B1	R—Q6
33 R—B3	R—Q8
34 Kt—R3?!	. . . .

I should have taken the draw
by repetition; but, with the mettle-
some spirit proper to a young man,
I prepared for a new sacrifice—
which should have cost me the
game.

| 34 . . . . | R—QB8 |

Better than 34 . . . R—QR8; 35
Kt—B4, R x P? 36 Kt—K5.

| 35 P—B4 | . . . . |

Sacrificing a Pawn, for 35 Kt—
B4? would be refuted by . . . B—
Kt2.

35	R—QR8
36 P—B5	B—B8
37 Kt—B4	R x P
38 Kt—K5	B—Kt7!

Preventing R—B7ch.

| 39 Kt—Q3 | B—B6 |
| 40 R—B4 | P—QR4! |

Realizing that if I took this Pawn
the ending would certainly be lost
for me, I saw my only chance in
aggressive counterplay. Therefore:

See through.

41 R—R4	P x P
42 R x Pch	K—Q1
43 Kt—B4	P—Kt6
44 Kt x Pch	K—B1

Position after Black's 44th move

Marco

Marshall

White's position has become desperate, as the hostile KtP must queen. I therefore try a last "swindle" with:

| 45 P—B6!? | .... |

If 45 R x Pch, K—Kt1 wins.

| 45 .... | B—K4? |

There was a win with 45 . . . P x P; 46 R x Pch, K—Kt1; 47 R—Kt7ch, K x R; 48 Kt—B5ch, K—R2! 49 Kt x R, B—Q5; 50 K—B3, K—R3; 51 K—K4, K—R4; 52 K x B, K x Kt etc.
The text gives White the opportunity to save himself in a manner which is reminiscent of some notable compositions!

46 P x Pch	K—Kt1
47 Kt—B5	R—R7ch
48 K—R3	P—Kt7
49 R—K7!	K—R2
50 R—K8	P—B3
51 R—R8ch	K—Kt3

52 R x R	P—Kt8 (Q)
53 P—Kt8 (Q) ch!	B x Q
54 R—Kt2ch	Q x R
55 Kt—R4ch	K—Kt4
56 Kt x Q	....

All forced since move 46! But now Black's lone Pawn becomes a threat.

56	P—B4
57 K—Kt2	P—B5
58 K—B3	P—B6
59 Kt—Q3	K—B5
60 Kt—K1	K—Q4
61 P—R4	B—Q3
62 P—Kt4	B—K2
63 P—Kt5	K—K4
64 K—Kt4	B—B1
65 Kt—B2	K—K5?

Having thrown away the win, Black now throws away the draw. Correct was 65 . . . K—K3; 66 P—R5, K—B2; 67 K—B5, K—Kt1 and the game is a draw, as the Knight cannot leave the vicinity of the· Black Pawn.

66 P—R5	K—Q6
67 Kt—R1!	....

Black had anticipated only 67 Kt—K1ch, K—Q7 etc. Now it is all over.

67	K—K5
68 P—R6	K—K4

Too late.

69 K—R5	K—B4
70 Kt—B2	B—Q3
71 Kt—Q4ch	K—K5
72 Kt—K2	P—B7
73 P—Kt6	B—R6
74 P—Kt7	K—Q6
75 P—Kt8 (Q)	K x Kt
76 Q—R2	Resigns

Surely one of the most notable fighting games on record.

23. Monte Carlo, 1904
(*Rice Gambit Tournament*)
RICE GAMBIT

The piquant final position is a worthy contribution to this opening, so famous for the many remarkable games produced from it.

F.J. MARSHALL   T. VON SCHEVE

White	Black
1 P—K4	P—K4
2 P—KB4	P x P
3 Kt—KB3	P—KKt4
4 P—KR4	P—Kt5
5 Kt—K5	Kt—KB3
6 B—B4	P—Q4
7 P x P	B—Q3
8 O—O	. . . .

The key move of the gambit.

8	B x Kt
9 R—K1	. . . .

These were obligatory moves of the tourney. Now the real play starts.

9	Q—K2
10 P—B3	. . . .

Of course not 10 P—Q4? B x Pch etc.

10	P—B6

Weak. For a better continuation, see the next game.

11 P—Q4	Kt—K5
12 R x Kt	B—R7ch
13 K x B	Q x R

Black is the exchange ahead, but his development lags badly, and his King will be exposed to lasting attack.

14 P—KKt3	O—O
15 B—Q3	Q x P(Q4)
16 P—B4	Q—KR4
17 Kt—B3	P—QB3

White was threatening to win some material with Kt—Q5, but . . . B—K3 was better than the text, as the Knight will now be established very strongly at Q6.

18 Kt—K4	P—KB4
19 Kt—Q6	P—B5!?

An ingenious attempt at counter-attack which doesn't quite come off. If now 20 B x P, R x B! 21 Kt x B, Kt—Q2 and Black has greatly improved his position. If, here, 21 P x R?, Q x Pch; 22 K—Kt1, Q—Kt6ch; 23 K—B1, Q—Kt7ch; 24 K—K1, P—B7ch and wins.

20 Q—K1!	P x Pch
21 Q x P	Kt—Q2
22 B—Kt5	P—B7

The Pawn looks dangerous! As . . . R—B6 is threatened, White combines attack and defense with his next move.

23 B—B5!	. . . .

Threatening to win with Kt x B etc.

23	Kt—Kt3
24 Kt x B	QR x Kt

If 24 . . . Kt x Kt; 25 B—K6ch, K—Kt2 (or 25 . . . R—B2; 26 R—KB1 and wins); 26 B x P, Q—K1; 27 B x Kt, R x B; 28 B—R6ch! and wins. If, here, 27 . . . P—B8(Kt)ch; 28 R x Kt, R x R; 29 B—R6ch! K—B2; 30 Q—Kt7 mate.

25 B—K6ch	R—B2

Or 25 . . . K—Kt2; 26 B x P! Q—K1; 27 B x R, Kt x B; 28 B—R6ch! etc.

26 R—KB1	R—K1
27 B x Rch	Q x B

If 27 . . . K x B; 28 R x Pch, K—Kt1; 29 P—Kt3 and wins.

28 Q x KtP	Q—Kt3

On 28 . . . Kt x P there follows 29 P—R5! K—R1; 30 Q—R4 and wins; or 29 . . . Q—Kt2; 30 R x P! P—KR3; 31 R—B6! winning.

29 R x P   Kt x P

Black is lost; if 29 . . . R—K5;
30 Q—B3, Q—K1 (30 . . . R—K1;
31 B—R6!); 31 R—Kt2 and wins.

30 P—R5   R—K5

Running into a problem-like finish, but if 30 . . . Q—Kt2; 31 R—
Kt2 or Q—R4 wins quickly.

31 B—R6!!   Resigns

The Final Position

Von Scheve

Marshall

White's unguarded Queen cannot
be captured either way!

---

24. Monte Carlo, 1904

(*Rice Gambit Tournament*)

RICE GAMBIT

The endless ramifications of this
opening gave us plenty of work.
Glancing through a magazine of
that time, I see the following
comment on my fourteenth move:
"An excellent innovation, which
Messrs. Marshall and Swiderski
analyzed the previous night from
10 in the evening to 3 in the
morning."

J. MIESES	F. J. MARSHALL
White	Black

1 P—K4	P—K4
2 P—KB4	P x P
3 Kt—KB3	P—KKt4
4 P—KR4	P—Kt5
5 Kt—K5	Kt—KB3
6 B—B4	P—Q4
7 P x P	B—Q3
8 O—O	B x Kt
9 R—K1	Q—K2
10 P—B3	Kt—R4

A far better move than 10 . . .
P—B6, which was played in the
previous game.

11 P—Q4	O—O
12 R x B	Q x P
13 R x Kt	. . . .

White gives up the exchange in
order to take the sting out of
Black's eventual attack with . . .
P—B6 etc.

13	Q x R
14 B x P	Kt—Q2

Realizing that it is important for
him to mobilize the Queen-side
pieces as rapidly as possible.

15 Kt—Q2	Kt—Kt3
16 B x P	B—Q2
17 B—QKt3	KR—K1

Black has completed his development in a most satisfactory
manner. His command of the K
file will take on more importance
as the game progresses.

18 P—B4	Q—Kt4!

A good move. It makes room
for the advance of the KRP; it
takes away the useful square KB4
from White's QB; and it induces
White to move his Kt, so that the
Queen will not be tied down to
its protection.

19 Kt—B1	. . . .

B—Kt3 would have avoided the

following forced exchange, but then . . . P—KR4—5 is much in Black's favor.

| 19 . . . . | QR—B1! |
| 20 B x Kt | . . . . |

If 20 P—Q6, Kt—R1 wins a Pawn.

20	P x B
21 Q—Q3	B—B4
22 Q—Kt3	P—R4
23 P—Q6	R—K7
24 B—Q1	P—R5
25 Q—QB3	R—K3
26 P—Q7	. . . .

White's maneuvers on the Queen-side are quite harmless. The game will be decided on the other wing.

26	R—Q1
27 P—Q5	R—K2
28 Q—Kt4	R(1) x P
29 B—R4	R—K7!

For if 30 B x R, B—K5 wins.

| 30 B—Q1 | R—K4 |
| 31 B—R4 | Q—B5! |

Decisive. The Rook still cannot be taken, because of the reply 32 . . . R—K7 and if 33 Q x P, B—K5! etc.

Position after Black's 31st move

Marshall

Mieses

| 32 Q x P | . . . . |

After 32 B—Q1 there are several winning methods, for example 32 . . . P—R6; 36 P—KKt3, P—R7ch!

| 32 . . . . | R—K7 |

Now 33 B—Q1 will not do because of . . . R—K8; 33 Q—B2, Q x Qch; 34 K x Q, R(2)—K2 and wins. This was the point of 31 . . . Q—B5!

33 B x R	B—K5!
34 Kt—K3	Q—B7ch
35 K—R2	Q—Kt6ch

Resigns

25.) Cambridge Springs, 1904
INDIAN DEFENSE

This was to be my last tournament game with Pillsbury.

F. J. MARSHALL   H. N. PILLSBURY

| White | Black |
| 1 P—Q4 | P—Q3 |

An unusual move which is bound to lead to a cramped game.

| 2 P—K4 | Kt—KB3 |

Here or on the next move Black should play . . . P—K4, which, despite its unattractive appearance, would at least hold the center.

3 Kt—QB3	P—KKt3
4 P—B4	B—Kt2
5 P—K5	P x P
6 BP x P	Kt—Q4
7 Kt—B3	Kt—QB3
8 B—QB4	P—K3?

As a result of his failure to play . . . P—K4, Black's position is anything but promising. The text makes matters still worse because of the hole created on Black's KB3.

Hence . . . B—K3 or . . . Kt—Kt3 should have been tried.

9 B—KKt5!	Kt x Kt
10 P x Kt	Kt—K2
11 O—O	P—KR3
12 B—B6!	B x B

Whether Black swaps or lets White do so, the important thing is that the KB disappears and the weakness of Black's KB3 becomes even more marked. As will be seen from the sequel, White is fully prepared to give up a Pawn.

13 P x B	Kt—B4
14 Q—K2	Q x P

It would have been wiser to play . . . P—KR4, although the outlook for Black's game would have remained poor.

15 P—Kt4	Kt—Q3

Position after Black's 15th move

Pillsbury

Marshall

16 Kt—K5	Q—K2

On 16 . . . Q—Kt4 there could follow 17 Kt x BP! Kt x Kt; 18 B x P, B x B; 19 Q x Bch, Q—K2; 20 Q x P, Q—K6ch; 21 K—R1, O—O—O; 22 R x Kt, Q x BP; 23 Q—B5ch, K—Kt1; 24 R—Q1 with a winning game.

17 B—Q3!	O—O

Necessary; if for example 17 . . . B—Q2; 18 Kt x BP, Kt x Kt; 19 B x P, R—KB1; 20 R x Kt, R x R; 21 R—KB1 and wins.

18 R—B2   . . . .

Played in order to double Rooks on the KB file (which will have decisive effect) and incidentally threatening 19 B x P! Note that this is not a threat with the KR on KB1.

18	K—Kt2
19 QR—KB1	B—Q2

Even the desperate expedient 19 . . . P—KB4 would be unavailing because of 20 Kt x P! K x Kt; 21 P x Pch and wins.

20 R—B6	R—KKt1

There is no defense against White's next move. If 20 . . . Q x R; 21 R x Q, K x R; 22 Kt x Bch etc.

21 Kt x KtP!	Q x R

Or 21 . . . Q—K1; 22 Q—K5 etc.

22 R x Q	K x R
23 Q—K5 mate	

26. Cambridge Springs, 1904

QUEEN'S GAMBIT

White wins a difficult and instructive ending.

F. J. MARSHALL	J. MIESES
White	Black
1 P—Q4	P—Q4
2 P—QB4	P x P

Mieses is fond of this defense because it leads to a fairly open game as a rule. Its one possible drawback is that White may obtain a lead in development which will make it difficult for Black to equalize.

3 P—K3	Kt—KB3
4 B x P	P—K3
5 Kt—QB3	P—B4
6 Kt—B3	B—K2
7 O—O	O—O

7 . . . Kt—B3 or . . . P—QR3 would have been more accurate.

8 Q—K2	P—QR3
9 P x P	B x P
10 P—K4	Kt—B3
11 B—KKt5	B—K2

Practically compulsory because of the threatened P—K5. But this Bishop will soon be exchanged, depriving Black's Q3 of protection and thus assuring White's control of the Q file.

12 QR—Q1	Q—B2
13 P—K5	Kt—Q2
14 B x B	Kt x B
15 B—Q3	Kt—KKt3
16 B x Kt	RP x B

Black must now be on guard against possible attacks by Kt—KKt5 and Q—K4—KR4.

17 R—Q6!	Kt—Kt3
18 KR—Q1	Kt—B5

Position after Black's 18th move

Mieses

Marshall

19 Q—K4!   . . . .

This enterprising sacrifice of the exchange must have come as a great surprise.

19 . . . .   Kt x R

If 19 . . . Kt x KtP; 20 R—QB1, Kt—B5; 21 R—Q4, Kt—Kt3; 22 Kt—KKt5, P—B3 (something has to be done about White's contemplated Q—R4); 23 P x P, P x P (if 23 . . . R x P; 24 Q—KR4); 24 Kt x P with a winning position.

20 P x Kt   Q—Q1

After 20 . . . Q—B3; 21 Q x Q, P x Q; 22 P—Q7, B—Kt2; 23 Kt—QR4, KR—Q1; 24 Kt—B5, R—R2; 25 Kt—K5, K—B1; 26 P—B4 Black would be subjected to unremitting pressure. It is understandable that an aggressive player like Mieses shies away from such a dreary prospect.

21 P—Q7   Q—K2

Or 21 . . . B x P; 22 Kt—K5 etc.

22 P x B(Q)	QR x Q
23 P—KR3	KR—Q1
24 R x Rch	R x R
25 P—R3	P—QKt4?

White's slight material advantage is enough to win, although the process is normally a lengthy one, since the Knights are often at a disadvantage against an agile Rook. The text makes it possible for White to exchange Queens.

26 Q—B6!   Q—Q3

If 26 . . . R—Q3; 27 Q—R8ch, Q—B1; 28 Q—Kt7 with advantage, or 27 . . . K—R2; 28 Kt—K4 winning a Pawn because of the threatened Kt—Kt5ch.

27 Q x Q	R x Q
28 K—B1	R—Kt3
29 K—K2	P—Kt5

Black plays to exchange as many Pawns as possible, because of the well-known drawing possibilities against the two Knights.

30 P x P	R x P
31 Kt—Q1	P—B3
32 K—Q3	P—Kt4
33 K—B3	R—B5

The Rook ultimately runs into trouble here; but against best play White would win by the admittedly laborious process of concentrating on the QRP, winning it and then advancing the passed QKtP.

34 Kt—Q4	P—Kt5

If now 35 Kt x P? P x P!

35 P x P	R x KtP
36 Kt—K3	R—B5
37 P—B3	P—K4

Loss of the Rook was threatened with P—KKt3.

38 Kt—K6	R—KR5

Now the KtP goes. After 38 . . . R—QR5 White would play as indicated in the note to his 33rd move.

39 Kt x P!	R—R8

If 39 . . . K x Kt; 40 Kt—B5ch.

40 Kt—K8	K—B2
41 Kt—Q6ch	K—K3
42 Kt—K4	R—B8ch
43 K—Q2	R—B1
44 P—QKt4	R—QR1
45 Kt—B5ch	K—Q3
46 K—B3	R—R2

If 46 . . . P—R4; 47 Kt—B4ch, K—B3; 48 Kt x Pch, R x Kt; 49 P x R winning the King and Pawn ending.

47 K—B4	R—R1
48 Kt—B5ch	K—B3

Or 48 . . . K—B2; 49 Kt—QKt3, K—Kt3; 50 Kt—K7 followed by Kt—Q5ch etc.

49 Kt x P	K—Kt3

If 49 . . . R x Kt; 50 P—Kt5ch.

50 Kt—B5	R—R7
51 Kt—K3	K—B3
52 P—Kt5ch	K—B2
53 K—Q5	. . . .

The shortest way is to go right after Black's King.

53	R—K7
54 Kt—B4	R x P
55 P—Kt6ch	K—Kt1
56 Kt—Q6	R—Q7ch
57 K—K6	Resigns

---

27. St. Louis, 1904

FOUR KNIGHTS' GAME

Black cheerfully gives up a Pawn in the opening to avoid the welltrodden and uninviting paths of the usual variations.

E. KEMENY	F. J. MARSHALL
White	Black
1 P—K4	P—K4
2 Kt—KB3	Kt—QB3
3 Kt—B3	Kt—B3
4 B—Kt5	B—B4
5 Kt x P	Kt—Q5

See the introductory comment. This line of play had a certain vogue at the time.

6 B—R4	O—O
7 Kt—Q3	B—Kt3
8 P—K5	Kt—K1
9 O—O	P—KB3

Black seeks compensation for the Pawn by playing to secure open lines for his pieces.

10 K—R1	P x P
11 Kt x P	P—Q3
12 Kt—B4	Q—R5

In keeping with Black's aggressive policy.

| 13 Kt x B | RP x Kt |
| 14 P—Q3 | . . . . |

A preferable course would have been 14 B x Kt, R x B; 15 P—Q3 and 16 B—K3.

| 14 . . . . | Kt—KB3 |

As a result of White's lapse, . . . Kt—Kt5 is threatened very strongly, and he must weaken the King-side.

| 15 P—B3 | R x B |

Only an exchanging combination, but it gains time for Black's attacking plans.

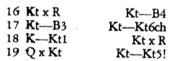

16 Kt x R	Kt—B4
17 Kt—B3	Kt—Kt6ch
18 K—Kt1	Kt x R
19 Q x Kt	Kt—Kt5!

Creating a new weakness and at the same time preparing to switch this piece to a stronger square.

20 P—KR3	Kt—K4
21 Q—B2	Q—R4
22 Q—Kt3	. . . .

Position after Whites' 22nd move

Marshall

Kemeny

| 22 . . . . | Kt x Pch! |

A perfectly sound sacrifice.

| 23 P x Kt | R x P |

If now 24 Q—Kt2, B x P wins; or if 24 Q—K1, all three captures of the KRP win!

| 24 Q—Kt5 | Q x Qch? |

Subsequently I discovered a much quicker win with 24 . . . Q x P! 25 B—B4, P—R3! 26 Q—Q8 ch, K—R2; 27 B—R2, Q—Kt5ch; 28 K—R1, R—B7 etc. However, the following ending is won without much trouble.

25 B x Q	R—Kt6ch
26 K—B2	R x B
27 P—KR4	R—Kt5
28 R—K1	. . . .

If 28 R—R1, K—B2 and the King joins the attack on the KRP.

28	K—B2
29 R—K4	R x R
30 P x R	. . . .

Threatening Kt—Kt5 or Kt—Q5; but 30 Kt x R would have been somewhat better.

30	P—B3
31 P—Kt4	P—QKt4
32 P—R4	P x P
33 Kt x P	P—QKt4
34 Kt—Kt2	B—K3
35 Kt—Q3	K—B3
36 K—K3	P—Kt4!

The first step of the winning plan: Black obtains an outside passed Pawn.

37 P x Pch	K x P
38 Kt—B4	B—R7
39 Kt—K2	B—K3
40 Kt—Q4	B—Q2
41 Kt—B3ch	K—B3
42 K—B4	P—R4

Second step: the outside passed Pawn ties down White's pieces.

| 43 P—K5ch | . . . . |

This hastens the end; Kt—R4 was in order.

| 43 . . . . | P x P ch |
| 44 Kt x P | K—K3 |

Third step: Black's King crosses to the Queen-side. If now 45 Kt—B3, K—Q4 and White is finally starved out of moves.

45 P—B4	P—R5
46 P x P	P x P
47 Kt—Q3	K—Q4
48 Kt—K5	P—R6

Resigns

---

28. Match, 1905
SICILIAN DEFENSE

In this game Janowski, whose love for the Bishops was proverbial, finds himself left with a miserably posted Knight against an admirably functioning Bishop!

D. JANOWSKI   F. J. MARSHALL

White	Black
1 P—K4	P—QB4
2 Kt—QB3	P—K3
3 Kt—B3	P—Q4

A line of play which can also arise in the French Defense (see for example Game no. 52). I adopted it frequently for a number of years and scored some pretty successes with it until the day arrived when I concluded that the variation had been analyzed excessively.

4 P x P	P x P
5 P—Q4	Kt—QB3
6 P x P	Kt—B3!?

This is the chief point of the variation. Black deliberately gives up a Pawn in order to gain time for effective development, at the same time provoking White to neglect his development in order to guard the extra Pawn.

| 7 B—K3 | B—K2 |
| 8 B—QKt5 | . . . . |

In a game played a few months later at the Ostend Tournament between Leonhardt and Tarrasch, the former introduced the far superior move 8 B—K2! The chief value of this move is that it avoids all the unpleasant consequences which arise in the present game from the subsequent pin with . . . B—Kt5.

| 8 . . . . | O—O |
| 9 O—O | . . . . |

Even now White would have done better to swallow his pride by playing 9 P—KR3. But with Janowski it was always a case of "all or nothing."

9	B—Kt5!
10 B x Kt	P x B
11 B—Q4	. . . .

White would have avoided the following difficulties by playing 11 P—KR3, B—R4; 12 P—KKt4, B—Kt3; 13 B—Q4. But of course that would involve a weakening of the King-side which he evidently didn't relish.

| 11 . . . . | Kt—K5! |
| 12 Kt—QR4? | . . . . |

It was a serious mistake to want to retain the QBP at the expense of permitting his King-side Pawns to be ripped up. 12 P—KR3 was absolutely essential here.

| 12 . . . . | Kt—Kt4 |

Threatening 13 . . . Kt x Kt ch; 14 P x Kt, B—R6; 15 R—K1, B x P!

| 13 B—K3 | B x Kt! |
| 14 P x B | P—Q5! |

It is clear that this cannot be answered by 15 B x P? (15 . . . Q x B).

| 15 B x Kt | . . . . |

Or 15 B—Q2, Q—Q4 and Black regains his Pawn with a very superior game.

| 15 . . . . | B x B |
| 16 P—KB4 | . . . . |

White is so discouraged that he relinquishes his only consolation—the extra Pawn! However, after 16 K—R1, Q—Q4 followed by . . . QR—K1—K3 and . . . R—R3 or . . . KR—K1, Black would have retained a commanding initiative.

16	B x P
17 Q—Kt4	Q—B3
18 KR—K1	QR—K1

Black means to secure mastery of the only open file. The innocent-looking text threatens . . . B x Pch!

| 19 Q—Kt2 | R—K3 |
| 20 QR—Q1 | . . . . |

There is not much point to this, but White ran out of good moves long ago. Here is a pretty variation indicated by Schlechter: 20 R x R, P x R; 21 Q x P, B x Pch: 22 K x B, Q—R5ch; 23 K—Kt1, Q x P ch; 24 K—R1, Q—R5ch; 25 K—Kt1, Q—Kt6ch; 26 K—R1 (if 26 Q—Kt2, Q—K6ch; 27 K—R1, R—B7; 28 Q—R8ch, K—B2; 29 Q—Kt7ch, K—B3 and wins), Q—R6ch; 27 K—Kt1, P—KR3 and wins.

20	KR—K1
21 R x R	R x R
22 K—B1	Q—K4
23 Q—B3	R—B3

Now that he has control of the K file, the Rook can be put to work against the exposed King. . . . B—K6 is threatened.

| 24 K—Kt2 | . . . . |

After 24 R—K1 there is a quick win with 24 . . . B—K6; 25 Q—Kt2, Q—R4 (threatening . . . P—KR3); 26 R—K2, R—Kt3 etc.

(see diagram next column)

| 24 . . . . | B xP |

A famous critic recommended 24 B—K6, overlooking that after 25

Marshall

Janowski

Q x B, Q—Q4ch; 26 P—B3, P x Q; 27 R x Q, P x R Black would win much more slowly than with the actual continuation.

| 25 Q—KR3 | P—KR3 |

Very simple!—if 26 Q x B, R x P ch etc.

26 P—QB3	Q—K7
27 R—KB1	B—K4
28 K—Kt1	. . . .

White might well resign. If 28 P x P, B x P and the KBP cannot be protected, for on either 29 Q—Kt3 or Q—R4, Black's Rook goes to Kt3 with fatal effect.

28	P—Q6
29 P—KB4	P—Q7
30 Q—B8ch	K—R2

White resigns. This was considered the best game of the match.

---

29. Ostend, 1905
(*Second Brilliancy Prize*)
GIUOCO PIANO

Rapid development and gains of time triumph over Pawn-grabbing.

F.J. MARSHALL   **A. BURN**

White	Black
1 P—K4	P—K4
2 Kt—KB3	Kt—QB3
3 B—B4	B—B4
4 P—B3	Kt—B3

The modern masters prefer a quieter type of game with 4 . . . Q—K2; 5 P—Q4, B—Kt3; this has the merit of minimizing White's attacking chances.

5 P—Q4	P x P
6 P x P	B—Kt5ch
7 K—B1!?	. . . .

Played on the spur of the moment! I didn't like 7 B—Q2, B x B ch; 8 QKt x B, P—Q4 because it is too simplifying; and I didn't like 7 Kt—B3, Kt x KP; 8 O—O, B x Kt; 9 P—Q5 because it is too complicated!

| 7 . . . . | Kt x KP? |

Burn was a fine defensive player, but this move sets him too tough a problem, for it leaves him with a disorganized and undeveloped position. Much better was 7 . . . P—Q4! which would have avoided these evils.

8 P—Q5	Kt—K2
9 Q—Q4	Kt—KB3
10 B—KKt5	Kt—Kt3
11 QKt—Q2	P—KR3

White has just the kind of game he was aiming for with his seventh move. If 10 . . . O—O, White can either continue to play for attack with 11 P—KR4; or he can cramp Black's game unbearably with 11 Kt—K4, B—K2; 12 P—Q6! P x P; 13 Kt x P etc. Somewhat better would be 11 . . . B x Kt; 12 B x B etc. but White would still have much the better of it.

| 12 R—K1ch | K—B1 |

Whereas White's King went to B1 voluntarily, Black plays his King here because he has to! Thus if 12 . . . B—K2? 13 B x Kt, P x B; 14 P—Q6! P x P; 15 Q x BP (threatening mate), R—B1; 16 Kt—K4!! and wins (16 . . . B x Q; 17 Kt x B mate!).

| 13 B—Q3! | B—K2 |

Relatively better was 13 . . . B x Kt; 14 B x B, P—Q3 although the outlook for Black's game would still be very poor.

| 14 KB x Kt | RP x B |

Or 14 . . . BP x B; 15 Kt—K5! Q—K1; 16 Q—Q3! and wins.

Position after Black's 14th move

Burn

Marshall

| 15 Kt—K5! | . . . . |

This leads to a short sharp finish. I saw the move in a flash, but its sequel had to be calculated with great exactitude.

15	P x B
16 Kt x KtPch	K—B2
17 R x Bch	K x Kt

17 . . . Q x R, leaving Black with Rook and Bishop for the Queen, would have lost more slowly.

| 18 Q—Q3ch | K—R3 |

Or 18 . . . K—R4; 19 R x KtP

R.d *wholeness.Rd.*
Rd.

and wins. With the Rook en prise and a piece to the good, Black seems to be getting out of his difficulties. But now comes the key move of the combination:

19 P—KR4!   P—Kt5

If 19 . . . Q x R; 20 P x P dbl ch, K x P; 21 Kt—B3ch, K—Kt5 (or 21 . . . K—B5; 22 P—Kt3ch, K—Kt5; 23 Q—Kt6ch, K x Kt; 24 Q—B5 mate); 22 Q—Kt6ch, K—B5; 23 P—Kt3ch and mate next move!

20 P—R5!   Kt x P
21 Q—B5   Resigns

For if 21 . . . P—KKt3; 22 R x Kt ch, P x R; 23 Q—B6 mate.

---

30.   Ostend, 1905
DUTCH DEFENSE

This is a real Fourth of July fireworks show from beginning to end!

F.J. MARSHALL   M. TCHIGORIN

White   Black

1 P—Q4   P—KB4

A form of the Dutch which often turns out to be too difficult for Black. Better is 1 . . . P—K3 and if 2 Kt—KB3 or P—QB4, P—KB4.

2 P—K4!   . . . .

A gambit which I have always loved to play!

2 . . . .   P x P
3 Kt—QB3   Kt—KB3
4 B—KKt5   P—B3
5 B x Kt   . . . .

This lets Black off too easily. 5 P—B3 gives a more lasting attack, for example 5 . . . P x P; 6 Kt x P, P—K3; 7 B—Q3, B—K2; 8 Kt—K5! O—O; 9 B x Kt! R x B; 10 Q—R5 with a mighty attack (Dr. Lasker-Pillsbury, Paris 1900).

5 . . . .   KP x B
6 Kt x P   Q—Kt3

Why not simply 6 . . . P—Q4; 7 Kt—B3, B—Q3 followed by . . . O—O with a good game for Black?

7 R—Kt1   P—Q4
8 Kt—Kt3   B—K3

In accordance with their temperaments, both players disregard the possibility of . . . Q—R4ch followed by . . . Q x P.

9 B—Q3   Kt—Q2
10 Q—K2   K—B2

As a result of his venturesome sixth move, Black cannot secure a normal development.

11 Kt—B3   R—K1
12 O—O   B—Q3
13 P—B3   Kt—B1
14 Kt—R4   B—KB4

It would have been more prudent to interpolate . . . B x Kt. In provoking the following combination Tchigorin must have thought that the seemingly trapped Knight would have no escape after move 18.

Position after Black's 14th move

Tchigorin

Marshall

15 Kt(4) x B!	R x Q
16 Kt x Bch	K—K3

If 16 . . . K—Kt1; 17 Kt x R!
P—Kt3; 18 P—QB4! P—QB4; 19
QP x P, Q x BP; 20 Kt—Kt5! P x P;
21 KR—B1! and wins!

17 Kt—B8!!	Q—B2
18 B x R	K—B2

18 . . . P—KKt3 would have led
to some pretty play; 19 KR—K1!!
P—KB4 (if 19 . . . K—B2; 20 B—
Kt4, P—KB4; 21 B x P! P x B; 22
R—K7ch, Q x R; 23 Kt x Q with
two Pawns ahead and an easy win;
or 20 . . . P—KR4; 21 R—K7ch
Q x R; 22 Kt x Q, P x B; 23 Kt—B8,
K—K3; 24 R—K1ch, K—Q2; 25
Kt x P, Kt—K3; 26 Kt x BP etc.) 20
B—B3ch, K—B3; 21 Kt—K7, Kt—
K3; 22 B x P! etc.
This sequel demonstrates that
White will be able to retain his
material advantage.

19 Kt—B5	Kt—K3
20 Kt(5)—Q6ch	K—Kt3
21 B—Q3ch	K—R4

Black hopes to get both Knights
for his Rook, but due to the exposed position of his King, White
always finds some new threat.

22 QR—K1	Kt—B5
23 R—K7	Q—R4
24 B—Kt1	. . . .

B—B2 would have been more exact; but in any event White's material and positional advantage
must triumph. The Queen cannot
contend against a Rook and two
minor pieces.

24	P—KKt3
25 P—KKt3	Kt—R6ch
26 K—Kt2	Kt—Kt4
27 B—Q3	R x Kt

Still trying to get both Knights.
The game was lost in any case, as
Black was helpless against the
threat of P—KR4 followed by B—
K2ch and Kt—B7ch.

28 Kt x R	Q—Q1
29 P—KR4	Q x Kt

If 29 . . . Kt—B2; 30 R x Kt,
Q x Kt; 31 R x Pch, K—Kt5; 32
P—B3 mate.

30 P x Kt	Resigns

---

31. Scheveningen, 1905
QUEEN'S GAMBIT DECLINED

A surprise sacrifice crashes
through Black's defense.

F.J. MARSHALL • O. DURAS

White	Black
1 P—Q4	P—Q4
2 P—QB4	P—K3
3 Kt—QB3	Kt—KB3
4 B—Kt5	QKt—Q2
5 P—K3	B—K2
6 Q—B2	. . . .

I was very fond of this move
at this stage of my career. Its
elastic character appealed to me;
for instance, it provides for Queen-
side castling in some instances.

6	P—B3
7 P x P	Kt x P
8 B x B	Q x B
9 Kt—B3	O—O
10 Kt x Kt	KP x Kt

And this Pawn formation is one
frequently seen in my games. In
recent years it has been adopted
a great deal, particularly by Flohr
and Reshevsky.

11 B—Q3	Kt—B3
12 O—O	R—K1
13 Kt—K5	P—KR3

Preparing to move his Knight,
so that he can undermine the commanding position of White's Knight.

14 P—B4	Kt—Q2

If 14 . . . Kt—K5; 15 B x Kt,

No Return + P Pr.

P x B; 16 P—B5 (not 16 Q x KP??
P—B3) with good attacking chances.

15 R—B3   . . . .

This move has the double object
of guarding the KP (Black was
threatening . . . P—B3) and of
placing the Rook in an attacking
position.

15 . . . .   Kt—B1
16 QR—KB1   P—B3
17 Kt—Kt6   Kt x Kt

Black has succeeded in dislodg-
ing the annoying Knight, but in
so doing, he has created targets
for attack which will be utilized
later on.

18 B x Kt   R—B1
19 P—B5   B—Q2
20 R—Kt3   B—K1
21 QR—B3   B x B
22 R x B   R—B2
23 P—KKt4   . . . .

White's attacking plan is clear.
He will advance his King-side
Pawns in order to open up av-
enues of attack against the Black
King.

23 . . . .   R—K1
24 P—KR4   Q—K5

An offer which White naturally
declines, since he wants to continue the attack and to avoid an
ending in which his Pawn position
would be unfavorable.

25 Q—B2   Q—Q6

To go Pawn-hunting with 25 . . .
Q—Kt8ch; 26 K—R2, Q x RP would
be very risky, to say the least,
for then the thrust 27 P—Kt5 would
be all the more powerful with
Black's Queen out of play.

26 P—Kt5   RP x P
27 P x P   P x P
28 R x KtP   R—B3
29 R—R3   R—K2

29 . . . Q—K5 gives an easier

defense. Black's pressure on the
Pawns hampers the execution of
White's attacking plans.

Position after Black's 29th move

Duras

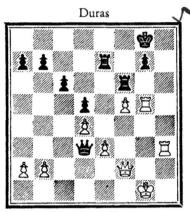

Marshall

30 K—R2   . . . .

At first sight it appears that 30
Q—R4 would have won, for example:

I   30 Q—R4, K—B2? 31 R x P
ch! and wins.

II   30 Q—R4, R x BP; 31 Q—
R8ch, K—B2; 32 R x Pch, K—K3;
33 R—R6ch! K—Q2; 34 R x Rch,
K x R; 35 Q—R7ch followed by a
Rook check, or 35 Q—Kt7ch, R—
B2; 36 Q—K5ch winning in either
event.

III   30 Q—R4, Q—Kt8ch; 31 K—
R2, Q—B7ch; 32 R—Kt2, Q x BP;
33 Q—R8ch, K—B2; **34 R x Pch,**
K—K3; 35 Q—B8ch, K—Q3; 36
Q—Q8ch, R—Q2; 37 R x Rch and
wins.

However, there IS a draw after
30 Q—R4 by 30 . . . **R—R3!!** 31
Q x R, Q—Q8ch; 32 K—B2, Q—Q7
ch; 33 K—Kt1 (if 33 K—Kt3 or
K—B3, R x Pch etc.), Q—K8ch; 34
K—R2, Q—B7ch; 35 R—Kt2, Q x R
ch; 36 K x Q, P x Q with equality.

30 . . . .   K—B2??

Running into a neat sacrifice.
. . . Q—K5 was still the move.

31 R x Pch!   **Resigns**

On 31 . . . K x R there is a
forced mate with 32 Q—Kt3ch, K—
B2; 33 R—R7ch, K—K1; 34 Q—
QKt8ch, K—Q2; 35 Q x Pch, K—
Q1; 36 Q x Rch; K—B1; 37 Q—B7
mate.
If 31 . . . K—B1; 32 R—Kt5 win-
ning without difficulty.

---

32. Barmen, 1905

QUEEN'S GAMBIT DECLINED

In which my opponent resigns
with a lot of play left.

F.J. MARSHALL   **C. SCHLECHTER**

White	Black
1 P—Q4	P—Q4
2 P—QB4	P—K3
3 Kt—QB3	B—K2
4 Kt—B3	Kt—KB3
5 B—Kt5	QKt—Q2
6 P—K3	O—O
7 Q—B2	. . . .

As played in the previous game.
This and White's next move point
to an attacking policy characterized by O—O—O.

7	R—K1
8 P—KR4	P—B3

Too conservative; 8 . . . P—B4
gives Black a freer game.

| 9 P—R3 | . . . . |

White is now content with simple positional play, for the cramped
state of Black's position will eventually bring its own punishment;
his QB, in particular, faces a
dreary future.

9	Kt—B1
10 B—Q3	P x P
11 B x P	Kt—Q4
12 P—K4!	Kt x Kt
13 Q x Kt	P—B3

This does not help matters, as
it weakens the diagonal KKt1—
QR7 in Black's camp. But Black's
choice of moves is sadly limited
because he cannot liberate himself
with the natural moves . . . P—K4
or . . . P—QB4.

14 B—K3	P—QR4
15 B—R2	B—Q2
16 O—O	Q—Kt1

The fact that Black finds it necessary to undertake such a clumsy
regrouping maneuver merely for
the purpose of bringing his QB to
a comparatively ineffective square,
shows how faulty his opening play
has been.

17 KR—Q1	R—B1
18 Q—Q2!	. . . .

White's logical goal is the push
to Q5, opening new lines of attack

18	B—K1
19 P—Q5!	BP x P
20 P x P	R—Q1

If 20 . . . P x P?? 21 Q x Pch and
wins. Or 20 . . . P—K4? 21 P—
Q6ch (this is the motif of the remaining play). Perhaps 20 . . .
B—B2 could have been tried, although it is anything but attractive.

21 B—KB4!	Resigns

The final position

Schlechter

Marshall

Ideas.

I knew my position was strong, but not that strong! A likely continuation would have been: 21 ... Q—R2 (if 21 ... B—Q3; 22 P x P! wins. If 21 ... P—K4; 22 P—Q6ch, K—R1; 23 Q—Q5 and wins); 22 P—Q6, Kt—Kt3 (White threatened to get three pieces for the Queen, and a fine position as well, with 23 P x B); 23 B x Pch, K—R1; 24 P—R5, Kt x B; 25 Q x Kt, B—B1; 26 R—Q5, B—B3; 27 Kt—R4! B x R; 28 Kt—Kt6ch, P x Kt; 29 P x P and mates in a few moves. However, Black preferred to bow to the inevitable.

---

33. Barmen, 1905

BISHOP'S OPENING

White embarks on an ingenious combination, which is topped by a better one!

P.S. LEONHARDT   F.J. MARSHALL

White	Black
1 P—K4	P—K4
2 B—B4	Kt—KB3
3 P—Q3	P—Q4
4 P x P	Kt x P

The same line of play as in Game No. 6—but here my opponent is a much finer player.

5 Kt—KB3	Kt—QB3
6 O—O	B—KKt5
7 R—K1	B—K2
8 P—KR3	B—R4

I was willing to lose the KP in order to provoke the following weakening move.

9 P—KKt4	B—Kt3
10 Kt x P	Kt x Kt
11 R x Kt	Kt—Kt3
12 B—Kt3	. . . .

The attempt to prevent Black from castling by playing 12 Q—K2 is pointless, as there follows 12 ... Kt x B; 13 P x Kt, P—KB3;

14 R—K6, K—B2; 15 Kt—B3, Q—Q2 and Black stands well.

12	O—O
13 Kt—B3	K—R1
14 B—Q2	B—Q3
15 R—K2!	. . . .

Very well played. The move prepares for doubling Rooks on the K file without loss of time, and also makes possible the excellent maneuver Q—B1—Kt2, adequately protecting the King-side.

15	P—KB4
16 Q—KB1	P x P
17 P x P	Q—R5
18 Q—Kt2	Kt—Q2

Hoping to get the Knight to K4, which is prevented by Black's reply. White's position is uncomfortable but quite playable.

19 QR—K1	Kt—B3
20 B—K6	B—B2

There is nothing in 20 ... B—K1; 21 Kt—K4, B—B3 because of 22 B—Kt5.

21 B—B5?	. . . .

Now White goes astray with some flashy combinative moves which soon recoil on him. Correct was 21 B x B! R x B; 22 P—Kt5, Kt—Kt5; 23 R—K8ch, R x R; 24 R x Rch, B—B1; 25 Kt—K4 and White has retained his material advantage with a satisfactory position.

21	P—KKt3

(see diagram next page)

22 Kt—K4!	. . . .

Forced, but quite pretty. The idea is if 22 ... P x B; 23 Kt x B with a very good game for White, as the Knight cannot be captured.

22	B—Q4!

A still better reply. Black now threatens ... P x B; and if 23 B—Kt5, Q x B and wins.

Position after Black's 21st move

Marshall

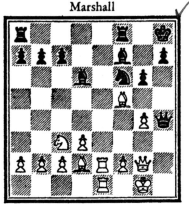

Leonhardt

23 B—K6!   Kt x Kt!

The refutation! But not 23 . . . B x B; 24 Kt x Kt and White has the advantage.

24 B x B   . . . .

Again forced. Black's next move establishes a won position.

24 . . . .   Kt x B
25 R x Kt   R—B5!
26 R—K4   P—B3!

A good move which drives off the Bishop from the defense. Luckily, White cannot interpolate 27 R x R?

27 B—Kt3   QR—KB1
28 R(2)—K2   B—B4!
29 P—Q4   B x P
30 R x R   R x R
31 P—Kt5!   . . . .

Another clever move which deserved a better fate. If now 31 . . . R—Kt5; 32 R—K8ch forcing mate!

31 . . . .   P—KR3!
32 R—K8ch   K—Kt2!
33 P x Pch   K—R2!

Good. If at once 33 . . . K x P; 34 Q—R2, Q x Qch; 35 K x Q, R x P ch and White's BP is protected. Black therefore entices the hostile Bishop away from Kt3.

34 B—Kt8ch   K x P
35 Q—R2   Q x Qch
36 K x Q   R x Pch
37 K—R3   R x P
38 P—Kt4   R—B6ch
39 K—Kt4   R—K6!

The ending is won, despite the Bishops of opposing color.

40 R x R   B x R
41 P—R4   B—Q7
42 P—Kt5   P x P
43 P x P   P—R4!
44 P x P e.p.   P x P
45 B—Kt3   K—Kt2
46 K—B3   K—B3

The winning process is clear: White's King can hold back only one Pawn, whereupon Black's King supports the advance of the other Pawn.

47 K—K4   P—R4
48 B—B2   P—Kt4
49 B—Q1   B—K8
50 K—K3   K—B4
51 B—B2ch   K—Kt5

White resigns. Both players have shown to advantage.

Time Space Material
T. S. M. F.   Force.

IV
COMMUTING TO EUROPE
(1906-1909)

34. Ostend, 1906

QUEEN'S GAMBIT DECLINED

The game is predominantly positional, but there are some neat tactical turns toward the end.

F.J. MARSHALL   R. SPIELMANN

	White	Black
1	P—Q4	P—Q4
2	P—QB4	P—K3
3	Kt—QB3	P—QB4
4	BP x P	KP x P
5	Kt—B3	Kt—QB3
6	B—Kt5	....

For some time this was my favorite line of play against the Tarrasch Defense; but later I switched to the more effective Schlechter-Rubinstein move 6 P—KKt3 after it had been introduced into master play in 1908.

6	....	B—K2
7	B x B	KKt x B
8	P x P	Q—R4
9	P—K3	O—O
10	B—Q3	Q x BP

Black is on the way to achieving a very fair development, but his position suffers from an ineradicable weakness: the isolated QP. Not only will White be able to exert pressure on this weakness; he will have a strong pressure on the central black squares Q4, QB5 and K5.

11	O—O	B—K3
12	P—QR3	KR—Q1
13	R—B1	Q—Q3

Weakness (handwritten margin note)

14	Kt—QKt5	Q—Q2
15	QKt—Q4	....

White has been able to post his QKt on the fine square Q4 with gain of time. Whatever piece White posts on this square will be strongly centralized and can never be driven away.

15	....	QR—B1
16	B—Kt1	....

Intending to force a weakening Pawn move with Q—Q3. Black decides to simplify, although his leaving the QB file in White's hands seems dubious policy.

16	....	Kt x Kt
17	Q x Kt	R x R
18	R x R	Kt—B3
19	Q—KR4	P—KR3
20	P—R3	....

Partly for restraint (. . . B—Kt5 is prevented) and also with some idea of attack by P—KKt4-5. This does not materialize.

20	....	R—K1
21	Q—KB4	Q—Q1
22	B—Q3	Q—R4
23	K—R2	P—R3

White has quietly improved his position move by move, incidentally compelling Black to admit that he has nothing better than waiting moves. White now strengthens his grip on QB5, further constricting Black's freedom of action.

24	R—B3!	Q—Kt3

He had no way of preventing White's next move.

Lift.

25 P—QKt4	R—Q1
26 R—B5	. . . .

A strong blockading move which has the additional merit of preventing . . . P—Q5.

26	K—B1
27 P—KR4	R—Q2
28 B—K2	R—Q1

28 . . . Q—B2 would lead to a lost game after 29 Q x Q, R x Q; 30 Kt—Q4 etc.

29 P—Kt3	K—K2?

Black wants to have his King in the center in the event an ending is reached; but at this stage this maneuver is too risky.

30 Kt—Q4	Kt x Kt
31 Q x Kt	P—B3?

. . . K—B1 was preferable.

32 Q—Q3	Q—Q3
33 Q—R7	R—KKt1

There was no good move: if 33 . . . K—B1; 34 Q—R8ch, B—Kt1; 35 P—K4! Q—K4 (if 35 . . . P x P or . . . P—Q5; 36 B—B4 wins); 36 B—B4! winning a Pawn. Black dare not play 36 . . . Q x P because of 37 R—B7, Q—K3; 38 Q x Pch, K—K1; 39 B—Q3 and wins.

Position after Black's 33rd move

Spielmann

Marshall

34 B—Kt4!	. . . .

The winning move!

34	B—B2
35 Q—B2!	R—Q1
36 R—B7ch	K—B1
37 R x P	K—Kt1
38 Q—QB5	P—Q5

Exchanging Queens would be equivalent to resignation.

39 Q—R7	Q—Q4
40 P x P	Q—R7
41 P—Q5!	. . . .

This pretty move initiates a forced win.

Σ F.

41	Q x QP
42 R—K7!	K—B1

White threatened B—K6! If 42 . . .P—B4; 43 B—R5! wins.

43 B—B3!	Q—R7

If 43 . . . Q—B5; 44 R—K4, or 43 . . . Q—Kt6; 44 R—K3 with the same point as in the actual play.

یمو)

44 R—K2	Resigns

He cannot guard against the threat of Q—K7ch. The concluding play is elegant in its simplicity.

---

35.   Ostend, 1906

(*Brilliancy Prize*)

QUEEN'S PAWN OPENING

An exciting game. White plays a very fine combination, but then falters and gives Black an opportunity to seize the advantage.

Init.

R. SWIDERSKI	F.J. MARSHALL
White	Black
1 P—Q4	P—Q4
2 Kt—KB3	P—QB4
3 P—K3	Kt—KB3

| 4 QKt—Q2 | Kt—B3 |
| 5 B—K2 | B—B4 |

This involves a Pawn sacrifice which is not quite sound. However, the unnaturally passive character of White's opening play is quite provocative!

6 P x P	P—K4
7 B—Kt5	Q—B2
8 P—QKt4	B—K2
9 B—Kt2	Kt—Q2
10 P—QR3	O—O
11 P—B4	....

Inviting Black's reply and beginning a combination.

11	B—Q6
12 Q—Kt3	P—K5
13 P x P	....

Evidently a prepared line, and an improvement on 13 B x Kt, as played by Swiderski against Spielmann in an earlier round. That game continued: 13 ... P x B; 14 P x P, P x P; 15 Kt—Q4, Kt—K4; 16 Q x P, B—B3; 17 Kt x P, QR—Q1; 18 Kt—Q6, Kt—B5; 19 Kt(4)—Kt5, Kt x B! 20 Q—Kt3, Q—B3; 21 Kt—Q4, B x Kt; 22 P x B, R x Kt! 23 Q x Kt, Q—K5ch and White resigned.
This gives us an idea of what to expect in the present game!

13	B x B
14 Kt x P	Kt(3)—K4
15 B x Kt	Kt x B
16 P—Q6	Kt—Q6ch
17 K—Q2	Q—B3
18 P x B?	....

Obvious—but not the best. Correct was 18 Kt—B3!! and White should win. After the text, Black seizes the initiative.

(see diagram next column)

18	Q x Kt!
19 P x R(Q)ch	R x Q
20 Kt—Q4	....

(see diagram next column)

Position after White's 18th move

Marshall

Swiderski

On 20 KR—KB1, Kt—B5! is very strong. The text seems conclusive, but Black has a good reply.

| 20 .... | Kt x KBP! |

So that if 21 Kt x B, Kt x R with a good attack (22 R x Kt? Q x KtP ch).

| 21 KR—KKt1 | R—Q1 |
| 22 QR—KB1? | .... |

Anticipating 22 ... B x R; 23 R x B, Q x P; 24 K—K1 and wins. 22 QR—K1 was a much better move.

| 22 .... | R x Ktch! |

A perfectly sound sacrifice.

| 23 P x R | Q x Pch |
| 24 K—B1 | .... |

Forced: 24 K—K1? Kt—Q6ch etc. Or 24 K—B2, B—Q6ch; 25 K—B1, Q—R8ch; 26 K—Q2, B x R etc.

| 24 .... | Q—R8ch |
| 25 Q—Kt1 | .... |

Some of the masters recommended 25 K—Q2, B x R; 26 Q—K3. But then Black wins with 26 ... Q—

Kt7ch; 27 K—K1, B—Kt4! Very pretty!

25	Q—B6ch
26 Q—B2	Q x Pch
27 K—Q2	. . . .

The Queen cannot interpose here because of . . . Kt—Q6ch, nor on the next move because of . . . Kt—K5ch.

| 27 . . . . | Q x Pch |
| 28 K—K3 | . . . . |

If 28 K—B1, Kt—Q6ch; 29 K—Q1, B—R5.

| 28 . . . . | Kt—Kt5ch |
| 29 K—B3 | Kt x Pch |

White resigns, for if 30 K—Kt3, Q—Kt5ch! 31 K—B2 (not 31 K x Kt, Q—R5 mate), Kt x R (threatening . . . Q—Kt6 mate); 32 R x Kt, Q—B5ch etc. Black's forces have co-operated with remarkable economy.

---

36. Ostend, 1906
QUEEN'S PAWN OPENING

One of my most exciting games. Burn's clever counter-attack beginning with move 20, made it the kind of position where "anything can happen."

| A. Burn | F.J. Marshall |
| White | Black |

1 P—Q4	P—Q4
2 Kt—KB3	P—QB4
3 P—B3	P—K3
4 B—B4	Kt—QB3
5 P—K3	Kt—B3
6 QKt—Q2	. . . .

This variation is one which has virtually disappeared from master play because it offers Black less trouble than he encounters in the Queen's Gambit. Black now has the choice of . . . Q—Kt3 followed by . . . B—K2, . . . B—Q2 and . . . QR—B1, and the simpler line of . . . B—Q3 intending . . . P—K4 eventually. He chooses the latter course.

6	B—Q3
7 B—Kt3	O—O
8 B—Q3	R—K1

Black is now ready for . . . P—K4. White's attempt to prevent this liberating move only leads to loss of a Pawn.

9 Kt—K5?	B x Kt
10 P x B	Kt—Q2
11 P—KB4	P—B5
12 B—QB2	Q—Kt3
13 K—B2	Q x P

And now he must win a second Pawn as well.   *Eagle.*

| 14 QR—B1 | Q x RP |
| 15 Q—K2 | P—B4 |

Now that Black has won the Pawns, he does not feel so happy! His Queen is out of play, his game undeveloped and there are storm clouds on the King-side.   *(must)*

16 P x P e.p.   *O.*

Naturally; he must keep the KB's attacking diagonal open.

16	Kt x P
17 B—KR4	R—B1
18 B x Kt!	R x B
19 Kt—B3	. . . .

Threatening B x Pch and thus gaining an important tempo for the attack.

| 19 . . . . | Q—R6 |
| 20 B x Pch!? | . . . . |

Now the fun begins. From this point on, Burn plays with desperate ingenuity, knowing full well that only a successful attack can out-weigh his material disadvantage.

| 20 . . . . | K x B |

Should I have declined the Bish-

op? After 20 . . . K—B1 White
has a strong attack with Kt—Kt5
threatening Q—R5, and Black lacks
the solace of being a piece ahead.

| 21 Kt—Kt5ch | K—Kt1 |

Forced. If 21 . . . K—Kt3; 22
Q—B2ch, R—B4; 23 P—Kt4 wins.
If 21 . . . K—R3; 22 Q—Kt4 with
decisive effect, for example 22 . . .
P—KKt3; 23 Q—R4ch, K—Kt2; 24
Q—R7ch, K—B1; 25 Q—R8ch, K—
K2; 26 Q—Kt7ch.

| 22 Q—R5 | . . . . |

Position after White's 22nd move

Marshall

Burn

| 22 . . . . | Kt—K4! |

A wild move which leads to
wonderfully interesting play.

23 Q—R7ch	K—B1
24 Q—R8ch	K—K2
25 Q x Pch	K—Q3!

The defense here must always be
aggressive! 25 . . . Kt—B2? is
refuted by 26 Kt—R7 threatening
Q—B8ch or Q x Rch.

| 26 K—Kt3 | . . . . |

Forcing Black's reply, now that
. . . Kt—Kt5ch is not available in
reply to Q x R. At the same time

the powerful advance of the KP is
prepared.

26	Kt—Q2
27 P—K4!	K—B3!
28 P—K5	Q—B1!!

After 28 . . . R—B1 or . . . R—
B4; 29 Kt x P Black's position
would rapidly disintegrate. The
text is therefore the best chance
to break the attack.

| 29 P x R | Q x P |
| 30 Q—Kt8 | . . . . |

A let-down after his superb attempt to turn the tables. 30 Q x Q
was indicated, followed by a nerve-
wracking race to queen, with a
result that would be very difficult
to forecast.

30	Kt—B4
31 Q—K8ch	B—Q2!!
32 Q x R	P—K4

Now I am in my element again.
This time it is White's Queen that
is out of play, and Black's attack
must win out, although he is a
Rook and the exchange down!

| 33 Kt—R3 | . . . . |

If 33 KR—B1, P x Pch; 34 K—B2,
Kt—Q6ch with a winning game.

33	Q—Kt3ch
34 K—B2	Kt—Q6ch
35 K—B1	. . . .

On 35 K—K3, Q—K5ch forces
mate in short order.

| 35 . . . . | Kt x R |
| 36 Kt—B2 | Q—B7 |

Threatens mate in two.

37 P—Kt3	Kt—Q6
38 Q x P	P—Q5!
39 Kt x Kt	B—R6ch
40 K—K1	P x Kt

White resigns. All's well that
ends well!

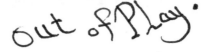

37. Ostend, 1906

QUEEN'S GAMBIT

As so often happened in his games, Janowski advances too impetuously and runs into a murderous attack.

F. J. MARSHALL	D. JANOWSKI
White	Black
1 P—Q4	P—Q4
2 P—QB4	P x P

It was about this time that Janowski took up the acceptance of the gambit, which remained a favorite with him to the end of his life. He played many beautiful games with this defense.

3 P—K3	P—QR3
4 B x P	Kt—KB3
5 Kt—KB3	P—K3
6 P—QR4	. . . .

This move has assets and liabilities. It prevents . . . P—QKt4 and therefore restrains Black to rather a modest development. On the other hand, it creates a hole at Q Kt4, which can be advantageously occupied by Black's QKt. It is also conceivable that this square may become a weakness in the endgame.

6	P—QKt3
7 Kt—B3	B—Kt2
8 O—O	Kt—B3
9 Q—K2	Kt—QKt5
10 P—K4	B—K2
11 B—KKt5	P—R3
12 B—B4	O—O

White has a fine free game, but Black's position, though cramped, is compact and free from weaknesses.

13 KR—Q1	R—B1
14 Kt—K5	Q—K1

This awkward-looking move is played in order to make . . . P—B4 possible.

15 R—Q2	. . . .

As . . . P—B4 may be expected momentarily, White prepares to occupy the Q file in force.

15	P—B4
16 P x P	B x BP
17 QR—Q1	Q—K2

This is possible because 18 R—Q7? would be refuted by 18 . . . Kt x R; 19 R x Kt, Q—B3. Hence, White's next move

18 B—KKt3	KR—Q1
19 B—R4	R x R
20 R x R	P—KKt4

An advance that may weaken Black's King-side critically, but on the obvious 20 . . . R—Q1 Janowski must have feared 21 R x Rch (not 21 Kt—Kt4? R x R; 22 Q x R, Kt x P!), Q x R; 22 Kt—Q3 (threatening P—K5 as well as Kt x Kt followed by B x P), P—KKt4; 23 B—KKt3, Kt x Kt; 24 B x Kt, P—QR4; 25 P—K5, Kt—Q4; 26 Kt—K4 and Black has weaknesses on both wings.

21 B—KKt3	R—Q1
22 R x Rch	Q x R
23 P—R4	Q—Q5?

Losing at least a Pawn. However, if 23 . . . B—KB1 or . . . K—Kt2; 24 Kt—Q3! is quite good.

24 P x P	Kt x P

If instead 24 . . . P x P; 25 Kt—B3 winning the KKtP and leaving Black with a lost game.

But now he succumbs to a surprise attack.

(see diagram next page)

25 Q—R5!	Kt x KtP

If 25 . . . Kt x B; 26 Q x Pch, K—R1; 27 Kt—Kt6 mate.

26 B x KP!	Q—Q7

Or 26 . . . P x B; 27 Q—Kt6ch, K—B1 (if 27 . . . K—R1; 28 Q x Pch,, Kt—R2; 29 Q—Kt6); 28 Q x

Position after Black's 24th move

Janowski

Marshall

Pch followed by Q x Kt with a winning attack.

27	B x Pch	K—B1
28	Q x Pch	K—K2
29	Q—Kt7	. . . .

Black was threatening . . . Kt—B6ch. As his position is now hopeless, he tries a last desperate gamble.

29	. . . .	B x Pch
30	B x B	Kt—R6ch

Hoping for 31 P x Kt? Q—B8ch; 32 K—R2, Q—R8ch; 33 K—Kt3, Q—Kt7ch winning the Queen.

31	K—R2!	Q x B
32	B—Q5ch	K—Q3
33	Kt—K4ch	. . . .

Good enough, but there was a mate in four by 33 Kt—B4ch, K—B4; 34 Q—K7ch, K—Q5; 35 Q—K5ch, K—Q6 (if 35 . . . K—B4; 36 Kt—K4 mate); 36 Q—K4 mate. After the text, Black resigned.

38.　Nuremberg, 1906

QUEEN'S GAMBIT DECLINED

My opponent in this game was a promising young German player who was subsequently killed in World War I.

F. J. Marshall	E. Cohn
White	Black
1 P—Q4	P—Q4
2 P—QB4	P—K3
3 Kt—QB3	P—QB4
4 BP x P	KP x P
5 Kt—B3	Kt—KB3

Surprisingly enough, this apparently obvious developing move is an inexactitude. . . . Kt—QB3 is the proper continuation.

6 B—Kt5	B—K3

If 6 . . . B—K2; 7 P x P is an embarrassing reply.

7 P—K4	. . . .

Equally strong, but simpler, is 7 B x Kt, Q x B; 8 P—K4. In either case Black finds himself in a serious predicament.

7	. . . .	BP x P

If 7 . . . QP x P; 8 B—Kt5ch as in the text, but not 8 Kt x P, P—B5!

8 B—Kt5ch!	QKt—Q2

Not 8 . . . Kt—B3; 9 KKt x P with an even stronger attack than in the text.

9 KKt x P	B—QKt5

If instead 9 . . . B—K2; 10 B x Kt followed by P x P wins a Pawn. Or if 9 . . . P x P; 10 Kt x B, P x Kt; 11 B x Kt, P x B; 12 Q—R5ch, K—K2; 13 O—O—O or R—Q1 and wins.

"It is remarkable," says Tarrasch, "that after so few moves in a Queen's Gambit Declined, Black's game should be so disorganized. White's attack is as strong as in a Muzio Gambit."

10 P—K5!	. . . .

This brings about the ruin of Black's King-side.

| 10 .... | P—KR3 |
| 11 P x Kt | B x Ktch |

This has to be interpolated hereabouts, else the Bishop will be lost later on by a Queen check at KR4.

12 P x B	P x B
13 Kt x B	P x Kt
14 P x P	KR—Kt1
15 Q—R5ch	K—K2
16 Q x Pch	K—B2

If 16 ... Kt—B3; 17 B—Q3 (threat: B—R7), K—B2; 18 B—Kt6ch, K x P; 19 R—Q1, K—B1; 20 R—Q3 and wins.

| 17 Q—R5ch | K—K2 |

If 17 ... K x P; 18 R—Q1! followed by R—Q3 leads to a quick win.

| 18 O—O | .... |

Had Black omitted ... B x Ktch, 18 Q—R4ch would now win the Bishop.

18	R x P
19 KR—K1	Kt—B3
20 Q—R3	Q—Q3
21 B—Q3!	QR—KKt1

The consolidation of Black's position is deceptive. With his King helpless in the center, he must soon succumb.

| 22 P—Kt3 | Kt—Kt5 |

Or 22 ... R—Kt4; 23 R—K2 followed by QR—K1 and Black's game becomes untenable.

| 23 B—B5! | Kt—K4 |

(see diagram next column)

| 24 B x P! | R—KB1 |

If 24 ... Q x B; 25 Q x Qch; K x Q; 26 P—KB4 and wins; or 24 ... Kt—B6ch; 25 K—R1, Kt x R; 26 R x Kt (also good is 26 B x R, Kt—B7; 27 R—QB1, Kt—R6; 28

Position after Black's 23rd move

Cohn

Marshall

R—K1ch, K—Q1; 29 B—K6) and White must win.

| 25 Q—R4ch | R—B3 |

On 25 ... K x B White wins with 26 Q—R6ch or 26 P—KB4.

26 B x P!	Q x B
27 Q—Q4!	K—K3
28 QR—Q1!	Resigns

For if 28 ... R—Q2; 29 R x Ktch, Q x R; 30 Q x R mate.

Tarrasch: "A magnificent game."

---

39. Nuremberg, 1906
QUEEN'S GAMBIT DECLINED

White wins by offering first one Bishop, and then the other!

F. J. MARSHALL	R. SPIELMANN
White	Black
1 P—Q4	P—Q4
2 P—QB4	P—K3
3 Kt—QB3	Kt—KB3
4 B—Kt5	B—K2
5 P—K3	QKt—Q2
6 Q—B2	....

A move which is encountered frequently in my games of this period.

6	O—O
7 Kt—B3	R—K1
8 R—Q1	P—QR3
9 P—QR4	. . . .

So that if 9 . . . P x P; 10 B x P and Black cannot play . . . P—QKt4. However, this move could be dispensed with, in favor of an immediate P x P, as played next move.

9	P—QKt3
10 P x P	P x P

Blocking the QB's diagonal, but if 10 . . . Kt x P; 11 Kt x Kt, P x Kt; 12 B x B, R x B; 13 Q—B6 etc.

11 B—Q3	B—Kt2
12 O—O	Kt—K5

Probably best. After 12 . . . P—B4; 13 P x P would be disagreeable, because of White's pressure along the Q file.

13 B—KB4	B—KB1

An illogical retreat. . . . B—KB3, preventing Kt—K5, would be more useful.

14 Kt—K5	QKt x Kt
15 QB x Kt	. . . .

I wanted to keep this Bishop's diagonal open; however, there is a lot to be said for 15 P x Kt, Kt x Kt; 16 P x Kt, P—Kt3; 17 B—K4 etc.

15	P—Kt3?

This plausible move loses a Pawn in a surprising manner. . . . P—R3 should have been played.

16 B x BP!	Q x B
17 Kt x Kt	Q—K2

If 17 . . . Q x Q; 18 Kt—B6ch and Black must play . . . K—R1.

18 Kt—B3	Q—Kt5
19 Kt—R2	. . . .

With this and the next move White only loses time and gives Black an opportunity to consolidate his position, until the winning procedure becomes really difficult.

There were at least two preferable plans: B—K2—B3 followed by Q—Kt1—R2 with pressure on the QP, or else Q—K2 followed by doubling Rooks on the QB file.

19	Q—R4
20 R—Kt1	KR—B1
21 Q—Q1	P—QKt4

Disposing of the threat of P—QKt4.

22 P—QKt3	B—B3
23 P x P!	. . . .

Getting rid of his somewhat shaky Pawn position on the Queenside. If now 23 . . . Q x Kt; 24 P x B, R x P and Black's QP and QRP are quite weak.

23	P x P
24 Kt—B1	B—Q2
25 Q—B3	B—K3
26 Kt—K2	Q—Kt5
27 P—R4!	. . . .

White is again in full command of the situation. He realizes that the defense of the weak QKtP is too heavy a task, and concentrates instead on combining pressure against the QP with aggressive play on the King-side.

27	R—R6
28 P—R5	R x P
29 P x P	RP x P
30 Kt—B4	. . . .

(see diagram next page)

Now one can appreciate the strength of the advance of the KRP. White threatens B x KKtP; Thus, if 30 . . . R—B3; 31 B x KKtP! P x B; 32 Kt x QP! Q—R6; 33 Kt—B6ch, K—Kt2; 34 Kt—K8ch, K moves; 35 Q x R—or 33 . . . K—B2; 34 Q x R, R x R; 35 R x R, Q—R7 (if 35 . . . K x Kt; 36 P—Q5); 36 R x P, K x Kt; 37 P—Q5 etc.

Position after White's 30th move

Spielmann

Marshall

Similarly, if 30 . . . R—K1; 31 B x KKtP! etc.

| 30 . . . . | R x R |
| 31 R x R | Q—R6 |

Somewhat better was 31 . . . Q—Q3; 32 R x P and Black can put up a longer resistance.

32 B x KKtP!   . . . .

In making this move, White had to appraise the position resulting from the exchange of Rooks and come to the conclusion that the passed QKtP can be neutralized.

32	R—B8ch
33 R x R	Q x Rch
34 K—R2	B—Q3

If 34 . . . P x B; 35 Kt x B, B—Q3ch; 36 P—Kt3, Q—B3; 37 Q—B6 and the game is over.

| 35 B—Q3 | Q—B3 |

White threatened Q—Kt3ch followed by Kt—Kt6ch with a quick win.

| 36 P—Kt3 | B x Kt |
| 37 Q x B | B—Q2 |

Simultaneously guarding against

Q—R6 and guarding the KtP against Q—Kt8ch. Now comes a final sharp phase in which White demonstrates that Black's passed Pawn is less dangerous than it seems. Accurate timing is the keynote, advance of White's KtP is the method.

38 P—Kt4	P—Kt5
39 Q—Kt8ch	K—Kt2
40 Q—K5ch	K—Kt1
41 Q—Kt5ch	K—B1
42 K—Kt3	P—Kt6
43 Q—K5	Q—Kt2
44 P—Kt5!	. . . .

Does White's attack have enough momentum? It hardly seems so!

44	P—Kt7
45 Q—R8ch	K—K2
46 Q—B6ch	K—K1
47 P—Kt6!	. . . .

Now the win is clear.

47	P—Kt8 (Q)
48 P x Pch	K—B1
49 B x Q	Q—Kt1ch
50 Q—B4	Q x B
51 Q—Q6ch	K x P
52 Q x Bch	K—B1
53 Q—Q8ch	K—Kt2
54 Q x P	Q—Kt8ch
55 Q—Kt2	Resigns

An interesting game in all its phases.

---

40. Nuremberg, 1906

QUEEN'S GAMBIT DECLINED

A positional game all the way. The exploitation of Black's Queenside weakness is interesting.

F. J. MARSHALL P. S. LEONHARDT

White	Black
1 P—Q4	P—Q4
2 P—QB4	P—K3

3 Kt—QB3	Kt—KB3
4 B—Kt5	B—K2
5 P—K3	O—O
6 Kt—B3	QKt—Q2
7 Q—B2	....

Regarding this move see also Game no. 32.

7	P—KR3
8 B—R4	P—B3
9 P—QR3	....

Trying to save a tempo instead of at once playing 9 B—Q3, P x P etc.

| 9 .... | R—K1 |
| 10 R—B1 | Q—R4 |

Not very promising in this position. 10 . . . P—R3, intending . . . P—QKt4, is better.

| 11 Kt—Q2 | .... |

The usual reaction to Black's Queen move. The idea is to answer . . . P x P with Kt x P, when White's KKt comes into play powerfully.

| 11 .... | P—K4 |

A freeing maneuver which does not quite succeed.

12 BP x P	Kt x P
13 B x B	Kt x B
14 Kt—B4	Q—B2
15 R—Q1	Kt—KKt3

(see diagram next column)

| 16 B—Q3! | .... |

An interesting move. The intention is to answer 16 . . . P x P with 17 B x Kt, P x Kt; 18 B x Pch! K x B; 19 Kt—Q6ch, K—B1 (not 19 . . . K—K2? 20 Q—K4ch); 20 Q—R7! and wins: 20 . . . Kt—B3; 21 Q—R8ch, Kt—Kt1; 22 Kt x R etc. or 20 . . . R—Q1; 21 Q—R8ch, K—K2; 22 Q x Pch, K—K3; 23 Q—B7ch, K—K4; Q—B5 mate.

| 16 .... | QKt—B1 |

Leonhardt

Marshall

| 17 P—Q5! | .... |

Leads to simplification which leaves White with the better ending.

| 17 .... | P—Kt4 |

Shakes off the pressure, but at the cost of creating serious weaknesses, as will soon become apparent.

18 Kt—Q2	P x P
19 Kt x QP	Q x Q
20 B x Q	B—Kt2

So that if 21 Kt—B7? KR—B1; 22 Kt x R, R x B; and the Knight is trapped.

| 21 B x Kt! | B x Kt |

Forced.

22 B—K4!	KR—Q1
23 B x B	R x B
24 Kt—K4	QR—Q1

White has a number of small advantages in this ending: Black's QKtP requires careful looking after; in short order a number of important squares in Black's camp, such as Q3, QB4 and QB2 become weak and subject to occupation;

White's King is in the center. Because of these weaknesses, Black dares not go in for general exchanges, for then White's King could dash across to the Queenside and win rapidly.

25 K—K2	Kt—K3
26 R x R	R x R
27 R—QB1!	K—B1
28 R—B8ch	K—K2
29 R—QKt8	....

White proceeds to apply the pressure. The text threatens Kt—B3, which if played immediately, would not yet bring results: 29 Kt—B3, R—Q2; 30 Kt x P, R—Kt2; 31 P—QR4, P—R3 regaining the Pawn.

29	P—R3
30 R—Kt6	Kt—B2
31 P—QKt4	P—B4

Creating new weaknesses, but there was no help for it. After the Tournament Book's recommendation 31 . . . R—Q1 there could follow 32 P—Kt4! and the subsequent centralization of White's King on K4; eventually Black would run out of moves.

32 Kt—Kt3	P—K5
33 Kt—R5	K—B2
34 Kt—B4	R—Q2
35 Kt—Kt6!	....

The winning move, for if 35 . . . K—K1; 36 R—Kt8ch, R—Q1; 37 R x Rch, K x R; 38 Kt—R4 winning a Pawn. Or 35 . . . R—Q4; 36 R—B6! and Black is in Zugzwang: he is helpless against 37 R x Ktch, K x Kt; 38 R—B6ch or simply 37 Kt—R4.

| 35 .... | K—Kt1 |
| 36 R—Kt8ch | K—B2 |

If 36 . . . K—R2?? 37 Kt—B8ch. If 36 . . . Kt—K1; 37 R x Ktch, K—B2; 38 R—QR8, K x Kt; 39 R x Pch K moves; 40 R—R5, R—Kt2 (if 40 . . . R—Q4; 41 P—QR4); 41 K—Q2 and wins.

37 Kt—K5ch	K—K2
38 Kt x R	K x Kt
39 R—Kt6	K—K2
40 P—Kt4!	P x P

Further material loss is now in store for Black.

41 R—Kt6	K—B2
42 R x KtP	Kt—Q4
43 R x P	Kt—B6ch
44 K—Q3	Kt x R
45 K x Kt	K—K3
46 P—KR4	P—Kt3
47 P—B4	K—B3

Or 47 . . . P—KR4; 48 K—Q4, K—B4; 49 P—K4ch! K x P (if 49 . . . K—Kt5; 50 P—K5 wins); 50 P—K5, K—B4; 51 K—Q5, P—Kt4; 52 P—K6 and wins.

| 48 K—B3 | K—K3 |
| 49 K—Kt4 | Resigns |

---

41. Nuremberg, 1906
QUEEN'S GAMBIT

Commenting on this game in the "Westminster Gazette" L. Hoffer wrote: "Marshall's score, whilst recording the game during its progress, bears the marks of queries at two of the most brilliant moves (18 Kt x RP and 20 Q—R5!). The inference naturally would be that Marshall launched into these sacrifices simply by intuition, without having taken the trouble to fathom the combination—and yet the game is a masterpiece!"

| F. J. MARSHALL | H. WOLF |
| White | Black |

1 P—Q4	P—Q4
2 P—QB4	P x P
3 Kt—KB3	Kt—KB3
4 Kt—B3	P—QR3
5 P—K3	P—K3

The attempt to hold the gambit Pawn by 5 . . . P—QKt4 would as usual be refuted by 6 P—QR4.

6 B x P	P—B4
7 O—O	Kt—B3

.... P—QKt4 followed by ... B—Kt2 may be better, in order to retain the option of playing the QKt to Q2.

8 P—QR3 ....

Initiating a plan of development which, perhaps, should not have had as much success as it achieves in the actual play. The better course is 8 Q—K2 and if 8 ... P x P; 9 R—Q1 recovers the Pawn advantageously.

8 .... Q—B2

This is a poor move, for after the QB file is opened later on, the Black Queen will be annoyed by a White Rook on the same file. Therefore 8 ... P—QKt4 followed by ... B—Kt2 was better.

9 Q—K2	P—QKt4
10 B—R2	B—Kt2
11 P x P	B x P
12 P—QKt4	B—Q3
13 B—Kt2	O—O
14 QR—B1	QR—Q1?

Very superficial play to leave the Queen on the same file with the hostile QR. Better was 14 ... Q—K2 and if 15 B—Kt1, Kt—K4 with a good game for Black. This method of play would have taken advantage of the fact that White has lost several tempi—with 8 P—QR3 and 11 P x P, and with taking an extra move to get his KB on the right attacking diagonal (10 B—R2 instead of 10 B—Q3).

For further discusion of this suggested line of play, see the next game.

15 B—Kt1	B—R1?
16 Kt—K4!	....

Very powerful, as it leads to formidable threats against both wings. The unfortunate position of Black's Queen proves fatal.

16 .... Kt—Q4

Black has no satisfactory move:
I 16 ... Kt x Kt; 17 B x Kt, Q—Kt3 (White was threatening to win a piece with 18 B x Kt, B x B; 19 Kt—Q4); 18 Kt—Kt5, P—R3; 19 Q—R5 (threatening Q x P!!), P—B4; 20 Q—Kt6 and wins.
II 16 ... Q—K2; 17 Kt x Ktch, P x Kt; 18 R x Kt, B x R; 19 Q—B2 winning the QB.
III 16 ... B—K2; 17 Kt x Ktch, P x Kt (if 17 ... B x Kt, 18 Q—B2! wins); 18 Q—B2, P—B4; 19 Kt—Q4, R—B1; 20 Kt x BP and wins.

17 Kt(4)—Kt5 P—Kt3

If 17 ... P—R3; 18 Q—B2, P—Kt3; 19 Kt x KP smashes Black's defense.

Position after Black's 17th move

Wolf

Marshall

18 Kt x RP!	K x Kt
19 Kt—Kt5ch	K—Kt1

Or 19 ... K—R3; 20 Q—Kt4 etc.

20 Q—R5!! P—B3

The only move. Naturally the Queen cannot be taken.

21 B x KtP! R—Q2

Again about the only move. If 21 ... Q—K2; 22 Kt x P and the attack goes on with unabated power.

22 Kt x P	R—R2!

A nice try, even though it fails.
The idea is if 23 Q x Kt? B x Pch;
24 K—R1, B—K4ch and Black
draws, since 25 B x Rch?? would
allow a mate after 25 ... Q x Bch.

23 B x Rch	Q x B
24 Q x Qch	K x Q
25 Kt x Rch	B x Kt
26 KR—Q1	. . . .

In addition to his material disadvantage, Black is burdened by
the awkward position of his pieces.
Further loss is inevitable.

26	Kt(3)—K2
27 P—K4	Kt—QKt3
28 R—B7	K—Kt1
29 B x P	Kt—Kt3
30 R—Q8	Resigns

He has no defense against R—
Kt7ch.

---

42.   Ostend, 1907

QUEEN'S GAMBIT

Schlechter undertakes to improve on Wolf's play, but comes to
grief against a surprise attack.

F. J. MARSHALL	C. SCHLECHTER
White	Black
1 P—Q4	P—Q4
2 P—QB4	P x P
3 P—K3	Kt—KB3
4 B x P	P—K3
5 Kt—KB3	P—QR3
6 O—O	P—B4
7 Kt—B3	Q—B2

The same inexactitude as in the
previous game. See the notes there
for preferable alternatives.

8 Q—K2	Kt—B3
9 P—QR3	P—QKt4
10 B—R2	B—Kt2
11 P x P	B x P
12 P—QKt4	B—Q3

13 B—Kt2	O—O
14 QR—B1	Q—K2

An improvement on Wolf's 14
... QR—Q1?

15 B—Kt1	QR—B1

Tarrasch demonstrates in the
Tournament Book that contrary to
first impression, 15 ... Kt—K4! is
perfectly feasible here. He con-
tinues 16 Kt x Kt, B x Kt; 17 Kt x
P (it was fear of this move that in-
duced Schlechter to play 15 ...
QR—B1), B x B; 18 R—B7, Q—K1!
19 Kt—Q6 (better than 19 R x B,
P x Kt; 20 Q x B, Q—B3; 21 R—K7,
KR—B1! when Black threatens
... K—B1 and White has nothing
better than 22 Q—Q4 giving up the
QRP), Q—Q1; 22 R x B, Q x Kt; 23
Q x B, Q—B3 and Black draws by
constantly attacking the Rook.

16 Kt—K4	Kt x Kt
17 B x Kt	P—B4

Black's game is uncomfortable,
and he gives way to his impulse
to drive away the Bishop, thereby
creating weaknesses in the center.

18 B—Kt1	P—K4

One thing leads to another . . .
in order to eliminate the weakness
of his K4, Black advances this
Pawn and thus opens up a new
attacking diagonal for the hostile
KB.

19 KR—Q1	P—K5?

A final error of judgment which
leaves White with a winning attack; but after 19 ... B—Kt1; 20
P—K4! Black's game would still
remain uncomfortable.

20 B—R2ch	K—R1

(see diagram next page)

21 Kt—Kt5!	Q x Kt

Forced. White was threatening
22 Q—R5 winning outright. If 21
... P—R3; 22 Kt—B7ch wins the
exchange; or if 21 ... B x Pch; 22

Position after Black's 20th move

Schlechter

Marshall

K x B, Q x Kt; 23 R—Q7 and wins.

22 R x B   KR—Q1

With the disappearance of Black's valuable Bishop, the black squares are all vulnerable, and White's far-ranging Bishops have a field day.

23 P—KR4!   . . . .

A surprise which leaves Black without a satisfactory defense! If now 23 . . . Q x RP; 24 B x Pch, K x B; 25 Q—Kt2ch, K—B1; 26 Q—R8ch, K—K2; 27 R—K6ch, K—Q2; 28 Q—Kt7ch, Kt—K2; 29 R—Q1ch K—B2; 30 Q—K5ch and mate next move.

23 . . . .   Q—Kt5

23 . . . Q—K2 has been recommended as a better defense, but Black is helpless against 24 R—K6!
I 24 . . . Q—KB2; 25 R(6) x Kt, Q x B; 26 R x R and then if 26 . . . B x R; 27 B x Pch, or 26 . . . R x R; 27 R x Rch, B x R; 28 B x Pch.
II 24 . . . Q—KB1; 25 P—R5!! R—Q3; 26 P—R6! and wins.
III 24 . . . Q—Q2; 25 P—R5, Q—Q7; 26 P—R6! Q x Q; 27 P x Pch, K—Kt1; 28 R—K8 mate.
Note that it was 23 P—KR4!

that made the latter variations feasible.

24 Q—Q2   R x R

White threatened R(1) x Kt.

25 Q x R   R—Q1

If 25 . . . P—B5; 26 B—K6, Q—Kt3; 27 Q—Q7 wins. Here again 23 P—KR4! proves its utility, for White's Queen would now be lost if the KRP had not advanced!

26 Q—B7   B—R1
27 B—Kt3   . . . .

Of course not 27 R x Kt?? R—Q8ch and mate next move.
But now Black cannot avoid a decisive loss of material.

27 . . . .   P—B5
28 R x Kt   R—KB1
29 Q—K7   Resigns

———

43. Ostend, 1907

QUEEN'S GAMBIT

One of my typical games with Janowski. You had to "get" him before he "got" you!

F. J. MARSHALL   D. JANOWSKI

White   Black

1 P—Q4   P—Q4
2 P—QB4   P x P
3 P—K3   P—K4
4 B x P   . . . .

4 P x P, Q x Qch; 5 K x Q, B—K3 gives an inferior ending for White.

4 . . . .   Kt—QB3
5 Kt—KB3   P—K5

Characteristic of Janowski's impetuous style. 5 . . . P x P was simpler and better.

6 KKt—Q2   P—B4

Creating weaknesses in his position; but after 6 . . . Kt—B3 the KP would be somewhat insecure.

7 O—O	B—Q3
8 Kt—QB3	Q—R5

Another premature attacking move which, however, has to be met with care.

9 P—KKt3	Q—R6
10 B x Kt!	. . . .

A very original conception. It forestalls . . . Kt—B3—Kt5 and also makes possible the following exchanging maneuver, which robs Black of an important attacking piece.

10	R x B
11 Kt—B4	B—Q2
12 Kt x Bch	P x Kt
13 P—QKt4!	. . . .

Another very good move. It is played to create a useful square for the Bishop at R3, and also to drive off Black's Knight after Black has castled.

13	P—KKt4

Threatening to nail down White's KBP with . . . P—Kt5, and then continue with . . . R—Kt3—R3. But this is all too wild and White has a good reply. Tarrasch suggests . . . Q—R3 as a more reasonable alternative.
Of course, if 13 . . . Kt x KtP? 14 Q—Kt3 wins.

14 P—B3	P x P
15 Q x P	R—Kt3
16 B—R3	O—O—O
17 QR—B1	. . . .

Despite Black's violent gestures, it is White who has the attack after all!

17	K—Kt1
18 Kt—Q5!	R—R3
19 R—KB2	R—K1

The threat of P—Kt5 has become critical. The alternative 19 . . . P—Kt4 would not be much better than the text.

Position after Black's 19th move

Janowski

Marshall

20 P—Kt5	Kt—K2

If 20 . . . Kt—R4; 21 B—Kt4, P—Kt3; 22 B x Kt, P x B; 23 Kt—B7 and it is all over. If 20 . . . Kt—Q1; 21 Kt—B7, R—K2; 22 Q—Q5, Kt—B2; 23 R—QKt2 and wins.

21 Kt x Kt	R x Kt
22 Q—Q5	R(2)—K3

The position is hopeless. If 22 . . . R x P; 23 B x Pch, K—R1; 24 Q—Kt8ch, R—K1; 24 Q x Rch, B x Q; 25 R—B8 mate.

23 B x Pch!	K—R1

Or 23 . . . R x B; 24 Q—Kt8ch etc.

24 R—B7	Resigns

---

44. Ostend, 1907

INDIAN DEFENSE

A little on the wild side, this one!

F. J. MARSHALL	A. BURN
White	Black
1 P—Q4	Kt—KB3

Extract.

2 Kt—KB3	P—Q3
3 B—B4	QKt—Q2
4 P—K3	P—KKt3
5 B—Q3	B—Kt2
6 QKt—Q2	O—O
7 P—KR4!?	....

Nowadays this move would be regarded with horror because of its anti-positional character; but I was determined to play for attack at all costs.

7	R—K1
8 P—R5	....

Consistent, but also almost unavoidable. Black was threatening . . . P—K4—5 very strongly.

8	Kt x P
9 R x Kt!?	....

Not analytically sound, but a nice "swindle" just the same.

9	P x R
10 B x Pch	K x B?

. . . K—B1 would have refuted the previous sacrifice. As Tarrasch puts it in the Tournament Book, Burn accepted all sacrifices "on principle"; but now, with a whole Rook to the good, he must lose by force!

Position after Black's 10th move

Burn

Marshall

11 Kt—Kt5ch	K—Kt3

If 11 . . . K—Kt1; 12 Q x P, Kt—B3 (or . . . Kt—B1); 13 Q x Pch, K—R1; 14 O—O—O followed by R—R1ch with fatal effect.

12 QKt—B3	P—K4
13 Kt—R4ch	K—B3
14 Kt—R7ch	K—K2
15 Kt—B5ch	K—K3
16 Kt x Bch	K—K2
17 Kt—B5ch	K—K3
18 P—Q5ch	K x Kt
19 Q x Pch	K—K5
20 O—O—O	Resigns

There is no defense to P—B3 mate. If 20 . . . P x B; 21 R—Q4 mate—this explains why White stopped to pick up the Bishop on move 16.

---

45.   Ostend, 1907

QUEEN'S GAMBIT DECLINED

Although this game is not very well known, it is one of my best.

F.J. MARSHALL   C. SCHLECHTER

White   Black

1 P—Q4	P—Q4
2 P—QB4	P—K3
3 Kt—QB3	P—QB4
4 BP x P	KP x P
5 Kt—B3	Kt—QB3
6 B—Kt5	B—K2
7 B x B	KKt x B

Regarding this variation, see also Game No. 34.

8 P—K3	O—O
9 P x P	Q—R4
10 B—Q3	Q x BP
11 O—O	B—K3
12 R—B1	Q—Kt3

As in the game quoted above, Black has a fair development, but suffers from the general helpless-

ness of the isolated QP and his
weakness on the black squares.

13	Kt—QR4	Q—Kt5
14	P—KR3	. . . .

Before playing his next move, he
cuts off the Queen from KKt5.

14 . . . .   P—KR3

. . . KR—Q1 looks preferable.

15	P—R3	Q—Q3
16	Kt—B5	QR—Kt1

Not a pleasant move to make.
He could have dislodged White's
QKt from its powerful post with
. . . P—QKt3, but this would have
created a certain amount of in-
security in the QB file and would
have made it difficult for him to
dispute the QB file later on because of the possibility of B—R6.

17 Q—K2   B—B4

Black's desire to exchange is
understandable, but the text is not
good, because it deprives the QP
of needed support. Evidently the
uncomfortable nature of his position is robbing Schlechter of some
of the necessary self-confidence in
his prospects.

18	B x B	Kt x B
19	KR—Q1	KKt—K2
20	P—K4	P—QKt3?

This may be said to be the decisive mistake, partly because it deprives the QKt of necessary protection, and partly because it results in the Queen being forced
back to a very bad square. It
would have been better to play 20
. . . KR—Q1, ruling out the reply
22 Kt—Q7 after 21 P—K5, Q—Kt3!

21 P—K5   Q—Q1

Not 21 . . . Kt x P; 22 Q x Kt!
Q x Q; 23 Kt x Q, P x Kt; 24 Kt—
Q7 and wins.

22 Kt—K4!   Q—B1

Position after Black's 22nd move

Schlechter

Marshall

23 Kt—B6ch!   . . . .

Initiating a surprise attack which
succeeds very rapidly because it
menaces both wings, and because
White is much more aggressively
developed than is Black.

23	. . . .	P x Kt
24	P x P	Kt—Kt3

If 24 . . . Q—K3; 25 Q x Q, P x Q;
26 P x Kt, Kt x P; 27 R—K1, K—
B2; 28 R—B7 followed by Kt—Q4
or Kt—K5ch with a won game.

25 Q—Q2!   . . . .

Q—Kt5 would regain the piece
at once, but the text is even more
forcing. The threat of Q x RP followed by mate, must now be met
by Black.

25 . . . .   Q—B4

If 25 . . . K—R2; 26 Kt—Q4
regaining the piece with decisive
advantage.

26	Q x RP!	Q x BP
27	R x Kt!	Q x P

If 27 . . . Q x R? 28 Kt—Kt5
forces mate.

28 R—Q4!   Q—Kt8ch

White threatened to win right off with R x Ktch etc.

| 29 | K—R2 | Q—B4 |
| 30 | R—KKt4 | Resigns |

As in our Barmen encounter, Schlechter's resignation comes somewhat too soon. However, there can be no doubt about the result; for example 30 ... QR—B1 (if 30 ... KR—B1; 31 either R x Ktch, P x R; 32 R x Pch, K—B2; 33 Q—R7ch etc.); 31 R(6)xKtch! P x R; 32 R—KR4! KR—Q1 (if 32 ... R—QB2; 33 Q—R8ch and 34 Q—R7ch); 33 Q—R8ch, K—B2; 34 R—R7ch, K—K3; 35 Kt—Q4ch and wins.

---

46. Carlsbad, 1907

QUEEN'S GAMBIT DECLINED

The chief feature of this game is the successful execution of a subtle positional combination.

F. J. MARSHALL	P. JOHNER
White	Black
1 P—Q4	P—Q4
2 P—QB4	P—K3
3 Kt—QB3	Kt—KB3
4 B—Kt5	B—K2
5 P—K3	O—O
6 Kt—B3	QKt—Q2
7 B—Q3	. . . .

Nowadays R—B1 is the favored move here.

7	P x P
8 B x P	P—QR3
9 O—O	P—Kt4
10 B—Kt3	P—B4
11 Q—K2	B—Kt2
12 KR—Q1	Q—Kt3

Black has obtained a very promising game. In order to disorganize his opponent's position, White now makes a move which despite its apparently obvious character, is the beginning of a positional combination ten moves deep!

| 13 P—QR4! | P—B5 |

Accepting the challenge. If instead 13 . . . P—Kt5; 14 P—R5! Q—B2; 15 Kt—Kt1 followed by QKt—Q2—B4 and White has achieved his objective without any risk whatever.

14 B—B2	P—Kt5
15 P—R5!	Q—B2
16 Kt—QR4	KR—B1
17 P—K4	P—Kt6
18 B—Kt1	Q x P

Black seems to have made marvelous progress. He has won a Pawn, and White's KB and QR are apparently out of play for the duration.

| 19 P—K5 | B x Kt |

The honeymoon is over. Now the seamy side of Black's maneuver begins to appear: he cannot play the "obvious" 19 . . . Kt—Q4, for then 20 Q—K4 is much in White's favor, as 20 . . . P—Kt3 or 20 . . . Kt—B1 would lose a piece.

20 Q x B	Kt—Q4
21 B x B	Kt x B
22 Kt—B5!	. . . .

Now White has the position he played for. 22 . . . Q x R? is of course refuted by 23 B x Pch, so that the Queen must retreat. White will then be free to carry out his basic idea: attack on the QBP, which should in due course lead to the capture of both the QBP and QKtP.

| 22 . . . . | Q—Q1 |

After 22 . . . Q—B2 White has a number of good lines, the most promising being 23 B—K4, R—R2; 24 Kt—Kt7 intending Kt—Q6 followed by KR—QB1.

| 23 Kt—Kt7 | Q—B1 |
| 24 Kt—Q6 | Kt—Q4 |

Now Black realizes that his position has its thorny aspects. If 24

... R—Q1; 25 Kt x QBP or if 24 ... R—B2; 25 Kt x KBP etc. Hence Black offers the exchange.

25 B—K4 . . . .

White is in no hurry, for if 25 ... R—Q1; 26 B x Kt, P x B; 27 Q x P with a winning position.

25	Kt(2)—Kt3
26 Kt x R	Q x Kt
27 R—R5!	. . . .

The Rook comes to life, prepared to render useful service.

| 27 . . . . | R—R2 |
| 28 Q—R3! | P—B4 |

The threat was 29 B x Kt, P x B; 30 Q x Qch, Kt x Q; 31 R x QP.

The text parries this threat, but creates a new weakness which is uncovered by White's next move.

29 P x P e. p.	Kt x P
30 R—QB5	Q—Q2
31 B—B6	Q—Q3
32 B—B3	Kt(B3)—Q4
33 B—Kt4	R—K2
34 P—Kt3	P—K4?

A natural attempt to free himself, but it creates weaknesses on the diagonal which are now exploited by White in a very subtle manner:

Position after Black's 34th move

Johner

Marshall

35 B—K2!! . . . .

Black's Q4 is the fatal weakness!

| 35 . . . . | P x P |
| 36 R—B8ch! | Kt x R |

Or 36 ... K—B2; 37 B x P winning in much the same way.

| 37 Q x Ktch | K—B2 |
| 38 B x P | K—Kt3 |

White threatened Q—B5ch as well as R x P. 38 ... Q—K3 would not do because of 39 Q x Qch, K x Q; 40 R x P, R—Q2; 41 B x P followed by a general exchange winning easily. Or 38 ... Q—K4; 39 Q—B5 and wins.

39 Q—Kt4ch	K—R3
40 Q—R4ch	K—Kt3
41 B x Kt	Resigns

---

47. Carlsbad, 1907

KING'S GAMBIT DECLINED

As so often happens in open games, a single move spells the difference between a fair position and a catastrophe!

F. J. MARSHALL	E. COHN
White	Black
1 P—K4	P—K4
2 P—KB4	B—B4
3 Kt—KB3	P—Q3
4 P x P	. . . .

A novel idea which was introduced into master practice in the present game. The object is to exert immediate pressure on Black's center; not by 5 Kt x P?? Q—R5ch, to be sure, but White has more effective methods at his disposal!

4	P x P
5 P—B3	B—KKt5
6 Q—R4ch!	. . . .

This surprise check is what gives life to the variation. 6 . . . Kt—B3 can be answered by 7 Kt x P, while if 6 . . . Q—Q2; 7 B—Kt5, P—QB3; 8 Kt x P!; hence Black must retreat his Bishop.

6	B—Q2
7 Q—B2	Kt—QB3
8 P—QKt4	. . . .

Another move which is part of the system. It drives Black's KB off the diagonal QR2—KKt8 (for if 8 . . . B—Kt3; 9 P—Kt5), but it has the drawback of weakening the Queen-side somewhat, so that Black can react later on with . . . P—QR4!

8	B—Q3
9 B—B4	Kt—B3
10 O—O	O—O
11 P—Q3	P—QKt4!?

A clever move which rules out the possibility of P—Kt5; but Marco is probably right in the Tournament Book when he recommends the more solid continuation 11 . . . P—QR4; 12 P—Kt5, Kt—K2; 13 B—Kt5, Kt—Kt3; 14 Kt—R4, Kt x Kt; 15 B x QKt, B—K2 etc.

12 B—Kt3   . . . .

Not 12 B x P, Kt x KtP! 13 Q—R4, Kt x QP etc.

12	P—QR4
13 P x P	Kt x RP
14 B—Kt5	Kt x B
15 Q x Kt	R—Kt1

Black is in difficulties, because the need for protecting the KP precludes his neutralizing the pin with . . . B—K2.

16 P—Q4!   B—K2

Making the best of it. The Pawn lost by this move can be regained with best play.

17 Kt x P   P—Kt5!

Weakening White's QP and

thereby assuring himself the necessary counterplay.

18 Kt—Q2	B—Kt4!
19 R—B2	P x P
20 Q x P	. . . .

The critical position.

Position after White's 20th move

Cohn

Marshall

20 . . . .   Kt x P?

This loses. Marco recommends 20 . . . Kt—Q4; 21 B x B (if 21 P x Kt, B x B; 22 Kt—K4, B—K2 with a good game for Black), Kt x Q; 22 B x Q, QR x B; 23 Kt—Kt3 (or 23 P—Q5, QR—K1), Kt—K7ch regaining the Pawn.

In this line of play, the following combination would have been impossible.

21 Kt x Kt	B x B
22 Kt x P!	R x Kt
23 R x R	K x R
24 Kt x Bch	K—B3

If 24 . . . K—Kt3; 25 P—KR4 wins.

25 Kt—K4ch	K—B2
26 Kt—Kt5ch	K—B3
27 P—KR4!	P—R3

There was no satisfactory defense. If 27 . . . K—Kt3; 28 Q—

B2ch etc. Or 27 . . . Q—Q4; 28
P—R4! B—R3; 29 R—K1 and wins.

28 Q—B3ch   Resigns

If 28 . . . K—K2; 29 Q—B7ch,
K—Q3; 30 Q—K6 mate. Curious!

---

48. Carlsbad, 1907

IRREGULAR OPENING

My famous opponent in this
game, Aron Nimzovich, was one of
the pioneers of the hypermodern
school. Born in Riga, he went to
live in Denmark at the end of the
last war. He was an extremely
sensitive and nervous man; while
playing, any slight noise upset him,
even the rattling of keys or money.
Smoking was obnoxious to him—so
he wasn't any too happy when
playing against cigar or pipe-smok-
ing opponents!

At the time this game was
played, Nimzovich was barely 20,
but he had already made quite a
name for himself.

A. NIMZOVICH   F.J. MARSHALL

White	Black
1 Kt—KB3	P—Q4
2 P—Q3	Kt—KB3
3 QKt—Q2	Kt—B3
4 P—KKt3	P—K4
5 B—Kt2	P—K5!

Realizing that Nimzovich was
bent on playing an Indian Defense
with colors reversed, I decided to
give up a Pawn to give the game
a character more congenial to my
style. Although this course involves an early exchange of
Queens, it leads to a fierce attack.

6 P x P	P x P
7 Kt—Kt5	P—K6!
8 P x P	P—KR3!

If 8 . . . Kt—KKt5; 9 QKt—K4,
Q x Qch; 10 K x Q, P—KR3 (or 10
. . . P—KB4; 11 P—KR3); 11 Kt—
R3 and Black is not making enough
headway.

9 KKt—K4   . . . .

If 9 Kt—R3 then simply 9 . . .
B—QB4 leaving White with a
wretched game.

9 . . . .   Kt—KKt5

Threatening to win the Queen
right off!

10 Kt—Kt3   . . . .

Not 10 Kt—KB3? Q x Qch; 11
K x Q, P—KB4 and wins.

10	Q x Qch
11 K x Q	B—KB4

Now 11 . . . P—KB4 would not
accomplish anything because of the
reply 12 P—KR3. Whereas if now
12 P—KR3? B x Kt wins a piece.

12 K—K1	Kt—Kt5
13 Kt—Q4	. . . .

The symmetrical play with the
Knights is amusing. 13 . . . P—B4
is to be answered with 14 P—QR3.
But there is a stronger move for
Black.

Position after White's 13th move

Marshall

Nimzovich

13 . . . .   O—O—O!

For if 14 Kt x B? Kt x Pch; 15
K—B1, R—Q8 mate!

| 14 P—KR3 | R x Kt! |
| 15 P x R | .... |

Or 15 P x Kt, B x Kt; 16 P x R, B x B; 17 KR—Kt1, Kt x Pch; 18 K—B2, B—K5 and wins.

| 15 .... | Kt x Pch |
| 16 K—Q2 | .... |

Tchigorin subsequently indicated the following saving line for White: 16 K—Q1! Kt(5)—K6ch; 17 B x Kt, Kt x Bch; 18 K—Q2, Kt x B; 19 Kt—B3, B—QKt5; 20 R—R2, B—K5; 21 P—K3! P—QB4; 22 K—K2, B x Kt; 23 P x B followed by QR—KKt1 etc.

16	Kt(5)—K6!
17 B—B3	Kt x R
18 K x Kt	Kt—B7ch
19 K—Q3	Kt—Kt5ch
20 K—K3	Kt—B7ch
21 K—Q3	Kt—Kt5ch
22 K—K3	Kt x P

White has got by comparatively well with the loss of only one Pawn; but he must lose in due course.

23 P—KKt4	B—Kt3
24 B—Q2	Kt—Kt5
25 R—QB1	B—K2
26 Kt—B5?	....

But this blunder hastens the end.

26	B—Kt4ch
27 K—B2	B x B
28 R—B4	P—Kt4
Resigns	

.49.   Vienna, 1908

TWO KNIGHTS' DEFENSE

A pleasing game. The attack is carried out with energy and finesse. Salwe was a very interesting type: a natural player, full of self-reliance and with little knowledge of the books. He had a knack of worming out of bad positions, but here he selected an opening variation that was too much for him.

G. SALWE	F.J. MARSHALL
White	Black
1 P—K4	P—K4
2 Kt—KB3	Kt—QB3
3 B—B4	Kt—B3
4 Kt—Kt5	P—Q4
5 P x P	Kt—QR4
6 P—Q3	....

6 B—Kt5ch has been revived of late years with fair success. The recommended line is 6 B—Kt5ch, P—B3; 7 P x P, P x P; 8 B—K2, P—KR3; 9 Kt—KB3, P—K5; 10 Kt—K5, B—Q3; 11 P—KB4, O—O; 12 O—O! B x Kt; 13 P x B, Q—Q5 ch; 14 K—R1, Q x KP; 15 P—Q4! and White, with his two Bishops and superior Pawn position, stands well.

6	P—KR3
7 Kt—KB3	P—K5
8 Q—K2	Kt x B
9 P x Kt	B—QB4
10 KKt—Q2	O—O
11 Kt—Kt3	B—Kt5
12 Q—B1	....

An ugly move which has been contemptuously described as "castling with the Queen!" But White has no choice, for if 12 Q—Q2, P—K6! It has already become apparent that Black's more rapid and aggressive development amply compensates for the sacrificed Pawn.

| 12 .... | B—Kt5ch! |

This important intermediary move was introduced into master practice in the present game.

| 13 P—B3 | .... |

(see diagram next page)

Creating a bad weakness at his Q3 which is subsequently exploited to the utmost, but there is no really satisfactory move:

The only.

Position after White's 13th move

Marshall

Salwe

I 13 B—Q2, B x Bch; 14 QKt x B, R—K1; 15 P—KR3, P—K6! with some interesting possibilities:

A. 16 P x B, P x Ktch; 17 K x P, Kt—K5ch, 18 K—B1, Q—Kt4ch; 19 P—B4, Q x KtP.

B. 16 P x P, R x Pch; 17 K—B2, R—K7ch; 18 K—Kt1, Q—K2! 19 Q—B4, P—KKt4! 20 Q—Kt3, B—B4; 21 K—R2, Kt—R4; 22 Q—B3, Kt—B5.

In either case Black should win. II 13 Kt—B3. This has been recommended by Fine in "Modern Chess Openings" as leading to equality, but it has recently been strengthened for Black in the following manner: 13 . . . P—B3! 14 P—KR3, B—KR4; 15 P—Kt4, B—Kt3; 16 P x P, P x P; 17 B—Q2, P—K6! 18 P x P, B x Kt; 19 P x B, B x P; 20 Kt—Q4, Kt—K5! with a winning position for Black (Luckis-Keres, Buenos Aires, 1939).

13 . . . .   B—K2
14 P—KR3   B—R4
15 P—Kt4   B—Kt3

White has had to drive away the Bishop in order to be able to castle Q side. But the King will not be safe in any event.

16 B—K3   Kt—Q2!
17 QKt—Q2   Kt—K4

18 O—O—O   P—Kt4!

A well-timed blow. He must open up attacking lines on the Queen-side.

19 P x P   Kt—Q6ch

This Knight is destined to remain a thorn in White's flesh throughout the game.

20 K—Kt1   Q x P
21 K—R1   . . . .

White intends P—KB4 and must therefore get his King off the hostile QB's diagonal. Attempts to save the Pawn would only lead to trouble:

I 21 P—QB4, Q—Q1 (stronger than 21 . . . Q—K4; 22 B—Q4, P—K6! 23 B x Q, Kt—Kt5ch; 22 K—R1, Kt—B7ch and Black has a perpetual check); and now that Black threatens . . . B—B3, he has time to force the opening of a file with . . . P—R3.

II 21 Kt—Q4, P—R3; 22 P—QB4, Q—Kt2; 23 Kt(2)—Kt3, P x P; 24 P x P, Q—R2; 25 P—R3, B x P! 26 P x B, Q x P; 27 R—Q2, P—QB4; 28 P x P e.p., KR—Kt1; 29 K—B2, R x Kt; 30 Kt x R, Q—Kt7ch; 31 K—Q1, Q x Ktch; 32 K—K2, Kt—B5ch! 33 B x Kt, Q—B6ch and wins. This variation, suggested by the Viennese player Krejcik, is not all forced, but gives some idea of Black's formidable attacking resources.

21 . . . .   Q x P
22 P—KB4   P—QR4!

Black need not bother about the threat to his QB, for example 23 P—B5, P—R5; 24 P x B, P x Kt and wins.

23 QR—Kt1   P—KB4
24 Kt—Q4   Q—R5!

(see diagram next page)

There is more to Black's last move than meets the eye. The plausible move 25 Kt x BP would be refuted in the following manner: 25 . . . R x Kt!! 26 P x R, Kt—

Position after Black's 24th move

Marshall

Salwe

Kt5!! (with a double threat of
mate); 27 P x Kt, P x P; 28 P—R3
(if 28 Q—B4ch, B—B2), B—B3! 29
K—R2, Q x Pch! 30 P x Q, R x P
mate!
Note also the alternative line
27 P—R3 (instead of 27 P x Kt),
Kt—B7ch; 28 K—R2, B—B2ch; 29
P—B4, KB x P! 30 P—Kt3, Kt—
Kt5ch; 31 K—R1, B—Kt7ch; 32
K x B, Q—R7ch; 33 K—B3, Q—B7
ch; 34 K—Q4, R—Q1ch; 35 K—B5
(or 35 K—K5, Kt—B3 mate), R—
Q4 mate (suggested by Marco).
Returning to the diagrammed
position, Marco also refutes 25
Kt(2)—Kt3 with 25 . . . Kt—Kt5!
26 P x Kt, P x P; 27 Kt—B1! P—
Kt6!! 28 Kt(4) x KtP, B—B2; 29
Q—Q1, Q x Pch! 30 Kt x Q, R x Kt
ch; 31 K x R, R—R1ch; 32 B—R7,
R x B mate.
Thus we may conclude that
Salwe's next move is best, although
it creates new weaknesses.

25 P—Kt3   Q—Q2
26 P x P   B x P
27 Q—Kt2   P—B4!

A nice move which freshens up
the attack. The occupation of the
long diagonal by Black's KB will
be decisive.

28 Kt x B   Q x Kt
29 Q x P   . . . .

Or 29 Kt x P, P—R5! with a
powerful attack. The text is answered in a surprising manner.

29 . . . .   B—B3!
30 Q—B4ch   K—R1
31 Kt—K4   . . . .

White appears to have consol-
idated his position, but now comes
a fresh surprise.

31 . . . .   QR—K1!

If now 32 Q x Kt, Q x Kt! and
wins, 33 Q x Q being answered by
. . . B x Pch.
Relatively best would have been
32 Kt—Q6, Q—K3; 33 Q x Kt, Q x B
with an ending in Black's favor.

32 Kt x B   R x Kt
33 B—B1   R(3)—K3

Black's strangle-hold on the K
file now decides in short order.

34 B—R3   R—K7
35 KR—Q1   Kt—K8!

As Marco shows, there is no de-
fense now:
I 36 KR—B1, Kt—B7ch; 37
R x Kt, Q x R; 38 B—Kt2, R—K8
and wins.
II 36 R—Q8, Kt—B7ch; 37 K—
Kt2, Kt x Bch; 38 Q x R, Q x Rch;
39 K x Kt, R x R and wins.
III 36 Q x R, R x Q; 37 R x Kt,
R x R; 38 R x R, Q x RP and Black
wins easily with his KRP.

36 B x P   Kt—B7ch
37 K—Kt2   Kt—Kt5ch

White resigns. One of my best
games.

---

50. Vienna, 1908

FOUR KNIGHTS' GAME

My young opponent in this game,
Richard Reti, later became an active proponent of the new theory
of flank development. A Czech who
lived a Bohemian existence, Reti
was lame, spoke with a high-

pitched voice, was a prolific writer of chess books and columns.

Reti was still in his teens in this his first big tournament. He drew three games and lost the rest, being completely outclassed. However, the shy young man acquired much valuable experience; soon he began to achieve the fame which was to be his in later years.

F. J. MARSHALL	R. RETI
White	Black
1 P—K4	P—K4
2 Kt—KB3	Kt—QB3
3 Kt—B3	Kt—B3
4 B—Kt5	B—Kt5

My favorite move here in earlier years was 4 . . . Kt—Q5.

| 5 O—O | O—O |
| 6 P—Q3 | B x Kt |

To avoid the difficulties which might arise after White's B—Kt5 and Kt—Q5.

| 7 P x B | P—Q3 |
| 8 B—Kt5 | Q—K2 |

This move, followed by the subsequent retreat of the QKt, is known as Metger's Defense, and a very good one it is, as Rubinstein has demonstrated in some fine games.

9 P—KR3	Kt—Q1
10 B—QB4	B—K3
11 Kt—Q2	P—KR3
12 B—K3	P—Q4

As one would expect from this rather colorless opening, White has not achieved a great deal. However, the text, despite its plausible appearance, leads to difficulties. The chief trouble, as will be seen, is Black's subsequent inability to get his QKt into the game. Hence the simple continuation 12 . . . B x B; 13 Kt x B, Kt—K3 suggests itself. The position would then be fairly level.

| 13 P x P | Kt x P |

14 B x Kt	B x B
15 P—Q4	P x P
16 P x P	P—KB4

Seemingly very strong, as it threatens . . . P—B5. But White has a good continuation.

| 17 R—K1! | Q—B2 |

Position after Black's 17th move

Reti

Marshall

| 18 P—QB4! | . . . . |

This looks surprising at first sight, but was already implied by White's previous move, as he is still menaced by . . . P—B5.

18	B x BP
19 Kt x B	Q x Kt
20 P—Q5!	. . . .

This was the position White aimed for. He is a Pawn down, but he has two good open files, while Black's Queen is cut off from the King-side, the Knight is out of play and the QBP is weak.

| 20 . . . . | R—B2 |
| 21 QR—B1! | Q—Kt4 |

If 21 . . . Q x RP; 22 B—B5 followed by R—K8ch with very strong pressure for the sacrificed Pawns.

| 22 B—B4 | P—B3 |

Now the QP becomes formidable; but after 22 ... R—QB1; 23 Q—Q4, P—R3; 24 R—K5, Q—Q2; 25 QR—K1 Black's game is unbearably difficult.

23 P—Q6	P—B4
24 Q—Q5	R—QB1
25 R—K7	Q—B3
26 P—Q7!	R—R1

He has no choice, since if 26 ... Q x Q; 27 R—K8ch coming out a Rook ahead.

27 R—K8ch	K—R2
28 Q x Q	P x Q
29 R—Q1	P—QR4
30 B—B7	R—R2
31 R x Kt!	Resigns

If 31 ... R x B; 32 R—R8ch etc.

---

51. Vienna, 1908

QUEEN'S PAWN OPENING

Rubinstein's inexactitude in the opening (a great rarity in his games) leads to a bad position from which he never recovers.

F. J. MARSHALL   A. RUBINSTEIN

White	Black
1 P—Q4	P—Q4
2 P—K3	Kt—KB3
3 B—Q3	P—B4

A more promising continuation against White's intended Stonewall formation is 3 ... Kt—B3! (threatening ... P—K4); 4 P—KB4, Kt—QKt5! virtually forcing the exchange of White's valuable KB.

4 P—QB3	P—K3
5 Kt—Q2	Kt—B3
6 P—KB4	B—Q3

And now ... B—K2 was much better, as this move later exposes Black to a strong attack by P—K4—5. The text threatens 7 ... P x P, compelling White to recapture with the QBP. But White's next move takes care of the threat.

7 Q—B3	B—Q2

This Bishop is out of play throughout the game.

8 Kt—R3	Q—Kt3
9 Kt—B2	O—O—O

Rightly fearing the attack that would come after 9 ... O—O; but the text is no improvement in this respect.

10 O—O	K—Kt1
11 P—K4!	....

This opening up of the game is much in White's favor. See also the note to Black's sixth move.

11	QP x P
12 KKt x P	Kt x Kt
13 Kt x Kt	B—K2
14 P x P	B x Pch
15 Kt x B	Q x Ktch
16 B—K3	Q—QR4
17 P—QR4	....

As a result of the thrust with the KP, White has developed with gain of time, obtained two Bishops and a lasting attack. The text prepares for P—QKt4, which, if played at once, could be answered by ... Q—R5.

17	Kt—K2
18 P—QKt4	Q—B2
19 B—Q4	P—B3
20 Q—B2	Kt—B1
21 KR—K1	....

To prevent ... P—K4. Black is now subjected to so much pressure that it is only a matter of moves until some material is gained.

21	KR—K1
22 Q—Kt3!	B—B3
23 P—Kt5	B—Q4
24 P—R5	B—B5
25 P—Kt6!	....

Position after White's 25th move

Rubinstein

Marshall

The attack has become very powerful, and White's last move forces the win of a Pawn.

25 . . . .   Q—B3

25 . . . P x P; 26 B x B, Q x B; 27 P x P would only hasten the end because of the opening of the QR file.

26 B x B   Q x B
27 Q x P   Kt—K2
28 Q x BP   Kt—B4
29 P—R6!   RP x P

Forced, else his King will be completely denuded of protecting Pawns. If 29 . . . Kt x B; 30 Q—K5ch! wins quickly.

30 Q—K5ch   K—R1

Not 30 . . . Q—B2?? 31 P—R7ch etc.

31 P x Pch   K x P
32 B—B2   . . . .

The valuable Bishop is to be preserved.

32 . . . .   R—Q4
33 Q—B6   Q—B3
34 KR—Kt1   R—Kt4

Or 34 . . . P—Kt4; 35 R—R7ch and wins.

35 R x R   Q x R
36 Q—B7ch!   . . . .

Forcing the exchange of Queens and winning a second Pawn.

36 . . . .   R—K2
37 Q—Kt8   Q—K1
38 Q x Q   R x Q
39 R—Kt1   K—B3
40 R x Pch   K—Q4

The rest is easy.

41 P—Kt3   R—QB1
42 R—Kt5ch   K—K5
43 K—Kt2   R—B3
44 R—K5ch   K—Q6
45 P—Kt4   Kt—K2
46 P—B5   Kt—Q4

If 46 . . . K x P; 47 P x P followed by B—R4 etc.

47 B—Q4   K—B5
48 K—Kt3   P x P
49 R x P   R—KKt3
50 R—B7   P—R4
51 R—KKt7!   R x R
52 B x R   P x P
53 K x P   Kt x P
54 B x Kt   Resigns

---

52. Vienna, 1908

(Second Brilliancy Prize)

FRENCH DEFENSE

Once again a struggle between superior development and an extra Pawn—a very uneven struggle at that!

J. MIESES	F. J. MARSHALL
White	Black
1 P—K4	P—K3
2 P—Q4	P—Q4
3 Kt—QB3	P—QB4

4 Kt—B3	Kt—QB3
5 B—K3	Kt—B3
6 KP x P	KP x P
7 P x P	B—K2

Beginning with a conservative defense, I have opened up the game by sacrificing a Pawn.

8 B—K2	O—O
9 O—O	R—K1
10 P—KR3	B—B4

Mieses has improved on Janowski's play in Game no. 28, so that we shall now have a real demonstration of the value of Black's superior development. White is welcome to the Pawn; he has lost a tempo to gain it, it is of no great value as it is doubled, and the prospects of future usefulness of the pieces obviously favor Black.

11 P—R3	P—QR4

Preventing the intended P—QKt4.

12 Kt—QR4	. . . .

Repeating Janowski's error. However, he hopes for a chance for P—B4 undoubling the Pawn, or else Kt—Kt6 in conjunction with B—KB4. But the opportunity never arises.

12	Q—B2

Developing, and also preventing B—KB4.

13 Q—B1	. . . .

Again angling for B—KB4.

13	QR—Q1!
14 B—Q3	Kt—K5!

Offering the exchange: 15 B—KB4, Q—Q2; 16 Kt—Kt6, Q—K3; 17 B—B7. But then comes 17 . . . B x RP! 18 B x R, Q—Kt5! with a very powerful attack. One possibility is 19 Kt—K1, B x BP! 20 B—B7, Kt x P! 21 R x Kt, R x Ktch! 22 Q x R, Q xP mate!

15 Kt—Q2	Q—K4

The coming King-side attack is already foreshadowed.

16 R—K1	Q—B3
17 B x Kt	. . . .

Against 17 P—QB4 Black has the powerful reply 17 . . . Kt—K4.

17	P x B
18 Kt—B1	. . . .

The only piece guarding the King-side. White is in for trouble.

18	Q—Kt3
19 Kt—Kt3	P—R4!
20 Kt x B	Q x Kt
21 P—QKt4	. . . .

Hoping for 21 . . . P x P; 22 P x P, Kt x P; 23 Q—Kt1. But Black naturally goes about his business on the other wing. It might have been better to try Kt—B3—K2.

21	Kt—K4
22 B—B4	Kt—Kt3
23 B—K3	Kt—R5!
24 B—B4	Q—Kt3
25 B—Kt3	. . . .

Warding off the attack for the moment. But now comes an absolutely decisive stroke.

25	B—Kt4!
26 Q—Kt1	R—Q7
27 Q—Kt3	P—K6!

The kill. There is no defense to this move, which cuts off the Queen from the defense of the King-side, and at the same time opens up the attack of the Rook along the seventh rank.

(see diagram next page)

28 Q—B3	. . . .

If 28 B x Kt, B x B and White is helpless.

28	P x Pch

Position after Black's 27th move

Marshall

Mieses

29 B x P   B—K6!

White resigns. A brilliancy prize game without a single combination! Thus the judges indicated their appreciation of the sledge-hammer blows with which the attack was carried out.

---

53. Prague, 1908

FOUR KNIGHTS' GAME

White goes Pawn-hunting for a distant Pawn on the Queen-side—with the usual result!

C. SCHLECHTER	F.J. MARSHALL
White	Black
1 P—K4	P—K4
2 Kt—KB3	Kt—QB3
3 Kt—B3	Kt—B3
4 B—Kt5	B—Kt5

This opening was very popular in pre-war days—so much so that Tarrasch once called it one of "the three milch cows of the tournament repertoire." Today it has all but disappeared.

5 O—O	O—O

6 P—Q3	P—Q3
7 Kt—K2	B—Kt5
8 P—B3	....

Leading to a King-side weakness whose influence is felt throughout the game. 8 Kt—Kt3 is preferable.

8	B x Kt
9 KtP x B	B—B4
10 Kt—Kt3	Q—B1
11 B x Kt	....

Otherwise this Knight may play to KKt3 via K2, threatening . . . Kt—R5 very strongly in some cases.

11	P x B
12 K—Kt2	Q—K3
13 P—KB4	P x P
14 B x P	P—Q4
15 P—K5	....

15 P x P was better. As the game goes, White's Bishop is soon hemmed in by White Pawns on white squares, and thus has very little scope.

15	Kt—Q2
16 P—Q4	B—K2
17 B—K3	P—B3!
18 P—KB4	P x P
19 BP x P	R x R
20 Q x R	R—KB1
21 Q—R6?	....

White underestimates his opponent's chances on the King-side. 21 Q—K2 was in order, but Schlechter probably feared 21 . . . P—B4 followed by 22 . . . P x P and 23 . . . P—B4.

21	P—R4!

This Pawn cannot be captured, for if 22 Kt x P, Q—Kt5ch; 23 Kt—Kt3, Q—B6ch etc.

22 R—KB1	....

White hopes to break the force of the attack with this proffered exchange. If 22 Q—K2, P—R5; 23

Kt—B1, Q—Kt3ch and Black has a winning game, for example 24 K—R1, Q—K5ch; 25 Q—Kt2, R x Ktch; 26 R x R, Q x B etc.

22	P—R5
23 R x Rch	Kt x R
24 Kt—B1	P—R6ch

Despite the few pieces left, Black's attack continues with undiminished force. If now 25 K—R1? Q—Kt5 forces mate.

25 K—B2	B—R5ch
26 K—K2	Q—Kt3
27 Q—Q3	. . . .

He has had to bring back the Queen to the defense after all.

27	Q—Kt7ch
28 K—Q1	Q x KtP
29 B—Q2	Q x RP
30 Q x P	Q—Kt8ch
31 K—K2	Q—K5ch
32 Kt—K3	B—Kt4

Black has won a Pawn, his Queen is strongly centralized, and he menaces the KP with the double advance of his BPs. The text was my sealed move at the midday adjournment, and the sequel was worked out as a win by the spectators! It requires only careful play, but it is quite interesting.

Position after Black's 32nd move

Marshall

Schlechter

| 33 Q—B8 | P—B4! |

If now 34 Q x P, P x P; 35 P x P, Kt—K3; 36 Q—B8ch, K—B2; 37 Q—Q7ch, B—K2 and the threat of . . . Kt x Pch or . . . Kt—B5ch is decisive. Or if 34 P x P, Q x P; 35 P—R3, K—B2 followed by . . . Kt—K3 winning easily.

34 Q—R8	B x Kt
35 B x B	P x P
36 P x P	P—B4!
37 P x P	Q—B5ch!
38 K—B3	P—Q5
39 B—B4	Q x P
40 K—K4	K—R2
41 Q—Q5	Q—B6!

Not 41 . . . Q x Qch? 42 K x Q and White's KP will cost the Knight. All that remains now for Black is to render this Pawn harmless.

| 42 P—K6 | . . . . |

Or 42 Q x P, Q x Qch; 43 K x Q, Kt—K3ch; 44 K—K4, Kt x B; 45 K x Kt, K—Kt3 and the outside passed Pawn wins for Black.

| 42 . . . . | Q—K8ch |
| 43 K—Q3 | . . . . |

43 K—B5, Q—Kt8ch comes to the same thing.

43	Q—B8ch
44 K—K4	Q—K7ch
45 K—B5	Q—R4ch
46 K—K4	Q—K7ch
47 K—B5	Q—Q6ch!
48 K—Kt4	Q—Kt3ch
49 K—B3	Kt x P
50 B—B1	Q—Q6ch
51 K—B2	Q—B7ch

White resigns. Although Black's RP never moved, its mere existence was a standing threat!

54. Duesseldorf, 1908

DUTCH DEFENSE

An inferior opening variation leads to a catastrophe for Black.

F.J. MARSHALL   R. SPIELMANN

White	Black
1 P—Q4	P—KB4
2 P—K4	P x P
3 Kt—QB3	Kt—KB3
4 B—Kt5	P—B3
5 P—B3!	....

For details about this variation, see Game No. 30, in which the weaker 5 B x Kt was played.

5	P x P
6 Kt x P	P—K3
7 B—Q3	B—K2
8 O—O	P—Q3

Black is afraid to castle, for White has an obviously powerful attacking formation. But to leave the King in the center is worse if anything. Black does better to avoid this difficult line of play altogether.

9 Q—K2	Kt—R3

In order to get the hostile KB off its strong diagonal (. . . Kt—QKt5) or else to give the KP additional protection.

10 P—QR3	Kt—B2
11 QR—K1	....

White continues to pile up pieces for the attack, while Black's pieces remain miserably huddled together. In such situations the combinations come of themselves.

11	P—QKt3
12 Kt—KR4	K—Q2

Not liking 13 B x Kt, B x B; 14 Q—R5ch, K—Q2 departs before he is smoked out; but the sequel is pitiable.

13 Kt—B5!	Q—KB1

The obstreperous Knight is immune: If 13 . . . P x Kt; 14 B x Pch, K—K1; 15 B x B, R x B; 16 R x Kt! P x R; 17 B x P and wins.

14 Kt x B	Q x Kt
15 Kt—K4	R—B1
16 Kt x Ktch	P x Kt
17 Q—B3	Kt—K1

If Black parts with the KBP, his position will fall apart in short order. But the text loses in a different way.

Position after Black's 17th move

Spielmann

Marshall

18 R x P!!	Q—B2

Or 18 . . . K x R (if 18 . . . Q x R; 19 B—B5); 19 Q—B5ch, K—B2; 20 Q x RPch, Kt—Kt2 (if 20 . . . K—K3; 21 R—K1ch); 21 B—Kt6 ch, K—K3; 22 R—K1ch etc.

19 R—K4	B—Kt2
20 R—KR4	Kt—Kt2
21 R x P	R—R1

This might be called a blunder if it were not for the fact that there is no defense against the threats of Q x P or B—KR6.

22 Q—R3ch	Resigns

A drastic demonstration of the value of superior development.

55. Lodz, 1908
QUEEN'S GAMBIT DECLINED

Time was of the essence in this game. It was truly a case of first come, first served.

F.J. Marshall   A. Rubinstein
White   Black

1	P—Q4	P—Q4
2	P—QB4	P—K3
3	Kt—QB3	P—QB4
4	BP x P	KP x P
5	Kt—B3	Kt—KB3
6	B—Kt5	B—K2

Deciding to give up a Pawn temporarily and thus avoiding Cohn's error in Game No. 38.

7	P x P	B—K3
8	R—B1	O—O
9	B x Kt	. . . .

There are various ways of playing to hold the Pawn, but that sort of policy is inconsistent with my style.

9	. . . .	B x B
10	P—K3	Q—R4
11	P—QR3	Kt—B3

Not 11 . . . Q x BP?? 12 Kt—QKt5 followed by Kt—B7.

12	B—Q3	Q x BP
13	P—KR4!?	. . . .

Indicating my aggressive intentions.

13	. . . .	Q—K2
14	Kt—KKt5	. . . .

The echo of my Paris game with Burn with 14 B x Pch would be unsound (14 . . . K x B; 15 Kt—Kt5ch, K—Kt3).

14	. . . .	P—KR3
15	Kt x B	P x Kt

The foregoing exchange may turn out to be beneficial or harmful for either player. On the one hand, Black has the open KB file for attacking purposes; on the other, the long diagonal leading to his KR2 has been opened for various threats by White.

16	B—Kt1	B x P!

This is not mere Pawn-grabbing; it is played with the following sacrifice in view.

17	P—KKt3	B x P!

Leads to a very dangerous attack—if only Black's King doesn't perish first!

18	P x B	Q—Kt4
19	Q—Q3	. . . .

Defense and attack.

19	. . . .	Q x KtPch?

This loses, despite its tempting appearance. Correct was 19 . . . Kt—K4! and Black's attack should succeed (20 Q—R7ch, K—B2; 21 R—B1ch, K—K2 and White has no good move).

20	K—Q2	R—B7ch
21	Kt—K2	Kt—K4

Too late. White has a beautiful forced win.

22	Q—R7ch	K—B2
23	R—B7ch	K—B3

Position after Black's 23rd move

Rubinstein

Marshall

Offhand, it looks as though I had "run out of gas," doesn't it? . . . but . . .

24 R x Pch!   Resigns

If 24 . . . P x R; 25 Q—K7 mate. Kaleidoscopic!

---

56. Lodz, 1908

QUEEN'S GAMBIT DECLINED

It often happens that it is quite easy to bring about a gain of material, but quite difficult to make that gain tell. Here is an instructive case in point.

F.J. MARSHALL   G. SALWE

White   Black

1	P—Q4	P—Q4
2	P—QB4	P—K3
3	Kt—QB3	P—QB4
4	BP x P	KP x P
5	Kt—B3	Kt—KB3

The same unfavorable move as in the previous game.

| 6 | B—Kt5 | B—K2 |
| 7 | P x P | B—K3 |

Thus far as in the previous game, but now I find an improvement.

8 P—K3!   Q—R4

Not good, as White can now maintain the extra Pawn with advantage; but after the alternative continuations 8 . . . B x P; 9 B—Kt5ch! or 8 . . . O—O; 9 B—K2, B x P; 10 O—O, B—K2; 11 Kt—Q4 (or R—B1) White still has the better game.

9	B—Kt5ch	Kt—B3
10	Kt—Q4	QR—B1
11	Q—R4!	Q x Q
12	Kt x Q	B—Q2
13	Kt x Kt	. . . .

Black was threatening . . . Kt x Kt.

13	. . . .	B x Kt
14	B x Bch	R x B
15	B x Kt	B x B

15 . . . P x B is answered in the same way.

| 16 | R—Q1 | R—R3 |
| 17 | P—QKt3 | O—O |

If instead 17 . . . R—R4; 18 O—O! maintaining his Pawn ahead —but not 18 R x P? P—QKt4; 19 P—B6, P x Kt! 20 R x R, B—B6ch etc.

| 18 | R x P | R—R4 |
| 19 | O—O | P—QKt3 |

If 19 . . . P—QKt4; 20 P—B6.

| 20 | KR—Q1 | R—B1 |

Position after Black's 20th move

Salwe

Marshall

White is temporarily two Pawns up; but he must lose one of them, and the position looks none too favorable, with his Knight somewhat out of play. The energetic continuation drives back the hostile Bishop and makes a loophole for White's King (threatening 21 P x P).

| 21 | P—KKt4! | P x P |
| 22 | P—Kt5 | B—K2 |

23 R—K5!   B—B1

If 23 . . . K—B1; 24 R—Q7, B—
Q1; 25 Kt x P! and wins, for ex-
ample 25 . . . R(4)x Kt; 26 R x Bch
or 25 . . . R x P; 26 Kt—Kt7, B—
Kt3; 27 Kt—Q6 or R x Pch or R(5)
—K7 winning easily in all cases.

24 R—Q7   R—R3

The threat was R—B5. The text
is compulsory, for if 24 . . . P—
Kt3; 25 R—K4 followed by R—KB4.

25 R—B5   P—B3

He might have tried the desper-
ate expedient 25 . . . P—B5?! for
instance 26 R(7)x BP, B—Q3; 27
R—Q7, R x Kt! 28 R x B, P—B6; 29
R—Q1, P—B7; 30 R—QB1, R x P;
31 R—Q5, R—Kt7; 32 R—Q2, R—
Kt8 and wins.
However, White would have an-
swered 25 . . . P—B5?! with 26
R(5)x P, P—B6; 27 Kt x P! (not
27 R—B7, R(3)—QB3; 28 R x R
(B8), R x R and wins), R x Kt; 28
R x P and with four Pawns for the
Piece, White must win.

26 P x P   P x P
27 Kt—B3   P—B5
28 P x P   . . . .

Of course not 28 Kt—Q5? P—B6;
29 Kt x Pch, R x Kt; 30 R x R, P—
B7 etc.

28 . . . .   R x BP
29 Kt—Q5   R—Kt5ch
30 K—B1   B—Kt2

Black's game is quite hopeless
now: his Bishop is dead, and
White's Knight has just come to
life.

31 P—KR3   R—KR5
32 R—B3   R—KR4
33 Kt—K7ch   K—B1
34 Kt—B5   R—Kt4
35 P—K4!   . . . .

Threatening R—B3 with fatal
effect.

35 . . . .   K—Kt1

Leads to loss of the exchange,
but there is no escape: if 35 . . .
R—B3; 36 R—QKt3, R—QKt3; 37
R—QB3, R—Kt1; 38 R(3)—B7 etc.

36 R—B3   P—R4
37 P—B4   R—KKt3
38 Kt—K7ch   K—R2
39 Kt x R   Resigns

---

57.   Match, 1908

QUEEN'S GAMBIT DECLINED

As in earlier examples of this
variation (compare Game no. 34
with Spielmann and Game no. 45
with Schlechter), Black suffers
from the weakness of his isolated
QP and his black squares.

F.J. MARSHALL   J. MIESES
    White   Black

1 P—Q4   P—Q4
2 P—QB4   P—K3
3 Kt—QB3   P—QB4
4 BP x P   KP x P
5 Kt—B3   P x P

Old-fashioned even for those
days. 5 . . . Kt—QB3 is the move.

6 KKt x P   Kt—QB3
7 B—B4   B—QKt5
8 P—K3   KKt—K2

More consistent was 8 . . . B x
Ktch, after which it would be a
question whether Black's QP is
weaker than White's QBP. But
Mieses evidently didn't care to
give me the two Bishops.

9 R—B1   O—O
10 B—K2   B—Q3
11 B—Kt3   Kt x Kt

Now White's Queen comes beau-
tifully into play on the strongly
centralized post Q4; but Black's
position remains uninviting in any
event.

12 Q x Kt   P—QKt3
13 B—Q3   . . . .

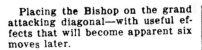

Placing the Bishop on the grand attacking diagonal—with useful effects that will become apparent six moves later.

13	B—Kt2
14 B x B	Q x B
15 O—O	KR—B1

Since White's reply is so strong, it may be wondered why Black did not play 15 . . . P—QR3. In that event, there would have followed 16 Kt—QR4, leaving Black the unappetizing alternatives 15 . . . P—QKt4; 16 Kt—B5 or 15 . . . Kt—B1; 16 B—B5.

| 16 Kt—Kt5! | Q—Q2 |
| 17 R x Rch! | . . . . |

Simple but forcible. As Black must guard the QRP, he cannot recapture with his Rook; and thus White secures control of the QB file with rapidly decisive effects.

| 17 . . . . | B x R |

If 17 . . . Q x R; 18 B x Pch! K x B; 19 Q—R4ch winning the Knight.

| 18 R—B1 | Kt—B3 |

Position after Black's 18th move

Mieses

Marshall

19 Q—KR4!   . . . .

With the amusing point that 19 . . . P—KR3? will not do because of 20 R x Kt! Or if 19 . . . P—B4; 20 Q—KB4 with a winning game (the chief threat is 21 Kt—B7, R—Kt1; 22 Kt x P).

| 19 . . . . | P—Kt3 |
| 20 Q—B6! | Kt—Kt5 |

Or 20 . . . B—Kt2; 21 Kt—Q6, Kt—Q1; 22 B—Kt5, Q—K3; 23 Q x Q, P x Q; 24 R—B7 and Black's position is quite hopeless.

The following invasion of the seventh rank must win very quickly.

| 21 R—B7 | Q—K3 |

If 21 . . . Q—K1; 22 Kt—Q6, Q—K3; 23 Q—Q8ch, K—Kt2; 24 Kt x P, Q x Kt; 25 R x Qch, K x R; 26 P—QR3! and wins.

| 22 Q—Q8ch | K—Kt2 |
| 23 Kt—Q6 | B—Kt2 |

If 21 . . . Kt x B; 22 Kt x P! Q x Kt; 23 R x Qch, K x R; 24 Q x Pch etc. For a moment the text seems to offer some hope.

| 24 Kt x P! | Resigns |

If 24 . . . R x Q; 25 Kt x Rch, K—B3; 26 Kt x Q and White remains the exchange ahead with an easy win.

---

58.   Match, 1908

QUEEN'S GAMBIT DECLINED

Evidently underestimating the pressure on his position, Mieses takes time out to grab an inoffensive Pawn. The results are grievous.

F.J. MARSHALL	J. MIESES
White	Black
1 P—Q4	P—Q4
2 P—QB4	P—K3
3 Kt—QB3	P—QB4
4 BP x P	KP x P
5 Kt—B3	Kt—QB3
6 P—KKt3	. . . .

Adopting the Schlechter-Rubinstein Variation, which had just begun to be fashionable.

6	B—K3
7 B—Kt2	Kt—B3
8 B—Kt5	B—K2

An uncomfortable position for Black; see the introductory comment on the previous game.

| 9 P x P | Q—R4 |

9 . . . B x P has been tried here, with none too happy results after the obvious and effective reply 10 QR—B1.

| 10 O—O | Q x BP |
| 11 R—B1 | R—Q1 |

An inferior move, as this Rook would have been more useful at QB1 later on. 11 . . . O—O was indicated.

12 Kt—QR4	Q—R4
13 Kt—Q4!	Kt x Kt
14 Q x Kt	O—O
15 Kt—B5	Q x P?

One could not imagine a more inopportune moment for Pawnhunting.

| 16 Kt x B | P x Kt |

The foregoing exchange has strengthened Black's QP, to be sure, but now the KP is very weak. White takes advantage of the absence of the hostile Queen to establish himself very strongly on the seventh rank.

17 R—B7	R—B2
18 B—R3	Q—R3
19 KR—B1	Q x P

Black's appetite grows by what it feeds on!

| 20 B—K3 | R—Q3 |

Permitting White's Queen to occupy K5, which was impossible earlier because of the reply . . . B—Q3. If instead 20 . . . Q—R3; 21 P—QKt4! and despite Black's

material advantage, his position is desperate (chief threat: R—R1, winning the exchange).

Position after Black's 20th move

Mieses

Marshall

| 21 Q—K5 | Q—R3 |
| 22 B—QB5 | Kt—Q2 |

Forced: any move of the QR would lose the exchange.

| 23 R x Kt | R x R |
| 24 B x KP | Q—B3 |

Black cannot shake off the pressure. If 24 . . . B x B; 25 R x B (threatening to mate with R—B8 ch or Q—Kt8ch), P—KR3; 26 B x R, R x B; 27 Q—K8ch wins.

| 25 B—K3 | Q—Q3 |
| 26 R—B8ch | B—Q1 |

If 26 . . . R—Q1? 27 Q x Q.

| 27 B x Rch | K x B |
| 28 Q—B5ch | B—B3 |

If 28 . . . K—Kt1; 29 B—B5 winning outright.

| 29 B—B5 | P—KKt3 |

Black's Queen cannot budge.

| 30 Q—R3 | Resigns |

If 30 . . . Q—K3; 31 Q x Pch, B—

Kt2; 32 R—B8 mate. Note that
after move 21, all of Black's moves
were forced!

---

59. Match, 1909

QUEEN'S GAMBIT DECLINED

A well-played positional game is
topped off with a neat sacrifice.

F.J. MARSHALL   J.R. CAPABLANCA

White	Black
1 P—Q4	P—Q4
2 P—QB4	P—K3
3 Kt—QB3	Kt—KB3
4 B—Kt5	B—K2
5 P—K3	Kt—K5

The idea of this variation is to
ease the pressure on Black's game
by exchanges.

6 B x B	Q x B
7 B—Q3	. . . .

Not the most exact, for now
Black could obtain a good game
with 7 . . . Kt x Kt; 8 P x Kt, P x P;
9 B x P, P—QKt3 etc.
For the modern method of beginning with 7 P x P see Game No. 109.

7	Kt x Kt
8 P x Kt	Kt—Q2
9 Kt—B3	O—O
10 P x P	P x P
11 Q—Kt3	Kt—B3
12 P—QR4	. . . .

A useful move. White foresees
that the hostile Queen-side Pawns
will be subjected to pressure.

12	P—B4

12 . . . P—B3 was less risky. The
text leads to difficulties.

13 Q—R3!	P—QKt3
14 P—R5	B—Kt2
15 O—O	Q—B2

Getting rid of the annoying pin.
But his troubles are not yet over.

16 KR—Kt1	Kt—Q2

Capablanca later confessed that
he never saw the reply to this
move. 16 . . . KR—Kt1 was best
under the circumstances, although
White would maintain the initiative.

Position after Black's 16th move

Capablanca

Marshall

17 B—B5!	KR—B1?

In order to save the Pawn threa-
tened by 18 B x Kt etc.
No better would be 17 . . . BP x
P; 18 BP x P, Kt—B3 with the pos-
sible continuation 19 R—QB1, Q—
Q1; 20 Kt—K5, R—K1; 21 P—R6,
B—B1; 22 Kt—B6, Q—B2; 23 B x
B, QR x B; 24 Kt—K7ch! Q x Kt;
25 R x R, Q x Q; 26 R x Rch coming
out the exchange ahead.
Best, however, was 17 . . . Kt—
B3.

18 B x Kt	Q x B
19 P—R6	B—B3
20 P x P	P x P
21 Q x P	. . . .

White has won a Pawn, and with
Kt—K5 or Kt—Q4 in the offing,
has a much superior position as
well.

21	QR—Kt1

Realizing that the position is

lost, Black desperately sets an ingenious trap.

| 22 R x R | R x R |
| 23 Kt—K5! | Q—B4 |

Threatens mate.

| 24 P—KB4! | R—Kt3 |

If 24 . . . R—Kt8ch; 25 R x R,
Q x Rch; 26 K—B2, Q—B7ch; 27
K—Kt3 and Black has not only
exhausted his checks, but his Bis-
hop is lost (27 . . . B—K1; 28 Q—
K7 or 27 . . . P—B3; 28 Q x B, and
the Knight cannot be captured).
Or 24 . . . P—B3; 25 P—Kt4!
after which Kt x B can be played
without having to fear perpetual
check (25 . . . Q—K5; 26 Kt x B,
R—Kt7; 27 Q x Pch! or 25 . . .
Q—B7; 26 Kt x B, R—Kt7; 27 Q x
Pch, K—B1; 28 Q—Q8ch, K—B2;
29 Q—K7ch, K—Kt3; 30 Q—K8ch,
K—R3; 31 Q—R5 mate).

| 25 Q x R! | Resigns |

Black' last hope was 25 Kt x B,
R—Kt8ch; 26 R x R, Q x Rch; 27
K—B2, Q—B7ch; 28 K—Kt3, Q—
Kt3ch with perpetual check.

---

60.   Match, 1909

(U.S.A. Championship)

DANISH GAMBIT

After achieving a perfectly satisfactory game, Black decides upon a wholly unmotivated Pawn
sacrifice; thereupon his game goes
steadily downhill.

F.J.MARSHALL	J.W. SHOWALTER
White	Black
1 P—K4	P—K4
2 P—Q4	P x P
3 P—QB3	P—Q6

Dull, but prudent: White's attacking aspirations are nipped in
the bud at once. For the complete
acceptance of the gambit, see
Game No. 82.

| 4 B x P | Kt—QB3 |

5 Kt—B3	P—Q3
6 B—QB4	Kt—B3
7 B—B4	B—K2

After 7 . . . Kt x P White would
regain the Pawn with 8 B x Pch,
leaving the Black King in a somewhat insecure state.

8 QKt—Q2	O—O
9 O—O	B—Kt5
10 R—K1	. . . .

Judging from the play that follows, it would have been worth-
while to interpolate P—KR3.

10	Kt—KR4
11 B—Kt3	Kt x B
12 RP x Kt	Kt—K4
13 B—B1	B—Kt4
14 Q—Kt3	. . . .

Black threatened to win a piece
with . . . KB x Kt.

| 14 . . . . | KB x Kt |
| 15 Kt x B | . . . . |

Position after White's 15th move

Showalter

Marshall

| 15 . . . . | B—K3? |

Much too optimistic. Simply . . .
P—QKt3 was in order.

| 16 Q x P | P—QR3 |

Black evidently believes that he can take advantage of the White Queen's position (17 B x P R—Kt1; 18 Q—R7, R—R1 with a draw). However, 16 . . . R—Kt1; 17 Q x RP, R x P would yield better drawing chances.

17 Kt—B3	Kt x Ktch
18 P x Kt	Q—Q2
19 Q—Kt4	. . . .

Guarding against . . . KR—Kt1. White now consolidates his position and prepares to make use of the extra Pawn.

19	KR—Kt1
20 Q—R3	P—QR4
21 QR—Q1	Q—B3
22 R—K3	P—B3
23 R—Q4	Q—Kt3
24 P—Kt3	P—QB4

Intending counterplay with . . .

P—R5; but this comes to nothing, and the weakness of the QP remains.

25 R—Q2	P—R5
26 P—QB4	P x P
27 Q x KtP	Q—B2
28 Q—Q1	R—Kt3
29 P—B4	. . . .

White has steadily gained ground; in due course P—K5 will be positionally decisive.

| 29 . . . . | Q—Kt1 |
| 30 R—Kt3! | . . . . |

Wins a second Pawn. If 30 . . . R.(1)—R3; 31 P—K5 etc.

30	R x R
31 P x R	R—R3
32 P—K5	Q—R2
33 R x P	P—Kt3
34 R x R	Resigns

V

CHAMPIONSHIP YEARS
(1910-1914)

61. Hamburg, 1910

MAX LANGE ATTACK

It was in this game, one of my most memorable tournament encounters, that I demonstrated the soundness of this famous old attack. Although the merit of my innovation 15 B—R6! has been hotly disputed for more than thirty years, no one has yet come forward with the refutation!

F. J. MARSHALL   DR. S. TARRASCH

White	Black
1 P—K4	P—K4
2 P—Q4	P x P
3 Kt—KB3	Kt—QB3
4 B—QB4	B—B4
5 O—O	Kt—B3

5 . . . P—Q3 gives an easier game. But Tarrasch evidently didn't dream that I had an improvement up my sleeve.

6 P—K5	P—Q4
7 P x Kt	P x B
8 R—K1ch	B—K3

These moves give us the Max Lange attack, one of the trappiest and trickiest lines in the whole realm of the openings.

| 9 Kt—Kt5 | Q—Q4 |

9 . . . Q x P? loses a piece (10 Kt x B, P x Kt; 11 Q—R5ch).

| 10 Kt—QB3 | Q—B4 |
| 11 QKt—K4 | . . . . |

The best move at this stage, for if 11 P—KKt4, Q—Kt3; 12 QKt—

K4, B—Kt3; 13 P—B4, O—O—O;
14 P—B5, B x P; 15 P x B, Q x P
(B4)—or 11 P x P, KR—Kt1; 12
P—KKt4, Q—Kt3; 13 QKt—K4,
B—K2; 14 P—B4, Q x P. In either
event Black should win.

11 . . . .   O—O—O

Likewise Black's best move. Rubinstein later suggested 11 . . .
B—KB1, but this is refuted by 12
Kt x BP! K x Kt; 13 Kt—Kt5ch,
K—Kt1; 14 P—KKt4! Q—Q4; 15
R x B, P x P; 16 R x P. Tarrasch,
to whom the move 15 R x B is due
in this variation, points out that
after 16 R x P White has the important square KB5 for his Rook, and
threatens Kt—B7 at once.

12 Kt x QB   . . . .

Again P—KKt4 would be a will-
o'-the-wisp, the continuation being
12 . . . Q—K4; 13 Kt—KB3, Q—Q4;
14 P x P, B x P; 15 P x R(Q), R x Q;
16 Kt—B6, Q x Kt; 17 Kt x B, Q x
Q; 18 R x Q, R—Kt1; 19 P—KR3,
P—KR4 and if anything the position favors Black.

12 . . . .   P x Kt
13 P—KKt4   Q—K4
14 P x P   KR—Kt1
15 B—R6!   . . . .

The new move. As will be seen,
the continuation entails putting
this Bishop completely out of play;
but Black's KR is similarly tied up,
and Black must always be on his
guard against the possibility of
White's Kt—B6 after P—Kt5 has
been played.

15 . . . .   P—Q6

(see diagram next column)

16 P—QB3   B—Q3?

Weak. The most promising continuation is 16 . . . P—Q7; 17 R—
K2, R—Q6; 18 Q—KB1! B—Kt3;
19 R—Q1, Kt—Q1. At this point
Fine, in "Modern Chess Openings,"
continues with Seibold's analysis
20 P—Kt5? Kt—B2; 21 Kt—Kt3,

Position after Black's 15th move

Tarrasch

Marshall

Q—Q4; 22 Q—R3, Kt—K4 and
Black has the better prospects.

However, Ulvestad, in some
clever analysis in his "Chess
Charts," has shown that White gets
the better of it with 20 Kt—Kt3!
(leaving the Bishop's diagonal open
for a decisive attack on the QP),
Q—Q4 (if 20 . . . Q—B3; 21 P—
Kt5, Q—B5;. 22 Q—R3 with advantage); 21 R(2) x P, Kt—B2; 22 R x
R, P x R; 23 R x P leaving White
with the better game.

17 P—B4   Q—Q4
18 Q—B3   . . . .

Not 18 Kt—B6? B—B4ch.

18 . . . .   B—K2

Threatening . . . B—B3. But this
is a sad comment on the previous
move of this Bishop.

19 P—Kt5   Q—KB4
20 Kt—Kt3   Q—B2
21 Q—Kt4   QR—K1?

Indirectly defending the KP, but
21 . . . P—Q7 would make a much
stronger fight for it. White could
not play 22 R x P? because of 22
. . . P—Q8(Q)ch; while if 22 R—
K4, B—B4ch; 23 K—R1, Kt—K2!
(with a view to . . . Kt—B4!) is
very strong.

22 R—K4!   . . . .

Commencing the final attack. In order to avoid the loss of the advanced Pawns, Black must weaken his King's position fatally; if 22 . . . Kt—R4; 23 QR—K1, K—Q2; 24 P—B5 and wins.

22	P—Kt4
23 P—QR4	P—R3
24 P x P	P x P
25 K—Kt2!	. . . .

Threatening to capture the KP, as Black's Bishop can no longer play to B4 with a check.

| 25 . . . . | Kt—Q1 |

Allowing White's pieces in with fatal effect; but if 25 . . . B—Q3; 26 Kt—R5 wins.

| 26 Q—B3 | Q—Kt3 |
| 27 R—Q4! | P—B3 |

Or 27 . . . B—Q3; 28 R x B, P x R; 29 Q—R8ch, K—Q2; 30 R—R7ch and mate follows.

| 28 R x Ktch | K x R |
| 29 Q x P | Resigns |

---

62. Hamburg, 1910
PETROFF DEFENSE

In this game I adopt a sacrificial counterattack which subsequently, despite the doubts expressed by many critics, managed to hold its own for almost twenty years. The flaw was there, but for many years it eluded discovery!

R. SPIELMANN   F. J. MARSHALL

White   Black

1 P—K4	P—K4
2 Kt—KB3	Kt—KB3
3 Kt x P	P—Q3
4 Kt—KB3	Kt x P
5 P—Q4	. . . .

A few years later 5 Q—K2 began

to have a great vogue; a continuation which, to my way of thinking, took most of the fun out of the Petroff.

| 5 . . . . | P—Q4 |
| 6 B—Q3 | B—Q3 |

. . . B—K2 is the customary development in this variation; but the text is played with a view to the play that follows.

7 O—O	B—KKt5
8 P—B4	O—O?!
9 P x P	P—KB4
10 Kt—B3	Kt—Q2?!

All according to plan.

11 P—KR3	B—R4
12 Kt x Kt	P x Kt
13 B x P	Kt—B3
14 B—B5	K—R1
15 P—KKt4	Kt x QP
16 Q—Q3	. . . .

Many years later the brilliant young British master Alexander discovered the refutation: 16 B—K6! B—B2; 17 Kt—Kt5! (wins the exchange), B x B; 18 Kt x B, Q—R5; 19 Q—Kt3! (threatening 20 B—Kt5 and thus extinguishing all of Black's attacking chances) and wins (Alexander—Mallison, Brighton, 1938).

The text is a fair move, but it leads to the kind of wide open game that I have always loved; and, as one would expect from an aggressive player like Spielmann, he finds himself uncomfortable on the defensive.

| 16 . . . . | Kt—Kt5 |
| 17 Q—K4 | B—B2 |

Now 18 B x P? is prohibitive because of 18 . . . B—Q4.

| 18 B—Kt5 | Q—K1 |
| 19 Kt—K5 | . . . . |

Both Q x Q and P—R3 have been recommended here; but the text is by no means fatal.

19 . . . .   B—Q4
20 Q—K2   . . . .

Practically compulsory, for if 20
Q—K3, R x B; 21 P x R, Kt—B7 or
20 Q—B4, Kt—Q6—in either case
with advantage to Black.

20 . . . .   Kt—B3
21 Q—Q3?   . . . .

After this White is definitely
lost. 21 KR—Q1 would have given
him a playable game, as 21 . . .
Kt x Kt fails after 22 P x Kt, B—B3
(not 22 . . . B x KP? 23 R x B, B—
R7ch; 24 K—B1); 23 R—K1 etc.

21 . . . .   Kt x Kt
22 P x Kt   Q x P

Black has a mighty attack now
which must bring results.

23 Q—KKt3   . . . .

If 23 P—B4, B—B4ch; 24 K—R2,
Q x KtPch with a winning game.

23 . . . .   Q x P!

This is not played for the sake
of Pawn-grabbing, but in order to
have White's QR en prise in some
variations.

24 Q—R4   . . . .

Position after White's 24th move

Marshall

Spielmann

24 . . . .   R x B

Every move hereabouts is played
with gain of time, and White
doesn't get a moment's rest.

25 P x R   Q—K4
26 Q—Kt3   Q x P

Stronger than the immediate 26
. . . Q—K5; 27 P—B3 etc.

27 Q—Kt4   Q—K4
28 KR—K1   . . . .

If 28 Q—Kt3, Q—K5; 29 P—B3,
Q—Q5ch; 30 Q—B2, B—B4; 31 Q x
Q, B x Qch winning easily.

28 . . . .   Q—R7ch
29 K—B1   R—KB1
30 K—K2   . . . .

On 30 B—K3 or Q—R4, Black
wins with . . . B—B6. Of course,
if 30 R—K2, Q—R8ch etc.

30 . . . .   Q x Pch
31 K—Q3   P—Kt4

White resigns; he has had
enough punishment. There is little
he can do against the threat of . . .
B—B5ch followed by . . . R—B6ch,
for example 32 B—Q2, B—B5ch; 33
K—B2, B—Kt5; 34 KR—Q1, R—
Q1; 35 Q—B4, R x Bch; 36 R x R,
Q x Q etc.

---

63. Hamburg, 1910

PETROFF DEFENSE

An incautious move by my opponent gives me the opportunity for
a surprising combination.

W. JOHN   F. J. MARSHALL

White   Black

	White	Black
1	P—K4	P—K4
2	Kt—KB3	Kt—KB3
3	Kt x P	P—Q3
4	Kt—KB3	Kt x P
5	P—Q4	P—Q4
6	B—Q3	B—Kt5

7 O—O	B—Q3
8 P—B4	O—O?!
9 P—B5?	....

Up to this point, the play was identical with that of the previous game, in which Spielmann played the superior 9 P x P. The text leaves White with rather a weak Pawn formation.

9	B—K2
10 P—KR3	B x Kt
11 P x B	....

Against 11 Q x B Black would quietly continue 11 . . . Kt—QB3! since 12 B x Kt, P x B; 13 Q x P, Q x P would win a Pawn directly.

| 11 . . . . | Kt—Kt4 |
| 12 P—B4 | Kt—K3 |

Avoiding the trap 12 . . . Kt x P ch? 13 K—Kt2, Q—Q2; 14 Q—R5 etc.

| 13 B—B5 | Kt—B3 |
| 14 B—K3 | B—B3 |

Leaving White no choice but to part with the more useful of his two Bishops. Black obtains a backward KP thereby, but it is easily defended and quite outweighed by the opening of the KB file. This latter factor enables him to exploit the weakening of the King-side caused by White's futile chase after the KKt (moves 11 and 12).

| 15 B x Kt | P x B |
| 16 Q—Q3? | .... |

In his anxiety to forestall the indicated attacking maneuver . . . Q—K1—Kt3ch, White completely overlooks the following sacrifice.

(see diagram next column)

| 16 . . . . | B x P! |

Quite sound. Black's attack now unfolds with terrible swiftness.

| 17 B x B | R x P |
| 18 B—B3 | .... |

Position after White's 16th move

Marshall

John

If 18 B—K3, R—B6 with a winning attack, for example 19 K—Kt2, Q—R5! 20 R—R1 (if 20 K x R, Kt—K4ch; 21 K—K2, Kt x Q; 22 K x Kt, Q—B5ch), P—Q5; 21 Q—B4 (or 21 Kt—Q2, P x B! and the Rook cannot be captured either way), Q—K5! 22 Kt—Q2, R x Pch! and wins.

18	P—Q5
19 B—Q2	Kt—K4
20 Q—KKt3	Kt—B6ch

Everything with gain of time!

| 21 K—Kt2 | .... |

If 21 K—R1, R—B3 and 22 . . . Q—Q4 will be decisive.

| 21 . . . . | R—B3 |
| 22 Q x Kt | .... |

There is nothing else left. But since White's King is exposed and his development is in arrears, he cannot last very long.

22	R x Q
23 K x R	Q—Q4ch
24 K—Kt3	R—KB1
25 P—B3	Q—K4ch

Leaving Black little choice, for

If 26 K—Kt2, R—B3 followed by
. . . R—Kt3ch; or if 26 P—B4, Q—
K7; 27 R—B2, Q—Q8 etc.

26 K—B2	Q—R7ch
27 K—K1	Q x P
28 P—B4	P—K4
29 Kt—R3	P x P

Or 29 . . . P—K5.

| 30 K—B2 | . . . . |

There was no defense against
the threat of 30 . . . R—K1ch.

30	Q—R7ch
31 K—K1	P—Q6
Resigns	

----

64. New York, 1911

(National Tournament)

DUTCH DEFENSE

This is the kind of game that
delights the spectators at a tourney.

F. J. MARSHALL	C. JAFFE
White	Black
1 P—Q4	P—KB4
2 P—K4	P x P
3 Kt—QB3	Kt—KB3
4 B—KKt5	P—KKt3
5 P—B3!	. . . .

As we saw in a similar position
in Game no. 54, this move subjects
Black to a disagreeably difficult
defense.

5	P—K6
6 Q—Q3	B—Kt2
7 Q x P	P—Q4

This leaves a hole at his K4 and
a backward KP; but after . . . P—
Q3 his position would also be most
unpleasant. The attempt to propi-
tiate the enemy by returning the
Pawn at move 5 has been unsuc-
cessful.

| 8 O—O—O | Kt—B3 |

| 9 B—Kt5 | Q—Q2 |

A sad move to have to make, but
if he allows B x Kt, his Queen-side
Pawns are hopeless, and White has
ideal squares for his Knights on
K5 and QB5.

10 KKt—K2	O—O
11 Kt—B4	. . . .

An effective spot for the Knight,
either for attacking purposes (as
in the game) or for strategical ob-
jectives (Kt—Q3 etc.).

11	P—K3
12 P—KR4	. . . .

Justifiably proceeding to the attack.

12	Kt—K1
13 P—R5!	. . . .

If Black thought that the
Knight's retreat would prevent this
move, he now finds that he guessed
wrong. The text involves a sacrifice which yields a lasting attack.

13	P—KR3
14 Kt x KtP	P x B
15 P—R6	B—R1

Position after Black's 15th move

Jaffe

Marshall

16 Q x KtP	Q—Q1

If 16 . . . B—B3; 17 P—R7ch, K—B2 (or 17 . . . K—Kt2; 18 Q—R6ch); 18 P—R8(Kt)ch and wins. Or 16 . . . K—B2; 17 R—R4 and wins, for example 17 . . . KR—Kt1; 18 Kt x Bch, R x Kt; 19 R—B4ch—or 17 . . . B—B3; 18 R—B4, KR—Kt1 (if 18 . . . K—Kt1; 19 R x B!); 19 Kt—K5ch, Kt x Kt; 20 Q—R5ch and wins.

17 P—R7ch	K—B2
18 Q—R6	Kt—Q3

If 18 . . . Kt—Kt2; 19 B x Kt, P x B; 20 Kt—K5ch, K—K1; 21 Q—Kt6ch winning the Queen.

19 P—KKt4	B—Q2
20 B x Kt	P x B
21 Kt—K5ch	K—K1
22 P—Kt5	Kt—B2

If 22 . . . Kt—B4; 23 Q—R5ch, K—K2; 24 Kt—Kt6ch, K—Q3; 25 Q—R2ch and wins.

23 Kt x Kt	R x Kt
24 P—Kt6	R—Kt2
25 Q x R	B x Q
26 P—R8(Q)ch	B x Q
27 R x Bch	K—K2
28 R x Q	R x R

After all the blood-letting, White has come out only a Pawn ahead, and a very puny-looking Pawn at that!

29 K—Kt1	R—KKt1
30 Kt—K2	. . . .

To the rescue!

30	K—B3
31 Kt—B4	P—B4

The natural move is 31 . . . B—K1, but then there follows 32 K—Q2, B x P; 33 K—B3 and White's King goes to B5 with a won ending.

32 Kt—R5ch	K—B4
33 P x P	B—K1

There were better drawing chances with . . . R x P.

34 P—KB4	B x P

It is too late for . . . R x P because of 35 Kt—Kt7ch and wins (35 . . . K x P; 36 R—B1ch).

35 R—Kt5ch	K—K5
36 Kt—B6ch	K x P
37 R—Kt1	R—B1

Unavoidable, for if 37 . . . R—Kt2; 38 Kt—R5ch and it is all over.

38 R x B	K—B4
39 Kt—R7	. . . .

Or 39 R—Kt7, K x Kt; 40 R x P etc.

39	R—B2
40 R x P	. . . .

I couldn't make up my mind about 40 R—R6, for although it would have left me with a piece to the good, the Knight would have been marooned for quite a while. The text, on the other hand, makes one more use of the hard-working Knight (if 40 . . . K x R; 41 Kt—Kt5ch) to lead into an easily won ending.

40	R x Kt
41 R—QR6	K—K5
42 R—R4ch	K—K4
43 P—B3	P—B3
44 K—B2	R—KKt2
45 R—KR4!	K—K3
46 R—R8	P—Q5

Desperation. If instead 46 . . . R—QB2; 47 R—Q8 followed by R—Q6ch and the advance of White's King with an easy win; or 46 . . . K—Q2; 47 R—R8, K—K3; 48 R—Q8 leading to the same line of play. The desperate text is likewise unavailing. The final moves were as follows:—47 P x P, K—Q4; 48 R—Q8ch, K—K5; 49 K—B3, R—Kt6 ch; 50 K—B4, R—Kt7; 51 R—K8 ch, K—B5; 52 R—K6, R x P; 53 R x P, R x P; 54 R—K6, K—B4;

55 R—K5ch, K—B3; 56 P—B6, R—
B7ch; 57 K—Q5, P—R4; 58 K—Q6,
R—B5; 59 P—B7, P—R5; 60 R—
B5, R x Pch; 61 K—B6, resigns.

---

65. New York, 1911

(National Tournament)

QUEEN'S GAMBIT

My opponent in this game, Albert B. Hodges, was chess champion of the United States in 1894-
96, and remained one of the finest
players in this country for many
years thereafter. Although he recently celebrated his 80th birth-
day, he is still active and retains
the presidency of the Staten Island
Chess Club.

F.J. Marshall	A.B. Hodges
White	Black
1 P—Q4	P—Q4
2 P—QB4	P—K3
3 Kt—QB3	P x P
4 P—K3	Kt—KB3
5 B x P	P—QR3
6 P—QR4	Kt—B3
7 Kt—B3	Kt—QKt5
8 O—O	. . . .

Regarding this variation see also
Game No. 37, in which Janowski
delayed the following advance for
quite some time.

8	P—B4
9 Q—K2	P x P

The idea of giving White an
isolated QP is often effective, as
Steinitz demonstrated. However,
the capture is made too hastily,
and opens up useful lines for White
at a very early stage.

10 P x P	B—K2
11 B—Kt5	B—Q2

Allowing the immediate thrust
of the QP; but after 11 . . . O—O
White has a strong counter in 12
QR—Q1.

12 B x Kt!	B x B
13 P—Q5	Q—K2
14 KR—K1	O—O

Black must lose a Pawn, but with
his usual resourcefulness, he has
prepared some clever counterplay.

15 P x P	P x P
16 B x Pch	B x B
17 Q x Bch	Q x Q
18 R x Q	Kt—Q6
19 R—Kt6	. . . .

Stronger than 19 R—K2, Kt x
KtP.

Position after White's 19th move

Hodges

Marshall

19	Kt x BP!

Not 19 . . . Kt x KtP; 20 Kt—Q5,
Kt—B5; 21 Kt x Bch followed by
R x KtP and White has retained
his material advantage.

20 Kt—Q5	. . . .

If 20 K x Kt? B—Q5ch winning
the Rook. White has had to return the extra Pawn, but the following moves assure him a lasting
positional advantage.

20	Kt—Q6
21 Kt x Bch	P x Kt

A basic point of the whole line of play is that Black must retake in this manner in order to be able to answer 22 R x KtP with . . . KR—Kt1 regaining his Pawn. Whereas after 21 . . . R x B; 22 R x KtP, Black cannot make good his material loss.

| 22 Kt—Q4 | KR—Q1 |
| 23 Kt—B5 | . . . . |

This is the position White was aiming for. The Knight cannot be dislodged from this powerful position, and White's Rooks likewise take up strong posts.

23	R—Q2
24 R—KB1	R—KB1
25 P—R5	Kt—B4
26 P—R3	Kt—R5

Black can do little but mark time. He has weaknesses on both wings, and pretty soon his King will be somewhat endangered.

27 R—Kt4	Kt—B4
28 R—B3	K—R1
29 Kt—R6	R—Q3

Allowing a neat finish. 29 . . . R—Kt2 was in order, although he would have had to succumb to the pressure in any event.

| 30 R—Kt4 | R—K3 |

Or 30 . . . R—Q6; 31 R x P!

| 31 R(3)—KKt3 | R(3)—K1 |
| 32 R—Kt8ch! | Resigns |

If 32 . . . R x R; 33 Kt—B7 mate.

---

66. San Sebastian, 1911

PETROFF DEFENSE

As I have always been looked upon as a player who seeks the decision in the middle game, I welcome the opportunity to acquaint the reader with some examples of my end-game play. Here is a game of which I am particularly fond.

R. TEICHMANN	F.J. MARSHALL
White	Black
1 P—K4	P—K4
2 Kt—KB3	Kt—KB3
3 Kt x P	P—Q3
4 Kt—KB3	Kt x P
5 P—B4	. . . .

Known as Kaufman's Variation, this move is seldom seen today. It was also adopted by Maroczy against me in the same tournament, with an exciting draw as the outcome. The object of the move was evidently to avoid the variation played in Game No. 62; but it leaves Black with an easy game.

5	B—K2
6 Kt—B3	Kt x Kt
7 QP x Kt	. . . .

If 7 KtP x Kt, O—O; 8 P—Q4, R—K1; 9 B—K2, B—B4; 10 O—O, Kt—Q2 likewise with excellent prospects for Black.

| 7 . . . . | Kt—B3 |
| 8 B—B4 | . . . . |

Anticipating Black's castling on the Queen-side, White prepares to follow suit.

8	B—Kt5
9 B—K2	Q—Q2
10 Q—Q2	O—O—O
11 O—O—O	P—KR3
12 P—KR3	B—K3
13 Kt—Q4	Kt x Kt
14 P x Kt	. . . .

If 14 Q x Kt, Q—R5; 15 K—Kt1, B—B3 with advantage to Black.

| 14 . . . . | Q—R5 |
| 15 P—QKt3? | . . . . |

Weakening the King's position. White apparently did not like the looks of the position after 15 K—Kt1, B x P; 16 P—QKt3, B x P; 17 P x B, Q x Pch; 18 Q—Kt2, Q x Qch—although this may have been his best course.

15	Q—R3
16 K—Kt1	B—B3
17 P—Q5	. . . .

Not liking . . . P—B4, he weakens his Pawn formation. 17 P—B5 might have been tried.

17	B—Q2
18 Q—B2	KR—K1
19 B—K3	Q—R4
20 B—Q4?	. . . .

A serious strategical blunder. In view of the fact that all but one of White's Pawns are on white squares, hemming in his KB, the logical exchange was by means of B—Kt4. The consequences of this mistake soon become evident.

20	B x B
21 R x B	R—K4
22 Q—Q2	Q—Kt3
23 R—Q1	QR—K1
24 B—B1	P—QR4!

Completely fixing White's Pawns on the Queen-side. Black's absolute control of the only open file, plus his superior strength on the black squares, soon result in a further restriction of White's forces.

25 R—B1	K—Kt1
26 R—B4	B—B4ch
27 K—Kt2	. . . .

If 27 B—Q3? R—K7 wins a Pawn.

27	P—Kt4
28 R—KB3	B—Kt3
29 R(3)—B3	R—B4!
30 P—B3	. . . .

If 30 P—B5, P x P; 31 R x P, Q—B3ch; 32 K—R3, R x BP; 33 Q x RP, Q—Kt7ch; 34 K—Kt4, R—K5ch winning easily.

But after the text the last remaining White Pawn has been moved to a white square, thus weakening White's KKt3. It is this weakness that ultimately causes White's downfall.

| 30 . . . . | Q—B4! |

Preventing . . . P—B5, which would now be good.

| 31 R—Q1 | R(4)—K4 |
| 32 Q—Q4 | . . . . |

If 32 B—Q3, B x B; 33 Q x B, R—K6; 34 Q—B2, R—K7; 35 R—Q2, Q—B7 and wins. Or 34 Q—B1, R—K7ch; 35 R—B2, Q—K6; 36 R—B1, Q—Q6 with advantage. Hence White decides to retain his inferior Bishop.

32	Q x Q
33 R x Q	R—K8
34 R—B1	R(1)—K6!

A strong positional move, and a key to the endgame.

35 R(4)—Q1	R x R
36 R x R	K—R2
37 R—Q2	R—K8
38 B—K2	K—Kt3
39 K—B3	K—B4
40 P—R3	R—B8ch

Position after Black's 40th move

Marshall

Teichmann

We now arrive at a remarkable Zugzwang position: a tempo-gaining series of moves is repeated four times, and there is nothing that White can do about it!

| 41 K—Kt2 | R—Kt8 |

42 B—Q1	R—K8!
43 B—K2	. . . .

White has nothing better: any other move gives Black a winning end-game. For example if 43 K—B3, R—K6ch; 44 K—Kt2, R—Q6 forcing the exchange of Rooks. Or 43 B—B2, B x B; 44 K x B, P—R5; 45 K—Kt2, P x P; 46 K x P, R—K6ch etc.

43	P—R4!
44 K—B3	R—B8ch
45 K—Kt2	R—Kt8
46 B—Q1	R—K8!
47 B—K2	P—KR5

Again the series of three moves has gained a tempo. The advance of the KRP is of great importance in the subsequent play.

48 K—B3	R—B8ch
49 K—Kt2	R—Kt8
50 B—Q1	R—K8!
51 B—K2	P—KB3!

The third tempo!

52 K—B3	R—B8ch
53 K—Kt2	R—Kt8
54 B—Q1	R—K8!
55 B—K2	P—B3

Having improved his position to the utmost, Black now decides to play for a win; the draw is always certain.

56 K—B3	R—B8ch
57 K—Kt2	R—Kt8ch
58 K—B3	P—Kt4!
59 P—Kt4ch	P x Pch
60 P x Pch	R x P
61 QP x P	P x P
62 R—Q5ch	K x P

Here Black could win a Pawn with 62 . . . K x R; 63 K x R, K x P; 64 K x P, P—Q4ch 65 K—Q4, K—Q3 but the position appears to be a draw.

63 R x Pch	K x R

64 K x R	K—K4
65 K x P	B—B2ch
66 K—Q3	K—B5
67 B—B1	K—Kt6

The desired position!

68 K—K3	B—Q4
69 K—K2	P—B4
70 K—K3	B—K3
71 K—K2	P—Kt5

The decisive break. The idea is to eliminate White's BP and RP by exchanges, then win the KtP and Black's RP will queen.

72 RP x P	. . . .

It has been suggested that 72 BP x P would have drawn, but this is incorrect. After 72 BP x P Black wins with 72 . . . P x P; 73 K—K3, B—Q2; 74 K—K2, B—Kt4ch! (not 74 . . . B—B3; 75 P x P, B x P; 76 B x B, K x B; 77 P—Kt5 and White queens in time); 75 K—K1, B—B3; 76 P x P, B x P; 77 B x B, (or 77 P—Kt5, P—R6; 78 P—Kt6, P—R7; 79 P—Kt7, B—Q4) K x B; 78 P—Kt5, P—R6 and Black wins because he queens with a check!

72	P x P
73 K—K3	B—Q2

If now 74 P—B4, K—R7; 75 K—B2, P—Kt6ch wins; or if 74 K—K2, B—Kt4ch! 75 K—K1, B—B3; 76 P x P, B x P as above.

74 P x P	B x P
75 K—K4	B—B1
76 K—K3	B—Q2

White resigns, since there is nothing to be done against . . . B—B3.

Commenting on this game, M. Albert Clerc, a first rank amateur of the Cafe de la Regence in Paris, said: "In all my observations of sixty years of chess, the most wonderful game as regards beauty of position and combination I ever saw."

67. Match, 1911
QUEEN'S PAWN OPENING

Leonhardt was a player with fine ideas, but in critical situations he often got into time pressure trying to make up his mind. As a result, he frequently blundered at crucial moments.

F.J. MARSHALL   P.S. LEONHARDT

White	Black
1 P—Q4	P—Q4
2 P—KKt3	. . . .

Did I really play this?! Such listless openings are rare in my games!

2	Kt—KB3
3 B—Kt2	P—B4
4 P—QB3	. . . .

Continuing in the same conservative manner. With 4 Kt—KB3 and 5 P—B4 I could have arrived at a Catalan formation which was to become so popular many years after this game.

4	P—K3
5 Kt—B3	Kt—B3
6 O—O	Kt—K5
7 QKt—Q2	P—B4
8 Kt x Kt	BP x Kt
9 Kt—K5	B—K2

After this he is soon in trouble. Leonhardt subsequently recommended the better line 9 . . . P x P; 10 P x P, Kt x Kt; 11 P x P, B—B4 or 10 Kt x Kt, P x Kt; 11 P x P, B—K2; 12 P—B3, P x P; 13 R x P, B—B3 etc.

10 P—B3	P x BP
11 R x P	B—B3
12 Kt—Kt4	. . . .

Maintaining the pressure. The Pawn-grabbing variation 12 Kt x Kt, P x Kt; 13 P x P, Q—K2; 14 B—K3, P—K4 doesn't look very attractive.

| 12 . . . . | P x P |

13 Kt x Bch	P x Kt
14 P x P	O—O
15 B—R6	R—B2

White has come out of the opening with the better game, as he has two Bishops and his opponent's Pawn position is somewhat shaky.

| 16 P—K3 | Kt—K2 |

I was prepared to give up the exchange here after 16 . . . P—K4; 17 P x P, B—Kt5; 18 Q—Kt3 with very strong pressure and prospects of recovering the exchange advantageously.

| 17 Q—Kt3! | K—R1 |

Of course if 17 . . . Kt—B4; 18 R x Kt. The text is a preparatory move which doesn't prepare.

| 18 QR—KB1 | Kt—B4 |

This is "asking for it," but the alternative 18 . . . Kt—Kt1 would leave Black with a very unpleasant game.

Position after Black's 18th move

Leonhardt

Marshall

| 19 R x Kt! | P x R |
| 20 B x P | R—K2 |

If 20 . . . R—QB2 White continues the attack with 21 P—Kt4! P x P; 22 P—K4 followed by P—K5.

21 P—K4!   Q—Kt3

If 21 . . . P x P; 22 R x P, R—
K1; 23 R—B7 and wins. The text
seems to offer the only hope, but
White's attack is of the kind which
rages undiminished even after exchange of Queens.

22 Q x Q   P x Q
23 P—K5!.   . . . .

This freshens up the attack. The
exchange is now regained, for if
23 . . . B—K3; 24 P x P, KR—K1;
25 P—B7.

23 . . . .   P x P
24 B—Kt5   B—K3

Or 24 . . . R—Kt2; 25 B—KB6,
P—K5; 26 R—B1—B7 and wins.

25 B x R   B x B
26 R x P   R x P
27 R—Kt5!   P—R4

Forced. The ending is now reduced to an easy win, as follows:
28 R x Pch, K—Kt2; 29 R x P, B—
B5; 30 B—R3, P—Kt4; 31 R—
K7ch, K—B3; 32 R x P, R—R8ch;
33 K—B2, Resigns.

---

68.   Match, 1911

MUZIO GAMBIT

Due to Leonhardt's failings mentioned in the previous game, this
seemed an eminently suitable opening for a serious match game! Nor
was my confidence misplaced.

F.J. MARSHALL   P.S. LEONHARDT

White	Black
1 P—K4	P—K4
2 P—KB4	P x P
3 Kt—KB3	P—KKt4
4 B—B4	P—Kt5
5 Kt—B3	. . . .

Adopting the MacDonnell Attack,
as in Game No. 17. It is a difficult
line to contend with, when the

minutes are ticking away at your
elbow.

5 . . . .   P—Q4

Black wants to open lines for
his pieces; but this remains no
more than a pious hope throughout the game.

6 B x P   P x Kt
7 Q x P   Kt—KB3
8 Q x P   B—K2

This looks ultra-safe, but it is
an error of judgment, exposing
Black subsequently to a strong attack along the long diagonal. Hence
8 . . . B—Kt2 was better.

9 O—O   O—O
10 P—QKt4!   . . . .

White means to get on the long
diagonal without loss of time, and
the value of placing the QB there
will be apparent soon enough. 10
P—QKt3 would not be as good, for
after 10 P—B3; 11 B—B4, P—Kt4
the KB would be driven off its
present powerful diagonal.

10 . . . .   P—QR4
11 B—Kt2   P x P
12 Kt—K2   R—R3

This Rook seems destined to
perform some valuable defensive
services; but this proves to be a
will-o'-the-wisp.

13 Q—R6!   . . . .

(see diagram next page)

13 . . . .   K—R1

To place the King in the hostile
QB's cross-fire is anything but desirable, but something has to be
done about the threat of R—B3—
Kt3ch.
Note the delightful possibility 13
. . . Kt—K1; 14 Q x Rch! K x Q;
15 R x Pch, K—Kt1; 16 R—Kt7
dbl ch and mate next move!

14 Kt—B4   R—Kt1

Position after White's 13th move

Leonhardt

Marshall

So as to be able to answer 16 Kt—R5 with . . . KR—Kt3.

15 B x BP   B—B1

Weakening himself on the terrible diagonal. But if 15 . . . Q—B1; 16 Kt—Kt6ch, R x Kt; 17 Q x Q ch, B x Q; 18 B x R with a winning game.

16 Q—R5!   . . . .

Whereupon Leonhardt comments sadly: "Against this there is no herb in the Pharmacopoeia of chess."

16 . . . .   R—Kt5

If he protects himself at once on the diagonal by 16 . . . B—Kt2 there is a nice smothered mate with 17 Kt—Kt6.

17 Kt—K6!   B—Kt2

Or 17 . . . R x Kt; 18 B x R, B—Kt2; 19 B x Kt, KB x B; 20 B x R and wins.

18 B x Kt   Resigns

---

69. Carlsbad, 1911
FRENCH DEFENSE
Black's opening play is too con-

servative and his middle game play is too risky. The two make a poor combination!

F.J. Marshall   A. Rabinovich

White   Black

1 P—Q4   P—K3
2 P—K4   P—Q4
3 Kt—QB3   P x P

Although Rubinstein played some fine games with this move, the general verdict (in which I concur) is that it gives White too many attacking chances.

4 Kt x P   Kt—Q2
5 Kt—KB3   KKt—B3
6 B—Q3   Kt x Kt
7 B x Kt   Kt—B3
8 B—Kt5   B—K2
9 B x Kt   P x B

Leaving his Pawn position somewhat weak, and practically committing himself to castling Queenside. 9 . . . B x B gives an easier game.

10 Q—Q3   . . . .

Threatening 11 B x KtP, B x B; 12 Q—Kt5ch. 10 Q—K2 was also good.

10 . . . .   P—B3

Now . . . P—KB4 is threatened.

11 Q—K3   P—KR4
12 O—O   . . . .

This is perfectly safe, as Black is not in a position to make use of the open KKt file. White foresees the inevitable . . . O—O—O, which will be answered by a general advance of his Queen-side Pawns.

12 . . . .   Q—B2
13 P—B4   B—Q2
14 QR—Q1   O—O—O
15 P—Q5!   . . . .

Striking while the iron is hot. Black is still in a quandary, for he must allow the deterioration of his Pawn structure in order to protect the QRP.

15	K—Kt1
16 Kt—Q4	B—Q3?

After this his game falls apart in short order. Relatively best was 16 . . . P—QB4, when White would retreat the Knight and continue with P—QR3 and P—QKt4.

17 P x BP	B x Pch
18 K—R1	P x P
19 Q—Kt3ch	. . . .

Naturally White prefers to play for attack rather than go in for 19 P—KKt3, P—R5! etc. However, if Black answers the text with 19 . . . Q—Kt2 there follows 20 Q x Q ch, K x Q; 21 K x B etc.

19	K—B1

19 . . . K—R1 is answered by 20 Kt—Kt5 and if 20 . . . Q—Kt1; 21 R x B, R x R; 22 B x Pch, R—Kt2; 23 R—Q1 — or 20 . . . Q—K4; 21 R x B, R x R; 22 B x Pch, R—Kt2; 23 Kt—Q6 etc.

20 P—B5	B—K4
21 Q—R4	P—B4

After 21 . . . B x Kt; 22 R x B White's threats (above all 23 R—QKt4) are too numerous to parry.

(see diagram next column)

22 Kt x QBP!   . . . .

This pretty sacrifice cannot very well be refused by 22 . . . B x Kt. The continuation would be 23 B x B, B x P; 24 Q—R6ch, K—Kt1; 25 QR—Kt1, R—Q7; 26 Q—Kt5ch, K—B1; 27 R x B and wins.

22	P x B
23 Q—R6ch	Q—Kt2
24 Q x Qch	K x Q
25 Kt x B	B—R5

Or 25 . . . B—Kt4; 26 Kt x P! White has an easy win.

Position after Black's 21st move

Rabinovich

Marshall

26 P—QKt3	R x R
27 R x R	B—B3
28 Kt x P	R—KB1

Equivalent to resignation, but if 28 . . . R—KKt1; 29 Kt—Q8ch, K—B2; 30 Kt x Pch etc. The final moves were: 29 Kt—Q8ch, R x Kt; 30 R x R, P—R4; 31 R—KR8, B—Q4; 32 R x P, K—B3; 33 R—R8, K x P; 34 R—QKt8, K—Q5; 35 R—Kt5, P—K6; 36 P x Pch, K x P; 37 K—Kt1, Resigns.

---

70. Carlsbad, 1911

QUEEN'S GAMBIT

I felt rather nervous when I sat down to play the Russian master Dus-Chotimirsky in the last round; I knew that he had received considerable coaching in anticipation of his game with me. My excitable opponent also showed signs of great nervousness. This amusing little game was the result of our meeting.

MARSHALL	DUS-CHOTIMIRSKY
White	Black
1 P—Q4	P—Q4

2 P—QB4	P—K3
3 Kt—KB3	P x P
4 P—K3	P—QR3
5 Kt—K5	. . . .

Steering away from book lines.

| 5 . . . . | Kt—Q2 |
| 6 Kt x Kt | . . . . |

A poor move which only develops Black's game. Simply 6 Kt x QBP was in order.

6	B x Kt
7 B x P	B—B3
8 O—O	B—Q3
9 Kt—B3	Q—R5

Black has developed with great rapidity.

| 10 P—B4 | Kt—B3 |
| 11 B—Q2 | Kt—Kt5 |

Already giving signs of suffering from a hallucination. . . . Kt—K5 was a good continuation.

| 12 P—KR3 | Q—Kt6?? |

Position after Black's 12th move

Dus-Chotimirsky

Marshall

My opponent made this move quickly, jumped up from his chair and went into the next room where most of the players were gathered.

In his broken English he said, "Poor Marshall dead!"

The players ran in and clustered round the table. I looked at the position and saw that he threatened mate in two ways, either with . . . Q x P ch or . . . Q—R7 ch. Very threatening, but the solution was simple enough. I just played:

| 13 Q x Kt | . . . . |

My opponent returned to the board and looked at what I had done. He threw over the pieces and in a loud voice exclaimed, "Oh, OH, Marshall not dead, I dead!"

---

71. San Sebastian, 1912
QUEEN'S GAMBIT DECLINED

A quiet positional game in which Black's minor inaccuracies finally add up to a major catastrophe.

F.J. MARSHALL   C. SCHLECHTER

White	Black
1 P—Q4	P—Q4
2 P—QB4	P—QB3
3 P x P	. . . .

A favorite continuation of mine. Black's game will not be so easy as first impressions seem to indicate.

3	P x P
4 Kt—QB3	Kt—KB3
5 Kt—B3	Kt—B3
6 B—B4	P—K3
7 P—K3	B—Kt5

This move does not exemplify Schlechter's usually excellent position judgment. Black's Pawn position is such that it condemns his QB to inactivity; hence he ought to retain his KB, playing . . . B—K2.

| 8 B—Q3 | O—O |
| 9 O—O | Kt—K2 |

The Knight maneuver loses time and accomplishes nothing of any value. Either ... Q—K2 or ... ... B—Q2 followed by ... R—B1 was in order.

10 R—B1	Kt—Kt3
11 B—Kt3	B—Q2
12 Q—Kt3	B x Kt
13 R x B	Kt—K5

Creating a serious weakness in his position; 13 ... B—B3 was safer, although White would maintain the initiative with Kt—K5.

| 14 B x Kt | P x B |

Position after Black's 14th move

Schlechter

Marshall

| 15 B—B7! | .... |

An important intermediate move. White wants to retake with the QP after a possible exchange of Knights on K5, in order to control Q6.

| 15 .... | Q—K2 |
| 16 Kt—K5 | B—B3? |

Not 16 ... Kt x Kt? 17 P x Kt winning the QKtP because of the threat of B—Q6 (see the previous note). But ... P—Kt3 was better than the text.

| 17 Kt x B | Q x B |

Hoping for 18 Kt x P, Q—R4 regaining the Pawn.

| 18 Kt—K5! | Q—Q3 |

Giving up a Pawn in order to diminish the pressure. If 18 ... Q—K2; 19 Kt x Kt, RP x Kt; 20 Q—B2, P—B4; 21 R—B7, Q—Kt5; 22 P—QR3, Q—Kt3; 23 R—B1 and Black will eventually succumb to the pressure.

| 19 Kt x Kt | RP x Kt |
| 20 Q x KtP | QR—Kt1 |

If 20 ... KR—Kt1; 21 Q x KP and wins.

| 21 Q x RP | R x P |
| 22 P—QR3 | .... |

White must stop to consolidate his position; once that is accomplished, the QRP will advance rapidly.

| 22 .... | Q—Q4 |
| 23 P—R3 | .... |

Creating a loophole and thus freeing White's Rooks for action.

| 23 .... | Q—R7 |

Threatening ... R x P!

24 R(3)—B1	Q—Kt6
25 P—QR4	R—R7
26 P—R5	Q—R6
27 R—B5	Q—Kt5
28 Q—R6	....

A new breathing spell to improve his position; but not 28 P—R6? Q—R5 winning the QRP.

| 28 .... | R—Kt1 |
| 29 Q—Q6 | Q—Kt2 |

White threatened R—B8ch.

| 30 KR—B1 | Q—Kt7 |
| 31 R(5)—B2! | R—R8 |

Absolutely forced. But White's reply is decisive.

| 32 Q x Rch | Q x Q |

33 R x R   Resigns

The QRP walks in.

---

72. San Sebastian, 1912

QUEEN'S GAMBIT DECLINED

Black runs into an inferior variation and is left with a permanently bad game.

F.J. MARSHALL   L. FORGACS

White   Black

1 P—Q4	P—Q4
2 P—QB4	P—K3
3 Kt—QB3	P—QB4
4 BP x P	KP x P
5 Kt—B3	Kt—QB3
6 P—KKt3	Kt—B3
7 B—Kt2	P x P

This exchange is questionable, for after the following recapture, White's KB strikes powerfully along the diagonal.

8 KKt x P   Q—Kt3

8 ... B—QB4 is better. The text neglects the development of the King-side, leaving Black's King in the center and exposed to hostile threats.

9 Kt x Kt   P x Kt

This exchange seems to have improved Black's prospects, for now his QP is no longer isolated. As will be seen, however, White's pressure on the long diagonal is stronger than ever.

10 O—O   B—K3

... B—KB4 would not prevent the advance of the KP, as there would follow 11 Q—R4 (threatening to capture the QP), R—Q1; 12 P—K4 with a very strong game.

11 P—K4!   ....

Reopening the diagonal and thus stamping the QBP as a serious

weakness. Black cannot reply 11 ... P—Q5 because of 12 Kt—R4, Q—Kt5 (if 12 ... Q—Q1; 13 P—K5!); 13 P—QR3, Q—Q3; 14 P—K5 etc.

11	Kt x P
12 Kt x Kt	P x Kt
13 B x P	B—QB4
14 Q—B2	QR—B1

White threatened P—QKt4!

15 B—B4   B—Q5

And here QR—B1 was threatened.

16 QR—K1!   O—O

Deciding to give up a Pawn; for if 16 ... P—Kt3; 17 B—Q5! or 16 ... Q x P; 17 B x Pch followed by Q—R4 with a winning advantage in either case.

17 B x Pch   K—R1
18 B—K5   ....

Position after White's 18th move

Forgacs

Marshall

White now seeks to work his Rook around to the KR file for a decisive attack. Thus if 18 ... Q x P? 19 B x B, Q x B; 20 R—R4, Q—Kt3; 21 R—KR4, P—Kt4; 22 B—Kt8ch etc.

18 ....   KR—Q1

If 18 . . . B x B; 19 R x B, P—
Kt3; 20 B x P, P x B; 21 Q x KtP
and wins.

| 19 B—B5! | QB x B |
| 20 Q x B | B x B |

If instead 20 . . . P—B3; 21 B x B,
Q x B; 22 R—K7 wins.

| 21 R x B | R—B1 |

Hastening the end, which, however, was already in sight; for
example 21 . . . Q x P; 22 KR—K1,
Q x P; 23 R(1)—K4 and there is
no defense.

| 22 Q—R3ch | K—Kt1 |
| 23 R—KR5 | Resigns |

If 23 . . . P—B3; 24 Q—K6ch
wins; if 23 . . . P—Kt3; 24 R—
R8ch, K—Kt2; 25 Q—R6ch wins;
if 23 . . . P—B4; 24 R—R8ch, K—
B2; 25 Q x Pch, K—K2; 26 R—K1
ch wins. A snappy affair!

---

73. Postyen, 1912

QUEEN'S GAMBIT DECLINED

Commenting on this game, Hoffer writes: "Masterly play, leading
up to a neat ending wherein White
is quite helpless. The play of
Marshall throughout reminds one
strongly of Pillsbury in his palmi-
est days."

My stout Russian opponent was
a great analyst, but as so often
happens, he did not possess the
same ability over the board.

S. ALAPIN	F.J. MARSHALL
White	Black
1 P—Q4	P—Q4
2 P—QB4	P—K3
3 Kt—QB3	Kt—KB3
4 B—Kt5	B—K2
5 P—K3	O—O
6 B—Q3	QKt—Q2
7 Kt—B3	P—QKt3

Having played against this de-

fense so many times, I had decided
to be on the receiving end for
once!

| 8 P x P | P x P |
| 9 O—O | . . . . |

As Rubinstein has shown in
some fine games, the continuation
Q—B2 followed by O—O—O is very
strong for White.

9	B—Kt2
10 R—B1	Kt—K5
11 B—KB4	P—QB4
12 Kt—Q2?	. . . .

What would Pillsbury have said
of this tame treatment of his pet
variation? Q—K2 should have been
played.

12	QKt—B3
13 B—K5	Kt x QKt
14 R x Kt	P—B5

Emboldened by his opponent's
rather weak continuation, Black
decides to play for the Queen-side
majority of Pawns. The proper
counter to this is the advance
P—K4; but, due to White's timid
play, it is not so easy to force
the move of the KP because of
the resulting weakness of White's
QP in most variations. Hence 14
P x Kt may have been preferable
on White's last move.

15 B—Kt1	P—QKt4
16 R—B1	R—K1
17 Q—B2	P—Kt3
18 KR—Q1	B—QB1

As the QB is not accomplishing
very much on Kt2, Black decides
to get rid of it by exchange. If
now 19 P—K4, Kt x P; 20 Kt x Kt,
P x Kt; 21 Q x KP, B—KB4 with
a good game.

19 Kt—B1	B—KB4
20 Q—Q2	B x B
21 R x B	Kt—K5
22 Q—K1	P—QR4

If Black holds his own in the

middle game, his Queen-side Pawns should prove decisive in the ending.

23 P—B3   B—Kt5!

Gaining time to keep the K file unobstructed, which will be an important factor in preventing P—K4.

24 Q—K2   Kt—Kt4

The Knight will have a useful retreat to K3.

25 B—Kt3   QR—B1
26 B—B2   B—Q3
27 Q—B2   Q—Q2
28 B—R4   Kt—K3
29 B—B6   . . . .

Still continuing the elaborate preparations for P—K4; if 29 P—K4, P x P; 30 P x P, Kt x P; 31 R x Kt, B—B4 and wins.

29 . . . .   Kt—B1

And now White could have played 30 P—K4; but after 30 . . . P x P; 31 P x P, Q—K3; 32 P—K5, B—K2; 33 B x B, R x B; 34 Kt—Kt3, P—B3 White's QP would become a serious weakness.

30 B—R4   P—B4

After this P—K4 is permanently out of the question, and Black can resume the march of the Queenside Pawns.

31 B—B2   . . . .

If 31 R—K1, P—Kt5; 32 P—K4? BP x P; 33 P x P, Q—Kt5 etc.

31 . . . .   P—Kt5
32 R—K1   P—R5
33 R—K2   P—Kt6
34 P x P   RP x P
35 Q—Q1   Kt—K3

White wanted to play B—K1—B3, but if now 36 B—K1, P—B5! 37 P x P, Kt x BP and . . . Kt—Q6 will be positionally decisive. Or if 37 P—K4, Kt x P! 38 R—Q2, P x P! 39 R x Kt, B—B4; 40 B—

B2, B x R; 41 Q x B, Q x Qch; 42 B x Q, P—K6 and the further advance of the KP wins a piece.

36 R—R1   Q—Kt2
37 K—R1   R—R1

Now Black obtains a new positional trump: control of the QR file.

38 R—Kt1   R—R7
39 B—K1   B—Kt5
40 B x B   . . . .

Hastening the end. He could have prolonged his resistance with B—Q2.

40 . . . .   Q x B
41 Q—K1   . . . .

If 41 Q—Q2, P—B6! But after the text, Black has a forced win.

41 . . . .   Q x Q
42 R(1) x Q   . . . .

If the other Rook recaptures, Black wins in the same way.

Position after White's 42nd move

Marshall

Alapin

42 . . . .   Kt x P!

Giving the Queen-side Pawns a chance to prove their worth.

43 P x Kt	R x R
44 R x R	P—B6
45 R—K1	R x P

Not 45 . . . P x P? 46 Kt—Q2, R—R8; 47 R—QKt1.

| 46 P—R4 | P—B5 |
| 47 K—Kt1 | R—QB7 |

White resigns; he is helpless.

---

74. Postyen, 1912

QUEEN'S GAMBIT DECLINED

White's dubious play in the opening enables Black to seize the initiative by sacrificing the exchange.

M. LOWTZKY	F. J. MARSHALL
White	Black
1 P—Q4	P—Q4
2 P—QB4	P—K3
3 Kt—QB3	Kt—KB3
4 B—Kt5	B—K2
5 P—K3	QKt—Q2
6 Kt—B3	O—O
7 R—B1	P—QR3

So that if 8 B—Q3, P x P; 9 B x P, P—Kt4; 10 B—Q3, P—B4 with a good game. However, I believe that 7 P x P, P x P; 8 B—Q3 gives White a slight positional advantage.

| 8 Kt—K5 | . . . . |

Premature.

8	Kt x Kt
9 P x Kt	Kt—Q2
10 B x B?	. . . .

B—B4 should have been played.

| 10 . . . . | Q x B |
| 11 P x P | . . . . |

After this Black has an easy game, but 11 P—B4 is answered by 11 . . . P x P; 12 B x P, Kt x P!

| 11 . . . . | Kt x P |
| 12 P—B4? | . . . . |

Weakening the KP. 12 B—K2 is best, but then Black gets the advantage with 12 . . . R—Q1; 13 Q—Kt3, P x P; 14 Kt x P, Q—Q3!

| 12 . . . . | Kt—Kt3 |
| 13 B—Q3 | . . . . |

Even now B—K2 was preferable.

13	R—Q1!
14 B x Kt	RP x B
15 Q—B3	P x P
16 Kt x P	. . . .

Position after White's 16th move

Marshall

Lowtzky

| 16 . . . . | R x Kt! |

"Marshall never hesitates to risk making a sacrifice when he sees it will give him a promising attack" (Burn).

| 17 Q x R | Q x Pch |

With White's King stuck in the center and thus permanently exposed to attack, Black has ample compensation for the exchange.

18 K—Q1	B—Kt5ch
19 K—B2	B—B4ch
20 K—Q1	Q x P

21 R—B4	Q—Kt4

Threatening to win the Queen with a Bishop check.

22 R—Q4	P—B3
23 Q—B3	R—K1
24 P—KKt4	. . . .

After which Black wins back the exchange. But the position was untenable in any event, for example 24 R—K1, B—B7ch etc.

24	B—K5!
25 Q—K2	. . . .

Or 25 R x B, Q—Q4ch etc.

25	Q—K4

Attacking both Rooks and thus forcing White's reply.

26 Q x B	Q x Q
27 R x Q	R x R

With two Pawns up, Black wins as he pleases.

28 P—KR3	P—KB4
29 K—Q2	K—B2
30 R—KKt1	K—B3
31 R—Kt3	R—Q5ch
32 K—B2	P—B5
33 R—Kt3	P—QKt4
34 P—KR4	P—Kt4
35 P—R5	K—K4
36 R—QR3	P—R4!

White resigns, as the KBP will soon cost the Rook.

---

75. Breslau, 1912

FRENCH DEFENSE

Perhaps you have heard about this game, which so excited the spectators that they "showered me with gold pieces!" I have often been asked whether this really happened. The answer is—yes, that is what happened, literally!

S. LEWITZKY	F.J. MARSHALL
White	Black
1 P—Q4	P—K3
2 P—K4	P—Q4
3 Kt—QB3	P—QB4

For other examples of this favorite variation of mine, see Games No. 28 and 52.

4 Kt—B3	Kt—QB3
5 KP x P	KP x P
6 B—K2	Kt—B3
7 O—O	B—K2
8 B—KKt5	. . . .

P x P is better. White does not handle the variation particularly well and Black soon has a fine position.

8	O—O
9 P x P	B—K3
10 Kt—Q4	B x P
11 Kt x B	. . . .

Weak. Black's Pawns are strengthened and the KB file is opened advantageously for Black. If White expected to profit from the "weakness" of the KP, he is soon undeceived.

11	P x Kt
12 B—Kt4	Q—Q3
13 B—R3	QR—K1
14 Q—Q2	. . . .

Another weak move, as Black promptly demonstrates. 14 P—R3 was decidedly better.

14	B—Kt5!

Now something has to be done about the threat of . . . P—Q5.

15 B x Kt	R x B
16 QR—Q1	Q—B4

Disposing of the threat of Kt—K4, and reviving the menace of . . . P—Q5.

17 Q—K2	. . . .

Feeling very uncomfortable because of the pin, White steers for what seems a clever exchanging combination. He could have put up a longer resistance with 17 P—R3, B x Kt; 18 Q x B, Q x Q; 19 P x Q — although it is clear that the ending would prove untenable.

17 ....   B x Kt
18 P x B   Q x P
19 R x P   ....

Regaining his Pawn, but losing the game. White's position can no longer be held.

19 ....   Kt—Q5
20 Q—R5   ....

Part of the combination: if 20 Q—K5, Kt—B6ch! 21 P x Kt, R—Kt3ch and wins.

20 ....   QR—KB1!

Better than 20 . . . P—KKt3? 21 Q—K5.

21 R—K5   ....

White must have relied on 21 R—QB5, overlooking 21 . . . R x P!

21 ....   R—R3
22 Q—Kt5   ....

Losing prettily, but if 22 Q—Kt4, Kt—B6ch wins easily enough.

22 ....   R x B
23 R—QB5   ....

Despair . . . but see what follows!

(see diagram next column)

23 ....   Q—KKt6!!!

The most elegant move I have ever played! The Queen is offered three ways, and White cannot accept the offer in any form: I 24 BP x Q, Kt—K7ch forcing mate; II 24 RP x Q, Kt—K7 mate; III 24 Q x Q, Kt—K7ch; 25 K—R1, Kt x Qch; 26 K—Kt1, Kt x R with a piece ahead.
Therefore:
White resigns.

Position after White's 23rd move

Marshall

Lewitzky

---

76. Breslau, 1912

SICILIAN DEFENSE

The first part of this game is of little interest because of White's feeble handling of the opening. But the second part abounds in lively play.

J. BREYER   F.J. MARSHALL
White   Black

1 P—K4   P—QB4
2 P—Q4   P x P
3 Kt—KB3   P—K3

Naturally I was not interested in maintaining the Pawn by getting a bad position after 3 . . . P—K4; 4 B—QB4 (not 4 Kt x KP?? Q—R4ch), followed by P—B3 etc.

4 Kt x P   Kt—KB3
5 Kt—QB3   B—Kt5
6 B—QKt5?   ....

Even as a youngster, Breyer had a leaning toward highly original moves; but this is going too far! Either 6 B—Q3 or Q—Q3 was in order.

6	Kt x P
7 O—O	Kt x Kt
8 P x Kt	B x P
9 R—Kt1	P—QR3
10 Kt—K2	B—B3

With two Pawns up and no technical difficulties, Black can win as he pleases; but the method actually selected is quite interesting.

11 B—Q3	O—O
12 Kt—Kt3	Kt—B3
13 P—KB4	B—Q5ch!

Utilizing the opportunity to put the Bishop on a more aggressive diagonal.

14 K—R1	P—B4
15 B—R3	R—B3
16 P—B3	B—R2

The Pawn could be taken, but Black is after bigger game.

17 B—Q6	P—QKt4
18 P—B4	R—R3

Threatening . . . R x Pch and mate next move.

19 P—KR3	B—Kt2

Threatening to win with . . . Kt—K4!

20 K—R2	Kt—Q5
21 P—QR4	Q—R5
22 P—B5	. . . .

This proves to be a futile attempt to block one of the attacking diagonals.

22	R—QB1!
23 P x P	P x P

If now 24 B x KtP, Kt x B; 25 R x Kt, B—R3 and wins.

24 R—Kt4	. . . .

(see diagram next column)

Having made all his preparations, Black is now ready to smoke out the White King.

Position after White's 24th move

Marshall

Breyer

24	B x KtP!

This cannot be answered by 25 R x Kt because of 25 . . . Q x Pch; 26 K—Kt1, Q x Kt and mate follows.

25 K x B	Q x Pch
26 K—B2	Q—R7ch
27 K—K3	Q x Ktch
28 K x Kt	P—K4ch!

This elegant move is decisive; if 29 K x P, R x B! etc.

29 P x P	R x Bch!
30 P x R	. . . .

30 K—B3, Q x Pch; 31 K—Kt3, Q—Q4ch is obviously hopeless.

30	R x P!
31 Q—Kt3ch	. . . .

Something has to be done about the threat of . . . Q—K4 mate. If 31 B—Kt1, Q—K4ch; 32 K—Q3, R—B6ch; 33 K—Q2, Q—K6 mate.

31	R—B5 dbl ch
32 K—Q5	R x R
33 Q x R	Q x Bch
34 K—K5	Q—K7ch

34 . . . B—B4 also does the trick. White resigned.

77. Match, 1912

PETROFF DEFENSE

During the quarter of a century from 1900 to 1925, Janowski and I must have played something like a hundred serious games. The following one is the most sparkling of the lot.

D. JANOWSKI	F.J. MARSHALL
White	Black
1 P—K4	P—K4
2 Kt—KB3	Kt—KB3
3 Kt x P	P—Q3
4 Kt—KB3	Kt x P
5 P—Q4	P—Q4
6 B—Q3	B—Q3
7 P—B4	....

A premature move, evidently played to avoid the variation which occurred in Game No. 62.

7 ....   B—Kt5ch

So that if 8 QKt—Q2, O—O; 9 O—O, B x Kt! 10 B x B, B—Kt5 with a fine game for Black.

8 K—B1   ....

But this has even less to recommend it.

8	O—O
9 P x P	Q x P
10 Q—B2	R—K1
11 Kt—B3?	....

This harmless-looking m o v e proves fatal. But also after 11 B x Kt, R x B; 12 Kt—B3, B x Kt followed by . . . B—Kt5, Black has the initiative.

| 11 .... | Kt x Kt |
| 12 P x Kt | .... |

(see diagram next column)

12 ....   Q x Kt!!

Before my opponent answered this surprise move, I heard him whisper, "Swindle!" He dare not

Position after White's 12th move

Marshall

Janowski

capture the Queen, for then Black mates with 13 . . . B—R6ch; 14 K—Kt1, R—K8ch; 15 B—B1, R x B mate.

| 13 P x B | Kt—B3 |
| 14 B—Kt2 | .... |

There is nothing better: 14 B—K3, B—R6; 15 KR—Kt1, R x B and wins.

14 ....   Kt x KtP!

And now a second combination, which leads to some interesting play.

15 B x Pch	K—R1
16 P x Q	B—R6ch
17 K—Kt1	Kt x Q
18 B x Kt	R—K7
19 R—QB1	QR—K1

Threatening . . . R—K8ch and also . . . R x B. White isn't given a moment's rest.

20 B—B3   R(1)—K6!?

Another inspired move, but the simpler 20 . . . R x B! 21 R x R, R—K3 finishes off the game at once.

21 B—Kt4   ....

If 21 P x R, R—Kt7ch; 22 K—B1, R x Bch (a little see-saw) followed by . . . R x Rch etc.

21 . . . .   R (6) x P!
22 B—Q1   R—B3!

White resigns. He has been punished drastically for his sins in the opening.

---

78. New York, 1913

(National Tournament)

QUEEN'S GAMBIT DECLINED

Black never has a chance after allowing his opponent to obtain the Queen-side majority of Pawns.

F.J. Marshall   O. Chajes

White	Black
1 P—Q4	P—Q4
2 Kt—KB3	Kt—KB3
3 P—B4	P—K3
4 P—K3	B—Kt5ch

An experiment which hardly seems worth-while. 4 . . . P—B4 is simple and good.

| 5 QKt—Q2 | O—O |
| 6 P—QR3 | B—Q3 |

Black's moves with this piece are unfortunate. . . . B—K2 was preferable.

7 B—Q3	QKt—Q2
8 O—O	P—QKt3
9 P—K4	P x KP
10 Kt x P	B—Kt2
11 Kt x B	P x Kt
12 B—B4	P—Q4?

A serious positional mistake which plagues Black for the remainder of the game. . . . Q—K2 was better, although White's game would remain freer.

| 13 B—Q6! | R—K1 |
| 14 P—B5 | P x P |

Black hopes to compensate for the hostile Queen-side majority by setting up a formidable center array; but it soon becomes clear that the center Pawns have little strength, since the advance of either one leaves them completely immobilized.

15 P x P	P—K4
16 B—Kt5	QR—B1
17 R—K1!	P—QR3
18 B—R4	B—B3
19 B x B	R x B
20 P—QKt4	P—K5

There is no other way to hold the KP. But now White's Knight takes up a magnificent position.

| 21 Kt—Q4 | R—QB1 |
| 22 Q—R4 | Kt—Kt5 |

He has nothing better, for if 22 . . . R—R1; 23 Kt—B6 wins the exchange. White could capture the RP at once, but he prefers to strengthen his position.

23 B—Kt3	P—KR4
24 Kt—B5	R—K3
25 QR—Q1	QKt—B3
26 Kt—Q4	R—K1
27 Q x P	R—R1
28 Q—Kt6!	. . . .

Decisive. If 28 . . . Q x Q; 29 P x Q and the queening of the QKtP wins at least the exchange.

(see diagram next page)

| 28 . . . | R x P |
| 29 P—R3! | Q x Q |

Or 29 . . . Kt—R3; 30 Q x Q, R x Q; and the Queen-side Pawns win easily.

| 30 P x Q | R x B |

With a sneaking hope that he may be able to hold his own on the Queen-side after the Bishop has been removed. But White has some neat tactical resources.

Position after White's 28th move

Chajes

Marshall

| 31 P x R | Kt—K4 |
| 32 Kt—B5 | K—B1 |

If 32 . . . R—Kt1; 33 Kt—K7ch followed by 34 Kt x P maintaining the advanced QKtP.

| 33 P—Kt7 | R—Kt1 |
| 34 R—R1 | P—Kt3 |

Of 34 . . . R x P; 35 R—R8ch, Kt—K1; 36 R x Ktch, K x R; 37 Kt—Q6ch etc.

35 R—R8	Kt(3)—Q2
36 R—QB1	Kt—B5
37 Kt—K3!	Resigns

If 37 . . . Kt—Q3; 38 R—B8ch etc.

---

79. New York, 1913

(National Tournament)

QUEEN'S GAMBIT DECLINED

This game starts out as a purely positional struggle, and yet Black's game collapses in amazingly short order!

F.J. MARSHALL   H. KLINE

White	Black
1 P—Q4	P—Q4
2 P—QB4	P—K3
3 Kt—QB3	Kt—KB3
4 Kt—B3	B—K2
5 B—Kt5	QKt—Q2
6 P—K3	O—O
7 R—B1	P—QKt3

. . . P—B3 has since become the favored move, mainly because it avoids any organic weaknesses.

| 8 P x P | P x P |
| 9 Q—R4 | . . . . |

An interesting move suggested by Duras. The idea is to bring about the exchange of Black's QB, in order to operate on the weakened white squares on Black's Queen-side.

| 9 . . . . | B—Kt2 |

Waste of time, since the Bishop will be exchanged very shortly. Modern theory therefore rightly favors the following Pawn sacrifice: 9 . . . P—B4! 10 Q—B6, R—Kt1; 11 Kt x P, Kt x Kt; 12 Q x Kt, B—Kt2; 13 B x B, Q x B; 14 Q—Kt5, Q x Q; 15 Kt x Q, P x P; 16 P x P, Kt—B3 with excellent positional compensation for the Pawn.

| 10 B—QR6 | B x B |
| 11 Q x B | P—B3? |

. . . P—B4 is better, although White would still be left with a clear positional advantage. After the weak text, the loss of a Pawn soon becomes compulsory.

(see diagram next page)

12 O—O	Kt—K5
13 B x B	Q x B
14 Q—Kt7!	KR—B1
15 Kt x P!	Q—Q3
16 R x P!	Resigns

Position after Black's 11th move

Kline

Marshall

---

80.   Havana, 1913

ALBIN COUNTER GAMBIT

One of my best games — an excellent example of positional maneuvering.

F.J. MARSHALL	D. JANOWSKI
White	Black
1 P—Q4	P—Q4
2 P—QB4	P—K4

To play t h i s counter-attack against a player of equal strength with the idea of gaining a point is ridiculous!

3 QP x P	P—Q5
4 Kt—KB3	Kt—QB3
5 P—KKt3	. . . .

Or 5 QKt—Q2.

5	B—K3
6 QKt—Q2	Q—Q2
7 P—QR3	KKt—K2
8 B—Kt2	Kt—Kt3

The crucial test of White's play in this opening is always whether or not Black can regain his Pawn

---

without incurring some positional disadvantage.

9 Q—R4	B—K2
10 Kt—Kt3	O—O—O

Black wants to have the QKtP protected when he finally plays to win the KP, but I like 10 . . . O—O here. It would then be unfavorable for White to play 11 KKt x P because of the continuation 11 . . . Kt x Kt; 12 Q x Q, Kt—B7ch; 13 K—Q1, B x Q; 14 K x Kt, Kt x P; and if 15 B x P?? QR—Kt1 followed by . . . B—QR5.

11 B—Kt5	K—Kt1
12 B x B	Q x B
13 O—O	B—Q2!

If 13 . . . KKt x P; 14 Kt x Kt, Kt x Kt; 15 B x P! with decisive advantage (15 . . . Kt x P; 16 B—Kt2 and Black's King is fatally exposed).

14 Kt—R5!	Kt x Kt

Good in appearance but actually bad is 14 . . . QKt x P; 15 Q—Kt3, Kt x Ktch; 16 Q x Kt, P—QB3 (if 16 . . . B—B1; 17 Kt—B6ch! P x Kt; 18 Q—Kt3ch, B—Kt2; 19 B x P and mate follows); 17 Q—Kt3 with considerable advantage.

15 Q x Kt	B—B3!

Very strong; White must now play the best moves to maintain the advantage.

16 KR—K1	P—Q6!

. . . B x Kt would be answered by 17 P x B. It would not be good to answer the text with 18 P x P? for then Black's Rooks would become too strong.

17 Q—Q2!	Q—B4
18 P x P	B x Kt
19 B x B	Kt x P

Black's position remains very menacing, and White must continue to play with great care.

20 R—K3	KR—K1

If 20 . . . Kt x BP? 21 Q—B3
wins. If 20 . . . Kt x Bch; 21
R x Kt, Q x BP; 22 P x Q, R x Q;
23 R x P still retaining his material
advantage.

| 21 QR—K1 | Q—Q5 |
| 22 B—Kt2! | P—KB3 |

Of course if 22 . . . Kt x BP? 23
Q—Kt4 is crushing.

23 R—K4!   . . . .

Decisive. Once the QP is able
to advance, Black's game deterior-
ates with terrible rapidity.

Position after White's 23rd move

Janowski

Marshall

23 . . . .   Q—Kt3

The pin on the Knight is fatal
for Black. Thus if 23 . . . Q x QP;
24 Q x Q, R x Q; 25 P—B4 etc. Or
23 . . . Q—Q2; 24 P—B4 leading
to a won ending for White.

24 P—Q4   . . . .

This highly desirable move comes
just at the right moment, for the
Knight still cannot move (24 . . .
Kt x P?? 25 R x R etc.). Black is
now driven back all along the line.

| 24 . . . . | R—KB1 |
| 25 Q—B3 | Kt—B3 |

26 P—Q5	Kt—K4
27 P—B5	Q—R3
28 B—B1!	. . . .

Up to now the Bishop has only
threatened to enter the game. But
this move leaves Black without
resource.

28	P—QKt4
29 P x P e.p.	Q—Kt2
30 P x BPch	Q x P
31 R—Kt4ch	Resigns

He must lose the Queen.

---

81.   Havana, 1913

PETROFF DEFENSE

This game was the deciding one
of the tourney. Capa staked all
to win and lost. The game is far
from perfect, but it reflects the
tense excitement of the occasion.

J.R. CAPABLANCA   F.J. MARSHALL

White	Black
1 P—K4	P—K4
2 Kt—KB3	Kt—KB3
3 Kt x P	P—Q3
4 Kt—KB3	Kt x P
5 P—Q4	P—Q4
6 B—Q3	B—Kt5
7 O—O	Kt—QB3

Deviating from my favorite 7 . . .
B—Q3. I felt that Capablanca
might have something up his sleeve
against that move, and I therefore
concluded that the text would be
more judicious.

8 P—B3   B—K2

Not best. 8 . . . B—Q3 should
have been played.

9 QKt—Q2   Kt x Kt

Although 9 . . . P—KB4 appears
good here, it might be difficult to
hold the position after 10 Q—Kt3

or 10 P—KR3 or 10 R—K1 or a combination of these moves.

10 B x Kt	O—O
11 P—KR3	B—R4
12 R—K1	Q—Q2?

A blunder; 12 . . . B—Q3 was better.

13 B—QKt5?   . . . .

He could have won a Pawn with 13 Kt—K5! Kt x Kt (not 13 . . . B x Q? 14 Kt x Q, KR—Q1; 15 Kt—K5! wins); 14 B x Pch, K x B; 15 Q x Bch etc.

13	B—Q3
14 Kt—K5!	B x Kt

I didn't like the looks of 14 . . . B x Q; 15 Kt x Q, KR—Q1; 16 QR x B, R x Kt; 17 P—QB4, B—B1; 18 P—B5 with a very superior position for White.

15 Q x B	B—B3
16 B—KB4	QR—K1
17 R—K3	R x R

An exchange which helps White to increase his command of the board. . . . R—K3 was preferable.

18 P x R	P—QR3
19 B—R4	P—QKt4
20 B—B2	P—Kt3
21 Q—B3	B—Kt2
22 B—QKt3	Kt—K2
23 P—K4!	P x P

Likewise after 23 . . . P—QB3; 24 R—K1 Black's game would remain uncomfortable.

24 Q x P	P—QB3
25 R—K1	Kt—Q4
26 B x Kt!	P x B

The foregoing exchange has enabled White to occupy the seventh rank with what should have been decisive effect. If instead 26 . . . Q x B; 27 Q x Q, P x Q; 28 R—K7 winning either the QP or the QRP.

27 Q—K7	Q—B1

. . . Q x Q loses a Pawn in short order, and if 27 . . . R—Q1?? 28 Q x Q, R x Q; 29 R—K8ch, B—B1; 30 B—R6 and mate follows.

28 B—Q6	P—R3

. . . R—Q1 (threatening . . . B—B1) appears better. Black's game has become quite difficult.

29 R—KB1!   . . . .

Threatening Q—R7 and thus creating a new weakness in Black's game.

29	P—B3
30 R—K1	R—Q1
31 B—B5	K—R2
32 Q—KB7	. . . .

The game was adjourned at this point for two days. I was a half-point ahead of Capa in the standing; to get first prize he would have to win this game, whereas a draw would give me undisputed first place. He has a winning position, but his anxiety eventually cost him the game.

32	Q—B4

Position after Black's 32nd move

Marshall

Capablanca

33 B—K7?   . . . .

A mistake, despite the fact that it not only attacks the Rook but threatens R—KB1 as well.

The proper course was 33 R—K7, R—KKt1; 34 R—R7, Q—B5 (threatening a perpetual check); 35 Q—B7! and Black is lost: if he declines the exchange of Queens, 36 B—B8 wins; if he exchanges Queens, the QRP or QP must fall.

33	Q—Q2!
34 K—B1	R—KB1
35 Q—K6	Q x Q

Black has not only succeeded in forcing an exchange of Queens in a manner unfavorable to his opponent; all the burdensome pressure on his position has been removed.

36 R x Q	R—K1
37 R—K2	K—Kt1
38 P—QKt3	K—B2
39 B—B5	R x R
40 K x R	P—B4

On entering the endgame, we find that Black has some advantage. My three Pawns on the Queen-side hold his four; whereas, on the King-side I shall be able to acquire a passed Pawn.

41 K—Q3	K—K3
42 P—B4	KtP x Pch
43 P x P	P—Kt4
44 P—Kt4	. . . .

This move has come in for severe criticism — in my opinion, unjustly so. True, it gives Black a passed Pawn; but it also fixes his King-side Pawns on black squares. The decisive mistake comes later on.

44	P—B5
45 B—Kt4	B—B3
46 B—B8	P x Pch
47 K x P	P—B6
48 P—Q5ch?	. . . .

The losing move. He could have drawn with 48 K—Q3; for example

48 . . . B x P; 49 B x P, K—B3; 50 B—B8, B—Kt3; 51 B—Q6 etc.

48 . . . .   K—K4

Now the damage has been done. White's QP is no match for the BP, which will have the active support of Black's King.

| 49 K—Q3 | K—B5! |
| 50 B—Q6ch | . . . . |

Or 50 P—Q6, K—Kt6! 51 B—K7, P—B7; 52 K—K2, K—Kt7 wins.

| 50 . . . . | B—K4 |
| 51 B—B5 | . . . . |

If 51 B x Bch, K x B; 52 K—K3, K x P, 53 K x P, K—Q5 and Black wins. A possible finish might be 54 K—K2, K—B6; 55 K—K3, P—QR4; 56 K—K2, P—R5; 57 K—K3, K—Kt7; 58 K—Q2, K x P; 59 K—B2, P—R6; 60 K—B1, K—Kt6; 61 K—Kt1, P—R7ch; 62 K—R1, K—R6; 63 P—R4, P x P; 64 P—Kt5, P—R6 and mate follows.

51	K—Kt6
52 K—K4	B—B5
53 P—Q6	P—B7

White resigns, for if 54 P—Q7, P—B8(Q); 55 P—Q8(Q), Q—B6ch; 56 K—B5 (or 56 K—Q4, Q—Q8ch), B—B2ch etc.

---

82.   Match, 1913
DANISH GAMBIT

Here is an echo of Game No. 68. There I adopted a Muzio Gambit in a match game, here I adopt an almost equally venturesome opening against an even stronger opponent.

F.J. MARSHALL	O. DURAS
White	Black
1 P—K4	P—K4
2 P—Q4	P x P
3 P—QB3	P x P

4 B—QB4   P x P
5 B x P   Kt—KB3

A little later, Schlechter was to introduce the superior defense 5 . . . P—Q4! 6 B x P, Kt—KB3! 7 B x Pch, K x B; 8 Q x Q, B—Kt5ch leaving Black with the better ending.

6 P—K5   P—Q4

This leads to a difficult game for Black. However, it is easy to understand that he did not relish retreating his Knight, which would have left him considerably in arrears with his development.

7 P x Kt!   P x B
8 Q x Qch   . . . .

The early exchange of Queens in such an opening as this, must have come as a great surprise to Black. However, White remains with a very strong attack and his powerful Pawn at KKt7 is bound to cause trouble.

8 . . . .   K x Q
9 P x P   B—Kt5ch
10 Kt—B3   R—K1ch

10 . . . R—Kt1 has been recommended, but after 11 O—O—Och Black is at a loss for a good reply. Thus if 11 . . . K—K1; 12 Kt—Q5 wins. If 11 . . . Kt—Q2 (or 11 . . . B—Q2); 12 Kt—Q5, B—Q3 (. . . B—K2 is answered in the same way); 13 Kt—B6! wins.

11 Kt—K2   B—KB4
12 O—O—Och   Kt—Q2
13 Kt—Q5   B—Q3
14 B—B6ch   Kt x B

The surrender of the exchange is compulsory, for if 14 . . . K—B1; 15 B—K7 with the same result (15 . . . B—K4; 16 B—B8).

15 Kt x Kt   . . . .

Position after White's 15th move

Duras

Marshall

15 . . . .   K—K2

The tricky alternative 15 . . . R x Kt?! is defeated by 16 P—Kt8(Q)ch, K—K2; 17 Kt—Q5ch, K—K3; 18 Kt x Pch! B x Kt; 19 R—Q6ch! etc.

16 Kt x R   R x Kt
17 R—Q4   K—B3

Black's King is still exposed to attack, and the advanced KKtP is still bothersome. Black's only hope of resistance lies in the two Bishops.

18 Kt—Kt3   B—R6ch
19 K—Q1   B—Kt3?

A serious loss of time. . . . B—Q6 should have been played at once.

20 P—B4   B—Q6
21 Kt—R5ch   K—Kt3
22 R—K1!   . . . .

A valuable gain of time, bringing the Rook into play at once.

22 . . . .   R—KKt1
23 R—Q5   P—KR3
24 R—K3   B—Kt7

White threatened 25 R—Kt3ch, K—R2; 26 Kt—B6 mate! But now White's Rooks gain the seventh rank, which will be fatal for Black's Pawns.

25	P—Kt4	B x P
26	P—B5ch	K—R2
27	R—K7	R—KB1
28	R x QBP	B—B6?

Shortens the agony; but after 28 . . . B—K5; 29 R(5)—Q7, B—B6ch; 30 K—B1, B x P; 31 Kt—Kt3, K—Kt1; 32 R x KtP White wins without much trouble.

| 29 | R x B | B—K4 |
| 30 | R x QBP | Resigns |

----

83. St. Petersburg, 1914

QUEEN'S GAMBIT DECLINED

This game begins as a positional battle, but it is soon enlivened by a clever combination on the part of my adversary. However, I go him one better, and he is left with a lost game.

F. J. MARSHALL   DR. O. S. BERNSTEIN

White	Black
1 P—Q4	P—Q4
2 P—QB4	P—QB3
3 Kt—QB3	Kt—B3
4 P x P	P x P
5 Kt—B3	P—K3
6 B—Kt5	. . . .

Played for variety's sake; the usual move is 6 B—B4. Black now gets the interesting notion of attempting to take advantage of the absence of this Bishop from the Queen-side.

6	Q—Kt3
7 Q—B2	Kt—B3
8 P—K3	B—Q2
9 P—QR3	R—B1
10 B—Q3	B—Kt5!?

A· clever move, typical of Bernstein's ingenious play. The idea is to answer 11 P x B? with 11 . . . Kt x KtP; 12 Q—Q2, Kt x Bch; 13 Q x Kt, Q x KtP. But White gains time with the following reply.

| 11 O—O | B x Kt |
| 12 P x B | Kt—QR4 |

Black has given his opponent a backward Pawn on an open file, but as Tarrasch notes in the Tournament Book, the position is not devoid of danger for Black, in view of White's open QKt file and the rather exposed position of Black's Queen.

13 QR—Kt1	Q—B3
14 KR—B1	Q—R5
15 Q—R2	Kt—K5

Beginning a combination which he expects will be decisive. And so it is, but not in the manner intended.

| 16 B x Kt | P x B |
| 17 Kt—K5! | P—B3 |

All according to plan.

| 18 R—Kt4! | R x P |

This is the move relied on; either 19 R x Q?? or 19 R x R?? would lead to mate, and in addition the QRP is attacked and White's minor pieces are both en prise.

(see diagram next page)

| 19 Q—Q2!! | R x Rch |
| 20 Q x R | . . . . |

Now comes the rude awakening. If 20 . . . Kt—Kt6; 21 Q—B7 wins. Black is lost.

20	O—O
21 R x Q	B x R
22 Q—B7	P—QKt3

Black's forces are so badly scattered that White has an easy win.

| 23 B—B4 | P x Kt |

Position after Black's 18th move

Dr. Bernstein

Marshall

| 24 B x P | R—B2 |
| 25 Q—Kt8ch | R—B1 |

The final moves now illustrate the tremendous power of the Queen against unorganized forces.

26 Q x RP	R—B2
27 Q—Kt8ch	R—B1
28 Q—B7	R—B2
29 Q—B8ch	R—B1
30 Q x Pch	Resigns

---

84. St. Petersburg, 1914

QUEEN'S GAMBIT

(*in effect*)

This was a very unusual kind of game, in which both players were continually called upon to make difficult decisions. I retain a memory of one curious quirk of the Doctor's: he always became very flushed when he was in a tight corner. There was a lot of flushing in this game!

DR. S. TARRASCH   F. J. MARSHALL

White   Black

1 P—Q4	P—Q4
2 P—QB4	P—K3
3 Kt—QB3	P—QB4

Good psychology. Tarrasch loved this defense, hence he did not like to play against it. This tendency was so pronounced that he did not care to play the strong Schlechter-Rubinstein Variation (as for example in Game No. 72), but instead favored an unduly conservative line, which he stubbornly claimed was best.

4 P—K3	Kt—KB3
5 Kt—B3	Kt—B3
6 B—Q3	QP x P
7 B x BP	P—QR3

Note that the opening has transposed into the realms of the Queen's Gambit Accepted.

8 O—O	P—QKt4
9 B—Q3	B—Kt2
10 P—QR4	P—B5!?

A fateful decision, which gives the whole game its specific character. Will the advanced Pawns prove strong or weak?

| 11 B—B2 | . . . . |

Turns out badly, as White's pieces are soon bottled up on the Queen-side. Better was (a) 11 P x P, P x P; 12 R x R, B x R; 13 B—Kt1 getting rid of the useless Rook or (b) 11 B—K2 with prospects of counter-action against the advanced Pawns.

11	P—Kt5
12 Kt—K4	B—K2
13 Q—K2	Kt—QR4
14 Kt x Ktch	P x Kt!

The logical recapture: it keeps White's Knight out of K5 and opens up the KKt file for counter-attack.

| 15 P—K4 | KR—Kt1 |
| 16 B—B4 | P—Kt6 |

White's QR will now be imprisoned until the 34th move!

17 B—Kt1	QR—B1
18 B—Q2	....

White naturally strives to undermine the protection of the Queenside Pawns.

18	Q—Kt3
19 R—B1	B—Kt5
20 B—B3	K—B1
21 Q—Q2	B x B
22 Q—R6ch	....

This has its pros and cons. White's forces are now badly divided, but his object was to prevent the maneuver . . . K—Kt2—R1.

22	K—K2

The King is safe here, contrary to appearances.

23 R x B	R—Kt3!

Position after Black's 23rd move

Marshall

Tarrasch

Tarrasch points out in the Tournament Book that 24 Q x P? would very likely be fatal for White because of his Queen's absence from the center. Here are two likely variations he gives:

I   24 Q x P? Kt—B3; 25 R x P! Kt x P! 26 R x R, Kt x Ktch; 27 K—B1, B x R; 28 P x Kt, Q—Q5 and wins.

II   24 Q x P? Kt—B3; 25 P—Q5, QR—KKt1! 26 P—Kt3, Kt—Q5; 27 P—K5, Kt—K7ch; 28 K—B1, Kt x R; 29 B x R, R x B; 30 P x Kt, B x P; 31 Kt—R4, B—K5; 32 Kt x Rch, B x Kt followed by . . . P—Kt7 and wins.

24 Q—R5	QR—KKt1
25 P—Kt3	R—Kt5!

In order to provoke the following weakening move.

26 P—R3	R(5)—Kt2
27 Q—R4	P—K4!

An aggressive parry to the threatened P—K5.

28 P x P	R x Pch
29 K—B1	R(6)—Kt3
30 P x Pch	Q x P
31 Q x Qch	....

I had expected 31 Q—R5 with a wild game in which both sides would have chances.

31	R x Q
32 Kt—Q2	B—B1
33 P—K5	....

Not 33 Kt x BP, Kt x Kt; 34 R x Kt, B x Pch; 35 K—K2, R—Kt7 with a winning advantage.

33	R—R3
34 B—K4	....

At last! It would still be bad to capture the QBP: 34 Kt x BP, Kt x Kt; 35 R x Kt, B x Pch followed by . . . R—Kt8.

34	B x Pch
35 K—K2	B—Kt5ch
36 K—K3	....

Not 36 P—B3, which would enable Black to double Rooks on the seventh rank by . . . R—R7ch and . . . B—R4.

36	R—R6ch
37 Kt—B3	B x Kt!
38 B x B	Kt—B3!

The object of the previous exchange was to free Black's Knight. The ending is difficult and interesting. Black must maintain his tactical threats in order to compensate for the prospective loss of the QBP and QKtP.

39 R—R1!   . . . .

If 39 R x BP?? R x Bch wins a piece.

39 . . . .   R x R
40 B x R   Kt x P
41 B—Q5   R—Kt5

Black's material advantage is deceptive, and the position is full of fight.

42 P—B4   K—Q3

So that if 43 B x QBP, Kt x Bch; 44 R x Kt, R—Kt7 winning the KtP with an easy victory.

43 B—K4   Kt—Q6!

Intending to answer 44 B x Kt with . . . R—Kt6ch and wins.

44 R x BP   R—Kt6ch
45 K—Q4   . . . .

If 45 B—B3, Kt—K8; 46 K—B2, R x Bch and wins.

45 . . . .   Kt x BP
46 R—B6ch   K—K2
47 R x P?   . . . .

A blunder which costs a piece. B x P would have drawn.

47 . . . .   Kt—K3ch!

If now 48 K—K5, R—Kt4ch; 49 B—B5, P—B3ch; 50 K—K4, Kt—B4ch etc.

48 K—B4   R—Kt5

A curious position: if 49 K—Q3, Kt—B4ch and if 49 K—Q5, Kt—B2 ch.

49 R—R7ch   K—Q3
50 K x P   . . . .

There is nothing better, for if 50 K—Q3, Kt—B4ch etc.

50 . . . .   R x B
51 R x P   Kt—B4ch
52 K—B2   R—K7ch
53 K—Q1   R—K2
54 R—B4   . . . .

If he swaps Rooks, the following position would eventually be reached: White: King on KR1, Pawns on QR5 and QKt2; Black, King on KKt6, Knight on QR3, Pawn on KR7. With White to move, the conclusion would be: 1 P—Kt4, Kt x P; 2 P—R6, Kt—Q6; 3 P—R7, Kt—B7 mate.

54 . . . .   R—R2
55 P—R5   R x P
56 P—Kt4   Kt—K3
57 R—KR4   R—Q4ch
58 K—B2   P—R4

White could have resigned here; the rest is given for the record: 59 K—Kt3, Kt—B2; 60 R—KB4, K—K4; 61 R—B7, Kt—Kt4; 62 R—B8, K—K5; .63 K—R4, Kt—Q5; 64 R—B7, R—Q1; 65 K—R5, R—KR1; 66 R—K7ch, K—Q4; 67 R—Q7ch, K—B3; 68 R—QR7, P—R5; 69 R—R6ch, K—Q4; 70 R—KB6, P—R6; 71 R—B1, P—R7; 72 R—KR1, K—K5; White resigns.

---

85. Mannheim, 1914

QUEEN'S GAMBIT DECLINED

This is the tournament which is famous for having been broken off abruptly by the opening of hostilities in World War I. Shortly after this game, my opponent bade me farewell and went off to the front.

F. J. Marshall   W. John

White   Black

1 P—Q4   P—Q4
2 Kt—KB3   Kt—KB3
3 P—B4   P—B3

4	P x P	P x P
5	Kt—B3	Kt—B3
6	B—B4	Kt—KR4

A radical method of at once getting rid of a piece which generally gives Black a lot of trouble (see Game No. 71!).

| 7 | B—K5 | P—B3!? |

The underlying idea is to gain possession of the center with his Pawns after getting rid of the Bishop.

| 8 | B—Kt3 | Kt x B |
| 9 | RP x Kt | P—K4 |

This cannot be answered by 10 P x P? because of . . . P—Q5! with a powerful attack.

To sum up the good and bad points of Black's strategy: he has gained the center, and a Bishop for a Knight — for which he has given White a dangerous open KR file and reconciled himself to certain tactical weaknesses on the King-side which temporarily impede his development.

| 10 | P—K3 | P—K5⁻ |

This is necessary, for should he insist on maintaining the tension in the center, his QP would become weak: 10 . . . B—K3; 11 Q—Kt3, Q—Q2; 12 R—Q1, R—Q1; 13 P x P, P x P (not 13 . . . P—Q5; 14 B—B4); 14 B—Kt5 — all of which indicates that . . . P—K5 is forced sooner or later.

11	Kt—Q2	B—K3
12	B—Kt5	P—QR3
13	B—R4	. . . .

White means to hold on to this Bishop, which should be useful in the event that an ending is reached; for most of Black's Pawns are on White squares and therefore vulnerable to the Bishop's attack.

13	. . . .	B—QKt5
14	QR—B1	QR—B1
15	P—R3	B x Kt

Depriving himself of the more useful of his two Bishops; . . . B—R4 seems preferable.

| 16 | R x B | P—QKt4 |
| 17 | B—Kt3 | K—K2 |

Protecting the Bishop against the threatened Kt x P, and preparing to bring the KR into play. Furthermore, the King is probably safer here than after castling into an open KR file.

| 18 | R—R4 | P—B4 |

Else Kt x P might again become feasible.

19	Q—R5	P—Kt3
20	Q—Kt5ch	K—Q2
21	Q x Qch	Kt x Q
22	R x R	K x R

I deliberately played for the ending, knowing that I had somewhat the better of it because of the theoretical advantage mentioned in the note to my thirteenth move.

| 23 | P—B3 | K—Q2 |
| 24 | P—Kt4 | Kt—B2 |

White strives to open up more lines for his pieces; but Black defends tenaciously.

25	KtP x P	KtP x P
26	P—Kt4	Kt—Q3
27	P—Kt5	K—K2
28	P—B4	Kt—B2
29	B—Q1	P—R3
30	P x P	R x P
31	R x R	Kt x R

Despite this simplification White still has the initiative.

| 32 | Kt—Kt3 | Kt—B2 |
| 33 | Kt—B5 | Kt—Q3? |

Usually so steady, John gets an "inspiration" here which costs him the game. He should have played 33 . . . B—B1 with good drawing chances.

| 34 | Kt x RP | Kt—B5 |

Regains the Pawn but loses the game.

35 K—K2   B—B2

If 35 Kt x KtP; 36 Kt—B7! maintains the advantage.

Position after Black's 35th move

John

Marshall

36 P—Kt3!   Kt x RP
37 K—Q2   K—Q3?

The only move to hold on was . . . P—Kt5, losing a Pawn but extricating the stranded Knight and considerably prolonging his resistance. White's reply seals the Black Knight's fate.

38 Kt—Kt4!   K—B2
39 K—B1   K—Kt3
40 K—Kt2   Kt—B5ch
41 P x Kt   QP x P
42 K—B3   K—R4
43 P—Q5   B—K1
44 P—Q6   K—Kt3
45 K—Q4   B—Q2
46 K—Q5   B—B1
47 Kt—B2   Resigns

An unconventional game all the way.

VI
CHAMPIONSHIP YEARS
(1915-1936)

86. New York, 1915

PETROFF DEFENSE

White's inexactitude in the opening leads to a quick catastrophe.

J. Michelsen   F. J. Marshall

White	Black
1 P—K4	P—K4
2 Kt—KB3	Kt—KB3
3 Kt x P	P—Q3
4 Kt—KB3	Kt x P
5 P—Q4	P—Q4
6 B—Q3	B—Q3
7 O—O	B—KKt5

8 Q—K2   . . . .

8 P—B4, with the idea of undermining the Knight, is stronger.

8 . . . .   P—KB4
9 P—B4?   . . . .

Too late now. Best was 9 P—KR3, B—R4; 10 P—KKt4! After this lapse, Black takes the initiative and decides the game with a few energetic strokes.

9 . . . .   Kt—B3!

If now 10 P—B5, Kt x QP! 11 Q—K3, Kt x Ktch; 12 P x Kt, P—B5; 13 Q—K2, B—KR6 (threatens . . .

Q—Kt4ch); 14 K—R1, B x R; 15 Q x B, Kt x P and Black has a winning position.

Position after Black's 9th move

Marshall

Michelsen

10 P x P	QKt x P
11 Q—K3	Kt x Ktch
12 P x Kt	Q—R5

What with his lack of development and exposed King-side, White has no defense against this sally. If 13 P—B4, B—B4; 14 Q—K1, B—B6 wins.

| 13 R—K1 | Q x RPch |
| 14 K—B1 | B—B4! |

Wins the Queen, for if 15 Q x B, Q—R8ch; 16 K—K2, Q x Pch; 17 K—B1, Q—R8 mate.

| 15 P x B | B x Q |

White could have resigned here. The remaining moves were: 16 B x B, Q—R6ch; 17 K—K2, Q x P ch; 18 K—B1, O—O; 19 Kt—Q2, Kt x Ktch; 20 B x Kt, Q—R6ch; 21 K—K2, QR—K1ch; 22 B—K3, P—B5; 23 R—R1, R x Bch; White resigns.

---

87. New York, 1915
FOUR KNIGHTS' GAME

White depends entirely too much on creating a positional weakness in my game; as it turns out, my attacking chances are more than enough compensation.

J. BERNSTEIN   F. J. MARSHALL

White	Black
1 P—K4	P—K4
2 Kt—KB3	Kt—KB3
3 Kt—B3	. . . .

What, no Petroff?!

3	Kt—B3
4 B—Kt5	B—Kt5
5 O—O	O—O
6 P—Q3	P—Q4

One of the many counter-attacks with which I have attempted to enliven this conservative opening.

7 P x P	Kt x P
8 Kt x Kt	Q x Kt
9 B x Kt	. . . .

I believe that 9 B—QB4! gives White a very good game. The text, it is true, gives White a favorable position for the endgame, but first he must survive the perils of the middle game.

9	P x B
10 Q—K2	R—K1
11 B—Q2	. . . .

P—Q4 can be answered effectively by . . . P—K5 or . . . B—Kt5. As for 11 Q—K4, Black simply replies 11 . . . B—Q3, after which the exchange of Queens would be all in his favor

| 11 . . . . | R—Kt1 |
| 12 B x B | . . . . |

White is anxious to rid his opponent of the weapon of the two Bishops, but in so doing he facilitates Black's chances of King-side attack.

| 12 .... | R x B |
| 13 P—QKt3 | R—Kt5 |

In view of the weakness of his Pawns, Black must play for attack.

| 14 KR—Q1 | P—QB4 |

Restraining P—Q4 for good, and also creating a good post for his Bishop.

15 Kt—K1	R—Kt3
16 Q—K4	Q—Q3
17 P—QB3	B—Q2
18 P—B3	....

In order to minimize the force of Black's next move; but the first King-side weakness is created thereby.

18	B—B3
19 Q—K2	R—R3!
20 P—KR3	....

The threat of . . . P—K5 has forced another weakness. Black steadily strengthens his position now in order to exploit the weaknesses.

20	R(1)—K3
21 R—Q2	R(K3)—Kt3
22 K—R1	....

K—B1 was probably a better way to parry the threat of . . . R x P.

| 22 .... | Q—K3 |

Already threatening 23 . . . R x P ch; 24 P x R, Q x P ch; 25 Q—R2, Q—B8ch and mate next move.

| 23 Q—B1 | .... |

If 23 Kt—B2, R x P ch; 24 P x R, Q x P ch; 25 Q—R2, Q x P ch and wins.

| 23 .... | R—Kt6! |
| 24 R—B1 | B—Q2! |

The KRP is the vulnerable target. White rushes reinforcements to his beleaguered King, but there is nothing to be done against the eventual sacrifice . . . B x P.

| 25 R(1)—B2 | .... |

The key variation here is 25 K—R2, Q—Kt3; 26 R(1)—B2, P—B4; 27 R—K2, P—KB5; 28 R x P, B x P! 29 P x B, R x P ch! 30 Q x R, R x Q ch; 31 K x R, Q—Kt6 mate.

| 25 .... | Q—KKt3! |
| 26 R—K2 | .... |

Or 26 K—R2, P—B4 followed by . . . P—KB5 as in the previous note.

Position after White's 26th move

Marshall

Bernstein

| 26 .... | B x P! |

Everything has been duly prepared, and the sacrifice is conclusive.

27 P x B	R(6) x P ch
28 R—R2	Q—Kt6
29 R x R	....

Or 29 Q—Kt1, R x R ch; 30 R x R, R x R ch; 31 Q x R, Q x Kt ch; 32 K—Kt2, Q—K7ch and the King and Pawn ending is an easy win.

| 29 .... | R x R ch |
| 30 Q x R | Q x Q ch |

As Black has a decisive material superiority, the rest is easy to understand. The game continued:

31 K—Kt1, P—B4; 32 R—K2, K—B2; 33 K—B2, P—KR4; 34 K—Kt1, Q—Kt6ch; 35 K—B1, P—R5; 36 R—Kt2, Q—B5; 37 K—K2, P—R6; 38 R—Kt1, Q—R7ch; 39 K—B1, Q x P; 40 R—R1, P—R7; 41 P—QB4, Q—Q7; White resigns.

---

88. New York, 1915

PETROFF DEFENSE

An interesting game after a rather dull beginning. The final phase is featured by a deep endgame conception.

A. KUPCHIK	F. J. MARSHALL
White	Black
1 P—K4	P—K4
2 Kt—KB3	Kt—KB3
3 Kt x P	P—Q3
4 Kt—KB3	Kt x P
5 Q—K2	Q—K2
6 P—Q3	Kt—KB3
7 B—Kt5	. . . .

As is well known, 7 Q x Qch makes the draw almost certain.

7	B—K3
8 Kt—B3	P—KR3
9 B—R4	P—KKt4

Black intends to castle Queenside, hence he need not fear any weakening effect from this advance. Furthermore, it makes possible the fianchetto development of his KB, and leaves White's QB rather out of play.

10 B—Kt3	B—Kt2
11 P—Q4	Kt—B3
12 O—O—O	. . . .

Threatening P—Q5. Note that Black has purposely avoided . . . P—Q4, partly in order to have this square available for his pieces and partly to avoid White's pieces having access to K5.

12	Kt—Q4!

So that if 13 Kt x Kt, B x Kt; 14 Q x Qch. K x Q with quite a favorable ending for Black: if 15 P—B3 (the threat was . . . B x Kt followed by . . . Kt x P), B x RP and if 15 B—K2, P—B4!

13 Kt x Kt	B x Kt
14 Q—Kt5	B x Kt
15 P x B	O—O—O
16 P—B3	K—Kt1
17 B—Q3	P—Q4
18 P—KB4	P—KR4

As previously forecast, White's QB plays an insignificant role.

19 KR—K1	Q—B3
20 P x P	Q x Pch
21 P—B4	Q—B3
22 P—B5	P—R5
23 B—K5	Q—R3ch
24 K—B2	B x B

Black continues in quiet positional fashion, and wins a Pawn now. At first sight it seems that he can win a piece with 24 . . . P—B3, but White has the resource of 25 KR—Kt1! P x B; 26 R—Kt6, Q—R2; 27 R x Kt, P—K5; 28 B—K2, Q x P and Black has won only a Pawn after all, and with Bishops of opposite color on the board, at that.

25 P x B	KR—K1
26 B—B1	Q—B5

White cannot save the Pawn, for if 27 R x P? Q—B7ch; 28 K—Q1, R x Rch; 29 Q x R, R—Q1 winning the Queen.

27 P—K6	P x P
28 P x P	R x P
29 R x R	Q—B4ch
30 Q—Q3	Q x R

Despite the win of the Pawn, Black now has considerable technical difficulties, because the position has been considerably simplified and because White's pieces are posted to good advantage.

31 B—Kt2	Kt—K2

32 R—Q2	P—B3
33 R—K2	Q—Q3
34 Q—Q4	Kt—Kt3
35 R—B2	Q x P!

This involves a far-sighted sacrifice of a piece; but if 35 ... Q—K4; 36 R—B6! with very strong drawing chances.

| 36 B—K4 | .... |

If now 36 ... Q—Kt8; 37 R—B8! Q—R7ch (not 37 ... Q x Q? 38 R x Rch, K—B2; 39 P x Q, K x R; 40 B x Kt and wins); 38 R—B2 and Black must go in for 38 ... Q—Kt6.

Or 36 ... Q—Q3; 37 R—B6, Q—R7ch; 38 R—B2 and again Black must resort to ... Q—Kt6.

Position after White's 36th move

Marshall

Kupchik

36	Q—Kt6!
37 R—Kt2	Q—B5!
38 B x Kt	Q x Q
39 P x Q	P—R6!

The point. If White plays 40 R—R2, then 40 ... R—Kt1 and the Bishop cannot retreat! Or if 40 R—Kt1 or 40 R—Kt5, Black replies 40 ... R—Kt1 followed by the winning advance of the KRP. Finally, if 40 R—Kt4, R—R1! 41

R—Kt1, R—Kt1! transposing into the same line.

40 R—K2	R—R1
41 R—K1	P—R7
42 R—KR1	R—Kt1
43 B—R5	....

Or 43 B—Q3, R—Kt7ch; 44 K—B3, K—B2 and Black wins by bringing his King to KKt6.

| 43 .... | R—Kt7ch |
| 44 K—Q3 | .... |

Interesting would have been 44 K—B3, K—B2; 45 P—R4, K—Q3; 46 P—Kt4, K—K3; 47 K—Q3, K—B4; 48 K—K3, R—Kt6ch (if 48 ... K—Kt4; 49 K—B3!); 49 K—B2, R—KR6; 50 B—Q1, K—B5 and wins; for example 51 K—Kt2, R—R1; 52 R x P, R x Rch; 53 K x R, K—K6; 54 K—Kt2, K x P; 55 K—B3, K—B5 and Black gets two connected passed Pawns, which must win for him.

44	R x P
45 B—K2	R x P
46 R x P	R—R6ch

This variation is likewise won for Black. The Pawns are too strong.

47 K—B2	P—R4
48 K—Kt2	R—K6
49 K—B2	P—Kt4
50 B—Q3	K—B2
51 R—R8	P—R5
52 R—R8	R—Kt6
53 R—R7ch	K—Kt3
54 R—R8	K—Kt2
55 R—KB8	P—Kt5!

A very important move, for now White's King is cut off from QB3, whereupon ... R—Kt5 becomes a real menace. If 56 B—K2, R—B6 ch with a winning position, likewise if 56 R—B2, R—Kt5 etc.

56 R—B7ch	K—Kt3
57 R—B8	R—Kt7ch
58 K—B1	P—R6!

59 R—Kt8ch	K—B2

White cannot play 60 R x P because of 60 . . . R—Kt8ch; 61 K—B2, P—R7 etc. Black now proceeds to take the remaining White Pawn, after which there is no more play left.

60 R—QR8	R—Kt5
61 K—B2	R x P
62 B—K2	R—K5
63 B—Q3	R—K6
64 R—R4	P—B4
65 K—Q2	R—Kt6
66 R—R5	P—B5
67 B—B5	K—Q3
68 B—B8	P—R7
69 B—Kt7	P—Kt6
Resigns	

---

89. New York, 1915

DANISH GAMBIT

For many years I played this opening in simultaneous and blindfold exhibitions with great success. However, I went to the well too often. The defenses to the Gambit were published and were available to the weaker players. When it was announced that Marshall was coming to give a "simultaneous," the boys all studied up the best defense. I finally gave it up!

Here is one of the games I played in a blindfold exhibition in which both players were without sight of the board.

F. J. MARSHALL   A. SCHROEDER

White	Black
1 P—K4	P—K4
2 P—Q4	P x P
3 P—QB3	P—Q4

A good way to decline the gambit.

4 KP x P	Q x P
5 P x P	P—QB4?

6 Kt—QB3!	. . . .

Sacrificing a Pawn for attack.

6	Q x QP
7 B—Kt5ch	B—Q2
8 Q—K2ch	B—K2
9 Kt—B3	Q—KKt5

Black is in great danger. If 9 . . . B x B; 10 Kt x B, Q—Q1; 11 B—B4, Kt—QR3; 12 R—Q1 or 10 . . . Q—Kt5ch; 11 B—Q2, Q x P; 12 O—O—in either case with a winning position for White.

10 Kt—Q5	K—Q1

Forced. But it is clear that Black's King cannot hold out long in the center in such an open position.

11 B—KB4	B x B
12 Q x B	Q—K3ch
13 B—K5!	. . . .

Very powerful. If now 13 . . . P—B3; 14 O—O—O! wins easily.

13	Q—QB3
14 Q x Q	P x Q

Or 14 . . . Kt x Q; 15 B x P etc.

15 Kt—B7	Kt—B3
16 Kt x R	Kt—R3
17 O—O—Och	K—B1
18 KR—K1!	Kt—Q4

The remaining play revolves about Black's vain attempt to capture the stranded Knight. If 18 . . . K—Kt2; 19 Kt—B7! Kt—QKt1; 20 B—Kt3, B—Q1; 21 Kt—K8! and wins.

(see diagram next page)

19 Kt—B7!	. . . .

Pretty and unexpected. The hitherto imprisoned Knight does his part, for if 19 . . . Kt(4) x Kt; 20 B x Kt and White remains a Rook ahead. Hence Black tries a different way.

Position after Black's 18th move

Schroeder

Marshall

19	Kt(3) x Kt
20 B x Kt	K x B
21 R x Kt	P x R
22 R x Bch	Resigns

---

90.   New York, 1918

INDIAN DEFENSE

Realizing that his position is lost, Janowski tries a desperate and ingenious swindle. Fortunately I have the resources to turn the sacrifice to my advantage.

F. J. MARSHALL   D. JANOWSKI

White   Black

1 P—Q4	Kt—KB3
2 Kt—KB3	P—Q3
3 P—B4	QKt—Q2
4 Kt—B3	P—K4
5 B—Kt5	. . . .

Nowadays 5 P—K4 and 5 P—KKt3 are the favored moves. But at the time this game was played, the best lines of play had not yet been evolved.

| 5 . . . . | B—K2 |
| 6 P—K3 | O—O |

7 Q—B2	R—K1
8 P x P!	P x P
9 O—O—O!	. . . .

An excellent idea. Black's position is so cramped that no counter-attack need be feared. White, on the other hand, has the undeniable advantages of attacking prospects and pressure on the Q file. The immediate threat is 10 Kt x P.

| 9 . . . . | B—B1 |
| 10 B—Q3 | P—KR3 |

B x Pch was threatened.

| 11 P—KR4! | P—B3 |

He cannot very well play 11 . . . P x B, for then 12 P x P regains the piece with a strong attack (12 . . . Kt—Kt5; 13 B—R7ch, K—R1; 14 B—Kt8ch and mate follows).

| 12 B x Kt! | . . . . |

Black was on the point of playing . . . Q—B2, but the text compels him to recapture with the Queen, leaving him in an awkward position.

| 12 . . . . | Q x B |
| 13 Kt—KKt5! | Kt—B4 |

Not 13 . . . P x Kt? 14 P x P and wins (14 . . . Q x KtP; 15 B—R7 ch, K—R1; 16 B—Kt8ch and mate follows).

| 14 B—R7ch | K—R1 |
| 15 P—QKt4! | P—K5 |

Avoiding the winning attack which would come after the retreat of the Knight, for example 15 . . . Kt—K3; 16 QKt—K4, Q—K2; 17 Kt—Q6, P x Kt; 18 P x P, Kt x P; 19 B—Kt6ch, B—R6 (if 19 . . . K—Kt1; 20 B x Pch wins); 20 R x B ch, Kt x R; 21 Kt x Pch, K—Kt1; 22 B—R7ch, K x Kt; 23 Q—Kt6 mate; or 15 . . . Kt—R3; 16 QKt—K4, Q—K2; 17 Kt—Q6, B—K3; 18 B—Kt8, P—KKt3; 19 B x P and wins.

| 16 P x Kt | B x P |

17 KKt x P   . . . .

B x P wins much more simply, as
the KKt cannot then be captured.

17	B—R6ch
18 K—Kt1	Q—K2
19 Kt—Q2	P—KKt3
20 B x P	P x B
21 Q x P	Q—Kt5ch

As the position is lost in any
event, Black tries a clever combination, which unfortunately has a
flaw.

22 Kt—Kt3	Q x Kt?!
23 Q x Rch	K—Kt2

Position after Black's 23rd move

Janowski

Marshall

White has no Queen check, and
if he tries to prevent the mate with
24 R—Q2? then Black wins with
. . . .B—B4ch. However . . .

24 R—Q7ch!   . . . .

This is the move that Black overlooked.

24	B x R
25 Q x Bch	K—Kt1
26 Q—Q4	. . . .

The mate is covered now and
White wins easily.

26	Q—Kt5
27 P—B5!	Q—Kt4
28 Q—Kt4ch	K—B1
29 R—Q1	R—K1
30 Q—B5ch	K—Kt1
31 Q—Kt6ch	K—B1
32 Q x Pch	K—Kt1
33 Q—Kt6ch	K—B1
34 ·Q—Q3	Q—Kt5

Since the exchange of Queens is
quite hopeless, Black prefers to
shorten the agony.

35 Q—Q4	Q—Kt4
36 Q—R8ch	K—B2
37 R—Q7ch	Resigns

---

91. New York, 1918

CENTER COUNTER GAMBIT

White misses too many chances
for equality and finally finds himself in a hopeless predicament.

O. CHAJES	F. J. MARSHALL
White	Black
1 P—K4	P—Q4
2 P x P	Kt—KB3
3 P—Q4	. . . .

After 3 P—QB4, P—QB3; 4 P x
P, Kt x P; 5 Kt—KB3, P—K4
White is a Pawn ahead, but his
position is a difficult one. The
best line is 3 B—Kt5ch! B—Q2; 4
B—B4, B—Kt5; 5 P—KB3, B—B4;
6 Kt—B3, QKt—Q2; 7 KKt—K2,
Kt—Kt3; 8 P—Q3, QKt x P; 9 Kt x
Kt, Kt x Kt; 10 Kt—Kt3, B—Kt3;
11 P—B4, P—K3; 12 O—O with a
fine game for White.

3	Kt x P
4 Kt—KB3	B—Kt5
5 B—K2	P—K3
6 O—O	QKt—B3
7 P—B4	Kt—Kt3
8 B—K3	B—K2

There is nothing to be gained

from 8 . . . B x Kt; 9 B x B, Kt x
BP; 10 Q—R4 etc.

| 9 Kt—B3 | O—O |
| 10 Q—Q2 | . . . . |

Needlessly weakening his Pawn
position. Simply P—QKt3 was in
order, avoiding the obligatory recapture with the KKtP next move.

10	B x Kt
11 P x B	P—B4
12 QR—Q1	P—K4
13 P—Q5	. . . .

Simpler and better was 13 P x P.
In an ending the exposed position
of White's King would not be serious, and it might be possible for
the two Bishops to make their
presence felt.

| 13 . . . . | Kt—R4 |
| 14 B x Kt? | . . . . |

A final mistake. This exchange
should have been avoided in favor
of 14 P—Kt3, and if then 14 . . .
P—B5; 15 B x Kt. In that case
White would at least have the consolation of greater mobility for his
KB after an eventual B—Q3. And
in addition, Black's Bishop would
have been shut out.

14	RP x B
15 K—R1	B—Kt4!
16 Q—B2	B—B5

Now White's sins come home to
roost. He is powerless against the
following attack.

17 KR—Kt1	Q—R5
18 R—Kt2	R—B3
19 QR—KKt1	R—KR3!

(see diagram next column)

Confronted by the threat of 20
. . . Q x Pch; 21 R x Q, R x R mate,
White indulges in a spite check.

| 20 R x Pch | K—R1 |

White resigns. If 21 R(7)—Kt2,
Q x Pch etc. If 21 R(1)—Kt2,
B x P wins.

Position after Black's 19th move

Marshall

Chajes

---

92. New York, 1920
(Metropolitan Chess League)

RUY LOPEZ

Over the years I have played
many interesting games in the
Metropolitan Chess League
matches, in which many of America's finest players have partici-
pated. The following game was
one of the most thrilling I have
played in these contests.

C. JAFFE	F. J. MARSHALL
White	Black
1 P—K4	P—K4
2 Kt—KB3	Kt—QB3
3 B—Kt5	P—QR3
4 B—R4	Kt—B3
5 Q—K2	. . . .

An old move which was to become quite fashionable a few years
later.

| 5 . . . . | B—B4 |
| 6 P—B3 | O—O?! |

A doubtful Pawn sacrifice, since
it is not clear just how Black is to

recover his Pawn after 7 B x Kt,
QP x B; 8 Kt x P, R—K1; 9 P—Q4
etc. 6 . . . P—QKt4 was more accurate.

7	O—O	P—QKt4
8	B—Kt3	P—Q3
9	P—QR4	. . . .

Frequently played in conjunction
with White's fifth move. As I did
not care to yield my opponent the
QR file with 9 . . . R—Kt1, the following advance was in order.

| 9 | . . . . | P—Kt5 |
| 10 | P—R5 | . . . . |

Preventing either . . . P—QR4
or . . . Kt—QR4. But he does not
profit much by the move.

10	. . . .	B—Kt5
11	P—Q3	R—Kt1
12	B—QB4	Q—B1

Not only guarding the QRP but
reserving the possibility of utilizing the Queen on the other wing.

| 13 | B—KKt5 | . . . . |

This has no great value. B—K3
was preferable.

| 13 | . . . . | Kt—K2 |

Black does not fear the doubling
of his Pawns, as he would thereupon have the open KKt file at
his disposal. The QKt is headed
for KB5.

| 14 | QKt—Q2 | Kt—Kt3 |
| 15 | Kt—Kt3 | P x P! |

Black operates on both wings—
the open QKt file will be useful
later on. If now 16 Kt x B, P x P!

| 16 | P x P | B—R2 |
| 17 | P—Q4 | . . . . |

Black's QRP is doomed; but he
has more than enough compensation on the other wing.

| 17 | . . . . | Kt—R4! |
| 18 | B x P | . . . . |

If instead 18 P—Kt3 (to prevent
. . . Kt—B5), P x P! 19 P x P, P—
B4! and Black's Knight comes to
K4 with fatal effect; or 19 QKt x P,
Kt—K4 and there is no defense
against KB x Kt.

| 18 | . . . . | B x Kt! |

Just at the right moment. If now
19 Q x B, Q x B; 20 Q x Kt, R x Kt
winning a piece. Thus the value
of Black's 15th move becomes apparent.

19	P x B	Q—R6
20	KR—Kt1	Kt(4)—B5
21	Q—B1	Q x P
22	P—R4	Kt—R6ch
23	K—R2	Kt x B
24	P x Kt	Kt—B5

White's King cannot escape, but
the remaining play is still quite interesting.

25	Kt—Q2	Q—R4ch
26	K—Kt3	Q x Pch
27	K—B3	R x R
28	R x R	P—KB4!

Opening a new line against
White's bedeviled King.

| 29 | R—Kt7 | P x P! |

Threatening . . . Q—Kt5 mate.

| 30 | BP x P | B x P! |
| 31 | Q—B4ch | . . . . |

Has Black miscalculated?!

(see diagram next page)

| 31 | . . . . | P—Q4!! |

This resource had to be foreseer
on move 28.

| 32 | Q x B | BP x Pch |
| 33 | Kt x P | . . . . |

Or 33 K—K3, Kt—K3ch.

| 33 | . . . . | Kt—K3ch |

White resigns; his Queen is lost
with check.

Position after White's 31st move

Marshall

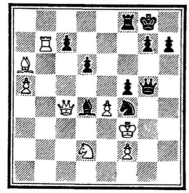

Jaffe

---

93. Atlantic City, 1920

(Best-played game prize)

BUDAPEST DEFENSE

A simple but somewhat subtle game. Although it is very quiet on the surface, I believe that the manner in which White manages to obtain and preserve a slight but winning advantage, is rather remarkable.

F. J. MARSHALL	S. T. SHARP
White	Black
1 P—Q4	Kt—KB3
2 P—QB4	P—K4

A defense which was at this time quite a novelty. I therefore determined to play safe, responding with a sound move, which, to be sure, leaves Black with a perfectly good game.

3 P—K3	P x P
4 P x P	P—Q4
5 Kt—KB3	B—Kt5ch
6 B—Q2	B x Bch
7 QKt x B	O—O
8 B—K2	P x P

Giving White an isolated QP, but also increasing his mobility.

9 Kt x P	Kt—B3
10 O—O	B—Kt5
11 Kt(4)—K5	B x Kt
12 Kt x B	Q—Q4

I should have preferred ... Kt—Q4 here. Black wants to increase his pressure on the QP, but, as will be seen, White has counterplay.

| 13 Q—R4 | QR—Q1 |
| 14 QR—B1! | .... |

In such situations my preference is always for an energetic counterstroke, rather than for a laborious defensive move such as KR—Q1.

| 14 .... | Kt x P |

The exchange of the rather sickly QP for the healthy QBP is of course quite pleasant for White; but Black probably has little choice, for on other moves, the possibility of B—Kt5 is annoying.

15 Kt x Kt	Q x Kt
16 Q x Q	R x Q
17 R x P	R—Q7

At first sight one would be inclined to put this position down as a quick draw, with a massacre of the Queen-side Pawns in the offing. But White sees a ray of hope in the superiority of his far-ranging Bishop against the rather limited Knight.

| 18 B—B4! | Kt—K1 |

The crucial variation was 18 ... R x KtP; 19 B—Kt3, P—QR4; 20 R x KtP, P—R5; 21 B x Pch and wins.

(see diagram next page)

| 19 R—K7! | .... |

Playing for a win. After 19 R x KtP Black has an easy draw with 19 ... Kt—Q3; 20 R—B7, Kt x B; 21 R x Kt, R x KtP etc.

Position after Black's 18th move

Sharp

Marshall

| 19 . . . . | Kt—Q3 |
| 20 B—Kt3 | R—Q1 |

. . . .R x KtP at once would lead to much the same kind of play. White regains his Pawn advantageously by doubling on the seventh rank.

21 R—B1!	R x KtP
22 P—KR3	P—KR3
23 R(1)—B7	R—KB1
24 R(B7)—Q7	Kt—B4
25 R x BP	R x R
26 B x Rch	K—B1
27 B—Kt6	. . . .

B—Kt3 is even more convincing, but the text does the trick.

| 27 . . . . | Kt—R5 |
| 28 B—K4 | P—KKt3 |

P—Kt3 was threatened.

29 R x P	R x RP
30 P—Kt3	Kt—B4
31 B x Kt	P x B
32 R—Kt5	P—QR4
33 R x Pch	K—Kt2

The ending is an easy win.

| 34 K—Kt2 | P—R5 |

| 35 R—QR5 | P—R6 |

The QRP looks nasty, but it can be stopped easily enough. White's winning plan is very simple. He advances his Pawns to the fourth rank and then brings his Rook to R6, preventing Black's King from coming to the third rank. Then White advances two Pawns to the fifth rank, forcing Black's King to the first rank with a check at QR7. The two Pawns then proceed to the sixth rank and Black's resistance is at an end.

36 P—Kt4	R—R8
37 P—R4	P—R7
38 P—B4	K—B2

On . . . K—Kt3 there simply follows R—R6ch, according to the winning method sketched above.

40 P—Kt5	RP x P
41 RP x P	K—Kt2
42 P—B5	Resigns

If 42 . . . K—B2; 43 R—R7ch, K—B1; 44 P—B6, K—Kt1; 45 P—Kt6, etc.

---

94. New York, 1921
GRECO COUNTER GAMBIT

This is a game from one of the many tourneys arranged by Edwin Dimock of New London for the purpose of testing various gambits.

As for my opponent, I first met him in Abo, Finland many years ago, when he was a very young man. Today he is a worthy and respected citizen of the U. S. A., but he has also had many honors conferred on him by the land of his birth for interesting America in Finnish problems. A former champion of the Marshall Club, and a very strong amateur, he can be counted on to give any master a tough fight.

F. J. MARSHALL	B. FORSBERG
White	Black
1 P—K4	P—K4

2 Kt—KB3	P—KB4
3 B—B4	. . . .

3 Kt x P is the simplest way to obtain an advantage.

3	P x P
4 Kt x P	P—Q4

Risky; . . . Q—Kt4! is customary.

5 Q—R5ch	P—Kt3
6 Kt x P	Kt—KB3
7 Q—K5ch	B—K2
8 B—Kt5ch	B—Q2
9 Kt x R	. . . .

If 9 B x Bch, QKt x B; 10 Q x B ch, Q x Q; 11 Kt x Q, K x Kt and Black's splendid position offers some compensation for his Pawn minus.

9	B x B
10 Kt—B3	B—R3

In order to prevent White from castling; but this Bishop is soon reduced to inactivity.

11 P—Q3	Kt—B3

If 11 . . . P x P; 12 B—Kt5 with a strong attack.

12 Q—Kt3	B—Q3?

Driving the Queen to a better square. Either 12 . . . Kt—Q5, with complications, or 12 . . . Q—Q2, intending . . . O—O—O, was in order.

13 Q—R4	P—Q5?

It had already become difficult to find a satisfactory continuation, but this makes matters worse.

14 Kt x P	B—K2
15 Kt x Ktch	B x Kt
16 Q—R5ch	K—Q2
17 Q—R3ch	. . . .

The right way was 17 Q—B5ch, K—K1; 18 O—O, B x Kt; 19 R—K1ch with a winning game.

17	K—K1
18 Q x P?	. . . .

It was still possible to transpose into the previous note.

18	Q—K2ch!
19 Q x Qch	Kt x Q
20 O—O	B x Kt

Black has the better of it now and should at least draw. White is well off in a material sense, having Rook and three connected passed Pawns for two minor pieces. But Black's forces are very well posted, and this should have been the decisive factor.

21 R—K1	K—B2
22 B—B4	Kt—Kt3
23 B—Kt3	P—B4
24 P—Kt3	P—Kt4!

This Pawn cluster is destined to become very dangerous.

25 P—QR4	P—B5!

Position after Black's 25th move

Forsberg

Marshall

26 RP x P	P x QP!
27 R x B	P x P

The Pawns have become quite formidable, especially since White's Bishop cannot cooperate in holding them back.

28 R—Q6	R—K1?

28 . . . R—QB1 would have won: 29 R—Q7ch (not 29 R—B6, R x R; 30 P x R, P—Q6; 31 P—B7, P—Q7 and wins), K—Kt1; 30 R—QB1, R—B6! and the threat of . . . P—Q6—7 is conclusive.

29 R—QB1	R—K7?

Again . . . R—QB1 is stronger; or 29 . . . P—Q6; 30 R x QP, B—Kt7 which gives good drawing chances.

30 K—B1	R—Q7
31 K—K1	R—Q6
32 R x BP	. . . .

Now White is out of the woods.

32	R—QB6
33 R—R2	R—B2
34 R(6)—R6	R—K2ch
35 K—Q1	Resigns

A great fighting game. Black missed several fine chances.

---

95. New York, 1922
(Metropolitan Chess League)

FRENCH DEFENSE

Dubious opening variations often acquire a good reputation because they are adopted with good results by first-class masters. In the hands of an amateur, such a line of play often leads to disaster.

F. J. MARSHALL   H. D. GROSSMAN

White	Black
1 P—K4	P—K3
2 P—Q4	P—Q4
3 Kt—QB3	P x P

The customary 3 . . . Kt—KB3 is better. The text gives up the center prematurely, with the result that White has a fine free game with attacking chances, while Black has meager prospects, especially with the problem of developing his QB. Rubinstein's success with this variation is truly unique.

4 Kt x P	Kt—Q2
5 Kt—KB3	B—K2
6 B—Q3	KKt—B3
7 Kt x Ktch	Kt x Kt

For the alternative . . . P x Kt in an analogous position, see Game no. 69.

8 Kt—K5	O—O
9 O—O	P—B4
10 P x P	B x P
11 B—KKt5	B—K2
12 Q—B3	Q—Q4

Black is subjected to a strong bind, and finds it difficult to develop his QB. Either . . . Kt—Q4 or . . . Q—B2 should have been tried, but he would have remained with the inferior game.

13 Q—K2	P—QKt3?

This is at once stamped as a mistake, but if instead 13 . . . B—Q2 the same reply is still very strong.

14 QR—Q1	Q—B4

Material loss was unavoidable, B x Pch being threatened.

15 B x Kt	B x B
16 Q—K4	P—Kt3

Position after Black's 16th move

Grossman

Marshall

Hoping to get by with the loss of "only" the exchange. But White's reply forces the gain of a whole piece.

17 Kt—Kt4!   Resigns

---

96. Match, 1923

QUEEN'S GAMBIT DECLINED

Although I missed the best continuation at a crucial point, I consider this game well worth inclusion because of the interesting character of the attack.

F. J. MARSHALL	ED. LASKER
White	Black
1 P—Q4	P—Q4
2 Kt—KB3	P—K3
3 P—B4	P—QB4
4 BP x P	KP x P

As has been seen from earlier games, this defense generally leads to a difficult game for Black because of the weakness of his QP.

5 Kt—B3	Kt—QB3
6 P—KKt3	Kt—B3
7 B—Kt2	B—K3
8 O—O	B—K2
9 P x P	B x P

In recent years the gambit 9 . . . P—Q5?! has been favored. It leads to a lively game but it is not quite sound, as White gets the better game with 10 Kt—QR4, B—B4; 11 B—B4! Kt—K5; 12 P—QKt4! Kt x KtP; 13 Kt x P, B—Kt3; 14 R—Kt1, P—QR4; 15 P—QR3, Kt—B3; 16 Kt x Kt, P x Kt; 17 R—Kt7 etc.

10 B—Kt5   P—Q5

. . . B—K2 is less aggressive, but also less risky.

11 B x Kt	Q x B
12 Kt—K4	Q—K2
13 Kt x B	Q x Kt
14 R—B1	Q—Kt3
15 Kt—Kt5!	B—B4

. . . . B—Q2 was safer. After 15 . . . . B x P White would recover his Pawn by 16 Q—R4, B—Kt6; 17 B x Ktch, P x B; 18 Q x Pch, Q x Q; 19 R x Q with the better ending because of the weakness of Black's Pawns.

16 P—K4!   P x P e p.?

Too light-hearted. Better would have been the variation subsequently suggested by Lasker: 16 . . . B—Kt3; 17 P—B4, P—Q6ch; 18 K—R1, O—O; 19 P—B5, P—KR3; 20 P x B, P x Kt; 21 R x P with a position which is difficult to appraise.

Position after Black's 16th move

Lasker

Marshall

17 R x Kt!   . . . .

Black's King will find no haven now.

17	P x R
18 Q—Q6	B—Q2

If 18 . . . QR—B1; 19 R—K1
wins.

| 19 Q—K5ch | K—B1 |
| 20 P x P | P—B3 |

He has no choice, for if 20 . . .
B—K1; 21 Kt—K6ch is decisive.

21 R x Pch!	P x R
22 Q x Pch	K—K1
23 Q x Rch	K—K2
24 Q—K5ch!	. . . .

Incomparably stronger than 24
Q x R, Q x Pch etc.

| 24 . . . . | K—Q1 |
| 25 P—KR4! | . . . . |

Creating a loophole for the King,
thus freeing White's Queen for the
attack.

25	K—B1
26 Kt—B7	P—QR4
27 Kt—Q6ch	K—Kt1
28 Kt—Kt5ch?	. . . .

Time pressure. There was a direct win with 28 Kt—B4ch! Q—B2;
29 Kt—Kt6! The same opportunity is missed two moves later.

28	K—Kt2
29 Kt—Q6ch	K—Kt1
30 Q—K7?	Q—B2

30 . . . R—R2 has been recommended as peferable, but after 31
Q—B8ch, K—B2; 32 Q—B4, K—
Q1; 33 Q—Kt5ch, K—B2; 34 Q—
K5, K—Q1; 35 K—R2 Black would
eventually succumb to the pressure. With two Pawns for the exchange and prospects of picking
up the KRP (yielding two passed
Pawns), and with all his pieces admirably placed, White would be
much better off than Black, with
his exposed King, sadly limited
pieces and weak Pawns.

31 Q—B8ch	K—R2
32 Kt—Kt5ch!	K—Kt3
33 Q x R	K x Kt

Running into a decisive attack,

but the game was lost in any event.

34 B—B1ch	K—Kt5
35 Q—B8ch	P—B4
36 Q—Kt7	P—B5
37 K—R2	Q—B3
38 Q—B3ch	K—Kt4
39 Q—Kt3ch	Resigns

An eventful game.

---

97. Match, 1923
QUEEN'S GAMBIT DECLINED

An unconventional game which
is characterized by original moves
on both sides.

ED. LASKER   F. J. MARSHALL

White   Black

1 P—Q4	P—Q4
2 Kt—KB3	P—K3
3 P—B4	Kt—KB3
4 B—Kt5	. . . .

During this period, I frequently
answered 4 Kt—B3 with . . . B—
Kt5.

4	QKt—Q2
5 P—K3	B—K2
6 Kt—B3	O—O
7 Q—B2	P—B4
8 R—Q1	Q—R4
9 BP x P	KP x P
10 B—Q3	P—KR3

B x Pch was threatened.

| 11 B—R4 | P—B5!? |

This move has strong and weak
points. It establishes the Queen-
side majority, but White can react
very strongly later on with Kt—
K5 or P—K4; and in addition,
Black's QP may be subjected to
strong pressure if White's Queen
ever lands on KB5.

| 12 B—R7ch | . . . . |

Loses time. B—B5 was stronger.

12	Kt x B
13 B x B	R—K1
14 B—Q6	QKt—B3
15 O—O	B—Kt5
16 QR—K1	R—K3

A useful gain of time. B—Kt3 was probably the best reply.

17 B—B4	B x Kt
18 P x B	Kt—R4
19 Q—B5!?	. . . .

As previously indicated, White's Queen is strongly placed here. Black has to play his very best now to avoid getting a disadvantage.

19	Kt x B
20 P x Kt	. . . .

A very interesting reply. White has no choice, for if 20 Q x Kt, Kt—Kt4; 21 K—R1, R—KB3 etc.

20	QR—K1

Position after Black's 20th move

Marshall

Lasker

21 R—K5	. . . .

21 Kt x P looks good here, for example 21 . . . R—Kt3ch; 22 Q x R! P x Q; 23 R x Rch, K—B2; 24 R—K5, Q—Q7; 25 KR—K1 with excellent prospects.

However, Black would answer 21 Kt x P with 21 . . . Q—Q1! (threatening . . . P—KKt3 or . . . R x R); 22 Kt—K3, Q x P with a good game.

21	Q—Kt3
22 R x P?	. . . .

This renunciation of the K file loses. Better was 22 Kt x P, Q x QP; 23 KR—K1 etc.

22	R—Kt3ch
23 K—R1	Q x KtP
24 Kt—K4	. . . .

Or 24 Kt—Q1, Q—K7; 25 Q—R3, Kt—B3; 26 R—K5, R x R; 27 BP x R, Kt—Q4 and wins.

24	Q—K7

Leaving White without an adequate defense.

25 Q—R3	R x Kt
26 P—B5	R—R5!

Forcing favorable simplification.

27 R—K5	Q—Q6
28 R—K3	R x Q
29 R x Q	P x R
30 P x R	P x P
31 R—Q1	R x P
32 K—Kt2	R—B4
33 R x P	Kt—B3
Resigns	

---

98. Lake Hopatcong, 1923

QUEEN'S GAMBIT DECLINED

It is delightful to observe how Black's advantage in development sweeps over all resistance. Open lines give him the initiative in short order.

A. KUPCHIK	F. J. MARSHALL
White	Black
1 P—Q4	P—Q4
2 Kt—KB3	P—K3

3 P—B4   Kt—KB3
4 Kt—B3   B—Kt5

Black has a wide choice here:
4 . . . QKt—Q2 or . . . B—K2 or
. . . P—B4 or . . . P—B3. However,
I like the text best, because of its
aggressive tendencies.

5 Q—Kt3   . . . .

Q—R4ch may be better.

5 . . . .   P—B4
6 BP x P   KP x P
7 P x P   . . . .

Here or next move B—Kt5 was
better. The text opens lines for
Black, and the following move is
too conservative.

7 . . . .   Kt—B3
8 B—Q2   B—K3

Already threatening to win a
piece with . . . P—Q5.

9 Kt—KKt5   O—O
10 P—K3   Kt—Q2!
11 Kt x B   P x Kt

Black has splendid prospects,
what with his superior development and the open KB file.

12 B—Kt5   Kt x P
13 Q—Q1   P—Q5!

With this energetic push Black
opens up the game further to his
advantage.

14 P x P   Kt x P
15 B—QB4   Q—R5
16 O—O   QR—Q1!

16 . . . Kt—B6ch followed by
. . . Q x B yields a winning positional advantage; but the text is
even more convincing.

17 B—K2   B x Kt
18 P x B   Kt—K5!

Decisive because of the pressure
on the Q file. There is no really
good counter to the threat of . . .
Kt x B followed by . . . Kt—B6ch.

Amusing would be 19 K—R1, Kt x
QB; 20 Q x Kt, Kt—B6 and the
Queen is lost just the same!

Position after Black's 18th move

Marshall

Kupchik

19 P x Kt   R x QP
20 Q—Kt3   Kt x B
21 Q x Pch   K—R1
22 P—Kt3   . . . .

There was no escape from material loss: if 22 KR—K1, Q x BPch;
23 K—R1, R—K5 and wins.

22 . . . .   Q—K5!
23 Q x Q   R x Q

If now 24 KR—K1, R(1)—K1
and wins. Hence White must lose
the exchange.

24 B—Q3   R—Q5
25 B—B2   Kt x R
26 R x Kt   P—QKt4
27 K—Kt2   R—Q7

The ending is an easy win.

28 B—Kt3   P—QR4
29 P—QR4   R—Kt7
30 B—Q1   R—Kt8
31 P x P   R—Q1
32 B—Kt4   R x R
33 K x R   P—R5

34 P—Kt6	R—QKt1

White resigns. This is one of my best games.

---

99. New York, 1924

QUEEN'S GAMBIT DECLINED

Neither master played perfectly in this game; but what a grand battle it was!

F. J. MARSHALL   DR. E. LASKER

White	Black
1 P—Q4	P—Q4
2 P—QB4	P—QB3
3 P x P	. . . .

A capture I have favored throughout my career, and with very good results.

3	P x P
4 Kt—QB3	Kt—KB3
5 Q—Kt3	P—K3
6 B—B4	Kt—B3
7 Kt—B3	B—K2

7 . . . Kt—QR4 is better, for if 8 Q—R4ch, B—Q2 gains time; or if 8 Q—B2, B—Q2 followed by . . . R—B1.

8 P—K3	Kt—KR4
9 B—Kt3	O—O
10 B—Q3	P—B4

Black is now on the point of setting up a strong central position with . . . Kt—B3—K5. White therefore decides to remove the Knight.

| 11 B—K5 | Kt—B3 |
| 12 B x Kt | R x B |

In a later game in this tourney (the famous encounter with Capablanca) Lasker retook with the Pawn, in order to keep White's KKt out of K5. One can see what a keen struggle revolves about the occupation of these center squares.

| 13 QR—B1 | B—Q3 |

14 Kt—QR4	Q—R4ch

Discouraging White from planting the QKt at B5, since 15 K—K2 would be answered strongly by . . . Kt—Kt5 and if 16 B—Kt1, P—QKt3! threatening . . . B—R3ch.

15 Kt—B3	R—Kt1

This soon leads to trouble. Either . . . Q—Kt5 or . . .Q—Q1 was in order.

16 O—O	P—QR3

The immediate . . . B—Q2 could be answered by Kt—QKt5, either removing the vital KB or else gaining control of the important square K5.

17 Kt—QR4	B—Q2

Threatening . . . Kt x P, but this is prevented easily enough.

18 Kt—B5	Q—B2

He cannot retreat . . . B—K1, for then comes 19 Kt x KtP, Q—B2; 20 Kt x B! R x Q; 21 Kt x B, Q—Q1; 22 Kt x Rch followed by P x R.

Position after Black's 18th move

Dr. Lasker

Marshall

19 Kt—K5!	. . . .

A very important stroke. Black

must not capture twice on this square, for example 19 . . . Kt x Kt; 20 P x Kt, B x P; 21 P—B4, B—Q3; 22 Kt—K4 etc.

19 . . . .   B—K1
20 P—B4   . . . .

Preferring to maintain the pressure rather than go in for 20 Kt x KP, R x Kt; 21 Q x QP, Q—K2; 22 B x P, Kt—Q1; White would have a material advantage, but Black's two Bishops would assure him of counterplay.

20 . . . .   Q—K2
21 P—QR3   R—R3

This attack can be parried easily enough, but Black has to do something in view of White's contemplated maneuver Q—Q1 followed by P—QKt4—5.

22 R—KB2   P—KKt4
23 P—Kt3   K—R1?

. . . P x P at once was better, for it would force White to retake with the KtP (he cannot interpolate 24 Kt x Kt? because of 24 . . . P x Kt attacking the Queen). White would still have the better game, but not to the extent of the actual continuation.

24 Q—Q1!   . . . .

Preparing for P—QKt4 and also making possible the recapture with the KP.

24 . . . .   P x P
25 Kt x Kt!   . . . .

Gladly giving up the occupation of K5 for the greater advantage of pressure against the backward KP.

25 . . . .   P x Kt

. . . B x Kt is the positional move, but Lasker wants the open QKt file.

26 KP x P   Q—KKt2?

Giving up a Pawn for what turns

out to be an inadequate attack; . . . P—R4 was more prudent and would still have left a lot of fight.

27 B x RP   B—R4
28 Q—Q2   R—Kt1
29 B—K2!   B—K1
30 Q—K3   . . . .

Guarding against the threat of . . . R x P! and at the same time beginning to turn the heat on the KP.

30 . . . .   R—B3
31 B—B1   . . . .

Making R—K1 possible in case of need and thus threatening Kt x P, which would have been refuted at this stage by . . . Q—K2.

31 . . . .   Q—K2
32 P—QR4!   . . . .

The advance of this Pawn will keep Black's pieces tied up.

32 . . . .   P—R4
33 R—Kt2   . . . .

In a won position, I begin to be over-cautious. P—R5—R6 was indicated, with a fairly rapid win in sight, as Black's "attack" was only a demonstration. The same comment applies with even more force to my next move.

33 . . . .   P—R5
34 Kt—Q3?   Q—QR2!

Now Lasker has a breathing spell.

35 P—Kt3   R—Kt2
36 Kt—K5   P x P
37 P x P   Q—Kt3
38 P—R5!   . . . .

Here I begin to play with renewed energy. As the QRP has been shorn of its terrors for Black, I utilize it to gain ground on the other side of the board.

38 . . . .   Q x RP
39 Kt x P   Q—Kt3

40 Kt—K5	R—QB2
41 R x R	Q x R
42 P—KKt4!	....

Beginning an attack which should have led to a quick win.

| 42 .... | P x P |
| 43 Kt x P! | R x P |

Or 43 ... R—Kt3; 44 P—B5 etc.

| 44 Q x P? | .... |

I gave a lot of thought to this move, but Lasker finds the flaw in it. Alekhine shows a simple win with 44 B—Q3! (threatening Q—R3ch with deadly effect), B—R4; 45 Kt—R6! R—B1; 46 Q—Kt5 and there is nothing to be done about the threat of Q—Kt8ch! This would have justified my 43rd move, which came in for baseless criticism.

| 44 .... | R x Bch! |
| 45 K x R | B—Kt4ch! |

Much better than the plausible 45 ...Q—B8ch, which would lose for him: 46 Q—K1, B—Kt4ch; 47 K—B2, Q—B5ch· 48 K—Kt1, Q x Pch; 49 K—R1, Q—Kt2 (if 49 ... Q—K5; 50 Q x Q, P x Q; 51 Kt—B6 and mate follows!); 50 Kt—K5! B x Kt; 51 R x Q, B x R; 52 Q—R4ch, K—Kt1; 53 Q—Q8ch etc.

| 46 R—K2 | .... |

There is nothing in 46 K—B2, Q—B7ch; 47 K—B3, Q—Q8ch; 48 R—K2, Q—Q6ch!

46	B x Rch
47 Q x B	Q—B2ch
48 Q—B2	K—Kt2

Not 48 ... Q x Qch? 49 K x Q and Black must lose the QP.

| 49 Kt—K3 | B—B5? |

Again running into a losing position. Edward Lasker showed a draw here with 49 ...B—R6! 50 Q x Qch, K x Q; 51 Kt x P, B—Kt7.

50 K—K2!	Q—B2
51 Q—Kt2ch	K—B1
52 Kt x P?	....

Letting the win slip out of his hands for the last time. After 52 Q x P Black would have a good many checks, but the ending would surely be lost.

| 52 .... | Q—B7ch |
| 53 K—B3 | B—Q7 |

The only move, but it draws.

54 Q—B1	Q x Pch
55 K—K2ch	K—K1
56 Q—B5	....

The beauty of Lasker's defense is seen in the variation 56 Kt—B6 ch, K—K2; 57 K x B, Q—Kt7ch; 58 K—K3, Q—B6ch; 59 K—K4, Q—B7ch; 60 K—K5, Q—B2ch; 61 K—B5, Q—B7ch; 62 K—Kt5 (if 62 Kt—K4, Q—B1ch etc.), Q—Q7ch followed by ... Q x P.

| 56 .... | Q—B5ch |
| 57 K x B | Q x Pch |

The game could be given up as a draw here.

58 K—K2	Q—B5ch
59 K—B2	Q—B4ch
60 K—Kt2	Q—Q3
61 K—B3	K—Q1
62 K—K4	Q—K3ch!

Drawn; a remarkable finish to a remarkable game. What a superb fighter Lasker was!

---

100.   New York, 1924

(Second Brilliancy Prize)

QUEEN'S GAMBIT DECLINED

My good-natured Russian opponent is often involved in brilliancy prize games; he has produced many brilliancies, and he has been the victim of them just as often!

F.J.MARSHALL   E.D.BOGOLJUBOW

White	Black
1 P—Q4	Kt—KB3
2 Kt—KB3	P—K3
3 B—Kt5	P—Q4

More exact would be 3 . . . P—B4, leading into a kind of Queen's Pawn Opening in which Black has an easier time equalizing than in the Queen's Gambit Declined.

4 P—K3	QKt—Q2

Here again . . . P—B4 is possible.

| 5 P—B4 | P—B3 |
| 6 P x P | . . . . |

A frequent move in my games. It is a good way to avoid the Cambridge Springs Defense.

| 6 . . . . | KP x P |
| 7 Kt—B3 | Q—R4? |

Black confuses his systems of defense. After the previous Pawn exchange, Black's Queen cannot accomplish anything useful here. Far better was the simple 7 . . . B—K2.

8 B—Q3	Kt—K5
9 Q—B2	Kt x B
10 Kt x Kt	P—KR3
11 Kt—B3	B—K2

. . . B—Q3 would offer better prospects. The more conservative text does not offer Black much opportunity to derive benefit from the two Bishops.

| 12 O—O | O—O |
| 13 P—QR3 | Q—Q1 |

This voluntary retreat does not speak well for Black's seventh move. However, it had already become apparent that the Queen was serving no useful purpose at R4.

| 14 QR—K1 | P—QR4 |

Waste of time. White's last move has indicated that he is not interested in Queen-side play and is intending action on the King-side. . . . B—Q3, now or next move, was decidedly preferable.

| 15 Q—K2! | Kt—B3? |

White was threatening 16 P—K4, when the Pawn could not be taken because of the winning reply 17 Q x P.
But 15 . . . B—Q3 would have parried this menace and prevented White's next move, which foreshadows a powerful attack.

| 16 Kt—K5 | B—Q3 |
| 17 P—B4 | P—B4 |

Desperately striving for counterplay against the attacking method which is common to such situations: B—Kt1 followed by Q—B2 and P—KKt4—5.

| 18 B—Kt1 | B—Q2 |
| 19 Q—QB2 | B—B3 |

White threatened Kt x QP. The text also contemplates the following defensive maneuver: 20 . . . P x P; 21 P x P, B x Kt; 22 BP x B, Kt—K5. White meets this plan with:

| 20 P x P! | B x P |
| 21 K—R1 | R—K1 |

After 21 . . . R—B1; 22 P—K4 would not be advisable; but White could continue with 22 Kt—Kt4, P—KKt3; 23 Kt x Pch, K—Kt2; 24 Kt x P, R x Kt; 25 Q x Pch with a good attack and three Pawns for the sacrificed piece. At all events, this was superior to the text.

| 22 P—K4! | B—Q5 |

There was no really good move here. Thus if 22 . . . P x P; 23 Kt x B, P x Kt; 24 Kt x P, Kt x Kt; 25 R x Kt, R x R; 26 Q x R, P—Kt3; 27 P—B5! and Black's position is quite hopeless.

| 23 Kt x B | P x Kt |

24 P—K5   Kt—Kt5
25 Q—R7ch   . . . .

Finally attaining the long-sought objective.

25 . . . .   K—B1
26 P—KKt3   Q—Kt3
27 B—B5!   . . . .

Initiating the final attack.

27 . . . .   Kt—B7ch

Position after Black's 27th move

Bogoljubow

Marshall

28 R x Kt!   . . . .

The most interesting way, although 28 K—Kt2 was also good enough (if then 28 . . . Q x P; 29 QR—Kt1 followed by R—Kt7 forces mate).

28 . . . .   B x R
29 Q—R8ch!   K—K2
30 Q x KtP   K—Q1

If 30 . . . B x R; 31 Q—B6ch, K—B1; 32 Q x RPch and mate in four follows.

31 Q—B6ch   R—K2
32 P—K6!   B—Q5

Other moves are no better: 32 . . . B x R; 33 P x P—or 32 . . . P x P; 33 R x P followed by Q—B8ch—

or 32 . . . Q—Q5; 33 R—K5 and wins.

33 P x P!   B x Q
34 P—B8(Q)ch   K—B2
35 R x Rch   B x R
36 Q x R

White threatened to win the Queen with 37 Q—B8ch, K—Q3; 38 Q—Q7ch, K—B4; 39 Kt—R4ch. After 36 . . .Q x P the Queen would be lost in the same way, while if 36 . . .Q—B7; 37 Q—B8ch followed by 38 Q—Kt8ch and 39 Q—R7ch still wins the Queen.

37 Q—R8!   Q—Q1
38 Q—K5ch   . . . .

White announced mate in five here: 38 . . . K—B4; 39 Kt—R4ch, K—B5 (if 39 . . .K—Kt4; 40 Q—K2ch, K x Kt; 41 B—B2 mate); 40 Q—B3ch, K—Kt4; 41 B—Q3ch, K x Kt; 42 Q—B2 mate.

---

101. New York, 1924

QUEEN'S GAMBIT DECLINED

A lively hard-fought draw with the present chess Champion. Born in Russia, Grandmaster Alekhine has lived for many years in France and served in the French Army. His greatest victory was the dethroning of Capablanca as World Champion in 1927. He lost the Championship to Dr. Euwe in 1935, made a magnificent comeback two years later to regain the title.

Full of life and endurance, Alekhine is extremely nervous; after making a move, he stares at his opponent and twirls a lock of hair. His reign as World Champion has helped chess, for he has put a great deal more pep into the game.

F. J. MARSHALL   DR. A. ALEKHINE

White	Black
1 P—Q4	Kt—KB3
2 Kt—KB3	P—K3

Nowadays my preference runs to
. . . P—KKt3 here.

3 P—B4	P—Q4
4 Kt—B3	P—B3
5 P x P	KP x P
6 B—Kt5	B—K2
7 P—K3	B—KB4

Taking advantage of the fact
that the Bishop's diagonal is not
blocked by the QKt at Q2.

8 B—Q3	B x B
9 Q x B	QKt—Q2
10 O—O	O—O
11 Q—B5!	. . . .

A very strong move and the key
to the following play. White's activities on the Queen-side are
clearly foreshadowed, indicating
the necessity for counter-action by
Black on the other wing. But, as
will be seen, the presence of
White's Queen at KB5 is awkward
for Black.

11	Kt—K5
12 B x B	Q x B
13 Kt x Kt!	P x Kt
14 Kt—Q2	Kt—B3
15 QR—B1	. . . .

Despite the equalizing tendency
of the previous exchanges, the
practical chances are all on
White's side. After this Rook goes
to B5, Black will have to be on his
guard against R—K5 and also
against the "minority attack" culminating in the advance of the
QKtP to Kt5, with lasting pressure
on Black's game.

15	KR—K1
16 R—B5	Kt—Q4
17 KR—B1	QR—Q1
18 P—QKt4!	. . . .

The more conservative P—QR3
would have led to the same continuation; but I wanted to give Black
something to think about.

18	P—QR3

Having convinced himself that
after 18 . . . Kt x KtP White would
obtain a very favorable ending
with 19 R—K5, Q—B3; 20 Q x Q,
P x Q; 21 R x Rch, R x R; 22 R—
Kt1, Kt x P; 23 R x P, P—QR4; 24
R—R7, R—Kt1; 25 R x RP, R—
Kt7; 26 Kt—B1, Kt—B8; 27 P—
Kt4! Kt—Q6; 28 R—KB5 etc.

19 P—QR3	R—Q3
20 P—Kt3!	. . . .

A many-sided move which serves
the following purposes: it opens
up a loophole for the King; it prepares a retreat for the Queen (Q—
R3—B1); in the event of . . . R—
R3 the continuation . . . Q—R5 is
automatically prevented; in the
event of . . . P—KKt3 followed by
. . . P—B4, the advance . . . P—B5
is prevented.

Black's position has become very
difficult. If 20 . . . P—KKt3; 21
Q—R3, P—B4; 22 Kt—B4 followed
by Kt—K5 with domination of the
black squares. And if 20 . . . R—
B3; 21 Q x P! Q x Q; 22 Kt x Q,
R x Kt; 23 R x Kt etc.

20	P—R3
21 Kt—Kt1!	. . . .

A simple but strong continuation.
The idea is to exchange Knights
with Kt—B3, after which the
Queen-side attack (P—QR4 followed by P—Kt5) can be resumed.
White hopes to give this plan decisive effect with a nice sacrifice
of the exchange, but the whole
idea is just barely parried by a
really magnificent counter-combination by Alekhine, involving the
sacrifice of a Rook and Knight!

21	P—KKt3
22 Q—R3	Q—Kt4!

The tension has reached its high-
est point: both combination and
counter-combination are now working against each other.

23 Kt—B3!	P—Kt3!

Watch this Pawn go right down
to KB7!!

24 Kt x Kt   . . . .

This move had been foreseen for
some time, as 24 R—B4? would not
do here because of 24 . . . KtxKP!

24 . . . .   P x R
25 Kt—B7!   . . . .

Seemingly leaving Black without
resource, for example 25 . . . R—
K2; 26 Q—B8ch, K—Kt2; 27 KtP
x P, R—B3 (if 27 . . . R x P; 28 R—
Kt1! wins); 28 R—Kt1 (threatens
R—Kt8), Q—B4; 29 Q x Q, R x Q;
30 Kt x P, R—R2; 31 R—Kt6 and
wins.
But . . .

Position after White's 25th move

Dr. Alekhine

Marshall

25 . . . .   P x QP!!
26 Kt x R   P x P!!

And not 26 . . . R—Q1? 27 Q—
Kt4! Q—K2; 28 Q x P! and wins.

27 Kt x R!   . . . .

This is by no means as obvious
as it seems. Consider the attractive line 27 P—B4!? P x P e. p.; 28
Kt x R, P—K7? (this looks strong
but it isn't!); 29 Q—B8ch, K any;
30 Q—R8ch! K x Q; 31 Kt x Pch
winning easily.
After careful study, however,
both players came to realize that

the substitution of 28 . . . P—B7ch!
(instead of 28 . . . P—K7?) draws
for Black. The proof: 29 K—B1!
P—K7ch!
I 30 K x KP, Q x R; 31 Q—B1,
Q—Kt7ch! 32 K—K3, Q—B6ch and
Black must win the Knight.
II 30 K x BP, Q x R; 31 Q—B8ch,
K—R2; 32 K x P, Q—B7ch; 33 K—
K3, Q—B6ch; 34 K—K4, Q—B7ch;
35 K—Q4, Q—B7ch! and White
can avoid a perpetual check only
at the cost of losing his Knight.

27 . . . .   P x Pch
28 K x P   Q—Q7ch
29 K—Kt1   Q—K6ch!

And not 29 . . . Q x Rch? 30 Q—
B1 and wins.

30 K—Kt2   Q—B6ch
31 K—Kt1   Q—K6ch
32 K—Kt2   Q—B6ch

Drawn by perpetual check. A
very thrilling game.

———

102. New York, 1924

THREE KNIGHTS' OPENING

This consultation game is featured by a number of sparkling
surprise moves.

E. B. EDWARDS   F. J. MARSHALL
C. E. NORWOOD   G. E. ROOSEVELT

White	Black
1 P—K4	P—K4
2 Kt—KB3	Kt—KB3
3 Kt—B3	B—Kt5

Throughout my career, I have
found this an interesting way of
by-passing the rather boring lines
of the Four Knights' Game.

4 B—B4   . . . .

Kt x P is more enterprising, and
at least permits White to obtain
two Bishops. After the text, Black
equalizes without much difficulty.

4	Kt—B3
5 O—O	P—Q3
6 P—Q4	B—Kt5!

Taking the initiative.

7 B—QKt5	O—O

The attempt to win a Pawn with 7 . . . B x QKt; 8 P x B, Kt x P could be met effectively in a number of ways, for example 9 P x P Kt x QBP; 10 B x Ktch, P x B; 11 Q—K1! with an excellent game.

8 B x Kt	P x B
9 P x P	. . . .

Q—Q3 was probably better. The text looks promising, but Black has a good reply.

9	B x QKt!

So that if 10 P x B, Kt x P and Black's superior Pawn position gives him the better game.

10 P x Kt	B x BP

With his two powerful Bishops, Black has the advantage.

11 Q—Q3	R—K1
12 P—B4	. . . .

To prevent . . . P—Q4; but, as the game goes, this precaution turns out to be futile.

12	R—Kt1
13 R—Kt1	Q—Q2
14 P—QKt3	. . . .

This natural-looking move is answered in a surprising way. Kt—Q4 was better.

14	P—Q4!

For if 15 BP x P, P x P; 16 Q x P, Q x Q; 17 P x Q. B—B4 and wins. As other ways of capturing the QP are answered in a similar manner, White cannot avoid losing a Pawn.

15 R—Q1	R x KP

If now 16 P x P, P x P; 17 Q x P,

Q x Q; 18 R x Q, B x Kt; 19 P x B, R—K8ch; 20 K—Kt2, R—Q1! 21 R—QB5, P—KR3; 22 R x P, R(1)—Q8 and wins, as the imprisonment of the Bishop must have fatal results.

16 B—Kt2	B x B
17 R x B	B x Kt
18 Q x B	. . . .

Allowing a neat reply, but if 18 P x B, Black replies . . . R—R5 or . . . R—K4 with an easy win due to White's ripped-up King-side.

Position after White's 18th move

Marshall and Roosevelt

Edwards and Norwood

18	P x P!

Very amusing: neither the Rook nor Queen can be captured!

19 R(2)—Kt1	Q—K3
20 P—KR3	P—KR3

In endings where only the heavy pieces are present, it is well to provide against surprise mates on the last rank with this loophole.

21 P—QKt4	P—QB4!

If now 22 P x P, R x R; 23 R x R, R—K8ch; 24 R x R, Q x Rch; 25 K—R2, Q—K4ch followed by . . . Q x P with an easy win.

22 P—Kt5   R—K1

As there is no immediate way of utilizing the passed Pawn, Black entrenches himself solidly on the K file, the immediate objective being to establish himself on the seventh rank. White cannot dispute this plan, for if either 23 R—Kt2? or R—Q2? then 23 . . . R—K8ch wins a Rook!

23 Q—B3   R—K7
24 QR—B1   Q—B4
25 R—B1   . . . .

He has no choice, for if 25 P—B3, Q—Kt4; 26 P—Kt4, Q—R5 wins.

25 . . . .   R(1)—K5
26 Q—R5   R—B5

Decisive, for if 27 P—B3, Q—Kt4; 28 R—B2, R x R; 29 K x R, R x Pch etc.

27 Q x RP   R(5) x P
28 Q—R8ch   K—R2
29 R x R   Q x Rch
30 K—R1   P—B6
31 Q—B3   . . . .

There was no defense against the further advance of the BP.

31 . . . .   Q x Q
32 P x Q   P—B7

White resigns, as . . . R—Q7 forces the game.

---

103. Baden-Baden, 1925
SICILIAN DEFENSE

One of the most valuable devices in master play is to confront an opponent with an opening line of play quite different from what he has anticipated. Thus in the present encounter Saemisch expects to play a quiet purely positional type of game; he is evidently upset when he finds that he must fight against an aggressive but rather puzzling line of play.

F. J. Marshall	F. Saemisch
White	Black
1 P—K4	P—QB4
2 P—QKt4	. . . .

The Wing Gambit. It is considered unsound, but I have had satisfactory results with it in my games.

| 2 . . . . | P x P |
| 3 P—QR3 | P x P |

It must be admitted that in none of the three games given with this variation did my opponents ever adopt the strongest reply, which is 3 . . . P—Q4! (See Special Analysis of Openings.)

| 4 Kt x P | P—Q3 |
| 5 B—Kt2 | Kt—QB3 |

. . . Kt—KB3 was more energetic. Black's passive policy soon places him in an extremely uncomfortable situation.

6 P—Q4	Kt—B3
7 B—Q3	P—K3
8 Kt—B3	B—K2
9 O—O	O—O

And hereabouts . . . P—Q4 was preferable. True, 10 P—K5 would shut in Black's QB, but it would do the same for White's QB.

10 P—B4	P—QKt3
11 Q—K2	B—Kt2
12 KR—Q1	R—K1
13 P—K5!	. . . .

White has steadily strengthened his position and is now ready for this advance, which creates further confusion in the enemy's ranks.

| 13 . . . . | Kt—Q2 |
| 14 Kt—QKt5! | Q—Kt1 |

Black could not have been very happy making this awkward move, but what to do? If 14 . . . P—Q4; 15 B—R3! and the QKt is eventually established very powerfully

on Q6. Or if 14 ...P x P; 15 P x P,
P—QR3; 16 Kt—Q6, B x Kt; 17
P x B and Black's game is extremely uncomfortable.

| 15 Q—K4 | Kt—B1 |

He decides to return the Pawn,
because in the process of recovering it, White must go in for exchanges which will relieve the
pressure somewhat. 15 ... P—Kt3
would have retained the Pawn but
would have left Black with a serious weakness on the black
squares.

16 P x P	B x P
17 Kt x B	Q x Kt
18 B—R3	Q—Q1
19 B x Kt	K x B
20 Q x RP	Q—B3
21 B—K4!	....

White still has the initiative;
Kt—K5 threatens to be very troublesome.

| 21 .... | Q—R3 |

Ridding himself of the middle
game dangers, but he is by no
means out of the woods.

| 22 Q x Q | P x Q |
| 23 Kt—K5 | Kt—Q1? |

After this the position is definitely untenable. He should have
played 23 ... Kt x Kt; 24 B x B,
QR—Kt1; 25 B—R6, Kt—B3; 26
B—Kt5, KR—B1 with very good
drawing chances.

| 24 B x B | Kt x B |
| 25 R—R3! | .... |

Despite the reduced material,
this gives White a strong attack.
Black's King-side Pawns are very
weak.

| 25 .... | P—B3 |

Something has to be done about
the threat of R—KB3.

| 26 Kt—Kt4 | K—K2 |

If now 27 Kt x RP, P—B4 and
White's Knight is in difficulties.

| 27 R—K1 | Kt—Q3 |
| 28 P—B5 | P x P |

... Kt—Kt4 at once may have
been better.

| 29 P x P | Kt—Kt4 |
| 30 R—KB3! | P—B4 |

The loss of a Pawn was unavoidable.

| 31 R x P | P—QR4 |

This advance leads to an exciting
finish.

| 32 R—B6 | R—R3 |
| 33 R x P | P—R5 |

Position after Black's 33rd move

Saemisch

Marshall

| 34 R—Q1! | .... |

Mating threats begin to make
their appearance (R—R7ch followed by R(1)—Q7 etc.).

34	R—KB1
35 Kt—K5!	R—B4
36 R—Q7ch	K—K1
37 R—QKt7!	Resigns

If 37 ... P—R6; 38 R—R8ch,
R—B1; 39 R—Kt8ch, K—K2; 40
R(R8) x R and wins.

104. Baden-Baden, 1925

QUEEN'S GAMBIT DECLINED

One of the few occasions on which I depart from my favorite method (3 P x P etc.) of handling the Slav Defense. The role played by the Bishops in the attack is noteworthy.

F. J. Marshall   A. Rabinovich

White	Black
1 P—Q4	P—Q4
2 P—QB4	P—QB3
3 Kt—QB3	Kt—B3
4 P—K3	P—K3
5 Q—B2	. . . .

Avoiding the Meran Variation (5 Kt—B3, QKt—Q2; 6 B—Q3, P x P; 7 B x BP, P—QKt4), which was highly thought of in those days.

| 5 . . . . | B—Q3 |
| 6 P—B4!? | . . . . |

With this sharp move, White announces his intention of maintaining mastery of the key square K5. On the other hand, Black will have the opportunity of reacting aggressively with . . . P—B4, with the likelihood that White's center will thereupon become rather shaky.

6	O—O
7 Kt—B3	P—B4!
8 B—Q3	Kt—B3
9 P—QR3	P—QR3?

A lapse which has serious consequences. Black intends 10 . . . BP x P; 11 KP x P, P x P; 12 B x P, P—QKt4; 13 B—Q3, B—Kt2 with a good game; but White's next move rules out that possibility.
Better was 9 . . . BP x P; 10 KP x P, P x P and Black's play against the isolated QP should give him good counter-chances.

10 P—QKt3!   P—QKt3

Since 10 . . . QP x P can be answered by 11 KtP x P, Black's plan has been nipped in the bud.

| 11 O—O | QP x P |
| 12 KtP x P | P x P |

Position after Black's 12th move

Rabinovich

Marshall

13 Kt—K4!   . . . .

This unexpected retort opens up the attacking diagonals for the Bishop and is therefore stronger than the routine 13 P x P. If now 13 . . . P x P; 14 Kt x Ktch, Q x Kt; 15 B x Pch, K—R1; 16 B—Kt2 with a very strong attack, for example 16 . . . Q x P; 17 B—K4, B—Kt2; 18 Kt—K5 and wins; or 16 . . . Q—R3; 17 B—K4, B—Kt2; 18 Kt—K5, B x Kt; 19 P x B followed by R—B3 with a winning attack; or 16 . . . Q—K2; 17 B—K4, B—Kt2; 18 Kt—Kt5 (threatening B x Kt followed by Q—R7 mate), P—B4; 19 Q—K2! Q—K1; 20 Q—B3 and wins.

| 13 . . . . | B—B4 |
| 14 K—R1 | P—R3 |

If 14 . . . P x P; 15 Kt x Ktch, Q x Kt; 16 B x Pch, K—R1; 17 B—Kt2 and the play proceeds pretty much as in the previous note—except that if 17 . . . Kt—Q5; 18 Q—K4 wins.

15 Kt x Ktch   Q x Kt

Or 15 . . . P x Kt; 16 B—K4, B—

Kt2; 17 R—Q1 regaining the Pawn advantageously.

| 16 B—Kt2 | B—Kt2 |
| 17 B—K4 | . . . . |

Not only regaining the Pawn, but actually threatening to win a piece with 18 P x P and 19 P—Q5.

17	P—Q6
18 B x P	Q—K2
19 Q—B3!	. . . .

Now the Bishops come into their own. Black must weaken his KP now, so that White also builds up a strong position on the K file.

| 19 . . . . | P—B3 |
| 20 QR—K1 | KR—Q1 |

It would have saved time to play the other Rook here.

21 B—Kt1	R—Q2
22 Q—B2!	P—B4
23 P—K4!	. . . .

Opens new attacking lines.

23	R—KB1
24 P x P	R x P
25 P—Kt4!	. . . .

Smashing Black's feeble blockade.

25	R x P
26 Q—R7ch	K—B1
27 B—Kt6	. . . .

Winning the Queen, for if 27 . . . Q—Q3; 28 Q—R8ch, K—K2; 29 Q—K8 mate or 27 . . . Q—Q1; 28 R x P etc.

| 27 . . . . | Q—B2 |

A last hope. If now 28 B x Q, R(2) x B; 29 K—Kt2, Kt—R4 with a somewhat inconvenient position for White, despite his great material advantage. However, there is a more exact course:

| 28 Q—R8ch! | Q—Kt1 |
| 29 R x P!! | Resigns |

Any attempt to stop R—K8 mate, such as 29 . . .R—Q1 or 29 . . . Kt—K2, allows 30 B x P mate. If either Rook goes to KB2, then 30 B x Pch! and mate next move.

---

105. Marienbad, 1925

SICILIAN DEFENSE

Far from being disposed to look a gift horse in the mouth, Black takes every Pawn which is offered him—with the usual result.

F. J. MARSHALL   K. HAIDA

White   Black

1 P—K4	P—QB4
2 P—QKt4	P x P
3 P—QR3	P—K3

As in Game no. 103, Black does not find the best defense.

4 P x P	B x P
5 P—QB3	B—K2
6 P—Q4	P—Q3
7 P—KB4	P—B4

Black probably fears that 7 . . . Kt—KB3 will be answered by 8 P—K5. However, the text is no improvement, as it creates weaknesses in the center.

| 8 Kt—Q2 | Kt—KB3 |
| 9 B—Q3 | . . . . |

More exact would have been P x P! at once; for here and on the next three moves, Black could play . . . P—Q4! making it possible for him to plant his KKt at K5 with strong defensive prospects.

9	O—O
10 KKt—B3	Kt—B3
11 O—O	P—QR3?

Too slow. Either 11 . . . P—Q4 or else 11 . . .P x P; 12 Kt x P, Kt x Kt; 13 B x Kt was in order.

| 12 P x P! | P x P |
| 13 P—Q5 | Kt x P |

It is understandable that Black prefers to go after a second Pawn rather than retreat the QKt into rather a dreary position.

14 B—B4   . . . .

This pin gives White a lasting attack.

14 . . . .   Q—Kt3ch

"Never miss a check." As it happens, this check only draws the Queen away from the defense, and in some variations permits White's QR to enter the attack with gain of time.

15 K—R1   B—K3

Position after Black's 15th move

Haida

Marshall

16 QR—Kt1   . . . .

Tartakover suggests the following line as more precise: 16 Kt—Kt3, Kt x KBP; 17 B x Bch, Kt xB; 18 Q—Q5, R—B3 (if 18 . . . Kt—Q1; 19 KKt—Q4 etc.); 19 B—Kt5, R—Kt3; 20 KR—K1, Kt—Q1; 21 KKt—Q4 and wins.

16 . . . .   Q—B2

. . . Q—B4 might have been better, although 17 Q—K2 would keep the attack in good repair.

17 Kt—Kt3!   . . . .

A third Pawn sacrifice!

17 . . . .   Kt x KBP
18 B x Bch   Kt x B
19 Q—Q5   Kt—Q1

If 19 . . . R—B3; 20 B—Kt5, R—Kt3; 21 KR—K1, Kt—Q1 (or 21 . . . Kt—K4; 22 QKt—Q4!); 22 QKt—Q4! with tremendous pressure, for example 22 . . . B x B; 23 Kt x Kt, Q—B2; 24 Kt(6) x B! R x Kt; 25 Kt x R and wins.

20 KKt—Q4   R—B3
21 R—K1   Q—B1

If 21 . . .Q—Q2? 22 Kt—B5 wins. There is no satisfactory defense.

22 Kt x Kt   Kt x Kt

Forced: if 22 . . .R x Kt; 23 Kt—Q4, Q—B4; 24 Q—Kt3 wins.

23 Kt—Q4   K—B2
24 R x P   . . . .

Another way was 24 B—Kt5.

24 . . . .   Q—B4

If 24 . . . R—Kt3 (to prevent B—Kt5); 25 B—R3 wins easily. Or if 24 . . . Q x P; 25 R x Kt, Q x B ch; 26 R—K1ch and wins.

25 R x Bch!   K x R
26 Q—Kt7ch   K—B1
27 Q x Rch   K—B2
28 Q—Kt7ch   K—Kt3
29 Kt x Kt   Resigns
A neat finish.

---

106. Marienbad, 1925

(Special Prize)

THREE KNIGHTS' OPENING

Yates was famous for his attacking play, which, however, is conspicuously absent in this game. Perhaps he was misled by the uneventful character of the first part of the game.

F. D. YATES   F. J. MARSHALL

White	Black
1 P—K4	P—K4
2 Kt—KB3	Kt—KB3
3 Kt—B3	B—Kt5

Regarding this opening, see also Game No. 102.

4 B—B4	P—Q3
5 P—Q3	B—K3
6 B—Kt3	Kt—B3

Black has already equalized, with an easy development in prospect.

7 O—O	P—KR3
8 Kt—K2	B x B
9 RP x B	P—Q4

The obvious reaction to the withdrawal of White's QKt.

10 Kt—Kt3	P x P
11 P x P	Q x Q
12 R x Q	B—B4
13 P—B3?	. . . .

A careless move. The cautious P—R3 was in order, with a perfectly level position.

13	Kt—KKt5
14 R—B1	O—O—O

Black has taken advantage of his opponent's lapse to seize control of the Q file, with consequences which soon appear.

15 P—QKt4	B—Kt3
16 P—R3	. . . .

(see diagram next column)

16	Kt x BP!

Of course. The sacrifice gives Black a lasting grip on the position, characterized by no less than three pins!

17 R x Kt	R—Q8ch

Position after White's 16th move

Marshall

Yates

18 Kt—B1	KR—Q1
19 P—Kt5	. . . .

This move looks weak at first sight, but closer examination demonstrates that White is in great difficulty, the chief threat being 19 . . . P—B4! 20 P x P, P—K5; 21 Kt—R2, Kt—K4 and the threat of . . . Kt—Q6 is decisive.

If 19 P—KKt3 (in order to free himself with K—Kt2), R(1)—Q6! 20 K—Kt2 (neither Knight can move), B x R; 21 K x B, R x Kt(6) ch and wins. Or 19 P—Kt4, R(1)—Q6; 20 Kt—R2 (if 20 K—Kt2, B x R similar to the previous variation), B x Rch; 21 K x B, R x RP and Black should win.

19	Kt—R4

The refutation of White's attempt to dislodge the Knight.

20 R x Kt	. . . .

He has no choice, . . . Kt—Kt6 being threatened.

20	R x B!

Much stronger than . . . B x R.

21 R—R4	R(1)—Q8
22 Kt—Q4	P x Kt

23 P x P   R x P!

White resigns. Curious: after
the exchange of Queens, his position collapsed like a house of cards
in only eleven moves!

---

107. Moscow, 1925

SICILIAN DEFENSE

When you play over an interesting attacking game, the moves and
combinations seem to come of
themselves. The fact is, however,
that a lot of hard work goes into
them. My fifteenth move, for example, took almost half an hour to
find and calculate its consequences.

F. J. Marshall   B. Werlinsky

White	Black
1 P—K4	P—QB4
2 P—QKt4	P x P
3 P—QR3	P—K4?

For the best move see Game no.
103. The text is definitely inferior,
as it allows White to obtain an attack of Evans Gambit character.
In some respects White's attack
here is even stronger!

| 4 P x P | B x P |
| 5 P—QB3 | B—B4 |

. . . B—K2 is safer, but leads to
a cramped game.

6 Kt—B3	Kt—QB3
7 B—B4	P—Q3
8 P—Q4	P x P
9 P x P	B—Kt3

Interesting would have been 9
. . . B—Kt5ch; 10 K—B1! (as in
my game with Burn at Ostend
1905), P—QR4 (White threatened
P—Q5 followed by Q—R4ch); 11
Q—Kt3 with a good attack.

10 O—O   B—Kt5

Threatening the QP. If 10 . . .

Kt—B3; 11 B—R3, O—O; 12 P—
K5.

11 Q—Kt3!   B x Kt

If instead 11 . . .B—KR4; 12 B—
Kt2 with powerful attacking pos-
sibilities, for example 12 . . . KKt—
K2; 13 P—Q5, Kt—R4; 14 R x Kt!
B x R; 15 B x P, KR—Kt1; 16 B—
Kt5ch and wins.
If 11 . . . Q—Q2; 12 Q x B! P x Q;
13 R x Rch, K—K2 (or . . . Kt—
Q1); 14 Kt—B3 with excellent
prospects.

| 12 B x Pch | K—B1 |
| 13 B x Kt | R x B |

. . . .B—KR4 offers better
chances.

| 14 Q x Bch | Q—B3 |
| 15 Q—R5! | . . . . |

The only way to keep up the
attack.

15 . . . .   Kt x P

15 . . . B x P looks too dangerous (16 R—R3! Kt—K4; 17 B—K3!
and Black is in trouble).

16 B—R3!   R—K1

If 16 . . . Kt—K7ch; 17 Q x Kt,
Q x R; 18 B x Pch with a winning
attack. Black's lack of development and the exposed position of
his King always tell against him.
The text is played to prevent
P—K5.

17 Kt—B3   R—K4

Sooner or later White's Knight
will occupy Q5 with decisive effect.
Black's position is very awkward.

18 Q—R3   Q—K3

Or 18 . . .Kt—B7; 19 Kt—Q5, R x
Kt; 20 Q—B8ch, K—B2; 21 Q x Kt,
R—KKt4; 22 QR—Q1 and Black's
QP is a troublesome weakness.

19 Q—Q3   P—Kt4

Partly with the idea of playing

the King to safer quarters, and also in the hope of taking the sting out of an eventual P—B4.

20 QR—Kt1!   B—B4

An unfortunate necessity, R x B being threatened.

21 B x B   P x B
22 P—B4!   ....

The position calls for the opening of new lin●s.

22 . . . .   P x P
23 R x P ch   ·K—Kt2

Likewise after 23 . . . K—K1; 24 R x P Black's position would be unpleasant.

24 R x P ch   K—R1
25 R (4)—B7   R—R4
26 P—K5!   Kt—B4

Black's position has become untenable. If 26 . . . Q—Kt3; 27 Q x Q followed by Kt—K4--B6 and wins.

27 Q—K4   P—R4

Of course if 27 . . . R—Q1; 28 Kt—Q5! just the same.

28 Kt—Q5   R—Q1

Position after Black's 28th move

Werlinsky

Marshall

29 R—B6   ....

Kt—B6 would also win.
At this point Black overstepped the time limit, but he was clearly lost: 29 . . . Q—B1 (not 29 . . . Q x Kt? 30 Q x Q, R x Q; 31 R—B8 mate); 30 R—QB7, Q—Kt1; 31 R—QKt6, Q—R1; 32 P—Kt4 and wins.

---

108. Moscow, 1925

QUEEN'S GAMBIT DECLINED

Rubinstein was not in good form in this tourney; but even after that explanation, his downfall after only twenty-five moves is striking!

F. J. MARSHALL   A. RUBINSTEIN

White	Black
1 P—Q4	P—Q4
2 P—QB4	P—K3
3 Kt—QB3	Kt—KB3
4 B—Kt5	QKt—Q2
5 P—K3	B—K2
6 Kt—B3	O—O
7 P x P	....

My trade-mark.

7	P x P
8 B—Q3	R—K1
9 O—O	P—B3
10 Q—B2	Kt—B1
11 QR—K1	....

This is the procedure I prefer. The moderns pin their faith to the "minority attack" with P—QR3 and P—QKt4 intending P—Kt5 in due course.

11 . . . .   Kt—K5

The customary freeing procedure. But White is prepared for it.

12 B x B	Q x B
13 B x Kt	P x B
14 Kt—Q2	P—KB4
15 P—B3!	....

White reasons that since he has

developed more rapidly and has more mobility, the opening up of the K and KB files should favor him.

15 . . . .   P x P
16 Kt x P   B—K3
17 P—K4   . . . .

Now we see why White played 11 QR—K1.

17 . . . .   P x P
18 R x P   QR—Q1
19 R—K5   P—KR3

Guarding against the unpleasant threat Kt—KKt5.

20 Kt—K4   Q—Kt5

This is not fatal, but it is surely unwise to remove the Queen from the center.   . . .Q—QB2 was safer.

21 P—QR3   Q—B5

. . . .Q—Kt3 should have been played. Black is courting serious danger.

22 Q—B2   B—B2?

After this he is definitely lost. Correct was 22 . . . Kt—Kt3 and if 23 R—QB5, Q—Q6.

Position after Black's 22nd move

Rubinstein

Marshall

23 P—QKt3!   Q x KtP?

Losing quickly, but 23 . . . Q—R3, recommended in the Tournament Book, would also prove inadequate. White would reply 24 R x R with these possibilities:
I 24 . . . R x R; 25 Kt—K5, B—Q4; 26 Kt—Q6, R—Q1; 27 Kt—B5 with the decisive threat of Q—Kt3.
II 24 . . . B x R; 25 Kt—K5, Kt—K3; 26 Kt—B6ch! P x Kt; 27 Q x P with an easy win.

24 Kt(3)—Q2!   Q—R7
25 Kt—QB3   Resigns

Triumph of the KB file! An original finish.

---

109. New York, 1926

(Metropolitan Chess League Match)

QUEEN'S GAMBIT DECLINED

Rook and Pawn endings proverbially abound in thorny technical difficulties. The concluding play in the following game is a good example.

F. J. MARSHALL   G. MAROCZY

White   Black

1 P—Q4   Kt—KB3
2 Kt—KB3   P—Q4
3 P—B4   P—K3
4 Kt—B3   B—K2
5 B—Kt5   O—O
6 P—K3   Kt—K5

As explained in Game no. 59, Black hopes to free himself by exchanging pieces. White selects what is nowadays considered the best continuation.

7 B x B   Q x B
8 P x P ·   Kt x Kt
9 P x Kt   P x P
10 Q—Kt3   R—Q1

. . . Q—Q3 is preferred at present. As will be seen, the Rook is not very well placed on the Q file.

11 B—Q3	Kt—B3
12 O—O	R—Q3?

Surprising from conservative Maroczy. . . . . R—Kt1 was better.

13 P—K4!   . . . .

Exploiting Black's last move to increase his command of the board (if 13 . . . P x P; 14 B x P, Q x B; 15 KR—K1 and wins).

13	B—Kt5
14 P—K5	R(3)—Q1

If 14 . . . R—R3; 15 Q x QP and Black has no compensation for the lost Pawn.

15 Kt—Q2   . . . .

In such situations, my preference is always for an aggressive move as against the rather uninspired capture of the QKtP, which more often than not leads to difficulties.

15	Q—Q2
16 QR—K1	QR—Kt1
17 Q—B2	P—KKt3
18 P—KR3	B—B4

Maroczy could not have been very cheerful about the ensuing break-up of his King-side, but after . . . B—K3 Black would have to contend with the duly prepared advance of White's KBP and KtP.

19 B x B	Q x B
20 Q x Q	P x Q
21 R—K3	. . . .

Going after the weak KBP, which cannot be maintained for very long.

21	Kt—K2
22 R—Kt3ch	K—B1
23 R—B3	K—Kt2
24 R—K1	QR—B1
25 Kt—B1	P—B4

Black must naturally seek counter-chances on the Queen-side. By

obtaining a Queen-side majority of Pawns, he deflects White's forces to that sector.

26 Kt—K3	P x P
27 P x P	R—B3

Realizing that passive defense will not do: 27 . . . K—Kt3; 28 R—Kt3ch, K—R3; 29 P—B4, R—KKt1 (White threatened R—Kt5); 30 R x R, R x R; 31 R—QB1 and Black's position is hopeless.

28 Kt x Pch	Kt x Kt
29 R x Kt	KR—QB1
30 R—K3	R—B8ch
31 K—R2	R(8)—B3
32 R—Kt3ch	R—Kt3
33 R—R3	. . . .

White wants to force the advance of the Queen-side Pawns so as to make them more accessible to attack.

33	P—QR3
34 R—QR5	P—Kt4
35 P—QR4	R—QKt1

Now that the QKtP becomes a threat, the remaining play must be handled with great care.*

36 R—B3	R—QB3
37 R—Kt3	R(3)—QKt3

Or 37 . . . R—B5; 38 P x P, P x P; 39 R(5) x P, R x R; 40 R x R, R x P; 41 K—Kt3 and wins.

38 P—B4	K—Kt3
39 P—Kt4	P—R4
40 K—Kt3	. . . .

White's Pawn mass is at last in action.

40	RP x P
41 KRP x P	P—B4
42 P x P	RP x P
43 R—QB3!	R(1)—Kt2

If 43 . . . P—Kt5; 44 R—B7! P—Kt6; 45 R(5)—R7! R—Kt1 (White threatened mate in two); 46 either R—Kt7 winning easily. The mating motif is now the predominant factor in the remaining play.

| 44 R—R8 | P—Kt5 |
| 45 R—Kt8ch! | K—R2 |

If 45 . . . R—Kt2; 46 P x Pch wins.

| 46 R(3)—B8 | P—Kt6 |

How is the Pawn to be stopped?!

47 R—R8ch	K—Kt3
48 R(B8)—Kt8ch	K—B2
49 R—B8ch	Resigns

The Final Position

Maroczy

Marshall

Actually the game was adjourned here, but Maroczy courteously resigned without further play. The most plausible continuation would have been 49 . . . K—Kt2; 50 P x P, P—Kt7; 51 P—B6ch, R x P (if 51 . . . K—Kt3; 52 K—Kt4, P—Kt8 (Q); 53 R(B8)—Kt8ch, K—B2; 54 R—Kt7ch, K—K3; 55 R—K8ch, R—K2; 56 R x R mate); 52 P x R ch, K—Kt3; 53 R—R1, P—Kt8(Q); 54 R x Q; and wins.
Or 49 . . . K—K2; 50 P x P, P—Kt7; 51 R(B8)—KKt8, K—Q2; 52 R—Kt7ch, K—B3; 53 R—R6ch, K—Kt4; 54 R x R(Kt7), R x R; 55 R—R1 and Black's Rook will be helpless against the passed Pawns.

110. New York, 1926
EVANS GAMBIT

Another game from a Dimock Tournament. Eddie Santasiere has been my good friend for many years, and in that time we have played quite a number of exciting games. Here is a struggle in which we both strive our utmost to win.

A. E. Santasiere   F. J. Marshall

White	Black
1 P—K4	P—K4
2 Kt—KB3	Kt—QB3
3 B—B4	B—B4
4 P—QKt4	B x P
5 O—O	. . . .

This is weaker than the customary 5 P—B3, but it was obligatory in the tournament. The best reply is 5 . . . Kt—B3.

| 5 . . . . | P—Q3 |

Now the game transposes into the usual lines of the Evans.

| 6 P—B3 | B—R4 |
| 7 P—Q4 | B—KKt5 |

An aggressive but risky reply. 7 . . . B—Kt3 (Lasker's move) is best.

| 8 Q—Kt3 | B x Kt |
| 9 P x B | . . . . |

Better than 9 B x Pch, K—B1; 10 B x Kt, R x B; 11 P x B, Q—Q2 or 11 . . . B—Kt3. Quite inferior would be 9 Q x P? B x KP; 10 P—Q5, QKt—K2; 11 Q—Kt5ch, P—B3 and Black is a piece ahead.

9	P x P
10 Q x P	Kt—K4
11 K—R1	. . . .

Avoiding the capture of the KBP with check, so that if now 11 . . . Kt x P? 12 Q—Q5 wins.

| 11 . . . . | R—Kt1 |

12 Q—R6	Kt x B

Beginning a series of exchanges to minimize White's attacking chances.

13 Q x Kt	P x P
14 Kt x P	B x Kt
15 Q x B	Q—B3

If now 16 Q x P, Q x Pch; 17 K—Kt1, Q—Kt5ch; 18 K—R1, Q—B6 ch; (not 18 . . . Q x Pch? 19 P—B3, Q—Kt2; 20 R—K1ch and wins) drawing by perpetual check. White therefore makes a last attempt to win which leads to exciting play.

16 P—K5!	P x P
17 R—K1	Kt—K2
18 R x P	R—Kt4!

White was threatening to win with B—Kt5 or B—R3.

Position after Black's 18th move

Marshall

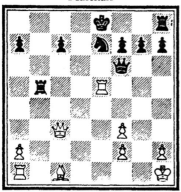

Santasiere

19 R x Ktch! •	K x R!

If 19 . . . Q x R; 20 B—R3 wins (20 . . . Q—Q2; 21 Q x KtP or 20 . . . Q—Kt4; 21 Q—B6ch, K—Q1; 22 Q—R8ch etc.

20 Q x Pch	K—K1
21 Q—B8ch	Q—Q1

22 Q—B6ch	Q—Q2
23 Q—R8ch	Drawn

A short but sharp battle.

---

111.   Chicago, 1926
QUEEN'S GAMBIT DECLINED

For a while the game proceeds on quiet positional lines; suddenly there is a dramatic interruption, followed by an abrupt finish.

F. J. MARSHALL   A. KUPCHIK

White	Black
1 P—Q4	Kt—KB3
2 P—QB4	P—B3
3 Kt—QB3	P—Q4
4 Kt—B3	P—K3

Subsequently the variation 4 . . . P x P; 5 P—QR4, B—B4; 6 Kt—K5 became very fashionable.

5 B—Kt5	QKt—Q2
6 P x P	. . . .

As in Game no. 100, I avoid the Cambridge Springs Defense.

6	KP x P
7 P—K3	B—K2
8 B—Q3	O—O
9 Q—B2	R—K1
10 O—O	Kt—B1
11 QR—K1	B—K3

In the event of 11 . . . Kt—K5 I intended continuing with 12 B x B, Q x B; 13 B x Kt, P x B; 14 Kt—Q2, P—KB4; 15 P—B3! as in my Moscow encounter with Rubinstein.

12 Kt—K5	KKt—Q2
13 B x B	R x B

. . . Q x B is more customary in such positions, but Kupchik foresees White's reply, after which it becomes desirable for Black to double Rooks on the K file.

14 P—B4	P—B3

15 Kt x Kt	Q x Kt
16 P—B5	B—B2

The position is rather reminiscent of my game with Duras (Game no. 31) played more than two decades earlier! We now have a struggle between White's attacking chances on the K-side and Black's counterplay in the center and on the other wing.

17 R—B3	QR—K1
18 Q—B2	P—KR3
19 P—QR3	Kt—R2

Hoping to be able to play . . . Kt—Kt4—K5.

20 P—KR4	Q—Q3

A few moves later, it will become clear that the Queen should have gone to B2, where it would have been protected by the Rook on K2. But this was difficult to foresee!

21 R—Kt3	K—R1
22 Kt—K2	P—QKt3
23 Kt—B4	P—B4?

The plan itself is good, but its execution is decidedly untimely. Some such move as . . . Q—Q2 or . . . Q—B2 was in order.

Position after Black's 23rd move

Kupchik

Marshall

24 R x P!	. . . .

A fatal surprise for Black. If 24 . . . K x R; 25 Q—Kt3ch and Black's Queen is lost after a Knight check.

24	Q—Q1
25 R—Kt3	P x P

A vain hope; White's reply is too strong.

26 Kt—Kt6ch	B x Kt
27 P x B	R x P

Or 27 . . . P x P; 28 Q—B4, Kt—B1; 29 Q x RPch, K—Kt1; 30 P—Kt7 and wins.

28 R(K1) x R	P x R
29 P—Kt7ch!	K—Kt1
30 Q—B5	Resigns

---

112. Chicago, 1926
QUEEN'S GAMBIT DECLINED

This game was played in the semi-final round, and I needed a win in order to come out ahead of Torre and Maroczy. The game proved worthy of the occasion!

F. J. MARSHALL	G. MAROCZY
White	Black
1 P—Q4	Kt—KB3
2 P—QB4	P—K3
3 Kt—QB3	P—Q4
4 B—Kt5	B—K2
5 P—K3	O—O
6 Kt—B3	QKt—Q2

Indicating that he is heading for the Orthodox Defense; he evidently does not care to repeat 6 . . . Kt—K5 as in Game no. 109, played a few months earlier.

7 R—B1	P—B3
8 B—Q3	P x P
9 B x P	Kt—Q4
10 B x B	Q x B
11 O—O	Kt(4)—Kt3

This leads to trouble. The simplest equalizing line is 11 ... Kt x Kt; 12 R x Kt, P—K4.

| 12 B—Kt3 | P—K4 |
| 13 P—Q5! | .... |

A powerful advance. Black appears to have nothing better than the following exchanges, which, however, result in the powerful centralization of White's Queen.

13	P x P
14 Kt x QP	Kt x Kt
15 Q x Kt	P—K5

Allowing the Knight to take up a very strong post at Q4, but he had no choice (if 15 ... R—K1; 16 R—B7 followed by KR—B1 with a won game).

| 16 Kt—Q4 | Kt—B3 |
| 17 Q—KKt5 | P—KR3 |

An awkward situation for Black, since he has so much difficulty developing his Bishop. White threatened 18 R x B! KR x R; 19 Kt—B5, Q—B1; 20 Kt—R6ch, K—R1; 21 Kt x Pch, K—Kt1; 22 Kt—Q6ch etc.

| 18 Q—B4 | Kt—K1 |

A disheartening move to be forced to make, but R—B7 must be prevented.

| 19 KR—Q1 | P—KKt4 |

Seriously weakening his position, but if instead 19 ... B—Q2; 20 Kt—B5, B x Kt; 21 Q x B, Kt—Q3; 22 Q—Q5, KR—Q1; 23 R—Q4 with a vastly superior position.

| 20 Q—Kt3 | B—Q2 |
| 21 P—KR4 | .... |

Taking advantage of Black's weakening of his King-side.

| 21 .... | P—QR4 |

Pointless. It would have been better to play some such move as ... Kt—Kt2 or ... Kt—Q3 or ...

R—B1, although a satisfactory defense was no longer possible.

| 22 P x P | P x P |
| 23 B—Q5! | Kt—Q3 |

Or 23 ... B—B1; 24 Kt—Kt5 threatening R—Q4 or Kt—B7. Now that the Knight has been drawn away from the protection of Black's QB2 after all, White's Rook invades the seventh rank.

| 24 R—B7 | QR—B1 |

Position after Black's 24th move

Maroczy

Marshall

| 25 R x B! | .... |

A nice sacrifice of the exchange which has an even neater sequel.

| 25 .... | Q x R |
| 26 Q x Pch | K—R2 |

If 26 ...K—R1; 27 Q—K5ch, P—B3; 28 Q—R2ch! K—Kt2; 29 Q x Kt etc.

| 27 Q—R5ch | K—Kt2 |

If 27 ... K—Kt1; 28 Q—Kt6ch, K—R1; 29 Q—R6ch, K—Kt1; 30 Kt—K6! wins.

| 28 Q—K5ch | K—R2 |
| 29 Kt—K6! | .... |

This clinches it. White simplifles into a won ending with two Pawns and a mighty Bishop for a Rook, with the likelihood of winning a third.

29	....	P x Kt
30	B x Pch	K—Kt1
31	R x Kt	Q—K2
32	Q—Kt3ch	....

And not 32 R x P??? R—B8ch; 33 K—R2, Q—R5 mate! The text forces the exchange of Queens, for if 32 . . . K—R1; 33 Q—R3ch, K—Kt1; 34 R x P, R—B8ch; 35 K—R2, Q—B2ch; 36 P—B4 and Black is helpless.

32	....	Q—Kt2
33	Q x Qch	K x Q
34	P—B4	....

Naturally much better than 34 R x P, R—B8ch followed by . . . R x P.

| 34 | .... | KR—Q1 |
| 35 | R—Kt6 | .... |

Much more forcing than 35 R x P, R—K1. The main thing is to keep up the pressure.

35	....	R—B2
36	R x KP	R—Q8ch
37	K—R2	R(2)—Q2
38	R—Kt6	R—K2
39	B x P	R x P
40	B—B3	R—Q7
41	K—Kt3	....

Now that the King is ready to take a hand, the end is in sight.

41	....	P—R5
42	P—B5	P—R6
43	K—B4	R x QKtP

Shortens the agony, but if 43 . . . R—K8; 44 P x P, R x RP; 45 K—Kt5 and Black cannot hold out much longer.

| 44 | R—Kt6ch | Resigns |

113. New York, 1927
QUEEN'S PAWN OPENING

An extremely instructive game from the psychological aspect. I get off to a poor start in the opening, and Vidmar presses me more and more uncomfortably. However, when he is on the point of deriving some tangible benefit from his good play, I find one resource after another; he loses patience, creates weak points in his position, and the counter-attack sets in. Watch the Black Knights get to work!

DR. M. VIDMAR	F. J. MARSHALL
White	Black
1 P—Q4	Kt—KB3
2 Kt—KB3	P—K3
3 P—B4	B—Kt5ch

3 . . . P—QKt3 is somewhat more promising.

| 4 B—Q2 | B x Bch |
| 5 QKt x B | .... |

Q x B is generally favored here, reserving the development of the QKt for QB3, where it has more scope in the center.

| 5 | .... | P—Q4 |

This involves Black in difficulties later on; for it leads to a Pawn formation in which the absence of Black's KB is inconvenient, while the remaining Bishop has trouble getting developed.

The proper course was 5 . . . P—Q3 followed by . . . Q—K2 and . . . P—K4. This would have avoided the drawbacks resulting from the text.

6 P—K3	O—O
7 Q—B2	QKt—Q2
8 B—Q3	P—KR3

Foreshadowing his next move.

| 9 O—O | P—B4!? |

The "safe" move is 9 . . . P—

B3; but is it really safe? It leaves Black with a badly cramped game, with the chances of developing his Bishop postponed indefinitely. The text leads to an open position more to my taste, even if it is White who chiefly profits by it.

10 BP x P	Kt x P
11 P x P	Kt—Kt5
12 B—R7ch	K—R1
13 Q—B4	Kt—R3
14 B—B2	Kt(2) x P
15 P—QKt4	Kt—Q2

White has driven the Knights back with great loss of time, but in the event that he does not achieve a decisive advantage, the advance of the QKtP may turn out to be seriously weakening.

16 KR—Q1	Kt—Kt3
17 Q—Kt3	Q—Q4
18 Q—Kt2	. . . .

Naturally declining the exchange, which would help Black considerably.

18	B—Q2
19 Kt—K4	. . . .

19 P—QR4 can be effectively answered by 19 . . .Q—Q3! Or if 19 B—K4, Kt—R5! 20 B x Q, Kt x Q; 21 B x KtP, Kt x R; 22 B x R, Kt—B6; 23 B—Kt7, Kt x KtP etc.

19	Q—QKt4
20 P—QR3	B—B3

Probably best in this position, which is awkward for Black because his Queen can so easily be subjected to attack.

21 Kt—Q4?	. . . .

Throwing away most of his advantage. Alekhine points out in the tournament book that either 21 Kt—K5 or 21 B—Q3 would have maintained the advantage.

21	Q—K4
22 P—B4?	. . . .

In order to make his next move possible, White weakens his center in a manner which subsequently proves irreparable. Q—Kt1 was preferable.

22	Q—B2
23 Kt x B	P x Kt

This Pawn is apparently an ugly weakness, and the Knight at R3 soon has to go to an even worse square. But, surprising as it may seem, Black's position has important resources!

24 B—Q3	Kt—Kt1
25 QR—B1	Kt—Q4

Beginning the counterplay based on the weakening of White's center.

26 Q—KB2	P—QR4!
27 P—Kt5	Q—Kt3!

Threatening two Pawns, and thus forcing White's reply, which leads to an obvious improvement of Black's game.

28 P x P	Kt x QBP
29 Kt—B5	QR—Q1
30 P—Kt4?	. . . .

This and the following move are evidently products of White's disappointment at not having achieved more tangible results. The natural outcome is that additional weaknesses are created in his position.

30	Kt(4)—K2
31 P—KR4?	R—Q4!

With this move the game reaches its crisis, for if White's forced reply had to be answered by . . . R(4)—Q1, White would obtain the better game with 33 R—Kt1.

32 P—K4	. . . .

(see diagram next page)

32	R—Q5!

This must have come as a sur-

Position after White's 32nd move

Marshall

Dr. Vidmar

prise to White. The idea is if 33
Kt—Q7, Q—Q1; 34 Kt x R, R x B;
35 R x R, Q x R and the Knight is
lost (36 P—B5, P x P; 37 KP x P,
K—Kt1; 38 P—B6, P x P etc.).

| 33 P—B5 | P x P |
| 34 KtP x P | Kt—K4! |

White's Pawn advances have
created good squares for the hostile Knights, and now the process
of retribution begins. 35 Q x R?
would of course lose the Queen.

35 B—K2	R x Rch
36 R x R	R—Q1
37 R x Rch	Q x R
38 P—B6	....

White welcomes exchanges in
the hope that they will make it
easier for him to defend his weaknesses; but this proves impossible.

38	Kt(2)—B3
39 P x Pch	K x P
40 K—Kt2	....

As Alekhine points out in the
Tournament Book, the ending is
as unfavorable for White as the
middle game, for example 40 Kt—
Q3, Kt x Kt; 41 Q—Kt3ch, K—R2;
42 B x Kt, Q—Q5ch; 43 K—B1,
Kt—K4 etc.

| 40 .... | Kt—Kt3 |
| 41 K—R3 | .... |

Or 41 P—R5, Q—Kt4ch; 42 K—
B1, Kt—B5 etc.

| 41 .... | Q—Q3! |

Threatening to win a piece with
. . . Kt—B5ch. White's position
continues to deteriorate.

| 42 K—Kt2 | Kt—Q5 |
| 43 Kt—Kt7 | .... |

A terrible place for the Knight;
but if 43 Kt—Q3, Kt x B; 44 Q x Kt,
Q x Kt winning a piece.

| 43 .... | Q—K4 |
| 44 K—B1 | Kt—B5 |

Strengthening his position (not
44 . . . Q x P? 45 Q x Pch etc.).

| 45 Q—Kt3ch | K—R2 |
| 46 B—Q3 | Kt(Q5)—K3! |

Threatening to win the Knight
with 47 . . . Q—R8ch and 48 . . .
Q—Kt7ch and thus compelling the
Bishop to join the Knight in exile.

| 47 B—R6 | Q—R8ch |
| 48 Q—K1 | Q—Kt7! |

Beginning the decisive attack.
Mating menaces are combined with
threats against White's minor
pieces. Thus if 49 Q—B2, Q—B8
ch; 50 Q—K1, Q—B3 winning a
piece.

| 49 Q—K3 | Q—Kt7ch |
| 50 K—K1 | Q—B7! |

Again threatening . . . Q—B3,
not to mention . . . Kt—Kt7ch.

| 51 Q—KB3 | Kt—Kt7ch |

51 . . . Q—B3 would have been
met by Q—B1.

| 52 K—B1 | Kt(3)—B5! |

Threatening the amusing mate
53 . . . Q—B8ch; 54 K—B2, Q—K8
mate!

53 K—Kt1	Kt x P
54 (—B1	Q x P
55 Kt—B5	Q—K6ch
56 K—R1	Q x Kt

If now 57 Q x Kt, Q—Q4ch and mate in two more moves. White tries a spite check before resigning.

57 B—Q3ch	P—B4!

White resigns, as he still cannot capture the Knight. An uncommonly instructive game.

---

114. London, 1927

(Best-played game prize)

NIMZOVICH DEFENSE

In this game I had the pleasure of using Nimzovich's own weapons against him, beginning with the choice of opening!

A. NIMZOVICH	F. J. MARSHALL
White	Black
1 P—Q4	Kt—KB3
2 P—QB4	P—K3
3 Kt—QB3	B—Kt5
4 Q—B2	. . . .

There is a wide variance of taste among the masters here. The text is the most usual, and probably the strongest.

4	P—Q4
5 P—K3	. . . .

This and his next move are rather slow. 5 P x P has been the favored move in recent years.

5	O—O
6 P—QR3	B x Ktch
7 P x B	P—QKt3

Having the better prospects of development, Black does not fear the two Bishops.

8 P x P	P x P
9 Kt—B3	P—B4

10 P x P	. . . .

Playing to give Black the "hanging Pawns." This plan is too mechanical, as Black has ample compensation: superior development, more terrain, easier access to the open files and good squares for his Knights. However, White must make an effort to open up the position for his Bishops, and the text is a beginning.

10	P x P
11 B—K2	Kt—B3
12 O—O	P—B5!

This looks bad at first sight, because it leaves the QP backward on the open file, and gives White's pieces command of his Q4; on the other hand, Black hems in the Bishops seriously (his prime objective) and gains a good square for his Knight at QB4.

13 R—Q1	Q—R4
14 Kt—Q4	B—Q2
15 P—B3	. . . .

Preparing an attempt to free himself in due course by P—K4.

15	KR—K1
16 R—Kt1	QR—Kt1

Preventing R—Kt5.

17 R x R	Kt x R
18 Q—Q2	Kt—R3

The Knight is headed for QR5.

19 P—K4!	. . . .

The only chance to gain some freedom.

19	Kt—B4!
20 P x P	Kt x P

Indirectly defending the QBP, for if 21 B x P? Kt—K6 wins.

21 B—Kt2	Kt—R5
22 B—R1	. . . .

The alternative was 22 R—QB1.

22	Kt (5) x P
23 B x P	Q—B4
24 QB x Kt	Q x B
25 B—Kt2	P—KR3
26 R—QB1	Q—R3

White has pretty well managed to work himself out of a difficult situation, and should now continue with 27 R—K1. Instead, he commits a serious mistake.

27 Kt—B5?　　　. . . .

This plausible move is refuted in an unexpected manner.

27	B x Kt
28 Q x Kt	Q—KKt3!
29 Q—Q2	B—Q6!

Strangely enough, this move leaves White without an adequate defense.

Position after Black's 29th move

Marshall

Nimzovich

30 R—B3　　　. . . .

There was no way out. For example 30 R—K1, Q—Kt3ch; 31 K—R1, R x Rch; 32 Q x R, Q x B. Or 30 Q—B3, R—K7; 31 P—Kt3, Q—Kt3ch; 32 Q—Q4 (if 32 Q—B5, Q x B or 32 K—R1, Q x B! and 33 Q x B? leads to mate), Q x B, 33 R—B8ch, K—R2; 34 Q x Bch, P—

Kt3 and White can resign, as he cannot parry both mating threats: one on the last rank with Queen or Rook, and the other by 35 . . . R—Kt7ch etc.

30 . . . .　　　**R—K7**

White resigns. A surprising finish.

115.　Bad Kissingen, 1928
(First brilliancy prize)

INDIAN DEFENSE

Although the favorite opening variations of the hypermodern masters are a far cry from the lines which were popular in my youth, I enjoy using these modern lines. It is amusing to see how the younger masters react to the use of their own weapons against them; as in the previous game, the distinguished author of "My System" comes a cropper.

A. NIMZOVICH	F. J. MARSHALL
White	Black
1 P—Q4	Kt—KB3
2 P—QB4	P—QKt3

In those days, the hypermoderns did not consider relinquishing the center as a matter of great importance. Subsequently, I came to the conclusion that 2 . . . P—QKt3 is out of order here; it should be delayed until White has played Kt—KB3 (say 2 . . . P—K3; 3 Kt—KB3, P—QKt3), or until Black can pin the QKt with his KB.

| 3 Kt—QB3 | B—Kt2 |
| 4 B—Kt5 | . . . . |

Much more to the point would be 4 Q—B2 to be followed by P—K4. White would then have a formidable center, leaving Black's QB out in the cold. The text now draws two drawbacks: the immediate development of the Bishop accomplishes little, and it neglects the desirable policy of advancing in the center.

4	P—K3
5 Q—B2	P—KR3!

"Putting the question" as recommended by Nimzovich!

6 B—R4	B—K2

The alternative was 6 . . . B—Kt5, more in accordance with my famous opponent's theory of remote control of the center. But I was anxious to do away with the pin on my KKt.

7 P—K4	O—O
8 P—K5?	. . . .

An impetuous and superficial advance which weakens the center Pawns. P—B3 or B—Q3 was the positional move.

8	Kt—Q4!

Did Nimzovich miss this reply?

9 B—Kt3?	. . . .

Losing valuable time, as this Bishop has no future. 9 B x B was much better.

9	Kt—Kt5

Nimzovich must have thought that this Knight would get into difficulties. If so, he didn't see ahead far enough.

10 Q—Kt3	P—Q4!
11 P x P e. p.	. . . .

There is hardly anything better, for if 11 P—QR3, P x P and White cannot retake either way. In addition, White is glad to get rid of his useless QB.

11	KB x P
12 O—O—O	. . . .

Very risky, but if 12 P—QR3, Kt(5)—B3 and the QP is doubly attacked; and meanwhile King-side castling is a long way off.

12	QKt—B3
13 B x B	Q x B

14 P—QR3	. . . .

This leads to a catastrophe. Relatively best was 14 Kt—Kt5 (not 14 Kt—B3 Kt—R4!), Q—K2; 15 P—QR3, Kt—R3 leaving Black with good attacking chances.

Position after White's 14th move

Marshall

Nimzovich

14	Kt x P!

An unexpected sacrifice which gives Black a lasting initiative because of his opponent's backward development.

If now 15 Q x Kt, P—QB4; 16 Q—R4, B—B3; 17 Q—R6 (a terrible place for the Queen), Q—B5ch; 18 K—Kt1, Q x BP; 19 KKt—K2, KR—Q1 with tremendous pressure.

15 R x Kt	Q x R
16 P x Kt	Q x KBP

In the Tournament Book, Tartakover gives the following variations to show the helplessness of White's position:

I 17 Kt—B3, B x Kt; 18 P x B, Q x KBP; 19 R—Kt1, Q—K6ch.

II 17 Kt—R3, Q—K6ch; 18 K—Kt1 (if 18 K—B2, KR—Q1), B—K5ch; 19 K—R2 (still worse is 19 K—R1, Q—B8ch; 20 K—R2, B—B7; 21 Q—R3, P—QR4; 22 P—Kt5, P—R5), P—QR4! 20 P—Kt5, P—R5! 21 Q—R3 (if 21 Q—Kt4, B—B7 or 21 Q—Q1, P—R6!), B—B7 with a winning game.

17 Q—Q1	KR—Q1
18 Q—K2	Q—B5ch
19 K—B2	P—QR4!

New lines must be opened. If now 20 P—Kt5, P—R5 with ... P—R6 to follow.

20 P x P	R x P
21 Kt—B3	R—R8
22 K—Kt3	P—QKt4!

For a moment the King seems safe, but Black's reply has freshened up the attack.

| 23 Q—K5 | . . . . |

If 23 P x P, B—Q4ch; 24 Kt x B, Q—R5ch; 25 K—B3, R x Kt; or 23 Kt x P, B—K5! threatening . . . P—QB3 or . . . B—Q6 with a winning game in all cases.

23	P x Pch
24 K—Kt4	Q—B8
25 Kt—QKt5	P—B4ch!

White resigns, for if 26 K x P, R—Q4ch; or 26 Q x P, Q x Pch and mate follows.

---

116. Budapest, 1928

QUEEN'S GAMBIT DECLINED

This game makes a pleasing impression because of the drastic way in which White is punished for his creation of weaknesses.

H. KMOCH   F. J. MARSHALL

White	Black
1 P—Q4	Kt—KB3
2 P—QB4	P—K3
3 Kt—QB3	P—Q4
4 B—Kt5	QKt—Q2
5 P—K3	B—Kt5

With the same aggressive tendencies as in Game no. 98.

| 6 P x P | P x P |
| 7 Kt—K2 | . . . . |

A clumsy move which is clearly inferior to the alternatives Q—R4 or B—Q3. '

7	P—B3
8 Q—B2	O—O
9 Kt—Kt3	P—KR3!

Well timed, for if 10 B—KB4, P—KKt4; 11 B—K5, Kt—Kt5 and Black wins a Pawn. Thus he is compelled to exchange, proving the inadequacy of his opening play.

10 B x Kt	Kt x B
11 B—Q3	R—K1
12 O—O	B—Q3
13 Kt—B5	. . . .

The excellent position of this Knight compensates to some extent for the fact that White has made very little of the opening moves.

13	B—B2
14 KR—K1	B—K3
15 P—B3?	. . . .

Possibly intending P—K4, but Black's surprising reply shows that the advance is faulty.

| 15 . . . . | B x Kt! |

Leads to Bishops of opposite color, but it enables Black to create a new weakness in White's Kingside and makes it possible for him to post his pieces favorably.

| 16 B x B | Q—Q3 |
| 17 P—KKt3 | R—K2! |

Training his guns on the rather weak KP.

18 QR—Q1	QR—K1
19 Q—Q3	B—Kt3
20 K—R1	. . . .

If 20 P—K4, P x P; 21 P x P, R—Q1 and White's center Pawns are dangerously weak (22 P—K5? R x P).

20 . . . .   P—Kt3!

Driving back the Bishop on an inferior diagonal.

21 B—R3   P—B4!

Black must take the initiative in the center. He does not fear the simplifying line 22 P x P, Q x BP; 23 Kt x P (or 23 Kt—R4, Q—R4 with advantage), Kt x Kt; 24 Q x Kt, Q x Q; 25 R x Q, R x P; 26 R—KB1 (if 26 R x R, R x R winning the BP because of the threat of . . . R—K8ch), R—K7 and despite the Bishops of opposite color, the ending is easily won for Black.

22 Kt—Kt5   Q—B3
23 P x P   B x P
24 Kt—Q4   Q—Kt3!

Forcing the win of a Pawn. White's game now disintegrates very rapidly.

25 Kt—Kt3   B x P
26 B—B1   P—R3
27 Q—Kt1   P—Q5
28 B—B4   . . . .

Very plausible, threatening Q x P ch. But there is an immediate refutation.

28 . . . .   Kt—Kt5!

White resigns. Somewhat premature, but he has no way of preventing the loss of the exchange.

(see diagram next column)

---

117. Hastings Christmas
Tournament, 1928-29

FRENCH DEFENSE

A narrow margin often separates "an uneventful draw" from a really interesting production with a decisive result. The difference is frequently due to some harmless-looking inexactitudes on the part of the loser.

The Final Position

Marshall

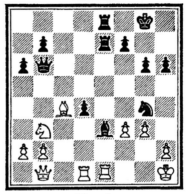

Kmoch

F. J. MARSHALL SIR G. A. THOMAS

White   Black

1 P—K4   P—K3
2 P—Q4   P—Q4
3 Kt—QB3   B—Kt5
4 P x P   . . . .

A tranquil continuation which does not inconvenience Black unduly. 4 P—K5 offers better prospects of securing the initiative.

4 . . . .   P x P
5 B—Q3   Kt—QB3
6 Kt—K2   KKt—K2
7 O—O   B—KB4

The position has taken on a fairly level appearance. White therefore plays for the Bishop-pair, which should assure him a slight advantage, microscopic though it may be with best play by Black.

8 P—QR3   B x Kt
9 P x B   O—O
10 P—QB4   . . . .

This is played with two objects in view: after . . . P x P; 11 B x P

White will have a more open game with scope for his Bishops; while in the event that his KB is removed, he will not have to fear the powerful maneuver . . . Kt—R4—B5, giving Black's QKt an admirable position.

10 . . . .   B x B

Instead of developing his opponent's game with this move, Black would have done better to further his own development with . . . Q—Q2.

11 Q x B	P x P
12 Q x P	Q—Q4
13 Q—Q3	QR—Q1
14 R—Kt1!	. . . .

This is reminiscent of Game no. 94. Instead of bothering to protect the QP, White plays to get his Rook on the seventh rank.

14 . . . .   Kt x P

The alternative was 14 . . . P—QKt3; 15 R—Kt5, Q—Q2; 16 B—Kt2 with a somewhat freer game for White.

15 Kt x Kt	Q x Kt
16 R x P	Q x Q
17 P x Q	R x P
18 R x BP	Kt—B1

Here are further similarities to the game with Sharp: White's Bishop is stronger than Black's Knight, and White hopes to double Rooks on the seventh rank.

19 B—K3   KR—Q1

19 . . . R x P? would lose: 20 KR—B1, Kt—Q3 (not 20 . . . Kt—Kt3? 21 B—B5); 21 B—B5, R—Q6; 22 R—Q7, R—B1; 23 R—K1 winning a piece.

20 P—QR4   R—R6?

Tempting but inferior. The best chance was 20 . . . R(6)—Q2, although after 21 R x R, R x R; 22 R—B1, Kt—K2; 23 K—B1 White would still have an edge because

of the weakness of Black's QRP.

21 KR—B1	Kt—Kt3
22 R x RP	Kt—B5

After 22 . . . Kt x P? 23 P—R3! the pin would be fatal for Black.

23 B—Kt5!   P—B3

Position after Black's 23rd move

Thomas

Marshall

24 P—R4!   . . . .

This powerful reply must have come as a great surprise. It combines a mating attack on the seventh rank with relief from Black's mating threat on the last rank.

24 . . . .   Kt—Kt7

If 24 . . . P x B; 25 R x Kt and Black is helpless against the coming R(4)—B7.

25 R(1)—B7!	P x B
26 R x Pch	K—B1
27 R x RP	K—Kt1
28 R(QR7)—Kt7ch	K—B1
29 R—Kt7!	K—Kt1

Forced.

30 P—KR5!   Resigns

The further advance of the KRP must obviously lead to a very

quick win. For example: 30 ...
R—Q3 (the threat was R(Kt7)—
Kt7ch followed by P—R6 and R—
R8 mate); 31 R(R7)—QB7, R—Q1;
32 P—R6 and Black has no defense
against the mating threat R—KR7
followed by R(Kt7)—Kt7ch, etc.

---

118. Hastings Christmas Tournament 1928-29

QUEEN'S PAWN OPENING

There is a lively contrast between the somewhat conservative
opening play and the dashing phase
which follows.

F. J. MARSHALL   G. M. NORMAN
White   Black

1 P—Q4	Kt—KB3
2 Kt—KB3	P—K3
3 P—B4	B—Kt5ch
4 QKt—Q2	....

Played as a welcome change
from the invariable B—Q2.

4	O—O
5 P—K3	P—QKt3
6 B—Q3	B—Kt2
7 O—O	....

White has handled the opening
in restrained style; but he is now
ready for the terrain-seizing advance P—K4, which induces
Black's reply, creating the danger
that the latter's QB will be buried
alive.

7	P—Q4
8 Kt—K5	P—B4
9 QKt—B3	....

Having ensconced himself very
strongly on K5, White now threatens to force the KB out of play
with P—QR3.

9	BP x P

Parrying the threat, but aiding
White's development by enabling
him to post the QB effectively.

10 KP x P	Kt—K5

"Imitation is the sincerest form
of flattery."

11 P x P	P x P
12 Q—Kt3!	....

Gaining time to exert pressure in
the center. The text will prove
particularly useful in the event of
Black's contemplated ... P—B4.

12	B—K2
13 B—KB4	P—B4?

A serious mistake: ... Kt—Q2
or ... Kt—QB3 was in order.

14 QR—B1!	....

At once taking advantage of
Black's lapse to impede the development of his Queen-side pieces.

14	P—KKt4?

Rendered desperate by the fact
that he cannot bring out his QKt,
he completes the ruination of his
position with this move.
If 14 ... Kt—Q2? 15 Kt x Kt,
Q x Kt; 16 R—B7 etc.
Or 14 ... Kt—R3; 15 B x QKt!
B x B; 16 Kt—B6, Q—Q2; 17 Q x P
ch! and wins.
But 14 ... K—R1 was preferable.

15 B—K3	K—R1

Intending . . . P—B5, which if
played at once would cost a Pawn
(16 B x Kt etc.). This is the critical stage: will White allow his QB
to be driven back?!

(see diagram next page)

16 B x Kt!	QP x B

Not much better would be 16 ...
BP x B; 17 Kt x P! B x Kt; 18
B x B, Q x B; 19 R—B7, B—R3; 20
Q x QP, B x R; 21 Kt—B7ch,
R x Kt; 22 Q x Q, R x R; 23 Q—
Q8ch winning easily.

17 Kt x P!	Q—Q4

The main variation was 17 ...

Position after Black's 15th move

Norman

Marshall

B x Kt; 18 B x B, Q x B; 19 R—B7!
B—B3 (if 19 . . . B—R3; 20 Kt—
B7ch, R x Kt; 21 Q x R and wins);
20 Kt—B7ch! R x Kt; 21 Q x R, B—
Q2; 22 Q—Q5! B—B3 (if 22 . . .
Q—Q1; 23 KR—B1 wins); 23 R—
B8ch, K—Kt2; 24 R—Kt8ch, K—
R3; 25 Q—Q6ch and Black can
resign.

18 R—B7!   . . . .

The shortest way.

18 . . . .   B x Kt
19 B x B   Q x Q

White threatened a quick win beginning with Kt—Kt6ch!

20 P x Q   B—Q4
21 B—K7   Resigns

For if 21 . . . R—K1 (or 21 . . .
Kt—R3; 22 R—Q7); 22 B—B6ch,
K—Kt1; 23 R—Kt7ch, K—B1; 24
R x KRP, R—B1; 25 Kt—Kt6ch,
K—K1; 26 R—K7ch, K—Q1; 27
R—K5ch etc.

A bright little game.

---

119. New York, 1929
(*Metropolitan League Match*)

QUEEN'S INDIAN DEFENSE

This game was played in the
most exciting match that has ever
taken place in these contests. It
occurred in the last match of the
season, with the Manhattan club
six points ahead of us; so that we
had to defeat that formidable ag-
gregation by 6½—1½. We did
just that!

F. J. MARSHALL   I. KASHDAN

White   Black

1 P—Q4   Kt—KB3
2 Kt—KB3   P—K3
3 P—B4   B—Kt5ch
4 B—Q2   Q—K2
5 Kt—B3   . . . .

The most popular move here is
5 P—KKt3. But I always like to
depart from the beaten path.

5 . . . .   P—QKt3
6 P—K3   B—Kt2

Since the continuation which actually occurs is in White's favor,
it would have been more accurate
to play at once for the command
of K5 with 6 . . . B x Kt; 7 B x B,
Kt—K5.

7 B—Q3   KB x Kt
8 B x B   Kt—K5
9 B x Kt!   . . . .

A good move which spoils
Black's plan of controlling K5. The
less energetic 9 Q—B2 would be
answered by . . . P—KB4.

9 . . . .   B x B
10 O—O   O—O
11 Kt—Q2   . . . .

The point of his 9th move. He
is now in a position to build up
a strong game in the center.

11 . . . .   B—Kt2
12 P—K4   P—Q3

13 Q—K2	Kt—Q2
14 QR—K1	P—K4
15 P—B4	P x QP
16 B x P	P—KB4?

Premature and risky. It is well-known that the player with the more constricted game stands to lose from the opening of new lines. Preferable, therefore, was 16 . . . P—KB3 with a cramped but solid game.

17 Q—Q3	QR—K1
18 Q—KKt3!	. . . .

Not 18 P x P, Q x R; 19 R x Q, R x Rch and Black has good winning chances. The text announces Whites' intention of utilizing the Bishop's long diagonal for attacking purposes—the result of Black's dubious 16th move.

18	Kt—B3

If 18 . . . P x P; 19 Kt x P, B x Kt; 20 R x B, Q—B2; 21 KR—K1 and White retains the initiative. In playing the text, Kashdan rightly felt that the loss of the Pawn was only temporary; but he failed to foresee that in regaining the Pawn he would give White the opportunity for working up a decisive attack.

19 P x P	Q—B2
20 Q—Kt5	P—KR3
21 Q—R4	Kt—K5

This was the move relied on.

22 Kt x Kt	R x Kt

Not 22 . . . B x Kt; 23 P—B6! with a powerful attack.

23 R x R	B x R
24 R—K1!	. . . .

Black must have underestimated the strength of this move. The Bishop must remain on K5 (if it moves, R—K7 is decisive) and if 24 . . . R—K1; 25 Q—Kt3 maintains the Pawn ahead with powerful pressure.

24	P—Q4
25 P x P	Q x QP

. . . . Q x BP is answered by Q—K7!

26 B x KKtP!	R x P

If 26 . . . K x B; 27 Q—K7ch regaining the piece and remaining with a clear Pawn to the good.

27 B—K5	K—R2

Forced. But now comes a sacrifice which wins by deflecting Black's Queen from the defense.

Position after Black's 27th move

Kashdan

Marshall

28 R x B!	Q x R
29 Q—K7ch	K—Kt3
30 Q—K8ch	K—R2
31 Q—Q7ch	. . . .

Q—R8ch would have won more rapidly. But since White is himself threatened with mate, he wants to gain time to "look around."

31	K—Kt3
32 Q—K8ch	K—R2
33 Q—R8ch	K—Kt3
34 Q—K8ch	K—R2
35 Q—R8ch	K—Kt3

36 Q—Kt8ch   . . . .

Now everything is in order.

36 . . . .   K—R4
37 Q—K8ch   K—Kt5

If 37 . . . K—R5; 38 B—B6ch
wins the Queen.

38 Q—Kt6ch   K—R5
39 B—B6ch   R x B
40 P—Kt3ch!   K—R6
41 Q—R5 mate

A pleasing finish.

---

120. Carlsbad, 1929
(*Fourth brilliancy prize*)

QUEEN'S PAWN OPENING

It cannot be repeated often
enough that players must beware
of setting out on marauding ex-
peditions before completing their
development. Here is a case in
point.

SIR G. A. THOMAS   F. J. MARSHALL

White   Black

1 P—Q4   P—K3
2 Kt—KB3   P—QB4

Offering White the opportunity
(which he ignores) of turning the
opening into a Sicilian Defense
with 3 P—K4.

3 P—B4   P x P
4 Kt x P   Kt—KB3
5 Kt—QB3   B—Kt5
6 Kt—Kt5   . . . .

Rightly fastening on the weakness in the Q file.

6 . . . .   O—O
7 B—B4?   . . . .

Too ambitious. Stronger was 7
P—QR3! forcing Black to an un-
welcome decision, and holding out
better prospects of exerting pressure on the Q file.

7 . . . .   P—Q4!

Eliminating his difficulties at one
blow. White expected only 7 . . .
Kt—R3; 8 B—Q6 leaving him with
a fine game.

8 P—K3   . . . .

Renouncing the originally intended 8 Kt—B7 because of 8 . . .
Kt—R4! which would give Black
two pieces for a Rook.

8 . . . .   Kt—B3

Still ignoring Kt—B7 which
would now be refuted by . . .
P—K4.

9 P—QR3   B—R4
10 P—QKt4   P—QR3!

Another unexpected retort. There
are many possibilities, all unfavor-
able for White. For example 11
Kt—Q6, Kt x P! 12 Kt x B, Kt—
B3!; or 11 P x B, P x Kt; 12 P x Kt
P, Q x P! 13 Q—Q2, P—K4! 14
P x Kt, P x B; 15 BP x P (if B—K2,
BP x P with a fine game), B x P;
16 B—K2, P—Q5; 17 P x QP, B x P
with much the better game.

White picks out a quieter line,
which is also not quite good
enough.

11 Kt—Q4   B—B2
12 Kt x Kt   P x Kt
13 B x B   Q x B
14 P x P   . . . .

White's procrastination in castling is strange, and on top of his
earlier losses of time, bound to
lead to trouble. However, if 14
B—K2, P—K4 leaves Black with
an excellent game.

14 . . . .   BP x P
15 R—B1   Q—K2
16 Q—Kt3   B—Kt2
17 P—B3   . . . .

His position is becoming uncomfortable. If 17 B—K2, P—Q5 is
annoying.

17 . . . .   P—K4!

Beginning a strong attack.

| 18 B—K2 | P—Q5 |
| 19 Kt—R4 | Kt—Q4! |

Leaving White no choice, for 20 P—K4, Kt—K6 would be intolerable.

| 20 P x P | P x P |
| 21 K—B2 | Kt—B5 |

White is now being punished for his previous inaccuracies.

Position after Black's 21st move

Marshall

Thomas

22 B—B4   . . . .

There appears to be no really satisfactory continuation. Some possibilities:

I 22 KR—K1, Q—Kt4; 23 P—Kt3, Kt x B; 24 K x Kt, P—Q6ch! 25 Q x P, KR—Q1; 26 Q—Kt3, R—Q7ch and wins.

II 22 QR—K1, QR—K1; 23 B—Q1, Q—Kt4; 24 P—Kt3, Kt—R6ch; 25 K—B1, R x Rch; 26 K x R, R—K1ch; 27 K—B1, Q—Q7 winning.

22 . . . .   P—Q6!

Decisive. If 23 KR—K1, P—Q7! If 23 QR—K1, Q—R5ch; 24 P—Kt3, Q—R6.

| 23 B x QP | QR—Q1 |

24 B x Pch   . . . .

Surrendering to the inevitable. If 24 Kt—B5 (or if White plays either Rook to Q1), Black wins with 24 . . . R x B! If 24 QR—K1, Q—Kt4; 25 B—B1, R—Q7ch wins.

| 24 . . . . | K x B |
| 25 QR—K1 | Q—Kt4 |

White resigns. His losses of time proved fatal.

---

121.   Carlsbad, 1929

(Special Prize)

QUEEN'S INDIAN DEFENSE

It is curious to observe how very often a perfectly good defense leads to a poor game when only one equalizing method has been neglected.

F. J. MARSHALL	E. CANAL
White	Black
1 P—Q4	Kt—KB3
2 Kt—KB3	P—K3
3 P—B4	P—QKt3
4 B—Kt5	. . . .

P—KKt3 is stronger. In answer to the text, Black should "put the question" to the Bishop a bit later.

| 4 . . . . | B—Kt2 |
| 5 P—K3 | B—K2 |

This is where Black misses his chance. Correct was 5 . . . P—KR3! 6 B x Kt, Q x B or 6 B—R4, B—Kt5ch; 7 Kt—B3 (not 7 QKt—Q2? P—KKt4! 8 B—Kt3, P—Kt5 winning a piece), B x Ktch with an excellent game for Black in either event.

6 B—Q3	Kt—K5
7 B x B	Q x B
8 B x Kt!	. . . .

An important gain of time—as in a similar position in Game no. 119.

8 . . . .   B x B
9 Kt—B3   B—Kt2
10 O—O   P—KB4

A difficult situation for Black.
A quiet continuation such as 10
. . . P—Q3; 11 P—K4 leaves him
with very poor prospects. But the
text can be answered effectively
with . . .

11 P—Q5!   . . . .

A powerful advance, based on
the tactical point that the natural
reply 11 . . . P—K4 is refuted by
12 P—Q6! (12 . . . Q x P; 13 Q x Q,
P x Q; 14 Kt—QKt5).

11 . . . .   O—O
12 Q—Q4   P—Q3

Black is now ready for . . . P—
K4. Hence White exchanges
Pawns, incidentally gaining an im-
portant outpost for his QKt.

13 P x P   Q x P
14 Kt—Q5   Kt—R3

Capturing the Knight would be
highly disadvantageous, for after
15 P x B, White would have an
easy time of it attacking the backward QBP on the open QB file—
not to mention the later possibility
of Kt—Q4—K6.

15 KR—Q1   P—R3
16 P—QR4   Q—B2

Intending . . . Kt—B4 followed
by . . . P—QR4. Hence White's
next move, which leaves Black's
Knight in an unenviable situation.

17 P—QKt4!   QR—K1
18 Q—Kt2?   R—K5
19 R—Q4   P—B3?

Beginning a faulty attempt to
free himself White's inexact play
could have been refuted by . . . P—
B4! White should have played 18
QR—B1 or Q—B3.

20 Kt—B4   Kt x P

Position after Black's 20th move

Canal

Marshall

21 R x P!   . . . .

Naturally not 21 Q x Kt? P—B4
etc. White's outpost at Q5 is gone,
but he has secured an even greater
advantage in his control of the
only open file.

21 . . . .   P—QR4

If 21 . . . R x BP? 22 Kt—K5
wins; likewise if 21 . . . Q x P? 22
Kt—Q2.

22 Kt—Kt6   Q—B2

He has little choice. If 22 . . .
KR—K1; 23 Kt(3)—K5, Q—B2;
24 R—Q7 wins.

23 QR—Q1   Kt—Q4

Again there is little that Black
can do (23 . . . R—B2; 24 R—Q8
ch, K—R2; 25 Kt—B8ch winning).

24 R(6) x Kt   P x R
25 Kt x R   K x Kt
26 P x P   Q—Q3

He cannot permit the further
advance of the QP; if 26 . . . R x
RP? 27 P—Q6 is decisive.

27 Q—B2!   K—Kt1
28 Kt—Q2!   R—R5?

Losing rapidly. ... R—K1 would have held out longer.

29 P—B4	R—Kt5

If 29 . . . Q x QP; 30 Kt—B3 wins. If 29 . . . B x P; 30 Kt—B3 followed by Q—Q2 wins. If 29 . . . R—R4; 30 Kt—B4 followed by P—Q6 wins.

30 Q x P	P—R4
31 Q x P	Resigns

A good positional game, except for one lapse.

---

122. Hamburg, 1930
(International Team Tournament)
QUEEN'S PAWN OPENING

In master chess, one can take nothing for granted. Whenever a particularly favorable possibility presents itself, one must be on guard against a trap.

F.J. MARSHALL   V. PETROV

White   Black

1 P—Q4	Kt—KB3
2 Kt—KB3	P—K3
3 P—B4	B—Kt5ch
4 B—Q2	Q—K2
5 P—K3	....

Seemingly harmless, but as will be seen, there are finesses to be mastered.

5	O—O

Here, for example, it would have been more exact to play 5 . . . P—QKt3. Then if 6 B—Q3, B—Kt2 and Black has prevented P—K4 without having had to resort to . . . P—Q4, which only blocks the QB's diagonal.

6 B—Q3	P—Q4
7 O—O	QKt—Q2
8 Kt—B3	B x Kt

It seems unwise to yield White the two Bishops so soon. Either

. . . P—QKt3 or . . .P—B4 seems perfectly feasible.

9 B x B	P—QKt3
10 R—B1	B—Kt2
11 P x P	P x P

Permanently blocking the Bishop's diagonal. 11 . . . B x P was preferable.

12 Q—Kt3!	....

A strong but provocative move. Black's obvious reply is readily refuted.

12	P—B4?

A serious mistake on top of the previous inexactitudes.

Position after Black's 12th move

Petrov

Marshall

13 P x P!	Kt x P
14 B x Kt!	....

The move that Black overlooked. If he plays 14 . . . Q x B there follows 15 R x Kt; or 14 . . . Kt x Q; 15 B x Q, Kt x R; 16 R x Kt. In either event White has two pieces for a Rook.

14	P x B
15 Q—Kt4!	K—R1

The position is lost. If 15 . . .

KR—K1; 16 B—B5 threatening Q—
KR4. If then 16 . . . Q—B1; 17
Q—KR4, Q—Kt2; 18 Kt—Q4 or 16
. . . B—B1; 17 Q—Kt4ch, K—R1;
18 Kt—Q4. In either event Black's
position would prove untenable
very quickly.

16 R x Kt!　　　　Resigns

If 16 . . . P or Q x R, 17 Q—KR4
and Black has no defense.

---

123. Liege, 1930

QUEEN'S INDIAN DEFENSE

It is curious how some players
seem to have the "Indian sign" on
other players. For example, while
Nimzovich won some nice games
from me, he lost a much larger
number to me and generally
seemed to start off with a defeatist
attitude!

F.J. Marshall	A. Nimzovich
White	Black
1 P—Q4	Kt—KB3
2 Kt—KB3	P—QKt3
3 P—K3	. . . .

Experience has shown that this
conservative-looking move h a s
more vitality than appears at first
glance.

3	B—Kt2
4 B—Q3	P—B4
5 O—O	P—K3

From a Hypermodern like my
opponent, one would have expected
. . . P—Kt3 here.

6 P—B4	B x Kt?

This move, which parts with a
useful piece and furthers White's
development at the same time,
cannot possibly be good. There
were several playable alternatives,
as for example . . . Kt—B3 or . . .
P—Q3 or . . . P—Q4 or . . . B—K2
or . . . Kt—K5.

7 Q x B	Kt—B3
8 P x P	B x P

Nimzovich must have intended
to play 8 . . . Kt—K4 here, but it
is clear that after 9 Q—K2, Kt x B;
10 Q x Kt Black would suffer from
a distressing weakness on the Q
file.

9 Kt—B3	O—O
10 R—Q1!	. . . .

The Q file is the Achilles heel
of Black's position.

10	Q—B2
11 P—QKt3	Kt—K4
12 Q—Kt3	Kt—R4
13 Kt—Kt5!	. . . .

An unexpected retort. Black cannot reply 13 . . . Kt x Q? without
losing some material, as for example 14 Kt x Q, QR—B1 (or 14
. . . Kt x B; 15 R x Kt, Kt—K7ch;
16 K—B1, Kt x B; 17 R x P!); 15
Kt x P! Kt x B; 16 Kt x R etc.

13	Q—Kt1
14 Q—R4	P—Kt3

Creating a new and serious
weakness on the long diagonal.
Better was 14 . . .Kt x B; 15 R x Kt,
Kt—B3; 16 B—Kt2, B—K2. However, after 17 P—K4 White would
have the makings of a good attack
with R—Kt3 or R—R3.

15 B—K2	Kt—Kt2
16 B—Kt2	P—B4?

The final mistake. . . . P—B3
was better, although his game had
already become quite disagreeable.

17 P—QKt4!	. . . .

P—B4 at once was also feasible,
but the text is even more forcing.

17	B x KtP
18 P—B4	Kt—B2
19 R x P	. . . .

White has a tremendous game.

He threatens Kt—B7 or B—KB3 or Q—B6.

19 . . . .   P—Kt4

Position after Black's 19th move

Nimzovich

Marshall

20 P x P   . . . .

Q x P could also have been played, but the text reduces Black to a helpless state soon enough.

20 . . . .   B—B4
21 Kt—B7   B x Pch
22 K—R1   P—K4

His game is untenable: If 22 . . . Q—Kt2; 23 Kt—Q5! winning the Queen. Or 22 . . . B x P; 23 Q x B, Kt x Q; 24 R x Ktch, K—R1; 25 R x Ktch and mate follows.

23 B—QB1   B x B
24 R x B   Kt—R1
25 P—B5!   Resigns

For if 25 . . . Kt—Kt3; 26 Q—R6, R—B2; 27 B—B4. Or 25 . . . P x P; 26 B—B4ch, Kt—B2; 27 B x Ktch, R x B; 28 Q—QB4, Q—KB1; 29 Q x Rch, Q x Q; 30 R x Q and Black's Rook hangs.

---

124. Liege, 1930
QUEEN'S INDIAN DEFENSE

Again the same timid-looking line of play proves its value. Inexactitude against these variations almost always leads to trouble.

F.J. MARSHALL   C. AHUES
    White   Black

1 P—Q4   Kt—KB3
2 Kt—KB3   P—K3
3 P—K3   P—QKt3
4 B—Q3   B—Kt2
5 O—O   P—B4
6 P—B4   B—K2

Thus far as in the previous game; but the text is an improvement on Nimzovich's . . . B x Kt?

7 Kt—B3   O—O

But this is rather dubious. The old-fashioned . . . P—Q4, restraining White's advance in the center, is preferable.

8 P—Q5!   . . . .

Doubtless a surprise. White has the better of it no matter how Black replies.

8 . . . .   P x P

8 . . . P—Q3 followed by . . . P—K4, although leaving him with a cramped game, would have offered better possibilities of resistance.

9 P x P   P—Q3

If instead 9 . . . Kt x P; 10 Kt x Kt, B x Kt; 11 B x Pch, K x B; 12 Q x B, Kt—B3; 13 R—Q1 winning a Pawn or 12 . . . Kt—R3; 13 R—Q1 with a decisive positional advantage.

10 P—K4   P—QR3

Hoping for a counter-advance with . . . P—QKt4—a possibility which is at once squelched by White.

11 P—QR4	R—K1
12 Kt—Q2!	....

With a double object: to make room for the advance of the BP, and to plant the KKt at the powerful post QB4, where it exerts strong pressure on K5, Q6 and QKt6.

| 12 .... | B—KB1 |

Black's rearrangement of his pieces doesn't amount to much; the fact is that he lacks the necessary terrain to dispose his pieces effectively.

13 P—B4	QKt—Q2
14 R—R3!	....

An interesting move. The intention is to utilize the Rook eventually along the rank.

14	P—Kt3
15 Kt—B4	Q—B2
16 P—B5	....

Further strengthening the pressure by opening the KB file. True, this cedes the usually valuable square K4 to Black; but, as the game goes, he is able to get precious little benefit from it.

16	B—Kt2
17 B—B4	Kt—K4
18 B x Kt	....

The Knight was too well posted. The text has the additional good feature of giving White a strong passed QP.

18	P x B
19 P x P	RP x P
20 R—Kt3	Kt—Q2
21 P—Q6!	....

This seems risky at first sight, because it looks as if the Pawn is advancing too far for its own good. But it always has adequate protection; and above all, the vital square Q5 is freed for White's pieces.

21	Q—Q1
22 Kt—K3	Kt—B3
23 B—B4	R—KB1
24 B—Q5	R—Kt1
25 B x B	R x B
26 Kt(B3)—Q5!	....

Position after White's 26th move

Ahues

Marshall

| 26 .... | Kt x Kt |

After 26 ... Kt x P there are some pretty possibilities: 27 Kt—K7ch, K—R2; 28 Kt(3)—B5 (threatening R—R3ch and mate next move), P x Kt (if 28 ... Kt—Kt4; 29 Q—Kt4, P x Kt; 30 Q x Kt, Q x P; 31 R—R3ch, B—R3; 32 Kt x P etc.); 29 Q—R5ch, B—R3; 30 Q x P(B5)ch, etc. winning.

In other words, the KP was bait, but fish don't always bite!

| 27 Kt x Kt | B—R3 |

Of course if 27 ... Q x P? 28 Kt—B6ch wins.

28 Kt—B6ch	K—Kt2
29 Q—Q5	B—B5

If the QR moves, 30 Q x KP wins easily.

30 Q x R	Q x Kt
31 P—Kt3	Q—Kt4

32 Q—K7	Q—Kt5
33 P—Q7	B—Kt4
34 P—Q8(Q)	B x Q

Or 34 ... R x Q; 35 R x Pch and mate follows.

35 Q x B	Q x P
36 R(3)—KB3	Q—Q4
37 R—K3	Resigns

---

125. New York, 1931

QUEEN'S INDIAN DEFENSE

A serious mistake in the opening leaves Black with a very poor game.

F. J. MARSHALL	M. Fox
White	Black
1 P—Q4	Kt—KB3
2 Kt—KB3	P—K3
3 P—B4	B—Kt5ch
4 B—Q2	Q—K2
5 Q—B2	P—QKt3?

Out of place because of White's next move, which will lead to a serious dislocation of Black's forces. Better was 5 ... B x Bch; 6 QKt x B, P—Q3; 7 P—K4, P—K4 maintaining the equilibrium in the center.

6 P—K4	B x Bch
7 QKt x B	P—Q3

Too late, as White's energetic continuation demonstrates.

8 P—K5	P x P
9 P x P	KKt—Q2
10 Q—K4!	P—QB3
11 Q—Kt4	O—O
12 B—Q3	. . . .

Threatening the ancient sacrificial line 13 B x Pch, K x B; 14 Q—R5ch, K—Kt1; 15 Kt—Kt5 and thus forcing a new weakness in Black's game.

12	P—KB4
13 P x P e.p.	Kt x P
14 Q—R4	. . . .

Threatening B x Pch. Black doesn't get a moment's peace.

14	Q—Kt5
15 O—O—O!	. . . .

In line with White's rapid development. The move involves no risk, since Black's development is so backward.

15	QKt—Q2
16 KR—K1	Kt—B4
17 B—B2	Kt—R5

A harmless demonstration.

18 Kt—Kt3	. . . .

Position after White's 18th move

Fox

Marshall

Black is lost. If 18 ... B—R3; 19 P—QR3! Q x BP; (if 19 ... Q—K2; 20 B x Pch); 20 R—Q4 wins. Or if 18 ... R—K1; 19 Kt—K5! (stronger than 19 P—QR3, Q—K2), B—Kt2; 20 P—QR3, Q—K2; 21 R—Q7! wins.

18	P—QKt4
19 P—QR3!	Q—K2

Forced: if 19 ... Q x BP; 20 R—Q4 wins the Queen!

20 B x Pch   K—R1

If 20 . . . K—B2; 21 Kt—K5ch, K—K1; 22 B—Kt6ch wins.

21 Kt—K5   Resigns

For if 21 . . . P—KKt4; 22 Q—R6, Q x B; 23 Kt—Kt6ch and mate next move.

---

126.   Prague, 1931

(International Team Tournament)

QUEEN'S GAMBIT DECLINED

My opponent's timid and superficial play soon leaves him with an inferior position. An instructive positional game.

M. MONTICELLI	F.J. MARSHALL
(Italy)	(U.S.A.)
White	Black
1 P—Q4	Kt—KB3
2 Kt—KB3	P—K3
3 P—B4	P—Q4
4 Kt—B3	B—Kt5

As in Game no. 98. Nowadays known as the Ragozin System, this line was played by myself and others long before the Russian master decided it was good.

5 Q—Kt3   . . . .

5 Q—R4ch, Kt—B3; 6 Kt—K5, O—O (or 6 . . . B—Q2) gives White no advantage.

5 . . . .   P—B4
6 P—QR3   . . . .

Waste of time; either 6 B—Kt5 or P—K3 would be preferable.

6 . . . .   B x Ktch
7 P x B   O—O
8 B—Kt5   BP x P
9 P(B3) x P   Kt—B3!

Not minding the doubled Pawns which I get two moves later.

10 P x P   P x P
11 B x Kt   P x B

. . . Q—R4ch was also good.

12 Q—B3   . . . .

Forestalling . . . Q—R4ch. At first glance, White appears to have an excellent game, in view of his opponent's disorganized Pawn structure. It soon becomes apparent, however, that this drawback is outweighed by Black's rapid development and his strong Queenside initiative.

12 . . . .   B—B4
13 P—K3   QR—B1
14 Kt—Q2   . . . .

Of course not 14 B—Q3?? Kt—K4 and wins. Black's play on the QB file, culminating in occupation of QB7, soon gives him a decisive grip on the position.

14 . . . .   Kt—R4
15 Q—Kt4   R—B7
16 B—Kt5   Q—Kt3

So that if 17 O—O, R x Kt etc.

17 Kt—B3   KR—B1
18 O—O   P—QR3!

Positionally decisive.

19 B—R4   R—Kt7!

Position after Black's 19th move

Marshall

Monticelli

The exchange of Queens is virtually forced, after which Black will have an easy win: two Pawns to one on the Queen-side, seventh rank and occupation of the weak White squares.

20 Q—K7   . . . .

Since this does not avoid the exchange, and in fact only gains time for Black by making an immediate . . . P—Kt4 possible, he should have played Q x Q directly.

20 . . . .   Q—K3
21 Q x Q   B x Q

21 . . . P x Q is desirable to round out Black's Pawns, but then 22 Kt—R4 is a good reply.

22 P—R3   P—Kt4
23 B—Q1   R—B6

The winning move. Black forces a powerful passed KtP.

24 Kt—R4   Kt—B5
25 P—R4   P—Kt5
26 B—Kt4   P—Kt6
27 B—B5   R—Q7

White resigns, as the KtP cannot be stopped. It is interesting to reflect that the Queen-side attack succeeded with all the speed which is characteristic of a direct King-side attack!

---

127. New York, 1932
(Metropolitan Chess League)

QUEEN'S GAMBIT DECLINED

Facing up to a tricky and puzzling attack still remains a man-sized job over the board, even though the subsequent annotations may demonstrate the task an easy one.

F.J. MARSHALL   D. GLADSTONE

White   Black

1 P—Q4   P—Q4

2 P—QB4   P—K3
3 Kt—QB3   Kt—KB3
4 B—Kt5   B—K2
5 P—K3   QKt—Q2
6 R—B1   P—B3
7 Kt—B3   O—O
8 Q—B2   P—KR3
9 B—R4   P—R3
10 P—QR3   P x P

Giving up the fight for the tempo. 10 . . . P—QKt4 leads to a totally different kind of game.

11 B x P   P—QKt4
12 B—R2   P—B4
13 Kt—K4   . . . .

The book line is 13 P x P, Kt x P; 14 B—Kt1, R—K1. The text is no better in an objective sense, but being a novelty, it gives my opponent more to think about.

13 . . . .   Q—R4ch
14 KKt—Q2   P x P
15 O—O!?   P x P

As will be seen, the acceptance of the speculative Pawn sacrifice is playable; but the return of the Pawn with 15 . . . P—Q6 is simpler.

16 P x P   Q—Kt3
17 Kt x Ktch   B x Kt?

This plausible move loses, whereas 17 . . . Kt x Kt would have left him with a satisfactory defense. After the text, White's attack crashes through to victory.

18 B—Kt1   R—Q1
19 Q—R7ch   K—B1

(see diagram next page)

20 Q—R8ch!   K—K2
21 Q x KtP!   . . . .

The move that Black overlooked. With Black's King wandering in the middle of the board, and with most of his pieces not functioning, the result is a foregone conclusion.

Position after Black's 19th move

Gladstone

Marshall

| 21 . . . . | Q x Pch |
| 22 K—R1 | B x B |

He has to take the Bishop for better or worse, for if 22 . . . Q—Q5 (or . . . Q—K4); 23 Kt—K4! wins rapidly.

| 23 Q x Pch | K—Q3 |
| 24 Kt—K4ch | K—Q4 |

Or 24 . . . K—K4; 25 Q—Kt7ch winning.

| 25 Q—R5ch | B—Kt4 |

Amusing would be 25 . . . P—K4; 26 Q—B7ch and wins; or 25 . . . Kt—K4; 26 KR—Q1ch etc.

26 Q—Q1ch!	Q—Q5
27 Q—Kt3ch	K—K4
28 Q—Kt3ch	K—Q4
29 Q—Q6 mate	

The last five moves give a good idea of the Queen's powers!

---

128.   Folkestone, 1933
(International Team Tournament)
QUEEN'S GAMBIT DECLINED
The crucial game in the last round. The U. S. team needed only one point out of four to retain the cup. With Fine, Kashdan and Simonson as my team-mates, it looked as though it were "in the bag" — but later the picture changed completely and I had to fight for a win!

F.J. MARSHALL	DR. K. TREYBAL
(U.S.A.)	(Czechoslovakia)
White	Black
1 P—Q4	P—Q4
2 P—QB4	P—K3
3 Kt—KB3	Kt—KB3
4 Kt—B3	B—K2
5 B—Kt5	O—O
6 P—K3	Kt—K5

The same defense as played by Capablanca (Game no. 59) and Maroczy (Game no. 110). I was surprised at Treybal's adoption of this simplifying line; all our team needed was a single point to hold the cup, and this move tends to result in a drawish position.

7 B x B	Q x B
8 P x P	Kt x Kt
9 P x Kt	P x P
10 Q—Kt3	R—Q1

. . . Q—Q3 is preferable.

| 11 B—Q3 | P—QB4 |

Threatening to win a piece with . . . P—B5. But my reply (another similarity to the Capablanca game) gives White strong pressure.

12 Q—R3	P—QKt3
13 O—O	Kt—B3
14 B—Kt5	P—B5
15 Q x Q	Kt x Q

The ending is somewhat in White's favor. Black has eliminated the pressure on his Pawns and has established the Queen-side majority. On the other hand, White has the better Bishop by far, and counterplay with P—K4 is indicated; however, if 16 P—K4? P—

QR3; 17 B—R4, P x P; 18 Kt—Q2, P—QKt4 winning a Pawn.

16 B—R4	B—B4
17 KR—B1	P—QR3
18 B—B2	P—QKt4

About this time, word came to me that Simonson and Kashdan had both lost their games and that Fine's position looked very bad. The cup seemed to be slipping from our hands. My own position was no better than my opponent's but I must now try to play for a win or the cup might be lost. It didn't look too promising; but I knew I was playing good chess and waited for any opportunity that was offered.

| 19 Kt—Q2 | B—K3? |

I was threatening P—K4, but 19 B x B is better—especially in view of the team score and the state of Fine's game. This looked like a weak move to me and I began to feel more optimistic.

| 20 KR—Kt1 | P—B4 |

Preventing P—K4, but reducing the scope of his Bishop still further.

| 21 P—QR3 | .... |

White is getting set to counter his opponent's logical plan: doubling Rooks on the QKt file followed ultimately by . . . P—Kt5. The alternative procedure—more promising perhaps—was P—QR4 with pressure against the Pawns.

| 21 . . . . | Kt—Kt3 |

. . . . Kt—B3 looks better, but would have led to much the same result, since White's Knight cannot be allowed to occupy K5.

| 22 P—B4! | .... |

Treybal must have forgotten all about this possibility, as P—K4 is the natural push for White to strive for in such positions.

22	KR—Kt1
23 Kt—B3	R—Kt2
24 Kt—K5	Kt x Kt
25 BP x Kt	QR—Kt1
26 R—Kt2	P—QR4
27 QR—Kt1	....

Just in the nick of time. Black's Queen-side advance is stopped, while White's KP will soon come to life in a surprising manner.

| 27 . . . . | K—B2? |

. . . P—Kt3 was a very necessary precaution here, as will be seen.

| 28 R—KB1! | .... |

The time is now ripe for attack. Black has made his first apparent mistake—or is it a snare? It occurred to me that Treybal might be luring me into moving my Rook, figuring that the Queen-side attack would carry the day. I decided that if I was to play for a win I would have to run that risk. My judgment told me that his last move had been a mistake.

| 28 . . . . | P—Kt5 |

Seemingly very formidable.

| 29 RP x P | P x P |

Position after Black's 29th move

Treybal

Marshall

30 P—Kt4!   K—Kt1

Treybal must have overlooked the advance of the KKtP in his calculations.
If instead 30 . . . P—Kt3; 31 P—K4!
I 31 . . . KtP x P; 32 R x Rch, R x R; 33 KtP x P and wins.
II 31 . . . QP x P; 32 B x P, R— Kt4; 33 R x P, R x R; 34 P x R, R x P; 35 P—Q5, B—B1; 36 P— K6ch, K—K2; 37 P x P etc.

31 P x BP   B—Q2
32 P—K6   . . . .

When you are attacking, make every move count. Don't let up or give your opponent any counterattacking chances. Every move must be a threat.

32 . . . .   B—B3
33 P x P   R x P
34 R x R   R x R
35 R—R1!   . . . .

The open file wins.

35 . . . .   K—B1

After 35 . . . R—Kt7 there is an interesting win with 36 R—R6!
I 36 . . . B—Kt2; 37 P—K7, K—B2; 38 R—K6, K—K1; 39 B— R4ch etc.
II 36 . . . R x B; 37 R x B, K— B1; 38 R—B8ch, K—K2; 39 R— B7ch, K—B1 forced; 40 R—B7ch! (gaining an important tempo), K— Kt1; 47 R—Q7 (threatens mate!), K—B1; 42 R x P and wins.

36 R—R6   B—K1
37 P—K4!   . . . .

Securing two passed Pawns which must win, as in the beautiful variation 37 . . . R—Kt7; 38 P x P, R x B; 39 P—Q6, P—B6; 40 R—R8, R—B8ch; 41 K—Kt2, P— B7; 42 P—Q7, R—Kt8ch; 43 K— R3! and wins. Or 37 . . . R—Kt7; 38 P x P! R x B; 39 P—Q6, R—Q7; 40 R—R8 and wins.

37 . . . .   R—Kt4

38 R—R8   K—K2

If 38 . . . R—Kt5 (in order to prevent White's next move); 39 P x P wins easily.

39 R x Bch   K x R
40 B—R4   Resigns

A most instructive ending after an unpromising beginning.

---

129. New York, 1934
(*Metropolitan Chess League*)

RETI OPENING

White concentrates on the Queenside, ignoring the menacing storm clouds on the other wing. In due course Black develops an attack which proves quite irresistible.

J. L. McCUDDEN   F. J. MARSHALL

White   Black

1 Kt—KB3   P—Q4
2 P—B4   P—K3
3 P—QKt3   P—QB4
4 P—Kt3   Kt—QB3
5 B—KKt2   B—K2!

For reasons that will be given later, this is stronger than the more obvious . . . Kt—B3.

6 B—Kt2   B—B3!
7 Kt—B3   KKt—K2
8 O—O   O—O
9 R—B1   B x Kt!

The strength of the Bishop has been demonstrated so convincingly in modern chess that this exchange comes as a great surprise. However, it is well motivated: Black has foreseen that after the intended advances with . . . P—Q5 and . . . P—K4, the KB would have little scope—hence its removal is in order.
The result is that Black retains his more effective Bishop—the one moving on white squares. Furthermore, the strength of White's Bis-

hops is greatly minimized by the fact that the position is one in which Bishops cannot accomplish a great deal.

10 R x B	P—Q5
11 R—B1	P—K4
12 P—Q3	B—Kt5
13 Q—Q2	Q—Q2
14 B—QR3?	....

White's plan is to break through on the Queen-side with an eventual P—QKt4, but this has little value unless preceded by P—QR3. The right course was 14 Kt—Kt5! followed by Kt—K4 and P—B4, and possibly P—QR3 and P—QKt4 later on.

| 14 .... | Q—Q3 |
| 15 P—Kt4 | .... |

Kt—Kt5 was still available.

15	P x P
16 P—B5	Q—Q2
17 B x P	P—KR3!

This useful move prevents Kt—Kt5—K4—Q6 and also, at some future time, the possibly annoying Q—Kt5. It is interesting to observe that White's attempt to extend the scope of his QB has not succeeded.

| 18 Q—Kt2 | .... |

Instead of beginning the pressure on the QKt file at once, he would have done better to retain the KB with some such move as KR—K1.

18	B—R6
19 Kt—Q2	B x B
20 K x B	Kt—Q4
21 B—R3	P—B4
22 Kt—B4	....

And now he tries to get the Knight into the game, but too much time is lost thereby. It is true that in closed positions time is not so important, yet so great an expenditure of time may prove to be a luxury, in view of Black's gaining strength in the center and on the King side.

| 22 .... | P—B5 |

Setting up the KB file as a valuable basis of attack.

23 Kt—Q6	QR—Kt1
24 Q—Kt3	Q—K3
25 QR—Kt1	K—R2
26 Q—B4	P x P

The defensive formalities attended to, Black resumes his attack on the King. If now 27 Kt x P, Kt—R4! 28 Kt x Kt, R x R; 29 R x R, R x P ch wins—an indication of the futility of White's Queen-side activities.

| 27 RP x P | .... |

Black is now ready for the final onslaught.

Position after White's 27th move

Marshall

McCudden

| 27 .... | Kt—B5ch! |
| 28 P x Kt | Q—Kt5ch |

Black's attack is perfectly sound because White's menaced King can secure no appreciable aid from his officers, who are busily engaged in conquering "scorched earth."

29 K—R2	R x P
30 Kt—K4	Q—R5ch
31 K—Kt2	R—Kt5ch

32 Kt—Kt3   R—KB1!

Decisive reinforcement of the attack: there is no good reply to his next move.

33 R—Kt1   R x Pch!
34 K x R   Q—R7ch
35 R—Kt2   R—B5ch
36 K—K1   Q x R

If now 37 Kt—K4, Q—B8ch winning the Rook.

37 R x P   Q x Ktch
38 K—Q1   R—B8ch
39 K—B2   Q—K8

There is no defense.

40 R—Kt5   Q—Q8ch
41 K—Kt2   Q—Kt8 mate

---

130. Warsaw, 1935
(International Team Tournament)

QUEEN'S GAMBIT

Here is another of those crucial team match struggles. It might have been—but wasn't!—one of my finest games. Maybe the tension was too great.

F. J. MARSHALL   E. GRUENFELD
(U.S.A.)   (Austria)

White   Black

1 P—Q4   P—Q4
2 P—QB4   P x P
3 P—K3   Kt—KB3
4 B x P   P—K3
5 Kt—QB3   P—B4
6 Kt—B3   P—QR3

My opponent is very well versed in the openings — particularly in this one, which is his favorite defense to 1 P—Q4.

7 P—QR4   Kt—B3
8 O—O   B—K2
9 Q—K2   P x P

10 R—Q1   P—Q6

Gruenfeld must have been in one of his extremely rare do-or-die moods, since Black has a drawing variation at his disposal here: 10 . . . P—K4; 11 P x P, P x P; 12 Kt x P, Kt x Kt; 13 Q—K5, Q—Q3!

11 B x QP   Q—B2
12 P—K4   Kt—KKt5

Judging from the subsequent play, Black would have been well advised to castle hereabouts.

13 P—KR3   KKt—K4

If he had intended 13 . . .Kt—Q5 here, the idea died aborning. After 13 . . . Kt—Q5; 14 B—Kt5ch, P x B; 15 R x Kt wins.

14 Kt x Kt   Kt x Kt
15 B—KB4   B—Q3

Black seems to have obtained a fair game, but the following move involves him in lasting difficulties.

16 B—Kt5ch!   K—K2

It is clear that 16 . . . P x B? would be disastrous.

17 QR—B1   Q—Kt1

Position after Black's 17th move

Gruenfeld

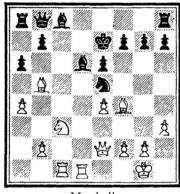

Marshall

| 18 B—Kt3? | .... |

I believe that I missed a superb brilliancy here. I could have played 18 R x B, Q x R (or 18 ... K x R; 19 Q—R5, P—B3; 20 Q—B7, P x B; 21 Kt x P mate); 19 R—Q1, Q—Kt1; 20 Kt—Q5ch, P x Kt; 21 P x P, P—B3; 22 P—Q6ch, K—K3; 23 B—B4ch, K—Q2; 24 B x Kt, P x B; 25 Q x P, R—K1; 26 Q x KtPch, K—B3; 27 B—Q5ch, K x P; 28 B—B7 ch, K—K2; 29 B—Kt8 mate.

| 18 .... | P—B3 |

Now Black gets a bit of a breathing spell to consolidate his position. If instead 18 ... P x B; 19 Kt x P, R—Q1; 20 R x B, R x R; 21 R—B7 ch, K—B3; 22 Q—R5 wins.

| 19 B—Q3 | B—Q2 |
| 20 B—Kt1 | P—KKt4 |

In order to hold P—B4 back, but he will pay for this weakening advance later on.

21 R—Q2	B—B3
22 QR—Q1	B—Kt5
23 B—QR2	Q—B2
24 R—B2	QR—Q1
25 R x R	Q x R
26 B x Kt	P x B

Black seems to have solidified his game somewhat, but the following move smashes up his position.

27 Kt—Q5ch!	P x Kt
28 P x P	B—Q2
29 Q x Pch	K—B2
30 R—B7	R—K1
31 Q—B5ch	....

Am I slipping here? Much more conclusive would have been 31 P—Q6ch, K—Kt3; 32 B—Kt1ch, K—R3 (if 32 ... K—B2; 33 Q—B5ch); 33 R x B, Q x R (not 33 ... R x Q? 34 R x P mate); 34 Q—B6ch, K—R4; 35 P—Kt4ch, and Black is either mated or loses the Queen.

| 31 .... | K—K2 |
| 32 Q—K6ch | K—B1 |

| 33 R x B | .... |

And here 33 Q—R6ch leads to a neat and quick win: 33 ... K—K2; 34 P—Q6ch, B x P; 35 Q—Kt7 mate. Or 33 ... K—Kt1; 34 P—Q6ch, K—R1; 35 B—Kt1, R—K8ch; 36 K—R2, R x B; 37 R x B, Q x R; 38 Q—B8 mate.

33	R x Q
34 R x Qch	R—K1
35 R x Rch	K x R
36 K—B1	....

Black resigned after a few more moves. The ending, of course, is an easy win.

---

131. San Juan, 1936
QUEEN'S GAMBIT DECLINED

So often a tenable position becomes unplayable after the ill-considered elimination of an important piece.

F. J. MARSHALL	P. GOTAY
White	Black
1 P—Q4	P—K3
2 P—QB4	Kt—KB3
3 Kt—KB3	P—Q4
4 Kt—B3	P—B3
5 B—Kt5	QKt—Q2
6 P x P	KP x P
7 P—K3	B—K2

After some transpositions, the game has now become identical with my Moscow encounter with Rubinstein (Game no. 108). The two games continue the same right up to White's 18th move!

8 B—Q3	O—O
9 Q—B2	R—K1
10 O—O	Kt—B1
11 QR—K1	....

According to the authorities, QB1 is the proper square; but as I am interested in forcing P—K4, I prefer the text.

11	. . . .	Kt—K5
12	B x B	Q x B
13	B x Kt	P x B
14	Kt—Q2	P—KB4
15	P—B3	P x P
16	Kt x P	B—K3
17	P—K4	P x P
18	Kt x P	. . . .

At last a deviation from the Rubinstein game! There I played 18 R x P.

| 18 | . . . . | Q—Kt5 |

If 18 . . . B—B4; 19 Q—Kt3ch and if 19 . . . Q—K3; 20 Kt—Q6, Q x Q; 21 P x Q, R x R; 22 R x R with advantage for White.

19	P—QR3	B—Kt6
20	Q—B2	Q—Kt3
21	Kt—K5	QR—Q1
22	Kt—B5	. . . .

Black has hopes of concentrating on the QP; however, White's superior mobility and attacking prospects seem to outweigh that possibility.

22	. . . .	B—Q4
23	R—K3	Q—B2
24	Q—B2	P—QKt3
25	Kt—K4	. . . .

Position after White's 25th move

Gotay

Marshall

| 25 | . . . . | B x Kt |

After the removal of this valuable piece, Black's position is bound to fall apart quickly . . . P—KR3 should have been tried.

| 26 | R x B | R x P |

Desperation. He has no good moves in view of the threatened R—B7 or Q—Kt3ch.

27	R x R	Q x Kt
28	Q—B2	Q—K6?

But this loses at once. . . . Q—K3 would have prolonged the game.

29	Q x Q	R x Q
30	R—Q8	Resigns

VII
RETIREMENT YEARS
(1937-1941)

132. New York, 1937
*(Marshall Chess Club
Championship)*

SICILIAN DEFENSE

Many a game which starts out
with unpromising opening play,
becomes intensely interesting later
on. This is the case here, where
my opponent is baffled by a long
series of surprise moves.

F. J. MARSHALL   D. POLLAND

White	Black
1 P—Q4	Kt—KB3
2 P—QB4	P—K3
3 Kt—KB3	P—B4
4 Kt—B3	. . . .

4 P—Q5! as in the following
game, is more vigorous.

4	P x P
5 Kt x P	P—QR3
6 P—K4	. . . .

Transposing into a variation of
the Sicilian Defense which gives
Black a good game.

6	B—Kt5
7 B—Q3	Kt—B3
8 Kt x Kt	QP x Kt
9 O—O	P—K4

Simple and good. White's KB
has little scope now, and his attacking chances are very slight.
The following attempts to gain
some initiative soon lead to trouble.

10 B—Kt5	P—R3
11 B—R4	B—QB4

The positional course would be
. . . B—K2 followed by . . . O—O
But Black does not fear complica-
tions.

12 K—R1	Q—K2
13 P—B4!?	P—KKt4!?

After 13 . . .P x P; 14 P—K5,
Q x P; 15 R—K1, B—K6 it is questionable whether White has enough
attack for the Pawns; but over the
board Black's game would be troublesome enough.

14 P x KP   . . . .

After 14 P x KtP the same reply
would still be available.

14 . . . .   Kt—Kt5

The exchange is now won for
Black, but . . . !

15 B—Kt3	Kt—K6
16 Q—R4!	Kt x R
17 R x Kt	B—K3?

. . . B—Q2 was much safer. White
now takes advantage of the available lines to make the most econ-
omical use of his lead in development.

18 Kt—Q5!!   P—Kt4

The lesser evil was 18 . . . Q—
Q1; 19 Kt—B6ch, K—B1. However,
Black does not yet appear to be in
any great danger.

19 Q—B2   P x Kt

If instead 19 . . . Q—Q1; 20 Kt—
B6ch, K—B1; 21 P x P attacking

223

the KB, with ample compensation
for the exchange.

20 KP x P   . . . .

Position after White's 20th move

Polland

Marshall

Black is a Rook up, but he is not
happy. Here are some of the possibilities:

I 20 . . . B—Q2; 21 P—K6, BP
x P; 22 B—Kt6ch, K—Q1; 23 Q—B3
threatening Q x Rch as well as Q—
R5ch and mate next move.

II 20 . . . B—B1; 21 P x P threatening P—Q6 and also P—Kt4 followed by Q—B6ch.

III 20 . . . . O—O—O; 21 P x B,
BP x P (or 21 . . . KtP x P; 22 Q x P
threatening B—KB2); 22 P x P
threatening B—B2 or P—Kt4.

20 . . . .   O—O

Apparently the safest course, for
if 21 P x B, P x P and the attack is
broken. But fortunately White has
a remarkable continuation at his
disposal.

21 R—B6!!   B—Q2
22 Q—K2   K—Kt2

He must get additional protection for his KR2; however,
he is helpless against the growing
concentration of White's forces on
the King-side.

23 Q—K4   R—R1
24 P—K6!!   B—K1
25 B—K5   Q x R

Despair; if 25 . . . K—B1; 26 P—
Q6! B x QP; 27 P x BP, Q x B; 28
P x B(Q)ch, K x Q; 29 R—K6ch etc.

26 B x Qch   K x B
27 P—Q6   . . . .

The advanced Pawns are deadly.

27 . . . .   R—Q1
28 Q—B5ch   K—Kt2
29 Q x B   P x P
30 Q—K5ch   K—Kt1
31 Q x KPch   B—B2
32 Q—B6   Resigns

For the QP advances victoriously.
A remarkable game.

---

133. New York, 1937
*(Marshall Chess Club
Championship)*

QUEEN'S PAWN OPENING

Here is one of these encounters
—rather frequent in my games—in
which an early exchange of Queens
does not prevent the subsequent
play from being extremely interesting. My young opponent in this
game is noted for his tactical skill.

F. J. MARSHALL   M. HANAUER

White   Black

1 Kt—KB3   Kt—KB3
2 P—B4   P—K3
3 P—Q4   P—B4
4 P—Q5   P—QKt4

This gambit was popular during
the twenties, but the following reply robbed it of much of its attrac-
tion.

5 B—Kt5!   Q—R4ch
6 Q—Q2   Q x Qch
7 QKt x Q   . . . .

The book move is 7 KKt x Q, in order to develop the QKt at QB3. However, the text also has its points, as it brings a new piece into play at once.

7	KP x P
8 B x Kt	P x B
9 P x QP	B—QKt2

Black has obtained the two Bishops at the cost of saddling himself with a seriously weakened Pawn position. The text is preferable to 9 . . . P—B4; 10 P—K4, P x P; 11 Kt x P, P—QR3 (if 11 . . . B—QKt2; 12 B x P, B x P?? 13 Kt—B6 ch); 12 P—QR4, P—Kt5; 13 Kt—K5, B—QKt2; 14 Kt—B4 with a fine game for White.

10 P—K4	P—QR3
11 Kt—R4	P—Q3

This safe and sane move is best. Inferior alternatives are (a) 11 . . . B—R3; 12 Kt—B5, B x Ktch; 13 K x B; (b) 11 . . . B—R3; 12 Kt—B5, B—B5; 13 Kt—QKt3, P—Q3; 14 P—Kt3, B—K4; 15 O—O—O; (c) 11 . . . B—R3; 12 Kt—B5, B—B5; 13 Kt—QKt3, P—B5? 14 Kt—B5, B—B1; 15 P—Q6 with an enormous positional advantage.

12 P—R4	P—Kt5

Black must have been reluctant to give his opponent the splendid square QB4 for his Knights; but if 12 . . . P—B5? 13 P x P, P x P; 14 R x R, B x R; 15 P—QKt3 etc.

13 Kt—B4	K—Q1

The King must be brought to QB2. If 13 . . . Kt—Q2? 14 Kt—B5 wins a Pawn.

14 B—K2	P—KR4

White threatened B—R5. It is interesting to see how the initial Pawn weaknesses lead to new Pawn weaknesses.

15 Kt—B5	K—B2
16 P—R4!	....

In order to fix the weak KRP on its present square.

16	Kt—Q2
17 Kt—Kt3	R—K1!

Well played. If now 18 B x P, B x P. Or 18 O—O—O, B—R3ch followed by . . . B—B5. Curious how Black can get some value from his Bishops even in this cramped position!

18 O—O	P—B4!

Another good move. However, I welcomed the opening of the K file, as I felt that my superior development would give me the first opportunity to make use of it.

19 Kt x BP	R x P
20 Kt (4)—K3	Kt—B3

The pressure against White's somewhat precarious QP will now give Black some much-needed counterplay.

21 B—B3	R—K4
22 QR—Q1	Kt—K5

. . . B—B1 was better, or even . . . B—R3. After the latter move, White could not have played 23 Kt x P? because of 23 . . . R x Kt! 24 Kt x B (or Kt x P), R x B.

23 KR—K1!	....

With threats on the K file which give him the upper hand.

23	B—B1
24 Kt—B4	R x Kt
25 B x Kt	R—B5
26 P—KKt3	R—Kt1

. . . R—B3 would leave Black in an uncomfortably passive position.

27 P—Kt3!	R x RP
28 B—R7	R—Kt2
29 R—K8!	R—Q5

(see diagram next page)

White has now obtained the position he was aiming for at move 27,

Position after Black's 29th move

Hanauer

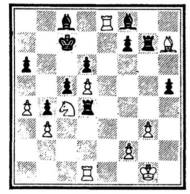

Marshall

and he should have continued with
30 R x R, P x R; 31 **B—Q3, R—Kt1;**
32 **Kt—Kt6!** (not 32 Kt x P? B—
Q2), K x Kt; 33 R x QB and White
will win both the QRP and KtP.
However, from now on both players
suffer from acute time pressure.

30 QR—K1?	R x B

With correct play, Black can slip
out.

31 R x B	R x P?

A blunder. . . . P—B4 was
necessary.

32 R—K7ch	. . . .

As so often happens when one is
short of time, White overlooks the
simple R x Bch, and instead finds
a more elaborate win!

32	B—Q2
33 R—QR8	R—Q8ch
34 K—Kt2	K—B3
35 Kt—R5ch!	K—Kt3
36 R x B	K x Kt
37 R—Kt7!	Resigns

There is nothing to be done
against R—Kt5 mate. An elegant
finish.

---

134. New York, 1937
(Metropolitan Chess League)

QUEEN'S GAMBIT DECLINED

This game is an interesting example of how a number of errors,
each one slight in itself, can finally
add up to a lost game.

A. KEVITZ	F. J. MARSHALL
White	Black
1 P—QB4	Kt—KB3
2 Kt—QB3	P—K3
3 Kt—B3	P—Q4
4 P—Q4	B—Kt5

We have reached a Queen's Gambit Declined in somewhat a devious
manner. After the timid reply that
follows, Black is at once certain of
a satisfactory position.

5 P—K3	O—O
6 B—Q3	P—B4

Freeing his position and disput-
ing the control of the center.

7 O—O	QP x P
8 B x P	P—QR3
9 P x P	. . . .

If 9 P—QR3, B x Kt; 10 P x B,
P—QKt4; 11 B—Q3, B—Kt2 leaving Black with an excellent position, despite his opponent's two
Bishops.

9	B x P
10 Q—B2?	. . . .

White's enterprise in avoiding a
probably quick draw after 10 Q x Q
is laudable, but the move he selects
is faulty. 10 Q—K2 was in order,
as it would have avoided the two
drawbacks of the text: putting
White's Queen on a file where it
will later be opposed by a Black
Rook, and giving up the protection
of White's KKt, which will later
lead to a weakening of the King-
side.

10	P—QKt4

| 11 R—Q1 | Q—K2 |
| 12 B—Q3 | .... |

B—K2 would avoid the later breaking up of the King-side, but then White's QKt would be barred from K4, and White would be restricted to an uncomfortably small amount of terrain.

| 12 .... | B—Kt2 |
| 13 Kt—K4 | QKt—Q2! |

Black still does not fear the two Bishops. After 14 Kt x B, Kt x Kt his generally aggressive position would outweigh the Bishop-pair.

| 14 B—Q2 | QR—B1 |

Leaving White's Queen in a poor position. As 15 Q—Kt1 is not inviting, the following weakening of White's King-side is inevitable.

15 Kt x B	B x Kt!
16 P x B	R x Kt
17 Q—Kt3	R—Kt4ch
18 K—R1?	....

After this White's game soon becomes untenable. K—B1 offered some defensive prospects.

| 18 .... | Kt—B4 |
| 19 Q—B2 | .... |

If 19 B—Kt4? Q—Kt2! wins at once.

| 19 .... | R—R4 |
| 20 B—R5 | .... |

Black threatened to win with 20 ... Q—B2; 21 P—B4, Q—Kt2ch; 22 K—Kt1, Q—B6. But the text is likewise ineffectual.

(see diagram next column)

| 20 .... | Q—Kt2 |

This is decisive. If 21 P—K4 (or 21 B—K4), Q—Kt1 wins; if 21 B—K2, Kt—Kt5 wins; and if 21 K—Kt2, R—Kt4ch winning.

| 21 R—KKt1 | Q x Pch |

Position after White's 20th move

Marshall

Kevitz

22 R—Kt2	Kt x B
23 Q x Kt	Kt—Kt5
24 K—Kt1	Kt x BP!
25 R—KB1?	....

Blundering in a lost position. If 25 R x Kt, R—Kt4ch; 26 K—B1, Q—R8ch wins.

| 25 .... | Q x Rch |

Resigns

---

135.   Stockholm, 1937

(International Team Tournament)

QUEEN'S INDIAN DEFENSE

Black makes a bad mistake in the opening, from whose evil effects he never recovers.

F. J. MARSHALL	O. LARSEN
(U.S.A.)	(Denmark)
White	Black
1 P—Q4	Kt—KB3
2 Kt—KB3	P—QKt3
3 P—KKt3	B—Kt2
4 B—Kt2	P—K3

Here or on the next move, ...

P—B4 would have been an excellent idea, as White would have been unable to push by with the QP.

| 5 O—O | B—K2 |
| 6 P—B4 | P—B4? |

But now this is distinctly inferior, because White's reply gives him an enormous advantage in terrain.

7 P—Q5!	P x P
8 Kt—R4	Q—B1
9 P x P	P—Q3
10 P—K4	O—O
11 Kt—B5	R—K1

Black suffers from a serious lag in development which can never be made up.

| 12 Kt—B3 | B—B1 |
| 13 B—Kt5 | P—QR3? |

His difficulties are already serious enough without being enhanced by the broken-up King-side which results from this move. . . . QKt—Q2 should have been played.

14 B x Kt	P x B
15 B—R3!	Q—Q1
16 Q—Kt4ch	K—R1
17 Q—R5	Q—B2
18 Kt—R6	B x Kt

Forced; if 18 . . . R—K2 or . . . K—Kt2; 19 B—B5 wins.

19 Q x B	Kt—Q2
20 P—B4	R—KKt1
21 B x Kt	Q x B
22 Q x BPch	R—Kt2

Black's game is hopeless: not only has he lost a Pawn, he is subjected to a formidable attack.

| 23 P—B5 | R—K1 |
| 24 QR—K1 | R—K4 |

If 24 . . . Q—Q1; 25 Q—R6 maintains the attack.

Position after Black's 24th move

Larsen

Marshall

| 25 Kt—K2! | K—Kt1 |

There is no defense against the coming inroad of the Knight. If 25 . . . R x KP; 26 Kt—B4, R x R; 27 R x R followed by Kt—R5 and wins.

26 Kt—B4	P—R3
27 Kt—R5	R—R2
28 Q x R!	Resigns

---

136. New York, 1939
(Metropolitan Chess League)

KING'S INDIAN DEFENSE

My opponent in this game is one of the most talented of the younger American masters. In the 1941 New York State Championship he tied for second prize with Reshevsky and Kashdan, after Fine.

| A. S. DENKER | F. J. MARSHALL |
| White | Black |

| 1 P—Q4 | Kt—KB3 |
| 2 Kt—KB3 | P—KKt3 |

A favorite defense of mine in recent years.

3 P—B4	B—Kt2
4 P—KKt3	O—O
5 B—Kt2	P—Q4
6 P x P	. . . .

I believe that 6 Kt—B3 or else O—O, P x P; 7 Kt—R3 is more promising. The text gives Black an easy game.

6	Kt x P
7 O—O	P—QB4

A temporary Pawn sacrifice which frees Black's game still further.

8 P x P	Kt—R3
9 P—B6	. . . .

In the hope of creating a weakness in Black's Pawn position; but the open QKt file and strengthening of the center are more than sufficient compensation. If instead 9 Q—Kt3, Kt(4)—Kt5! followed by . . . B—K3 with a good lead in development and the prospective regain of the QBP in short order.

9	P x P
10 Kt—Q4	. . . .

After 10 P—K4, Kt—Kt3 the diagonal of White's KB would be blocked and his white squares would be weak.

10	B—Kt2
11 Kt—QB3	Q—Kt3!

Let it never be said that I shrink from Pawn sacrifices! The text required consideration of the following line of play: 12 Kt x P, Kt x Kt; 13 Kt x Pch, K—R1; 14 P x Kt, B x B; 15 K x B, Q—K3; 16 B—R3, KR—K1; 17 Q—R4, Kt—B2; 18 Kt—B6, Kt—Q4 and although Black is momentarily two Pawns down, he has the better game.

12 P—K3	Kt x Kt
13 P x Kt	P—QB4!
14 Kt—K2	B x B

As a result of this transaction Black is left with a strong KB

against a weak QB.

15 K x B	Q—B3ch
16 P—B3	KR—Q1
17 Q—B2	. . . .

Or 17 Q—Kt3, R—Q6 followed by . . . QR—Q1 with unpleasant pressure on White's position.

17	Kt—Kt5
18 Q—Kt3	Q—R3
19 QR—Kt1?!	. . . .

If 19 Kt—B4, Kt—Q6 maintains the pressure. White therefore goes in for a combination which, however, proves unprofitable for him.

19	Q x Ktch
20 R—B2	Q—K8!

Leaving White little choice, since 21 P x Kt, R—Q8 leaves him badly trussed up.

Position after Black's 20th move

Marshall

Denker

21 B—Q2	Q x B
22 R x Q	R x Rch
23 K—R3	Kt—Q6

Black has three pieces and a strong attack for the Queen; he must win with best play.

24 Q—Kt7	R—K1?

But this is an inexactitude which makes the win difficult. Correct was 24 ... R—Q1; 25 Q x KP, B—B1! 26 Q x RP, Kt—K4 with a winning attack.

| 25 Q x RP | Kt—B7ch |
| 26 K—Kt2 | .... |

He has no choice (26 K—R4?? B—B3 mate).

26	Kt—K5ch
27 K—Kt1	Kt—Kt4
28 R—Kt8	....

Now it becomes an exciting struggle between the advance of White's QRP and the attack against the White King.

28	Kt x Pch
29 K—B1	Kt x Pch
30 K—Kt1	Kt—B6ch
31 K—B1	Kt—R7ch
32 K—Kt1	Kt—B6ch
33 K—B1	Kt—R7ch
34 K—Kt1	R x R
35 Q x Rch	B—B1
36 P—R4	....

Isn't it amazing that this Pawn succeeds in advancing only one more square throughout the rest of the game!

36	Kt—B6ch
37 K—B1	R—QR7
38 Q—R8?	....

Too far afield. Q—Kt5 would have made a much harder fight of it.

| 38 .... | Kt—Q7ch |
| 39 K—K1 | .... |

If 38, K—K2, P—B5! is very strong.

39	Kt—Kt6
40 Q—Q5	R—R6
41 Q—B4	B—Kt2
42 K—Q1	....

Hoping to take advantage of the rather awkward position of Black's pieces; but he only hastens the end. A waiting course would have been better.

42	P—R4!
43 K—B2?	Kt—R4
44 Q—Kt5	R x Pch
45 K—Q1	Kt—B5
46 P—R5	....

At last. But Black can banish all danger by giving up his Knight.

| 46 .... | R—Q6ch |
| 47 K—K1 | .... |

If 47 K—B1, B—Kt7ch wins the Queen.

| 47 .... | R x Pch |
| 48 K—B1 | .... |

Or 48 K—B2, B—Q5; 49 K—Kt2, Kt—K4; 50 P—R6, P—B5; 51 Q—Kt8ch, K—R2; 52 P—R7, R—K7ch wins.

48	Kt x P!
49 Q x Kt	R x P
50 Q x P	P—K4
51 Q—B6	K—R2

White resigns, as he is helpless against the Pawns. A thrilling encounter!

---

137. New York, 1940

(Marshall C. C. Championship)

SICILIAN DEFENSE

The fact that White does not develop a single piece in his first fourteen moves is surely a striking violation of all basic principles! But White's exclusive use of Pawn moves is justified by Black's faulty development of his Knights.

F. J. MARSHALL	H. ROGOSIN
White	Black
1 P—K4	P—QB4

2 P—QKt4   P x P
3 P—QR3   Kt—QB3?

As in earlier examples of this gambit, Black does not find the proper reply. But the text is particularly weak, since Black must lose further time with this piece.

4 P x P   Kt—B3?

This makes matters worse. . . . Kt x P had to be played.

5 P—Kt5   Kt—Q5?

Black's reluctance to retreat to QKt1 is natural, but the text only leads to new trouble.

6 P—QB3   Kt—K3
7 P—K5   Kt—Q4
8 P—QB4   Kt(4)—B5?

. . . Kt—Kt3 was necessary; the text leads to the loss of a piece. The helplessness of the Knights is pathetic.

9 P—Kt3   Kt—Kt3
10 P—B4   . . . .

Rogosin

Marshall

There is no way out for Black. If 10 . . . Kt—B2; 11 P—B5! Kt x P; 12 P—Q4 and the piece is lost!

10 . . . .   Kt(Kt3) x BP
11 P x Kt   Kt x P

12 P—Q4   Kt—Kt3
13 P—R4   . . . .

Threatening to win the other Knight as well!

13 . . . .   P—K3
14 P—R5   B—Kt5ch
15 B—Q2   . . . .

The Pawns have done their work well and White can now reply on his pieces to make use of the gains achieved thus far.

15 . . . .   B x Bch
16 Kt x B   Kt—K2
17 Kt—K4   Kt—B4
18 P—R6!   P—KKt3

After 18 . . . Kt x RP there would have followed 19 Kt—Q6ch, K—K2; 20 R x Kt, P x R; 21 Q—R5, Q—Kt1; 22 Kt—B3 and Black's position is in a bad way.

19 Kt—B6ch   K—B1
20 Kt—B3   P—Q3
21 Kt—Kt5   P x P
22 P x P   Q x Qch

Black's position is so hopeless that the removal of the Queens brings no relief.

23 R x Q   K—K2
24 R—R3   P—Kt3
25 B—Kt2   QR—Kt1
26 Kt(5) x RP   Resigns

For if 26 . . . R—Q1; 27 R x R, K x R; 28 Kt—B8 followed by the advance of the RP.

---

138. New York, 1940
(*Exhibition Match*)

QUEEN'S GAMBIT DECLINED

Dr. Lasker's last serious games were played in this match; he died about six months later. We contested the following game at the Astor, in the playing enclosure in which the U. S. Championship was taking place. I am sure that that gallant old warrior must have shared my feelings, as I looked around at today's youthful stars— Reshevsky, Fine and the others, and thought of all the old tournaments in which we had had so many stirring encounters, and all our famous rivals: Pillsbury, Tarrasch, Janowski and so many others . . . they are only memories now.

	F J. MARSHALL	DR. E. LASKER
	White	Black
1	P—QB4	P—K3
2	Kt—KB3	Kt—KB3
3	Kt—B3	P—Q4
4	P—Q4	QKt—Q2
5	B—Kt5	B—K2
6	P—K3	O—O
7	Q—B2	P—B4

This has been a fashionable variation of late; however, it leads to an isolated QP for Black, which, as has been observed in earlier games, leaves Black with lasting disabilities.

8	BP x P	Kt x P
9	B x B	Q x B
10	Kt x Kt	P x Kt
11	B—Q3	P—KKt3
12	P x P	Kt x P
13	O—O	. . . .

The positional significance of the isolated QP is now clear: White has a splendid square for his Knight at Q4 and a generally freer position; Black's Bishop has little scope and his position is rather uncomfortable and holds out little promise.

| 13 | . . . . | P—Kt3 |

He wants to protect the isolated Pawn; but I should prefer more aggressive tactics such as . . . B—Kt5.

| 14 | QR—B1 | P—QR4 |

In order to maintain the Knight at B4. The incidental threat, by the way, is 15 . . . Kt x B; 16 Q xKt, B—R3. However, Black's Pawn position is certainly not benefitted by this advance.

| 15 | KR—Q1 | B—Kt2 |
| 16 | Kt—Q4 | . . . . |

The Knight is ideally posted.

16	. . . .	KR—B1
17	Q—K2	Q—B3
18	P—KR3	. . . .

In such positions, in which both sides intend to occupy an open file (the QB file here), it is well to guard the last rank against surprise attacks.

18	. . . .	R—B2
19	R—B3	QR—QB1
20	KR—QB1	. . . .

The doubling of the Rooks favors White's more aggressive position, since Black's Knight at B4 is pinned.

| 20 | . . . . | Q—K4 |
| 21 | P—R3 | P—R5 |

Black is in a quandary; he does not want to allow his Knight to be driven off by P—QKt4, but the text creates a serious weakness.

| 22 | B—Kt5! | R—R1 |

Loss of material was unavoidable. Thus if 22 . . . Kt—Kt6; 23 R x R, R x R; 24 R x R, Q x R; 25 B x P, Kt x Kt; 26 P x Kt, Q—B8ch; 27 B—Q1! and wins.

(see diagram next page)

| 23 | B x P!! | . . . . |

A neat sacrifice with several interesting points.

| 23 | . . . . | R x B |
| 24 | P—QKt4 | Q—K1 |

Or 24 . . . Kt—K3 (if 24 . . . Kt—

Position after Black's 22nd move

Dr. Lasker

Marshall

Kt6; 25 R x R, Kt x Kt; 26 Q—Q1 etc. or else 24 . . . Kt—Kt6; 25 R x R, Kt x R; 26 Q—B2); 25 R x R, Kt x R; 26 Q—B2, R xRP; 27 Q x Kt, Q x Q; 28 R x Q, B—R1; 29 P— Kt5 with a winning position.

| 25 Q—B2 | .... |

Not 25 P x Kt? R x Kt.

25	R—K2
26 P x Kt	P x P
27 R x P	R x KP

Attempting counterplay. If instead 27 . . . R x RP there might follow 28 Q—Kt2, Q—R5 (or 28 . . . R—R1; 29 Kt—Kt5 with a winning game); 29 R—B8ch! B x R; 30 R x Bch, K—Kt2; 31 Kt—B5 mate!

28 P x R	Q x Pch
29 Q—B2	Q x Kt
30 Q x Q	R x Q
31 R—R5!	....

The quickest way, the threat being R—B7.

31	R—QB5
32 R x R	P x R
33 R—QB5	B—R3
34 P—QR4	Resigns

139. New York, 1941

(Marshall Chess Club Championship)

KING'S INDIAN DEFENSE

An interesting Pawn sacrifice turns a predominantly positional defense into an aggressive counterattack.

A. E. SANTASIERE   F. J. MARSHALL

White	Black
1 Kt—KB3	Kt—KB3
2 P—B4	P—KKt3
3 Kt—B3	B—Kt2
4 P—K4	....

P—Q4 would have been more exact, as Black's reply indicates.

4	P—K4!
5 P—Q4	P x P
6 Kt x P	O—O
7 B—K2	R—K1
8 P—B3	P—B3!

Black's h i t h e r t o inexplicable avoidance of the almost obligatory . . . P—Q3 now becomes clear. He intends to advance the QP two squares, even at the cost of sacrificing a Pawn.

| 9 Kt—B2 | P—Q4!? |
| 10 BP x P | .... |

A very puzzling position, but 10 KP x P, P x P; 11 Kt x P, Kt x Kt; 12 Q x Kt would have been relatively better.

| 10 . . . . | P x P |
| 11 Kt x P | .... |

No better is 11 P x P, Q—Kt3! with a very awkward position for White.

11	Kt x Kt
12 Q x Kt	Q—B2
13 Q—B4	Kt—B3
14 Kt—K3	....

White's position is anything but enviable; the omission of castling ultimately proves disastrous, but 15 O—O, B—K3; 16 Q—R4 (if 16 .Q—Q3, QR—Q1; 17 Q—K3, Kt—Q5 etc.), P—QR3 likewise leaves him with a poor game.

Black has indeed obtained excellent value for the Pawn.

14 . . . .   B—K3

He does not fear the seemingly formidable 15 Kt—Q5, which is simply answered by . . . Q—Q1 with a view to . . . Kt—Q5 and . . .R—B1.

15 Q—B2   B—K4!

Virtually decisive, since White has little to hope for from 16 P—KR3, B—Kt6ch etc.

16 P—KKt3   . . . .

Position after White's 16th move

Marshall

Santasiere

16 . . . .   B x Pch!

Relying on his superior development.

17 P x B	Q x Pch
18 K—Q1	QR—Q1ch
19 B—Q2	Kt—Q5

Since a Queen move is refuted by . . . Kt x P, White tries an ex-

change of Queens; but this also proves inadequate.

20 Kt—B1	Kt x Q
21 Kt x Q	Kt x R
22 P—K5	. . . .

Despair; if instead 22 P—Kt3, B x Pch; 23 P x B, Kt x P; 24 Kt—B1, R x Bch; 25 Kt x R, R—Q1 etc.

22	B x P
23 P—B4	Kt—Kt6
24 Kt—K4	R x Bch

White resigns.   Triumph of the open lines!

---

140. New York, 1941
(*Marshall C. C. Championship*)
FRENCH DEFENSE

I was deeply moved by Santasiere's tribute written in connection with this game:

"Yet one more brilliant game from a really unique and universally beloved personality. It is not often that the world is treated to the fresh, rare, sparkling genius of a Frank Marshall. Speculative play has been his passion, and many an important point it has cost him! But we love and honor the brave spirit that can scorn the point, for the play! Incidentally, it is amazing to note that the last decade has witnessed a definite growth rather than decline in Marshall's allaround chess ability. His style is more eclectic, more steady—even more brilliant. If only he had now great physical endurance! But the years take their toll. Even Marshall must resign to so implacable a foe. But as long as chess is played, his name will be synonymous with glorified brilliance."

F. J. MARSHALL	L. LEVY
White	Black
1 P—K4	. . . .

In this tournament I had discovered, to my great amusement, that the Danish Gambit was still capable of cutting a wide swath among my young opponents. They are at home in the Slav, Catalan and other modern wrinkles, but some of the older openings seem to baffle them.

1 ....   P—K3

Levy, being an aggressive and very gifted young player, prefers to steer the game into different channels.

2 P—Q4   P—Q4
3 Kt—QB3   Kt—KB3
4 B—Kt5   B—Kt5
5 Kt—K2   ....

A good move. I don't care for 5 P x P, as I used to like Black's position after 5 ... Q x P in the days when I played this defense.

5 ....   P—KR3?

Deciding to sacrifice a Pawn; but the gambit has little to recommend it.

6 B x Kt   Q x B
7 P—QR3   B x Ktch
8 Kt x B   O—O
9 P x P   R—K1
10 B—K2   ....

P x P was also feasible, but I prefer to seize the initiative as soon as possible.

10 ....   Q—Kt4
11 Q—Q2!   ....

As long as I had to give back the Pawn, I preferred to do it in a manner which would either yield a strong attack (as in the game) or else leave Black without any play whatever (after ... Q x Qch).

11 ....   Q x KtP
12 O—O—O   P x P

After 12 ... Q x BP the strongest line would probably be P—KR4 followed by harrying moves against the Black Queen. With such an enormous lead in development and with a formidable attack, White is bound to have an easy time of it in any event.

13 QR—Kt1   Q x BP

... Q—R6 would not make much difference, as White's attack would proceed along similar lines.

14 R—Kt3   B—-K3
15 R—B1   Q x RP
16 Q—B4   K—-R1

White threatened R x Pch. His attack has become devastating.

Position after Black's 16th move

Levy

Marshall

17 B—B3   ....

Another way was 17 Q—K5! and Black is helpless: 17 ...P—KB3; 18 R x BP, Kt—Q2; 19 R—B8ch etc.; or 17 ... R—Kt1; 18 B—Q3! Kt—B3; 19 R x KtP! winning the Queen. However, the method selected is just as quick.

17 ....   B—B4
18 B—Kt2   B—Kt3

This attempted barricade collapses very rapidly, ruining Black's hope of maintaining resistance after loss of the Queen.

19	R—R1	Q x Rch
20	B x Q	R—K8ch
21	K—Q2	R x B
22	R x B!	. . . .

Crushes all resistance.

22	. . . .	P x R
23	Q—B8ch	K—R2
24	Kt x P	Resigns

There is nothing to be done about the coming Kt—K7.

INDEX OF OPENINGS

PART THREE

SPECIAL ANALYSIS OF OPENINGS

For many years, my good friend Tom Emery and I have spent several hours a week together, talking and playing chess. Like all chessplayers, we love to "analyze" our games, to discuss the moves and the possibilities of side variations.

Free from the tense atmosphere of the competitive contest and the constant ticking of the time-clock, these peaceful and friendly discussions have been unusually productive of new ideas and new moves in the openings.

A few of the variations we have analyzed are presented below.

THE KING'S GAMBIT

One evening Tom and I were going over some of the games I played at the King's Gambit Tournament in Vienna, 1903.

"Why don't we see games like that any more?" he asked me. "Nobody seems to accept the King's Gambit nowadays. Why is that?"

It is true that, in modern master play, the King's Gambit is rarely accepted. In a way, it is a pity. A great deal of beauty has been taken from our noble game. No more Muzios, Cunninghams, Kieseritzkys, or Rice Gambits. Perhaps hypermodern chess has doomed all gambits.

However, you can hardly blame the masters. As a matter of fact, I would refuse to accept the King's Gambit myself in a tournament game. It gives White a strong attack and your opponent may have studied some variation with which you are not familiar. With the clock ticking, defensive moves are hard to find. White has so many strong continuations at his disposal, the game becomes very difficult for the second player.

Paul Keres, the young Estonian grandmaster who recently finished second to Botvinnik in the Sextangular Match-Tourney in Russia, often plays the Gambit and con-

siders the opening as good as any other. His continuation against the acceptance is as follows:

1 P—K4, P—K4; 2 P—KB4, P x P; 3 Kt—QB3, Q—R5ch; 4 K—K2, P—Q3; 5 Kt—Q5, B—Kt5ch; 6 Kt—B3, B x Ktch; 7 P x B, K—Q1 (QKt—R3 can also be played); 8 P—Q3, P—KKt4; 9 B—Q2, B—Kt2; 10 B—K1, Q—R4; 11 P—KR4! P—QB3; 12 Kt—B3, Kt—K2; 13 B—Kt2, P—Kt5; 14 P x P, Q x Pch; 15 B—B3.

This is just one of the many continuations for White. Others begin with 3 Kt—KB3, 3 B—B4, 3 Q—B3, 3 B—K2 and even 3 K—B2, as played by Steinitz! In all cases, Black is exposed to constant danger and must make the correct defensive moves.

In a serious game, therefore, it is safer and better to decline the gambit. One of the best ways to do this is by means of the Falkbeer Counter-Gambit. Here, the opening moves are 1 P—K4, P—K4; 2 P—KB4, P—Q4; 3 KP x P, P—K5.

Analyzing this opening, Tom and I found a new move in the continuation known as the Keres variation, viz:

4 P—Q3, Kt—KB3; 5 Kt—Q2 (Keres' move), P x P (here Keres recommends 5 . . . B—KB4 but we prefer the text); 6 B x P, Kt x P; 7 Kt—K4, Kt—Kt5!

Position after 7 . . . Kt—Kt5

The strength of the last Black move has apparently been overlooked. In a correspondence game (Keres—Malmgren, 1934), Black played 7 . . . B—K2 and White soon obtained a definite advantage. 7 . . . Kt—Kt5 is much more powerful. If Black can exchange White's KB, the attack loses much of its force.

A possible continuation would be:

8 B—Kt5ch, B—Q2; 9 B x Bch, Kt x B; 10 Kt—KB3 (If 10 P—QR3, Q—K2; 11 Q—K2, Kt x Pch; 12 Q x Kt, Kt—B3), Kt—B4 and Black has a good game.

(Publisher's Note: Other continuations of this move, as analyzed by Olaf I. Ulvestad, are given in CHESS CHARTS, Issue No. 3, now in process of publication. Mr. Marshall and Mr. Ulvestad both discovered this strong reply for Black in independent analysis.)

THE MAX LANGE ATTACK

In the notes to the 16th move of Game No. 61, we referred to the continuation 16 . . . P—Q7; 17 R—K2, R—Q6; 18 Q—KB1, B—Kt3, etc.

Quite recently, Emery and I found a new defense here for Black which looks promising. Instead of 18 . . . B—Kt3, we recommend 18 . . . Q—Q4! and after 19 QR—Q1 (. . . P—Q8(Q) was threatened) Kt—K4!;

20 Kt—B6 (if 20 Q—Kt2, Kt—B6ch; 21 K—B1, Kt—R5; 22 Q—Kt1, Kt—B6 draws. Here, if 21 K—R1, Kt—R5; 22 Q—Kt1), Q—B6; 21 Kt x R (if 21 P—Kt5, Kt—Kt5), Q x Pch; 22 K—R1, Q—B6ch; 23 K—Kt1 and the game is a draw. If 23 Q—Kt2, Q x R and Black has the advantage.

SICILIAN DEFENSE
(Wing Gambit)

This gambit leads to some beautiful combinations and positions. Like all gambits, the idea is to secure a strong center, quick development and a chance for combinations.

In the variation which begins 1 P—K4, P—QB4; 2 P—QKt4, P x P; 3 P—QR3, P—Q4 (best); 4 KP x P, Q x P, there are some interesting possibilities for White after 5 Kt—KB3.

If 5 . . . B—Kt5; 6 P x P, B x Kt; 7 Q x B, Q x Q (better than 7 . . . Q—K4ch; 8 K—Q1, Q x R; 9 Q x KtP); 8 P x Q. White's doubled pawns are a hindrance but with two Bishops and the more open game, we still prefer White.

If 5 . . . P—K4; 6 P x P, B x P and we reach the position shown in the diagram below.

Position after 6 . . . B x P

White then has the choice of three moves, with the following variations:

I 7 P—B3, B—B4 (If 7 . . . B—Q3; 8 Kt—R3, QKt—B3; 9 B—B4, Q—K5ch; 10 B—K2, KKt—B3; 11 Kt—QKt5, B—Kt1; 12 R—R4, Q—B4; 13 B—R3 with a good game for White. Here, if 12 . . . Q—Kt8, 13 P—Q4 wins); 8 Kt—R3, QKt—Kt5, K—Q1 (apparently best); 10 KKt—Q4, QKt—B3; 11 Q—R4, Kt—B3; 12 B—R3 and White can castle on the Q-side with a good game.

II. 7 Kt—R3, P—K5; 8 Kt—QKt5, K—Q1; 9 KKt—Q4, QKt—B3; 10 P—QB4, Q—Q2; 11 B—Kt2, Kt—B3; 12 Q—R4, B—B4; 13 Kt—Kt3, P—QKt3; 14 Kt x B, P x Kt; 15 B—K2 or 15 B—B3 and White threatens to castle with good prospects.

III. 7 B—R3, Kt—QB3 (if 7 . . . B x B, 8 R or Kt x B); 8 B x B, Kt x B; 9 Kt—QB3, Q—B4; 10 B—Kt5 ch, Kt—B3; 11 R—R5, P—KB3; 12 Q—R1, Kt—K2; 13 Kt—K4, Q x P; 14 P—Q3! and the Black Queen is in danger of being captured.

PETROFF DEFENSE

This opening is seldom used to-day. It used to be one of my favorites and I won a lot of games with it. However, later analysis showed that White could force an even position with 5 Q—K2. When this move was played against me in my matches with Dr. Lasker and Capablanca I stubbornly refused to exchange Queens and insisted on playing for a win. As a result, I lost both games. Unfortunately, there seems to be little left for Black after this move. By exchanging Queens, of course, the game is probably a draw so there is nothing inherently wrong with the defense. Between players of equal strength there is no reason why Black should not adopt the defense, as an even position is quickly reached. Against a weaker player, however, it is questionable whether Black should play the Petroff; it gives White an easy game. Even a weak player, with the White pieces, can worry the strongest master and make it difficult for him to find a

win. The best line for Black is as follows:

1 P—K4, P—K4; 2 Kt—KB3, Kt—KB3; 3 Kt x P, P—Q3; 4 Kt—KB3, Kt x P; 5 Q—K2, Q—K2; 6 P—Q3, Kt—KB3; 7 B—Kt5, Q x Q ch; 8 B x Q, B—K2; 9 Kt—B3, P—QB3; 10 O—O—O, P—KR3. With equal play on both sides, the game should be drawn, whether the Bishop retreats or captures the Knight.

RUY LOPEZ
(Marshall Variation)

I have made some changes in my variation of the Ruy Lopez which tend to strengthen it. The opening moves of this line are as follows:

1 P—K4, P—K4; 2 Kt—KB3, Kt—QB3; 3 B—Kt5, P—QR3; 4 B—R4, Kt—B3; 5 O—O, B—K2; 6 R—K1, P—QKt4; 7 B—Kt3, O—O; 8 P—QB3, P—Q4; 9 P x P, Kt x P; 10 Kt x P, Kt x Kt; 11 R x Kt.

Position after 11 R x Kt

Here our analysis deviates from previous play. In this position, 11 . . . Kt—B3 or 11 . . . B—Kt2 have hitherto been played. We now recommend the following:

11 . . . P—QB3! 12 P—Q4, B—Q3; 13 R—K1, Q—R5! 14 P—KKt3, Q—R6; 15 B x Kt, P x B; 16 Q—B3, B—KB4; 17 Q x P (as . . . B—K5 was threatened), QR—K1; 18 R x R, R x R; 19 B—Q2, B—K5 and Black should win.

TWO KNIGHTS' DEFENSE
(Wilkes-Barre Variation)

This variation was first published, named and analyzed by the author. It has possibilities for Black. The opening moves are:
1 P—K4, P—K4; 2 Kt—KB3, Kt—QB3; 3 B—B4, Kt—B3; 4 Kt—Kt5, B—B4.

I called the continuations beginning with 4 . . . B—B4 the Wilkes-Barre variation. The usual move is 4 . . . P—Q4. There are two main lines, as follows:

Position after 4 . . . B—B4

I 5 B x Pch, K—K2; 6 B—Kt3, R—B1; 7 O—O, P—KR3; 8 KKt—B3, P—Q3; 9 P—KR3 (if 9 Kt—R4, Kt—KKt5; 10 Kt—Kt6ch, K—K1; 11 Kt x R, Q—R5 etc.), Kt x P; 10 P—B3, Q—K1; 11 P—Q4, B—Kt3; 12 Q—K2 with a difficult position.

II 5 Kt x BP, B x Pch; 6 K x B, Kt x Pch; 7 K—Kt1, Q—R5; 8 Q—B1, R—B1; 9 P—Q3, Kt—Q3; 10 Kt x Ktch, P x Kt; 11 Q—K2, Kt—Q5; 12 Q—Q2, Q—Kt5 and Black wins.

THE VIENNA GAME

This is a very conservative opening, against which we tend to favor the Black side. One of the standard lines is as follows:
1 P—K4, P—K4; 2 Kt—QB3, Kt—KB3; 3 P—B4, P—Q4; 4 BP x P, Kt x P.

Position after 4 . . . Kt x P

Here some masters play 5 Q—B3, whereupon Black's best reply appears to be 5 . . . Kt—QB3 (although 5 . . . P—KB4 has been tried) and is usually followed by 6 B—Kt5, Kt x Kt; 7 KtP x Kt. An optional possibility here is 7 Q x Kt, Q—R5ch; 8 P—Kt3 (8 K—B1 is also possible), Q—K5ch; 9 K—B2, Q x R; 10 B x Ktch, K—Q1; 11 Kt—B3, P x B; 12 P—Q4, threatening B—Kt5ch. This line is complicated but playable.

After the more usual 5 Kt—B3, one variation continues: 5 . . . B—QB4; 6 P—Q4, B—QKt5; 7 Q—Q3 (if 7 B—Q2, P—QB4; 8 B—Kt5ch, Kt—B3; 9 O—O, O—O; 10 B x Kt, P x B; 11 P—QR3, B x B; 12 P x B, P x P; 13 P x P, P—KB3 with the threat of 14 . . . B—R3), P—QB4; 8 P x P.

At this point we recommend 8 . . . B—KB4 (instead of 8 . . . Kt x P) and if 9 Q—K3, O—O; 10 B—Q2, Kt—QB3. Or if 9 Q—Kt5ch, Kt—B3; 10 Q x KtP, B—Q2! In all cases, we prefer Black.

THE NIMZOVICH DEFENSE
(King's Pawn Opening)

This irregular defense was often played by Tschigorin. We cannot recommend it, as it is contrary to all theory. We suggest the following line for White:

1 P—K4, Kt—QB3; 2 P—Q4, P—Q4 (if 2 ... P—K4, 3 P x P, Kt x P; 4 P—KB4, QKt—B3; 5 B—K3), 3 P x P, Q x P; 4 Kt—KB3, P—K4 (best); 5 P—QB4 (also playable is 5 Kt—B3, B—QKt5; 6 B—Q2, B x Kt; 7 B x B, P x P; 8 Kt x P, Kt x Kt; 9 B x Kt), Q—K5ch; 6 B—K2, P x P; 7 O—O, B—K2 (if 7 ... B—KB4; 8 R—K1, O—O—O; 9 Kt—Kt5) 8 R—K1! Q—Kt3 (if 8 ... B—KB4; 9 Kt—R3, O—O—O; 10 KKt—Kt5, B x Kt; 11 B x B, P—B3; 12 B—B3, Q—Q6; 13 Q—R4, P x B; 14 QR—Q1 wins the Q); 9 Kt x P and White has the advantage.

ALEKHINE'S DEFENSE

The idea behind Alekhine's move (1 ... Kt—KB3) is to tempt White to make premature pawn moves, but we believe Black loses too much time with this Knight. However, it is an interesting game and we suggest the following new lines.

1 P—K4, Kt—KB3; 2 P—K5, Kt—Q4; 3 P—QB4, Kt—Kt3; 4 P—Q4, P—Q3; 5 P—B4, P x P; 6 BP x P.

Position after 6 BP x P

At this point the usual move is 6 ... Kt—B3 with a playable game. A possibility for Black, however, is 6 ... P—Kt3 and this move should be tested. White's best reply is probably 7 P—B5 and if 7 ... Kt—Q4, 8 B—QB4. Against other con-

tinuations, Black obtains the advantage, e. g.

I 6 ... P—Kt3; 7 QKt—B3, B—Kt2; 8 B—K2, P—QB4; 9 P x P, Q x Qch; 10 K x Q, KKt—Q2 and Black has good chances.

II 6 ... P—Kt3; 7 Kt—KB3, B—Kt5; 8 B—K2, P—QB4; 9 B—K3 (if 9 P—Q5, B—Kt2; 10 B—B4, QKt—Q2), P x P; 10 Kt x P, B x B; 11 Q x B, B—Kt2; 12 KKt—B3, Kt—QB3 and Black stands better.

THE RETI-ZUKERTORT OPENING

Reti did 'a great deal to popularize this opening, although I believe Zukertort was the first to play it. It belongs to the hyper-modern school and the object is to obtain indirect control of the center. The typical moves are as follows:

1 Kt—KB3, Kt—KB3; 2 P—B4, P—B4; 3 P—KKt3, P—KKt3; 4 B—Kt2, B—Kt2; 5 O—O, O—O; 6 Kt—B3, Kt—B3; 7 P—Q3.

Position after 7 P—Q3

Here Black is supposed to duplicate White's move with 7 ... P—Q3 but we feel that 7 ... P—Q4 should be tried. Then, if 8 P x P, Kt x P; 9 Kt x Kt, Q x Kt and Black stands better, for if 10 Kt—Kt5, Q—Q2 or Q—Q1.

FOUR KNIGHTS' GAME

Another conservative opening. In one variation a strong move was suggested by Tom Emery, as follows:

1 P—K4, P—K4; 2 Kt—KB3, Kt—QB3; 3 Kt—B3, Kt—B3; 4 B—Kt5, P—QR3? (4 ... B—Kt5 or B—K2 are better moves for Black); 5 B x Kt, QP x B; 6 Kt x P, Kt x P; 7 Q—R5! (Emery's move), Kt—Q3; 8 P—Q4, B—K3; 9 B—B4, B—K2; 10 O—O—O, O—O; 11 KR—K1 and White has the advantage.

GIUOCO PIANO

Instead of analyzing this opening, we give below a game played between Tom Emery and Miss Vera Menchik, woman champion of the world, at Biarritz, March, 1939, just prior to Mr. Emery's forced evacuation. The game well illustrates the opening.

Tom Emery	Vera Menchik
White	Black
1 P—K4	P—K4
2 Kt—KB3	Kt—QB3
3 B—B4	B—B4
4 P—B3	Kt—B3
5 P—Q4	P x P
6 P x P	B—Kt5ch
7 Kt—B3	Kt x KP

7 ... P—Q4 is sounder, as demonstrated in a test of this variation in a tournament, many years ago, suggested by Mr. Dimock of New London, Conn.

| 8 O—O | B x Kt |

If 8 ... Kt x Kt; 9 P x Kt, B x P; 10 Q—Kt3, B x R; 11 B x Pch, K—B1; 12 B—Kt5, Kt—K2; 13 R—K1 and White should win.

| 9 P—Q5 | .... |

Known as the Moller Attack. Many beautiful games have been played with this attack, mostly in White's favor.

9	B—B3
10 R—K1	Kt—K2
11 R x Kt	P—Q3

Too slow. Black should castle.

| 12 B—KKt5 | B x B |
| 13 Kt x B | B—B4 |

Position after 13 ... B—B4

Apparently powerful, but unsafe. Black should have castled.

| 14 Q—B3 | .... |

A beautiful attacking and developing move. A rook is sacrificed.

| 14 .... | B x R |

If 14 ... B—Kt3; 15 QR—K1 wins, or if 14 ... Q—Q2, 15 QR—K1 or 15 B—Kt5!

15 Q x Pch	K—Q2
16 Q—K6ch	K—K1
17 Q x B	Q—Q2
18 R—K1	P—QR3
19 Kt x P	K—Q1
20 Kt—Kt5	....

Every move is a picture. Now Kt—B7ch is threatened.

20	R—K1
21 Kt—K6ch	K—B1
22 Kt x P	Resigns

CPSIA information can be obtained at www.ICGtesting.com
Printed in the USA
LVOW11s2357100314

376862LV00004B/355/P